Transformative Approaches to Social Justice Education

Transformative Approaches to Social Justice Education is a book for anyone with an interest in teaching and learning in higher education from a social justice perspective and with a commitment to teaching all students. This text offers a breadth of disciplinary perspectives on how to center difference, power, and systemic oppression in pedagogical practice, arguing that these elements are essential to knowledge formation and to teaching. *Transformative Approaches to Social Justice Education* is structured as an ongoing conversation among educators who believe that teaching from a social justice perspective is about much more than the type of readings and assignments found on course syllabi.

Drawing on the broadest possible definition of curriculum transformation, the volume demonstrates that social justice education is about both educators' social locations and about course content. It is also about knowing students and teaching beyond the traditional classroom to meaningfully include local communities, social movements, archives, and colleagues in student and academic affairs.

Premised on the notion that continuous learning and growth is critical to educators with deep commitments to fostering critical consciousness through their teaching, *Transformative Approaches to Social Justice Education* offers interdisciplinary and innovative collaborative approaches to curriculum transformation that build on and extend existing scholarship on social justice education. Newly committed and established social justice pedagogues share their experiences taking up the many difficult questions pertaining to what it means for all of us to participate in shaping a more just, shared future.

Nana Osei-Kofi is Director of the Difference, Power, and Discrimination Program, and Associate Professor of Women, Gender, and Sexuality Studies at Oregon State University.

Bradley Boovy is Associate Professor of Women, Gender, and Sexuality Studies and World Languages and Cultures and co-facilitator with Nana Osei-Kofi of the Difference, Power, and Discrimination Academy at Oregon State University.

Kali Furman is a PhD Candidate in Women, Gender, and Sexuality Studies at Oregon State University writing her dissertation about the Difference, Power, and Discrimination Program.

The *Teaching/Learning Social Justice* Series

The Teaching/Learning Social Justice Series explores issues of social justice—diversity, equality, democracy, and fairness—in classrooms and communities. "Teaching/learning" connotes the essential connections between theory and practice that books in this series seek to illuminate. Central are the stories and lived experiences of people who strive both to critically analyze and challenge oppressive relationships and institutions, and to imagine and create more just and inclusive alternatives.

Edited by Lee Anne Bell, Barnard College, Columbia University

Actions Speak Louder than Words
Community Activism as Curriculum
Celia Oyler

Practice What You Teach
Social Justice Education in the Classroom and the Streets
Bree Picower

Active Learning
Social Justice Education and Participatory Action Research
Dana E. Wright

Storytelling for Social Justice
Connecting Narrative and the Arts in Antiracist Teaching, Second Edition
Lee Anne Bell

Transformative Approaches to Social Justice Education
Transformative Approaches to Social Justice Education
Nana Osei-Kofi, Bradley Boovy, Kali Furman

For more information, please visit: https://www.routledge.com/Teaching-Learning-Social-Justice/book-series/SE1023

Transformative Approaches to Social Justice Education
Equity and Access in the College Classroom

Edited by Nana Osei-Kofi, Bradley Boovy and Kali Furman

NEW YORK AND LONDON

First published 2022
by Routledge
52 Vanderbilt Avenue, New York, NY 10017

and by Routledge
2 Park Square, Milton Park, Abingdon, Oxon OX14 4RN

Routledge is an imprint of the Taylor & Francis Group, an informa business

© 2022 Taylor & Francis

The right of Nana Osei-Kofi, Bradley Boovy, and Kali Furman to be identified as the authors of the editorial material, and of the authors for their individual chapters, has been asserted in accordance with sections 77 and 78 of the Copyright, Designs and Patents Act 1988.

All rights reserved. No part of this book may be reprinted or reproduced or utilised in any form or by any electronic, mechanical, or other means, now known or hereafter invented, including photocopying and recording, or in any information storage or retrieval system, without permission in writing from the publishers.

Trademark notice: Product or corporate names may be trademarks or registered trademarks, and are used only for identification and explanation without intent to infringe.

Library of Congress Cataloging-in-Publication Data
Names: Osei-Kofi, Nana, editor. | Boovy, Bradley, editor. | Furman, Kali, editor.
Title: Transformative approaches to social justice education : equity and access in the college classroom / Edited by Nana Osei-Kofi, Bradley Boovy, Kali Furman.
Description: New York, NY : Routledge, 2021. | Includes bibliographical references and index.
Identifiers: LCCN 2020044468 (print) | LCCN 2020044469 (ebook) | ISBN 9780367551049 (hardback) | ISBN 9780367551032 (paperback) | ISBN 9781003091998 (ebook)
Subjects: LCSH: Social justice Study and teaching (Higher) | Educational equalization. | Education, Higher Curricula. | Education, Higher Aims and objectives.
Classification: LCC LC192.2 .T73 2021 (print) | LCC LC192.2 (ebook) | DDC 370.11/5 dc23
LC record available at https://lccn.loc.gov/2020044468
LC ebook record available at https://lccn.loc.gov/2020044469

ISBN: 978-0-367-55104-9 (hbk)
ISBN: 978-0-367-55103-2 (pbk)
ISBN: 978-1-003-09199-8 (ebk)

DOI: 10.4324/9781003091998

Typeset in Baskerville
by Taylor & Francis Books

To Isabelle Brock (1981–2018)
Senior Instructor of English
Oregon State University

Contents

Foreword by Alma Clayton-Pedersen and Frank Hernandez   ix
Acknowledgements   xii
Introduction   xiv
NANA OSEI-KOFI, BRADLEY BOOVY, AND KALI FURMAN

SECTION 1
Archives and Power: Engaging History Collaboratively   1

1. Student Activism and Institutional Change: A History of The Difference, Power, and Discrimination Program at Oregon State University   3
KALI FURMAN

2. Collaborations between Professors and Archivists: Engaging Students with their Local Community History   21
NATALIA FERNÁNDEZ

3. Scripting Change: The Social Justice Tour of Corvallis   40
NATCHEE BLU BARND

SECTION 2
Frameworks for Transformative Pedagogies   63

4. Universal Design for Instruction and Institutional Change: A Case Study   65
STEPHANIE JENKINS AND MARTHA SMITH

5. Critical Pedagogy Online: Opportunities and Challenges in Social Justice Education   87
JENNY N. MYERS

6. Peace Literacy, Cognitive Bias, and Structural Injustice   105
SHARYN CLOUGH

7 From Here to There: Educating for Wholeness   124
   ERICH N. PITCHER AND CHARLENE C. MARTINEZ

SECTION 3
Destabilizing Dominant Narratives   141

8 "The Tree of Anger": Queer and Trans Studies in the Difference, Power, and Discrimination Program at Oregon State University   143
   H. RAKES AND QWO-LI DRISKILL

9 Reflections on Race/Ethnicity, Gender, and Labor in the Latinx Studies Classroom   158
   MARTA MARÍA MALDONADO

10 Talking About Class   174
   ALLISON L. HURST

11 Teaching About Race in the Historically White Difference, Power, and Discrimination Classroom: Teacher as Text   189
   BRADLEY BOOVY AND NANA OSEI-KOFI

SECTION 4
Rethinking Approaches to Disciplinary Content   205

12 Religious Bias, Christian Privilege, and Anti-Muslimism in the Difference, Power, and Discrimination Classroom   207
   AMY KOEHLINGER AND KRYN FREEHLING-BURTON

13 ¡Sí, se puede! Teaching Farmworker Justice in the Land-Grant University   228
   RONALD L. MIZE

14 Listen up, STEM: We Don't Just Teach Facts   246
   GLENCORA BORRADAILE

15 "Show, Don't Tell": Teaching Social Justice at the Source   266
   MARISA CHAPPELL AND LINDA M. RICHARDS

16 Afterword   283
   SUSAN M. SHAW

   Bios   290

   Index   298

Foreword

Are you frustrated by the challenge of taking one step forward and two steps backward in your efforts at curriculum transformation that engages with systems of oppression?

Are you lamenting that you've not yet found effective ways to engage students with content concerning disciplinary, local, and national realities of injustice?

Do you wish the courses you teach could enhance all students' learning so that they are equipped with knowledge and a critical consciousness in service of contributing to structural changes that help build a more just world?

Congratulations! You've found the right publication to assist you!

This collection is a reflection of work that emerges from the Difference, Power, and Discrimination (DPD) Program at Oregon State University which is as near perfect as an institution-wide program can get. The DPD Program is a unique, productive, highly successful and time-tested program. Its emphasis is on curricular transformation, critical interdisciplinary engagements, and creative collaborations. It works with instructors across disciplinary locations to encourage their critical innovations for teaching students about the social ills of discrimination and about the power yielded to implement structures of discrimination and their impact at the individual and structural levels. These social ills not only have a negative impact on individuals; they also affect groups, communities, social systems, and nations. This program is clearly distinctive in its focus and insistence on engaging with questions of power, effective in its implementation, and serves as a model for any higher education institution regardless of size, location or affiliation.

We, Drs. Alma Clayton-Pedersen and Frank Hernandez, are privileged to write this foreword about the DPD Program because of our personal and professional relationship with the program's director, Dr. Nana Osei-Kofi. As an administrator and scholar, she is transnationally and locally informed as well as clearly passionate about the Program, which prompted her to invite us to conduct a program review of it in 2015 and submit a report to help guide its ongoing evolution. Our team, which included Jonathon McPhetres who was then a graduate student, spent four days interviewing faculty, administrators, staff, and students engaged with the program. We also reviewed program documents, course syllabi, and previous program development recommendations. Our insights as early readers of this collection and especially as reviewers of the Program and its history allow us to write with clarity and conviction.

The DPD Program has evolved over its nearly 30-year history. Yet, it remains a work in progress because its multi-discipline and multi-course curricula have an evolutionary design that is locally aware and responsive to living histories. It includes a summer faculty professional development component. The Program also evolves by taking into account adopting the lessons learned from regularly reviewing, enhancing, and incorporating new content into faculty development offerings and course design. It focuses on historical and new knowledges and embeds current events that provide contexts for its focus on the persistence of inequities in society, with a focus on the United States, challenging and resisting the all-too-common practice of locating social inequities elsewhere, rather than in our immediate environment. This better ensures that all students understand and have the knowledge to address discrimination and inequities effectively when they are witnessed and experienced. While it is not guaranteed that learners will use their knowledge and skills, having them offers learners an opportunity to do so; while not having them makes it highly unlikely. It remains an exemplary prototype that needs to be amplified and expanded to other institutions and nations to address global racial tensions, especially *now* in the midst of the COVID-19 pandemic and persistent publicly enacted racial injustices.

The deaths of George Floyd, Michael Brown, Natasha McKenna, Eric Garner, Breonna Taylor, Ahmaud Arbery, Sandra Bland, and Michelle Cusseaux, among many others, have raised our nation's awareness of the violence and daily injustices that Black people face in the United States. These daily injustices are part of a long history of a not-yet-eradicated epidemic of violence in the U.S. that, while centered in the Black community, also extends into LGBTQ communities, Indigenous communities, and all communities of color. The data on the COVID-19 pandemic also shows a disproportionately negative impact on Black, Brown, and Indigenous communities and underscores the health inequities these communities face in the U.S. These awakenings by those inside and outside communities of color have energized others across the globe to demand equity and justice for Black people and others who are marginalized. DPD courses at Oregon State University offer deep insights about such disparities here in the United States and provide exemplary guidance on how to address them in the classroom and in the world beyond. We are convinced that embedding such learning experiences as an academic requirement can increase our nation's ability not only to grapple with but also to resolve these destructive inequities – especially when addressed from an intersectional systems of oppression perspective.

Since 1992–93, all undergraduate students at OSU have been required to take a minimum of one, three-credit DPD course to fulfill the university's Baccalaureate Core curriculum requirements. Building on this distinctive institutional history, this volume of selected course development, content, and implementation strategies is timely and urgent. Most importantly, each DPD course examines the different ways inequities are laid bare and offers strategies to address them regardless of discipline or students' majors. Taking at least one DPD course increases students' awareness of the disproportionate challenges and structural injustices that marginalized communities face. Minimally, the one-course requirement ensures students are exposed to knowledge and can develop understanding and skills to address the barriers to achieving a world in which everyone regardless of identity or group belonging, can thrive and fully realize their potential. Students are encouraged to enroll in more than one DPD course and some do.

In different ways, the four sections of this book focus attention on various approaches faculty can use to reframe subject matter content while also attending to effective instructional practices. That is, practices should engage all students more deeply in the subject matter through a full understanding of learners' capacities. The keys to the DPD Program's success are derived from an understanding that each faculty member brings valuable insights as well as a willingness to take pedagogical risks in the name of the development of coherent and effective plans for achieving the desired student learning outcomes. However, participating instructors must be vigilant to define clearly to students what those learning outcomes are, and then link them to effective practices that learners can enact in real-world settings. Said differently, it is not enough to possess knowledge; we must know how it can be used to achieve intended goals, especially as these pertain to social justice!

The DPD Program at OSU offers a prototypical structure and evolutionary content for higher education to finally address the destructive effects of interlocking systems of oppression, discrimination, and exclusion; social ills grounded in negative perceptions of group and individual differences, and relations of power. For these reasons, we think you truly have found a model program that can guide our higher education systems, institutions, and their faculties towards the moral high ground.

Acknowledgements

As editors, we would like to first thank the Kalapuya people whose land Oregon State University sits on and on which we completed this volume. We are greatly appreciative of the Coalition of Concerned Student Leaders whose demands resulted in the creation of the DPD Program close to three decades ago, as there would be no Program without these student activists' labor. We also want to recognize the first Director of the DPD Program, Annie Popkin, for the foundational work she did in the early years, as well as those who followed in this role: Barbara Paige, Mina Carson, Joan Gross, Susan Shaw, Jun Xing, and Michelle Bothwell. We extend our thanks to the over 300 faculty members who have participated in the DPD Academy over the life of the Program, and from whom we continuously learn how to most effectively do the work of curriculum transformation for social justice across all fields and disciplines.

This book would not be possible without the support of Alix Gitelman, Vice Provost for Undergraduate Education, which is where the DPD Program is housed at OSU, nor would it have come into being if it were not for our colleagues who contributed to this text, and who share our deep commitments to attending to matters of difference, power, and discrimination in everything we do as academics. We are grateful to Alma Clayton-Pedersen and Frank Hernandez for contributing the Foreword to our book and to Susan Shaw for the Afterword. We are also very appreciative of Matthew Friberg and Jessica Cooke at Routledge for enthusiastically working to bring this book to press. A special thank you goes out to Adela C. Licona for gifting us with her artwork on the cover of this book. Last but certainly not least, thank you to our students, who every day help us become better educators, and better advocates for socially just institutions of higher education.

Kali Furman: This project serves as a reminder that the best work and growth happens in community. I am thankful to my co-editors, Bradley and Nana, for bringing me into this project, particularly Nana, who has been my chair and mentor throughout my doctoral work. I am profoundly grateful for the people who have helped me grow as a social justice educator and feminist scholar, whose love, support, and teachings have enabled me to be the person I am today. A special thank you to Jeff Kenney, Charlene Martinez, Natchee

Barnd, Michelle Bothwell, Jess Caldwell-O'Keefe, and Riley Caldwell-O'Keefe for your friendship and mentorship. I would be remiss if I didn't express my heartfelt gratitude to the students I've worked with through my time in Student Affairs; you bring such joy and hope to this world and have taught me so much about the fight for justice. Last, but never least, to my family, partner, and friends, thank you for your unwavering support and love; I couldn't do this work without you.

Bradley Boovy: This volume has reinforced for me the importance of collaboration and community in all aspects of academic work and activist scholarship. I am grateful to my co-editors Kali Furman and Nana Osei-Kofi. Special thanks to Nana for inviting me to join her as co-facilitator of the DPD Academy several years ago. Our work together has been the defining experience of my time at OSU. Thank you to the many friends and colleagues who have offered guidance and encouragement, in particular Hester Baer, Natchee Barnd, Kit Belgum, Susan Bernardin, Benita Blessing, Jennifer Creech, David Crew, Qwo-Li Driskill, Patti Duncan, Michael Floyd, Kryn Freehling-Burton, Sabine Hake, Sebastian Heiduschke, Mariana Ivanova, Jonathan Kaplan, Amy Koehlinger, Janet Lee, Marta Maldonado, Ron Mize, Adam Schwartz, Susan Shaw, Lily Sheehan, Mehra Shirazi, Carrie Smith, Maria Stehle, and Beverly Weber. Finally, I am grateful to my family in Louisiana and my family in Oregon, in particular, James Tarr and Barbara Muraca, for their love and support.

Nana Osei-Kofi: Bradley Boovy and Kali Furman, working with you on this project has been an outstanding experience of teamwork at its best. Thank you for a truly joyful collaboration, every step of the way. To Patti Duncan, Qwo-Li Driskill, Mehra Shirazi, Kryn Freehling-Burton, Ron Mize, Lily Sheehan, Natchee Barnd, Marta Maldonado, Adam Schwartz, Michelle Bothwell, Susan Shaw, Janet Lee, Charlene Martinez, Tyson Marsh, Lena Sawyer, Adela Licona, Daryl Smith, Mel Michelle Lewis, and Antonia Darder, your dedication to doing what it takes to strive toward greater educational, social, and economic justice has served as an inspiration for the work that it took to put this book together, and for this I am deeply appreciative. To my given and chosen family spanning the United States, Ghana, Sweden, and Luxemburg, thank you for your encouragement, love, and support. To Diane Kendall, thank you for your love and for reminding me each day of what it means to be brave, to strive to live up to our highest ideals and values, and to keep on doing the work because it is the right thing to do.

Introduction

Nana Osei-Kofi, Bradley Boovy, and Kali Furman

As we write this introductory chapter, we are in the midst of COVID-19, a global pandemic that has shut down the world in a manner never before experienced in modern history. We are also at a historical juncture in which the murders of Tony McDade, Breonna Taylor, George Floyd, and Ahmaud Arbery have fueled protests against police brutality, white supremacy, and anti-Black racism in the United States and around the world and given rise to an unprecedented public awareness of structural racism. In many ways this is an impossible time to focus on writing. And at the same time, it is a perfect time to focus on writing. This writing. What we see in our own backyard, across the United States, and in many other parts of the world, makes the ongoing urgent need for the type of teaching we take up in this book, centering questions of difference, power, and discrimination, painfully evident. Amid claims that we are all in this together, the reality is that COVID-19 does discriminate. Jointly, these crises of pervasive white supremacy and anti-Black racism along with the COVID-19 pandemic magnify historical and contemporary systemic inequities, and their material consequences. With evidence of who and what is valued in a profoundly unequal society of intersectional stratification, this book works from and attends to the uneven and unjust conditions under which we are living, with a focus on transforming undergraduate curricula in ways that are attentive to matters of difference, power, privilege, and oppression, across all fields and disciplines.

As social justice pedagogues, our inspiration for this book is informed by a longstanding truth articulated among others, by Toni Morrison (in Hult, 2016) in her suggestion that "if there is a book that you want to read, but it hasn't been written yet, then you must write it" (p. 327). We have put together an edited volume that builds on the excellent work that already exists on social justice education, and at the same time attends to the ways in which the manifestation of social and economic injustice is always historically and contextually specific, thus shifting in various ways over time. This recognition, therefore, requires that we as educators keep learning and keep growing in our commitments to facilitating and fostering critical consciousness in our classrooms, in order that students may see the world and come to understand it through a social justice lens, fully recognizing how we all participate in shaping a shared future.

In pursuit of these goals, we invited an interdisciplinary group of faculty members with deep commitments to the advancement of social justice in higher education to contribute to this book. As a way of modeling the type of engagement we seek to advance, the process for putting this text together has been highly collaborative, intentionally crossing disciplinary boundaries and pushing back against the many silos that often serve as limiting factors in realizing commitments to institution-wide curriculum transformation. As we worked together, we developed a peer-review process where we reviewed each other's drafts ahead of a three-day contributor retreat. At this retreat, each contributor, or contributor pair, was provided with a time slot to workshop their chapter. During our time together, we also had the opportunity to talk about our collective vision for the book as a whole, as well as what the future might hold for social justice teaching and learning in U.S. higher education. We shared meals, had engaging and intense conversations, learned from each other, and also laughed a lot. We were able to be in community in ways that are all too uncommon for those of us who labor in the academy.

What we witnessed through this process was in many ways an object lesson in the transformative power of collaboration, as the contributors to this book fully embraced the risks and joys of collaboration in service of meaningful social and curriculum transformation. The willingness of our contributors to make meaning of the process of collaboration with each other across disciplines and institutional locations, and to learn from each other, was truly inspiring in ways we hope are evident to readers throughout the chapters of this book.

Transformative Approaches to Editing, Authoring, Teaching, and Administering: A Relational Practice

So, who are we, the editors of this book, and for whom is it intended? As editors, we come to the notion of advancing how we do social justice education in colleges and universities from varied histories and commitments to socially just transformative teaching and learning practices. Nana has been a faculty member for close to 20 years, directing social justice-focused programs for the majority of this time. Bradley is a recently tenured faculty member whose disciplinary training is in German literary and cultural studies, and who comes to social justice pedagogies through activist commitments and community engagement. Kali, who is completing her PhD in Women, Gender, & Sexuality Studies, has worked in the area of student affairs for five years with programs that focus on supporting marginalized students and providing social justice-focused educational programming and training.

As we have worked on this volume, it has pushed us and challenged us, and appropriately so, to critically and earnestly reflect on what brings us to this work. For Kali, being a PhD candidate, the answer to these questions have often come easily as the articulation of a rationale for one's work is central to the doctoral completion process. Describing the experiences that inform her drive to create change through curriculum transformation, Kali says,

I was raised in a rural white working-class community in Northern Idaho, and I always viewed education as my way out of my hometown. In college I began to take classes in history and gender studies and these courses gave me the opportunity to understand systems of privilege and oppression and make meaning of my own complex experiences within these systems. My time in gender studies courses led me to get involved with my campus' Gender Equity Center and introduced me to the world of Student Affairs. My dedication to social justice education began with my own transformative education experiences but grew to be grounded in relationships and being in community with undergraduate students. A major theme that emerged from my work with students was hearing about the barriers they were facing in college, particularly those inside the classroom as they were experiencing hostile environments and difficulty with faculty. These experiences deepened my research interests in social justice education and commitment to better preparing faculty to support students from historically underrepresented groups, incorporating social justice issues into college curricula across the institution, and working for more equitable, just learning environments for all students.

For Bradley, the work has meant a deeper reckoning with his own past as a white queer man raised in a context where racism and white supremacy structured daily social interactions and how he moved in and around New Orleans and the city's historically white suburbs. Bradley reflects,

My education through graduate school did not provide much exposure to social justice or critical pedagogies, beyond a few women's studies, sociology, and Latin American studies courses in undergraduate and limited engagement with critical language pedagogies in graduate school (Spanish and German Studies). Until I went through the DPD faculty seminar after starting my position at Oregon State in 2012, social justice education meant simply adding an author of color, a woman author, or a queer author to my syllabus. Although the content of the readings and discussions in the DPD seminar were certainly necessary, equally important were the conversations and collaborative visioning that we engaged in. It was through these conversations – many with colleagues whose work is included in this volume – that I began to understand social justice education in structural terms: as curriculum transformation, to be sure, but also as an activist position from which to engage in transforming the institution and higher education more broadly.

Nana grew up in a family of educators from very different parts of the world (Ghana and Sweden), where questions of social justice were part of her every day. Describing how she became involved with social justice education, she says,

In some ways I wonder if I ever truly had a choice! Growing up, my mother's side of the family was deeply rooted in socialist labor movements. To work for the rights of working people was much more than being involved in different campaigns and actions, it was a defining identity and way of being in the world. Both my father and my maternal grandmother were also heavily invested in addressing conditions on the African continent with attention to those nations that at the time of my childhood had yet to achieve independence, as well as those grappling with the realities of post-independence. That is to say, the conversations I heard at home growing up, were often defined by questions of social justice and economic justice. As a young adult I experimented with doing something other than working in education, as this maybe seemed all too familiar to me. However, after some time working in both the non-profit world and the corporate world, it was clear to me that doing work in education, as part of a commitment to social justice, was and is, to this day, what I call home.

We envision this volume as a book for *anyone* with an interest in teaching and learning in higher education from a social justice perspective and with a commitment to teaching *all* students. It aims to offer a breadth of disciplinary perspectives on how to enter the stream by incorporating or building new courses as well as by collaborating in ways that take up a lens or framework that centers difference, power, and discrimination as essential to disciplinary knowledge building and to teaching. All too often, issues that concern matters such as race, class, gender, sexuality, (dis)ability, environmental sustainability, and nation are treated as "add-ons" or dealt with as discrete areas of engagement during predetermined class sessions, rather than being conceived of as fundamental to a critical understanding of all forms of disciplinary knowledge.

This book is structured as an ongoing conversation among educators and collaborators who take the position that teaching from a social justice perspective is about much more than the type of readings and assignments that we put on our course syllabi. Drawing on a broad definition of curriculum transformation, it is as much about how our positionality as educators informs how we show up in the classroom as it is about the content of our courses. It is about the degree to which we understand the students we are charged with teaching, the type of pedagogical approaches we employ as individual instructors and as social justice educators innovating through collaboration. It is also about teaching beyond the traditional classroom to include local communities, labor movements, archives, and colleagues in student and academic affairs. Through relational collaboration and with a context-informed, place-based grounding, this project seeks to demonstrate the possibilities of transformative approaches to social justice education across disciplines.

Context

This volume comes out of Oregon State University's Difference Power, and Discrimination Program, a distinctive faculty development program now in its 28th year, designed to facilitate focused and productive faculty engagement with contemporary, multidisciplinary scholarship on issues of power, oppression, and systemic injustice; critical pedagogies; and curriculum transformation. While we envision this as a book for educators in all types of higher education institutions, it is important to say something here about our specific context, working, teaching, and learning within a land-grant institution. We hope this will inspire readers to interrogate their respective institutional contexts as part of advancing social justice education. It is also our hope that the hyper-local, place-based approach that serves as the foundation for this book and that has lent success to the DPD Program, functions as a resource for those who might seek to create similar programs to think critically and creatively about their institutional context.

Located in Corvallis, Oregon State University is in the traditional territory of the Ampinefu Band of the Kalapuya people. As a land-grant institution, Oregon State traces its history to the first Morrill Act of 1862, through which the land-grant system was first established. Although the first Morrill Act is often understood as a landmark piece of legislation in the history of U.S. democracy, the Act and the institutions that it enabled cannot be fully grasped apart from broader histories of genocide and relocation of Indigenous peoples, enslavement of Africans and their descendants, and U.S. settler colonialism and imperialism more generally. Tellingly, while the land granted through the enabling act belongs to Indigenous people, it was not until a full 132 years later in 1994 that tribal colleges and universities were assigned land-grant status.

Passed in the midst of the Civil War, the 1862 Act was principally motivated by the federal government's need to ensure that the country would not be without the infrastructure to support a robust agricultural system in the event that the confederate states won the War (Collier, 2002). In 1890, the second Morrill Act provided for the expansion of the 1862 Act by making it a requirement that 17 southern states establish separate institutions for Black students in order to continue receiving funding for white land-grant colleges. The distinction between institution and college is important in the language of the 1890 Act insofar as it signaled critical distinctions in higher education for Black and White students. While the historically white 1862 land-grants benefitted from legislation such as the 1887 Hatch Act, which established agricultural experiment stations, the 1890 Black land-grants were not given nearly the same amount of financial support to develop robust research and educational initiatives on a par with their 1862 counterparts (Christy et al., 1992; Humphries, 1992). The growth and development of the 1994 tribal land-grants has followed a similar pattern as the 1890 Black land-grants, with notable disparities in resources between historically white institutions and tribal colleges and universities (Phillips, 2003). These differences in access to financial support and other resources between the 1862 land-grants on one hand, and the 1890 and 1994 land-grants on the other, point to the ongoing impact of settler colonialism and systemic racism in educational legislation and appropriation of state and federal funding into our present moment.

As an institution that bears the legacy of these systems of oppression and their contemporary ongoing manifestations, Oregon State University is a contested space in which students, faculty, staff, and administrators continually navigate their positions in relation to institutional power structures. For many Oregon State University students, activism has been a central component of their university experience. Student activists have had a profound effect on the institution over the course of its history, shaping institutional change and leaving behind a legacy of action. Student activists have created lasting change on our campus in many different ways, from the existence of our seven cultural resource centers to the Difference, Power, and Discrimination Program itself. As a program brought into being as a result of student activism and their demands that we as educators do our job with all students in mind, we ultimately have students to thank for this book project becoming a reality.

The history of the DPD Program has its roots in the fall of 1990, when, following a series of racially motivated incidents on campus and consistent reports from marginalized students about a chilly campus climate, a coalition of student leaders prepared a detailed letter outlining six proposals for ways to address these issues. The students, recorded in the archives by the collective name *Concerned Student Leaders*, delivered their demands to then university president John Byrne. Among the items in the letter was a proposal that the institution create a "series of courses dealing with cultural and ethnic diversity, as well as racism/discrimination and their origins" (Concerned Student Leaders, 1990, pp. 17–18). In their response to the students, the University administration agreed to this item and tasked the Faculty Senate Baccalaureate Core Committee (BCC) to create a framework for adding a course dealing with issues of diversity to the Baccalaureate Core requirements for the university. The BCC worked throughout the 1990–1991 academic year to develop an initial proposal for what they called the "Affirming Diversity" course. They recommended to the Faculty Senate that a multi-disciplinary committee be created and tasked with developing the full proposal and all of the logistics for the course in the 1991–1992 academic year. This group, the Affirming Diversity Course Development Committee, worked to research similar courses across the United States, gathered input from students, faculty and staff, and assembled the final proposal that was submitted to and approved by the Faculty Senate in May 1992, creating the Difference, Power, and Discrimination Program. For more about the early history and development of the DPD Program, see *Teaching for Change* (Xing et al., 2007), Kali Furman's chapter in this volume, and Susan Shaw's Afterword.

The essence of the DPD program is made up of two elements: a multi-disciplinary selection of course offerings that meet the DPD Baccalaureate Core general education requirement and a faculty development seminar that provides faculty with the tools to aid in the creation of DPD courses. All courses in the DPD category of the Baccalaureate Core must meet a set of 10 criteria:

1   Be at least three credits;
2   Emphasize elements of critical thinking;
3   Have as their central focus the study of the unequal distribution of power within the framework of particular disciplines and course content;
4   Focus primarily on the United States, although global contexts are encouraged;
5   Provide illustrations of ways in which structural, institutional, and ideological discrimination arise from socially defined meanings attributed to difference;
6   Provide historical and contemporary examples of difference, power, and discrimination across cultural, economic, social, and political institutions in the United States;
7   Provide illustrations of ways in which the interactions of social categories such as race, ethnicity, social class, gender, religion, sexual orientation, disability, and age, are related to difference, power, and discrimination in the United States;
8   Provide a multidisciplinary perspective on issues of difference, power, and discrimination;
9   Incorporate interactive learning activities (e.g., ungraded, in-class writing exercise; classroom discussion; peer-review of written material; web-based discussion group); and
10 Be regularly numbered departmental offerings rather than blanket number courses.

Additionally, there are three learning outcomes for all DPD courses:

1   Explain how difference is socially constructed;
2   Using historical and contemporary examples, describe how perceived differences, combined with unequal distribution of power across economic, social, and political institutions result in discrimination;
3   Analyze ways in which the interactions of social categories such as race, ethnicity, social class, gender, religion, sexual orientation, disability, and age, are related to difference, power, and discrimination in the United States.

These learning outcomes are the same for all DPD courses and are listed in syllabi in addition to any course-specific learning outcomes designed by faculty.

In the 1992–1993 academic year, eight DPD course sections were offered at Oregon State University; a number that has steadily grown over the past 28 years, with 242 course sections being offered in the 2017–2018 academic year. The growth in the number of DPD courses offered is also reflected in student enrollments. In the 1992–1993 academic year 239 students enrolled in a DPD course. By 2017–2018, this number had grown to 8,262. DPD courses are offered across disciplines, with courses being housed in the College of Liberal

Arts; the College of Public Health and Human Sciences; the College of Education; the College of Earth, Ocean, and Atmospheric Sciences; the College of Science; and the College of Engineering.

Since the first faculty seminar in the summer of 1992, over 300 faculty members have participated in the immersive seminar experience. As it stands today, the DPD Academy is designed to facilitate faculty engagement with contemporary scholarship on issues of difference, power, and discrimination, critical pedagogies, and curriculum transformation. Faculty apply to participate in the Academy and work to revise an existing course or develop a new course that meets the DPD course criteria for the Baccalaureate Core. The DPD Academy consists of sixty hours of programming divided between a 45-hour summer institute and three to five follow-up sessions held throughout the academic year following the summer institute. Faculty are compensated via participant stipends for participating in the DPD Academy. The editors and contributors to this volume have all participated in or helped to facilitate the DPD Academy over the years, and the diversity of their experiences and the resulting work from the seminar are reflected in their contributions in the chapters that follow.

Overview of the Book

Any effort at fundamental curriculum transformation is a deeply political endeavor that must transcend our classroom practices. To create educational environments where students must critically engage with questions of difference, power, privilege, and oppression demands that we as educators take up these very same types of questions in relation to our disciplinary communities, the institutions in which we labor, and the larger society in which we live. While these are not matters that we take up exhaustively throughout this text, we believe it is important to mention these factors as essential to the realization of the type of pedagogical work with which the contributors to this volume engage. Drawing on a wide range of literatures, contributors candidly share and theorize from their own efforts and experiences in the classroom, and offer specific pedagogical suggestions, as well as resources for further engagement.

Section 1: Archives and Power: Engaging History Collaboratively opens with Kali Furman's chapter titled "Student Activism and Institutional Change: A History of the Difference, Power, and Discrimination Program at Oregon State University" wherein she draws on archival materials to examine student activism and faculty responses to student demands that led to the creation of the Difference, Power, and Discrimination Program. Reflecting on her own experiences working with student activists in the present, Furman insists on the need to take up the role of student activism in any effort to understand social justice-informed institutional change in U.S. higher education, noting that this often means lifting forth historical lessons hidden in plain sight. In the chapter that follows, "Collaborations between Professors and Archivists: Engaging

Students with their Local Community History," Natalia Fernández provides a framework and multiple examples of how faculty and archivists can work collaboratively across disciplines to not only engage with institutional histories but also histories of local communities, with a focus on minoritized populations, which all too often are missing from the official histories of communities. The final chapter in this section, "Scripting Change: The Social Justice Tour of Corvallis" by Natchee Barnd offers a powerful example of a faculty member in an ethnohistory methodology class, working collaboratively across disciplines, with students, archivists, and the local community, to create a series of social justice tours. Barnd highlights student work as a way to illustrate the power of experiential learning, speaking to the importance of institutions of higher education engaging with the local communities in which they are situated, while also offering specific suggestions for how similar projects can be realized within any institution of higher education.

Section 2: Frameworks for Transformative Pedagogies is made up of four chapters that in different ways highlight strategies to shift pedagogical practices toward greater justice and equity for all students. In "Universal Design for Instruction and Institutional Change: A Case Study," Stephanie Jenkins and Martha Smith offer a detailed overview and account of various ways to effectively use Universal Design for Instruction (UDI) to improve access for all students. Drawing on their collaborative efforts to promote UDI at Oregon State University, they share ways to incorporate UDI into all elements of course design, while also offering an honest assessment of both the benefits and obstacles they have experienced as a result of their collaborative efforts. Jenny Myers addresses the absolute necessity of intentionality in online course design where social justice is of import in "Critical Pedagogy Online: Opportunities and Challenges in Social Justice Education." In this chapter she notes that while online education can increase access globally, it simultaneously presents a great risk of re-creating colonizing educational structures, norms, and biases. Reflecting on her experiences with teaching a course on the social dimensions of sustainability, Myers recounts her efforts to create a just, sustainable community of learners online. In "Peace Literacy, Cognitive Bias, and Structural Injustice," Sharyn Clough introduces and offers a framework for the incorporation of Peace Literacy in the teaching of subject matter pertaining to questions of injustice. She describes how she uses a classroom art exercise to bring awareness to the ways in which individually held cognitive biases interact with and perpetuate structural levels of injustice. She also discusses how she situates her work in the classroom within a Peace Literacy framework, which can provide both educators and students with new ways to both learn about and work to dismantle structural injustice. The final chapter in this section, "From Here to There: Educating for Wholeness" by Erich Pitcher and Charlene Martinez focuses on the role of healing as part of social justice education. Drawing on their collaborative work with an arts and social justice living learning community for first-year undergraduate students, Pitcher and Martinez describe different pedagogical practices aimed at healing and wholeness, not only for students, but also for educators, and changemakers generally. Guided by the question of what it means to work toward the twin goals of justice and wholeness in higher education, they identify and discuss sentipensante pedagogy as a framework that seeks to achieve wholeness as part of teaching for social justice, as well as within higher education more broadly.

Section 3: Destabilizing Dominant Narratives centers pedagogical approaches to the taken for granted. In "'The Tree of Anger': Queer and Trans Studies in the Difference, Power, and Discrimination Program at Oregon State University," H. Rakes and Qwo-Li Driskill use their development of Queer Studies curricula and a degree minor to discuss what it means to both create courses and use pedagogical approaches that seek to uproot multiple forms of oppression. Focusing on the need for queer and trans people-of-color critiques in Queer Studies, Rakes and Driskill speak to the erasure and tokenization of race and colonization as dominant characteristics of the field and offer specific examples of how they have disrupted these notions in their own practices as well as how they work to move students from the personal to the political and from theory to practice. Also addressing the multiple roots of oppression, in "Reflections on Race/Ethnicity, Gender, and Labor in the Latinx Studies Classroom," Marta Maldonado offers critical pedagogical approaches to teaching about race/ethnicity, gender, and labor. Centering unlearning as a way to encourage students to become aware and critically question the ways race, class, and gender shape thoughts, actions, and emotions, Maldonado shares strategies from her Latinx Studies courses that go beyond simply providing information and, instead, aim to help learners see and pursue future possibilities for positive social transformations at the individual and the structural level. Allison Hurst's chapter, "Talking About Class," describes different ways to break the silence about class in response to what is an all-too-common absence of engagement with this important topic in many courses, even in spaces where other social justice-related content is covered. Drawing on her own experiences as a working-class academic, Hurst shares activities and exercises from her own classrooms whereby students have the opportunity to explore class at the macro level, and from there move towards examinations of their own class identities and culture. Throughout, Hurst highlights the importance of recognizing that a deep understanding of class goes beyond dollars and cents, and that class must also be understood in relation to other intersecting identities. Working with the concept of the teacher as embodied text, in "Teaching about Race in the Historically White Difference, Power, and Discrimination Classroom: Teacher as Text," Bradley Boovy and Nana Osei-Kofi use their experiences of being differently racialized and gendered by students to discuss how their awareness of the ways in which students read them has shaped their teaching practices in relation to matters of race, racialization, and racism. In so doing, they not only consider faculty-student relationships, but also highlight the significance of engaging with matters of race at a historically white land-grant institution.

Section 4: Rethinking Approaches to Disciplinary Content includes four chapters that offer perspectives on how to work with disciplinary content and remain attentive to difference, power, and discrimination. "Religious Bias, Christian Privilege, and Anti-Muslimism in the Difference, Power, and Discrimination Classroom" by Amy Koehlinger and Kryn Freehling-Burton addresses ways to challenge commonly held beliefs about Christianity especially, and religion generally, in the U.S. As a response to identified misconceptions, they offer pedagogical strategies to help students develop more complex understandings of religion in history as well as in contemporary society, with attention to interrupting and challenging anti-Muslimism. Additionally, they provide approaches to help facilitate students' critical reflections on religion in their own lives as an effective way to create awareness and knowledge that pushes against dangerous, oppressive, and discriminatory ways of thinking about religion. In "¡Sí, se puede! Teaching Farmworker Justice in the Land-Grant University," Ronald Mize recounts his experiences with teaching farmworker justice courses and shares his process for implementing experiential learning approaches developed by ethnic studies scholars in these courses. He also offers a broad overview of farmworker justice courses taught nationally, while at the same time both raising critical questions about the institutional contexts in which these courses are taught and centering questions of the politics of engagement with farmworker justice at land-grant universities. In "Listen Up, STEM: We Don't Just Teach Facts," Glencora Borradaile compares two experiences teaching in STEM classrooms (engineering and computer science) and the results of her efforts to support both undergraduate and graduate students' understanding of individual, institutional, and structural discrimination. As Borradaile describes and reflects on her experience, she not only shares from the classroom, but also takes up broader challenges in relation to how social justice content is often seen as something out of place in STEM. Her work demonstrates the possibilities and challenges of different models of incorporating social justice content into STEM classrooms, and as the only chapter that includes content on graduate education, demonstrates how lessons from teaching graduate students are also applicable to the undergraduate context and vise-versa. This section concludes with "'Show, Don't Tell': Teaching Social Justice at the Source" by Marisa Chappell and Linda Richards. In this chapter the authors explore the use of primary sources as a pedagogical approach to allow students to discover important historical lessons for themselves, with a focus on deepening their understanding of unequal power relations and their development of historical empathy. Pointing to this as an effective way to address difference, power, and discrimination in a history course, Chappell and Richards describe ways they foster critical analyses and appreciation for complexity in their classrooms, in addition to their focus on historical empathy. The book concludes with an Afterword by feminist religious studies scholar and former DPD Director Susan Shaw. It is our hope that jointly the chapters of this book will inspire creativity, risk-taking, collaborative endeavors, and foremost, institutional change, premised on commitments to teaching all students, and to working to radically transform how and what we teach, in service of equity and justice.

References

Christy, R.D., Williamson, L., & Williamson Jr, H. (1992). A century of service: The past, present, and future roles of 1890 land-grant colleges and institutions. In R. D. Christy, & L. Williamson (Eds.), *A century of service: Land-grant colleges and universities, 1890–1990* (pp. xiii–xxv). Routledge.

Collier, J. (2002). Scripting the radical critique of science: The Morrill Act and the American land-grant university. *Futures, 34*, 182–191. https://doi.org/10.1016/S0016-3287(01)00057-X

Hult, C.A. (2016). *The handy english grammar answer book*. Visible Ink Press.

Humphries, F. (1992). Land-grant institutions: Their struggle for survival and equality. In R.D. Christy, & L. Williamson (Eds.), *A century of service: Land-grant colleges and universities, 1890–1990* (pp. 3–12). Routledge.

Johnson, E.L. (1981). Misconceptions about the early land-grant colleges. *The Journal of Higher Education, 52*(4), 333–351. https://doi.org/10.1080/00221546.1981.11780153

Phillips, J.L. (2003). A tribal college land grant perspective: Changing the conversation. *Journal of American Indian Education, 42*(1), 22–35. https://eric.ed.gov/?id=EJ668564

Xing, J., Li, J., Roper, L., & Shaw, S. (Eds.). (2007). *Teaching for change: The Difference, Power, and Discrimination model*. Lexington Books.

Section 1
Archives and Power: Engaging History Collaboratively

1 Student Activism and Institutional Change

A History of The Difference, Power, and Discrimination Program at Oregon State University

Kali Furman

In 1990 a group of Oregon State University student organizers sent a letter to then university president John Byrne with a series of proposals for addressing the climate on campus for underrepresented students following a series of racist incidents on campus. Among the student proposals was an item insisting that "the University must develop and implement a series of courses dealing with cultural and ethnic diversity, as well as racism/discrimination and their origins" (Xing et al., 2007, p. 14). This letter started a chain of events that ultimately led to the creation of the Difference, Power, and Discrimination (DPD) Program. The creation of the DPD Program and its continued survival at the institution is due to the combined efforts of multiple actors including students, faculty and staff, the faculty senate, and DPD Program administrators. Each has parallel histories that intersected for the purpose of establishing and maintaining the DPD Program on campus. Through the use of university archival materials that span the past twenty-eight years, this chapter examines the relationship between student activism, faculty involvement, and institutional change in the history of the Difference, Power, and Discrimination Program at Oregon State University. Drawing on this as a foundation, I also reflect on my own experiences working with student activists and learning from a long history of student activism at Oregon State University about how we as teachers and practitioners can account for legacies of student activism and institutional memory.

The student organizers who addressed the university president in 1990 were not an anomaly in the history of the institution, but rather another generation in an ongoing legacy of student activists at Oregon State. This history is one I was largely unaware of when I came in 2013 to Oregon State University to pursue a master's degree in Women, Gender, and Sexuality Studies. When I arrived at Oregon State my knowledge about student activism was relatively limited. I was familiar with particularly famous historical forms of activism such as the Student Nonviolent Coordinating Committee (SNCC) and had some experiences as an undergraduate student planning student actions. I spent my first three years on campus working for the Diversity and Cultural Engagement office and through my work with undergraduate students began to understand the university's student activist culture that continues from this historical legacy.

DOI: 10.4324/9781003091998-2

In the eight years I've been at Oregon State there have been numerous incidents on campus that have spurred student action and, in turn, an institutional response. As these events have unfolded, I have had the opportunity to learn from students participating in these actions, as well as from university faculty and staff whose institutional memories include actions from previous student generations that have echoed the patterns happening in contemporary events. I experienced first-hand the tensions present in supporting student activism while serving as an employee of the institution and navigating bureaucratical structures while helping students to subvert them. These experiences have prompted my research interests in the ebbs and flows of institutional memory in relationship to student activism, faculty involvement, administrative responses, and institutional change more broadly. To examine how these patterns function in the history of the Difference, Power, and Discrimination Program, it is important to understand the history of racism in Oregon and Oregon State University's student activist history.

Oregon's Racial History and Student Activism at Oregon State University

In the United States, the state of Oregon has a reputation for being a highly progressive liberal state but, in reality, the state operates from a place of white liberalism – meaning people who proport to be "liberal" but still uphold beliefs, practices and policies that continue to support oppression such as racism or classism. For example, in liberal communities such as Portland, Corvallis, and Eugene NIMBYism (an acronym for Not in My Back Yard) is commonplace. The majority of the population support policies that actively harm the large local houseless populations, such as opposing the creation of new low-income housing developments. As the writer, organizer, and spoken word artist Walidah Imarisha (2013) has shown through her critical work on the history of Black people in Oregon, the state was founded as "a white Utopian homeland" (p. 12). The state's history of anti-Black racism predates its official statehood. In 1844 the provisional Oregon government passed Black exclusion laws, including a "Lash Law" that required all Black people residing in the state be whipped twice a year (Imarisha, 2013, p. 13). Oregon was the only state in the United Sates that was founded with an explicitly anti-Black clause in its constitution that forbade Black people from living in the state. Also included in the state constitution was a prohibition on Chinese Americans owning property, as well as filing or working on mining claims (Wilson, 2017). Oregon's legacy of racism continues to this day and is evidenced in the gentrification of historically Black Portland communities like Albina – which were created by the use of redlining – and discrepancies in housing, income, education, and incarceration rates for Black Oregonians as compared to their white counterparts (Imarisha, 2013, p. 19). Oregon's history of white supremacy and its ongoing legacy contributes to low numbers of people of color living in Oregon and attending Oregon State University. This also influences the ways in which racism manifests in the state and at the institution. A strong dynamic I observed while working in student affairs at Oregon State University is the divergent ways that white students, especially those from rural communities, and students of color experience our campus.

Oregon has a population-dense urban corridor ranging from the cities of Portland to Eugene; however, most of the state outside this corridor is composed of rural communities. I have often seen students from backgrounds not dissimilar from my own, small rural predominantly white working-class communities, express that Oregon State University is the most diverse place they've ever lived. In the same conversations students of color will state that Oregon and Oregon State University are the whitest places they've ever lived. These differences contribute to the divergent ways that students experience campus and how they navigate the institution and broader Corvallis community. Oregon State University is a predominantly white land-grant Research I institution located in Corvallis, Oregon. Founded in 1868, Oregon State University is located on the traditional territory of the Mary's River or Ampinefu Band of the Kalapuya people who were forcibly removed to the Siletz and Grand Ronde reservations beginning in 1855. Oregon State has a heavy STEM focus and is one of only two universities in the United States to have Land-Grant, Sea-Grant, Space-Grant, and Sun-Grant designations. The university currently has an enrollment of 32,011 students and of those 25% are students of color[1] (About Oregon State University, n.d.). Oregon State University has been shaped by whiteness through the legacy of racism in the state of Oregon and through dominance of white students, staff, and faculty on campus throughout the institution's history.

Oregon State University, like many institutions of higher education, has a long history of racism and, accompanying that, a rich history of student activism. Over the course of its history, Oregon State University has seen multiple marches, walkouts, and other forms of student protest in response to racism, homophobia, sexual violence, and other bias incidents. For example, in 1969, the Black Student Union walked out of the university after a racist incident with the head football coach, Dee Andros, when he threatened to expel a Black student athlete, Fred Milton, over his facial hair. In addition to the walk out the Black Student Union organized a sit-in, a class boycott, and started an underground newspaper, *The Scab Sheet*. These actions led the university to create the Educational Opportunities Program and in the years that followed two of Oregon State University's seven cultural resource centers opened – the Native American Longhouse (1971) and the Centro Cultural Cesar Chavez (1972) (Oregon Multicultural Archives & Students of ALS 199, 2013). This pattern of student activism and institutional moves to create offices or programs to address issues around diversity and inequity continues today.

A contemporary example of this pattern occurred in 2015. That year students of color at the University of Missouri began a series of protests addressing the racist and homophobic campus climate. These protests sparked further student actions at multiple institutions across the United States, including Oregon State

University. On November 11, 2015 three students, two of color and one white, and some of whom were queer, sent a letter to the senior administrators of Oregon State University calling out the administration for not doing enough to make OSU's stated vision of creating a collaborative, inclusive and caring environment a reality for students of color. In their letter the students wrote,

> Many students of color have experienced acts of racial violence on our campus that have gone unacknowledged and unaddressed. Furthermore, students of color are not experiencing the sense of security or the space to have their voice be heard on campus that they are entitled to.
> (Armas et al., 2015)

The students demanded upper administration presence at a student of color speak out on the evening of Monday, November 16, 2015 at Gill Coliseum (the campus basketball arena). Over 500 people attended the Student of Color Speak Out event on campus and an estimated 3,000 watched the event from a live stream hosted by the university (Rimel, 2015). This event was attended by then university president Ed Ray, along with several other senior administrators. Eventually these actions led the university to create an Office of Institutional Diversity and hire a Chief Diversity Officer.

These events speak to the current state of student activism at Oregon State University and reflect the longer history of the institution. Such patterns of student demands and administrative responses are also visible in the history of the Difference, Power, and Discrimination Program on campus, which began in the early 1990s following a series of racist incidents and student organizing. In the history of these cycles of student actions and institutional responses at Oregon State University we can begin to see patterns emerge that demonstrate the importance of institutional memory and collaborations between students, staff, and faculty to create institutional change.

1990 Student Organizing

On October 20, 1990 an African American male student at Oregon State University was verbally assaulted with derogatory racist remarks from a group of white men in a moving van while in a restaurant parking lot in Corvallis. The student wrote down the vehicle license plate number and saw that the van had several decals associated with a campus fraternity. The student followed the van back to the fraternity house and left a written request for an apology. The next day he received a phone call from the van's driver, an Oregon State Alumni and fraternity member. The driver told the student that he and the other men in the van, who were also alumni and one active OSU student, acted the way they did because they had been drinking (Jaramillo, 1991). After, word began to spread on campus about this incident and students began to organize. On October 23, three days after the incident, the Board of Directors of the Memorial Union held an emergency meeting. At that meeting the coordinator of the Lonnie B. Harris Black Cultural Center announced that the center would be closing indefinitely in protest of the "increased incidents of racial bigotry on campus and in the community, as well as the lack of responsiveness from university administration" (Jaramillo, 1991, p. 2). This closure and the ensuing student conversations about their experiences prompted a significant increase in accounts of racial harassment and discrimination that had gone unreported and further assertions that the university administration was unresponsive to incidents that were reported to the institution (Jaramillo, 1991).

Following this action by student leaders at the Lonnie B. Harris Black Cultural Center, on October 24 Oregon State University President Byrne and other administrative leaders (the Vice Presidents of the institution and the Faculty Senate President) published an open letter stating that the university "will not tolerate cultural insensitivity or racial, ethnic, sexist, or homophobic harassment" and to reaffirm the university's "commitment to increasing the ethnic/cultural diversity on campus and in the greater community" (Jaramillo, 1991, Appendix A). The letter was published in the student newspaper, *The Barometer*, and sent to all faculty, staff, student leaders, and the residence halls (Jaramillo, 1991). The Lonnie B. Harris Black Cultural Center reopened on October 26 after students felt like the institution was beginning to move on these issues. During his annual Charter Day address on October 29 President Byrne announced he would form a commission to investigate the extent of racism on campus and the surrounding community and the committee would be charged with making recommendations to him based on the results of their investigation. Much of the history that is recounted in this section is made possible through the documentation of the President's Commission on Racism and their official report, submitted to President Byrne in 1991.

Just one day after the President's announcement that he would create the commission on racism, members of the student government, the Associated Students of OSU (ASOSU), lodged a complaint that other organization members told racist and sexist jokes at an unofficial social event following an ASOSU retreat and that ASOSU failed to take action prohibiting or sanctioning the behavior (Jaramillo, 1991). On October 31 hundreds of students, faculty, staff, and administrators attended a three-hour "Town Meeting" in the Memorial Union lounge to discuss racism on campus. The stories shared at the town hall demonstrated the prevalence of racism in all areas of campus and in the greater Corvallis community. In summarizing the stories shared during the event, the President's Commission on Racism wrote that the issues brought up included:

> The behaviors and actions of administrators, faculty, and staff; interactions between and among students; curricula entrenched primarily in western civilization and Eurocentric thought, and generally insensitive to other cultures; and support of an array of extracurricular activities that reinforced a narrow and oftentimes denigrating attitude toward those outside the mainstream culture. These factors created and maintained an

> unwelcome and insecure learning, working, and living environment for 'minority' students, faculty, and staff.
>
> (Jaramillo, 1991, p. 3)

Following this description of the events that transpired at the Town Meeting, the President's Commission report moves on to describe the work of their committee. Notably, in the commission's report on the racist incidents in the fall of 1990, they excluded a direct action organized by student leaders, a letter sent to the president by student organizers three days after the public meeting.

On November 3, 1990 concerned student leaders presented President Byrne with a letter containing six proposals to confront campus-wide discrimination. These included adopting a zero tolerance policy for all forms of "racist and discriminatory behavior;" developing and implementing a "series of courses dealing with cultural and ethnic diversity, as well as racism/discrimination and their origins;" and making a "firm commitment to the existence of cultural centers" (Concerned Student Leaders, 1990, pp. 17–18). The students' fourth proposition was that the proposed office of Minority Affairs should have the name and scope to reflect its mission and suggested that the title for the office be the "Vice President for Equality Affairs" (Concerned Student Leaders, 1990, p. 19). Additionally, students proposed that an educational program for all faculty, staff, and university employees should be created to deal with topics of cultural and ethnic diversity, as well as discrimination. The final proposal put forth by students was to have an external entity conduct an evaluation of the Affirmative Action Office due to concern over the "ineffectiveness" of the Affirmative Action Office (Concerned Student Leaders, 1990).

On November 8, 1990 President Byrne wrote a letter responding to each of the Concerned Student Leaders' proposals. In response to their proposal for the creation of a series of courses addressing diversity and discrimination, Byrne wrote,

> the Office of Academic Affairs, the Vice President for Student Affairs, the Faculty Senate Curriculum Council, and the Baccalaureate Core Committee will institute at least one new course, or significantly modify existing courses, to deal with issues of cultural awareness.
>
> (Kaattari, 1991, p. 23)

The Baccalaureate Core Committee (BCC) then became tasked with "creating a framework in which a course addressing issues of openness and diversity might be implemented as a required course in the University's Core Curriculum" (Sayre, 1991).

The BCC sought feedback from campus stakeholders and students throughout the winter term in 1991 and on May 12 the Baccalaureate Core Committee sent their recommendations on creating an "Affirming Diversity" course together with a draft of a course rationale and criteria to the Faculty Senate Executive Committee. The initial rationale stated:

One of the chief aims of a liberal education is to provide a forum in which the diverse points of view of the entire community can be meaningfully articulated, understood, and evaluated. Every effort must be made to create a climate for learning in which intolerance and insensitivity, racism, sexism, ageism, homophobia, religious discrimination, and discrimination against the handicapped, can neither thrive nor endure. The university should be a place that affirms diversity. As a community, it must appreciate difference. The existence of such an atmosphere is in fact central to our ability to appreciate and benefit from liberal education itself.

(Sayre, 1991)

Along with this rationale the Baccalaureate Core Committee put forth five criteria for the proposed Affirming Diversity course.
These included:

- studying the "origins and effects" of all kinds of discrimination;
- promoting the "creation of an atmosphere of openness and sensitivity to others as human beings";
- fostering "openness to the ideas and perspectives of others";
- focusing on "a wide range of appropriate issues and examples"; and
- having a multidisciplinary approach.

(Sayre, 1991)

In addition to providing an initial course title, rationale, and criteria, the Baccalaureate Core Committee provided the recommendation that there should be a "broad-based and multi-disciplinary" committee created "consisting of individuals deeply committed to the idea of the course, to develop it in all its particulars during the 1991–92 academic year" (Sayre, 1991). This group, the Affirming Diversity Course Development Committee, began its work in October 1991 and created the proposal for the Difference, Power, and Discrimination baccalaureate category that would ultimately be adopted by the Faculty Senate in the spring of 1992 (Xing et al., 2007).

Program Creation

The Affirming Diversity Course Development Committee (ADCDC) held its first meeting on October 14, 1991. The committee was chaired by Joan Gross, an Assistant Professor in Anthropology, and included faculty members from the History, Chemistry, Political Science, Anthropology, Women Studies, Human Development and Family Science, and Counseling programs, as well as staff from the Educational Opportunities Program, and an ex officio committee member from the Office of Multicultural Affairs. In their first meeting the committee laid out their meeting structure for the term and began discussion of the course format. Determining the format, scope and placement of the course in the Baccalaureate Core were the main objectives of the committee and, as such, members began by gathering information from other universities who offered courses similar to the one being designed by the committee. Additionally, the committee made clear that the expectation from the Baccalaureate Core Committee and Faculty Senate was to work closely with faculty and students in their efforts to design the course and consequently the Affirming Diversity Course Development Committee (ADCDC) prioritized creating and sending a questionnaire to faculty and students to gather their input (Affirming Diversity Course Development Committee, 1991b). The course development committee met every two weeks throughout the 1991–1992 academic year.

During fall term, the ADCDC focused on information gathering and coming to a consensus on the format of the course. During meetings, committee members reported back on their research about other universities who offered a similar diversity focused course. The institutions discussed in the meeting minutes included UC Berkley, UC Santa Barbara, the University of Washington, the University of Santa Cruz, SUNY Courtland, the University of Oregon, and the University of Michigan. While the initial course rationale and criteria provided by the Baccalaureate Core Committee was for a single course, members of the Affirming Diversity Course Development Committee were learning from other institutions, such as SUNY Courtland and UC Santa Barbara, that they had a designated category under which students could choose from several courses on different topics that fit within the category's criteria.

At their third meeting, members of the ADCDC felt a consensus had been reached in the group

> that this area needs to be part of the life of the university and done in a more positive fashion than the WIC [Writing Intensive Curriculum] was. Faculty would not have to develop entirely new courses; old courses could be re-worked.
> (Affirming Diversity Course Development Committee, 1991b)

The committee left this meeting with a charge for each of the members to consider "the possibility of re-organizing the whole idea of the course into an area (like the existing Cultural Diversity BCC requirement) from which students could choose a course from a list of four or five" (Affirming Diversity Course Development Committee, 1991b). Ultimately, the committee decided to create a designated category with multiple course offerings, though this was a major point of discussion and debate throughout the committee's work.

At the November 25 meeting, members of the Affirming Diversity Course Development Committee received a report on the results of the faculty survey sent out at the end of October. 260 faculty surveys were returned to the committee. Eighty-four faculty members responded saying that they would be willing to teach a course in the area being developed by the committee and 94 said that they would be willing to help formulate the course. The committee viewed these "as very encouraging numbers, with a much higher return rate and higher volunteer rate than expected" (Affirming Diversity Course Development Committee, 1991c). Resistance to the proposed course was revealed in a thread of conversation throughout the committee's meetings during their fall meetings, with one committee member noting during the initial meeting that "getting any more than one three-credit course approved would be virtually impossible. The resistance from colleges on campus who think that the current Baccalaureate Core is too intrusive on their majors would be extremely difficult to overcome" (Affirming Diversity Course Development Committee, 1991a). The comments coded as "negative" in the faculty survey results discussed on November 25 were described as having to do with "the difficulties inherent in a course such as we are proposing" (Affirming Diversity Course Development Committee, 1991c). Some of these difficulties discussed by the Affirming Diversity Course Development Committee included the monetary costs of the course as originally envisioned, as well as the staffing that would be required to have enough faculty and graduate teaching assistants to teach the courses.

On December 9, 1991 following their research about best practices at other institutions, surveys from faculty, and discussion amongst the committee members, the Affirming Diversity Course Development Committee reached the consensus "that the single-course model would not help us achieve our goals" (Affirming Diversity Course Development Committee, 1991d). At this point in the committee's work, a discussion began about whether the title of "Affirming Diversity" was most appropriate for the category. The issue around what to call the category continued throughout the ADCDC meetings in winter term. The majority of the meeting on December 9 focused on solidifying the committee's decisions on the course model. These decisions included the move away from a single course to having multiple course offerings under an umbrella category in the Baccalaureate Core and the development of a summer seminar to support faculty in exploring issues of diversity and discrimination in order to develop courses in their disciplines, with a goal of having a cohort of 10–20 faculty in a seminar that coming summer. Additionally, the ADCDC planned to write a faculty forum paper containing the committee's proposed model to inform faculty and gather their input. Finally, following in the model of SUNY Courtland, the course model could potentially simultaneously meet both an "Affirming Diversity" Baccalaureate Core requirement and another area of the existing core requirements.

On January 9, 1992 committee chair Joan Gross was invited to update the Faculty Senate on the developments of the committee. In a memo to the ADCDC, Gross wrote that "there were less oppositional voices" during her presentation to the senate and reported that there was dissatisfaction around the potential names of the course category (the name discussed at the Faculty Senate meeting was "Confronting Prejudice and Discrimination") (Gross, 1992). In January and February of 1992, the Affirming Diversity Course Development Committee continued to refine their proposal and made it available to the faculty senate, as well as published it in *The Barometer* to solicit feedback from the campus community.

On March 5, 1992 during a committee meeting, a primary topic of discussion was pushback against the proposal, in particular a faculty forum paper by Steven T. Buccola, a professor in the Department of Agricultural and Resource Economics, titled "'Diversity' Courses: Blueprint for an Illiberal Education." Buccola argued that "[t]he proposed course requirement doesn't promote curricular diversity; it promotes an ideological agenda" (Buccola, 1992). Buccola's criticism against the proposal focused on how it confined diversity to "a very narrow subset of human characteristics" and that the proposal was not a form of liberal education but rather was "illiberal, unacademic, and insulting and thus an illegitimate expenditure of dwindling University resources" (Buccola, 1992). While Buccola's response serves as an example of one form of resistance to the proposed model, the committee minutes noted that most discussion occurring was actually centered on the title of the category itself. One member of the committee suggested taking out words like "diversity," "tolerance," "sensitivity" and "acceptance" "as they seem to be loaded words which initiate an immediate response" (Affirming Diversity Course Development Committee, 1992). Members noted some support for the alternative title of Difference, Power, and Discrimination (DPD).

In April and May of 1992, the Affirming Diversity Course Development Committee moved to the final stages of preparing their proposal for the faculty senate. The committee decided on the title "Difference, Power, and Discrimination" because of its "focus on systems of oppression" and because the courses "that met this requirement would deal with oppression not in terms of hierarchies but rather in terms of the interlocking nature of multiple oppressions" (Xing et al., 2007, p. 10).

On May 7, 1992, the final proposal for the Difference, Power, and Discrimination category of the Baccalaureate Core was presented to the Faculty Senate for a vote. The Affirming Diversity Course Development Committee had determined the most strategic choice of implementation was to make the category part of three of six flexible preexisting floating credits already included in the Baccalaureate Core, avoiding the addition of any new credits to the 51 general education credits required at the time (Xing et al., 2007). The proposal put forth to the senate had been unanimously endorsed by the Faculty Senate Baccalaureate Core Committee and was approved by the full Faculty Senate (Xing et al., 2007). In Spring of 1992 Annie Popkin was hired as the acting director of the new DPD Program – housed in the College of Liberal Arts – and in the summer of 1992, she ran the first faculty seminar.

The actions of students in the fall of 1990, the response of the Oregon State University administration, the subsequent work of faculty and staff serving on the Affirming Diversity Course Development Committee, and the support of the faculty senate are what led to the creation of the DPD Program. The coalition of the DPD Advisory Council, faculty, staff, and students are also responsible for saving the program when it faced elimination in a series of budget cuts in 1998.

Program Challenges

During the 1997–1998 academic year the DPD program director position was empty following the Fall 1997 resignation of the director who had been hired in 1995 (Gross et al., 1999). The administration absorbed the annual budget of the program leaving it without funds that year. In the spring of 1998, the DPD Advisory Committee submitted a proposal to fund the program at about half the original level of approximately 100,000 dollars, which was initially rejected. Emails between DPD advisory board members and articles from *The Daily Barometer* [2] show the quickly organized efforts by faculty, staff, and students to prevent the elimination of the program.

On February 23, 1998 an advisory committee member sent an email to alumni of the DPD seminar informing them that the DPD Advisory Committee was holding a meeting with the Associate Provost for Academic Affairs, the Director of Undergraduate Academic Programs, and the Dean of the College of Liberal Arts to discuss the future and funding for the DPD program and that "given the general climate of budget cuts, we do not anticipate good news" (L. Roberts, personal communication, February 23, 1998). The email asked alumni to contact the administrators and share the impact of the DPD seminar on their teaching and the Baccalaureate Core classes that emerged from the seminar (L. Roberts, personal communication, February 23, 1998a). These emails provide first-person narratives about the impact of the program for faculty. A professor who attended the seminar and created a graphic design DPD course wrote,

> I know I never would have developed this type of course without the DPD Faculty Seminar as the impetus. I also feel it is so important for students at OSU to be exposed to classes that discuss these issues. I realize we are in a time of financial crisis and there must be corners cut, but I feel the DPD faculty seminar provides a wonderful opportunity for faculty to network and dialogue on some very crucial topics.
> (A. Marks, personal communication, February 25, 1998)

Another professor wrote that the DPD "curriculum requirement is forward thinking, fits the mission and goals of the University and is important to the preparation of our students for future leadership" (N. Vanderpool, personal communication, February 26, 1998). It was not just individual faculty who wrote in favor of funding the program, but other campus entities as well.

The President's Commission on Campus Climate also wrote a letter to administrators advocating for the funding and continuation of the program. The chair of the commission wrote,

> OSU has gained much attention for this innovative curricular development. It is an important part of our students' core curriculum. It would be a tremendous loss if the program is not continued. OSU continues to

need the DPD program. We urge the administration to respond affirmatively to this need.

(M. Bonnichsen, personal communication, March 13, 1998)

After meetings and conversations with university administrators, on April 16, 1998, the DPD Advisory Committee followed up on an invitation to submit a detailed funding proposal and interim budget to maintain the program. Their proposal included funding for an interim director at a .5 FTE, 9-month contract hiring an individual to run the faculty seminar in the summer of 1998, a stipend of $2500 for each faculty member, with a maximum of ten individuals, to participate in the summer seminar, as well as funds for clerical support (Foster et al., 1998a). The budget request totaled $56,396 (Foster et al., 1998a). On May 3, the DPD Advisory Council was informed by the Associate Provost for Academic Affairs that the DPD Program was not funded by the university budgeting process. The potential source remaining for funding was through the Provost's office. On May 5 the DPD Advisory Council submitted another amended request for funding to the Associate Provost, asking for $16,552 to fund the interim director and provide clerical support (Foster et al., 1998b). On May 13 the Advisory Council was informed that this funding proposal had also been declined by the Provost's office (A. Hashimoto, personal communication, May 13, 1998).

These decisions caused push back from across campus, with faculty members writing emails to university administrators, including then university president Paul G. Risser, and a flurry of op-ed and forum pieces in *The Daily Barometer*. DPD Advisory Council member, Dr. Lani Roberts published an op-ed in *The Daily Barometer* calling out the administration for failing to fund the DPD program and arguing that such actions were irresponsible, hypocritical and immoral. She wrote that

> Oregon State University postures itself publicly as being 'diverse by choice' and valuing diversity. To present ourselves to the public in this manner and not support the educational imperatives that provides substance to the claim is disingenuous; it is talking the talk but not walking the walk.
>
> (Roberts, 1998b)

In an article in *The Daily Barometer* about the lack of funding for the DPD Program, several of Roberts' students were quoted stating how valuable the DPD course they took with her was for them.

A junior majoring in general science said,

> [f]or me, it's just been a tremendous eye-opener, as far as seeing these things that are occurring in our society that we are basically conditioned to ignore.... It's not until you take a class like this that you really start to see those things happening.
>
> (Pesznecker, 1998, p. 6)

Another student, a junior in computer engineering, argued that

> [i]t's important that people take these classes, because in order for situations in society to improve, more people are going to have to open their eyes and their minds to this. It's not the responsibility of minority groups, it's the responsibility of the dominant culture as well.
>
> (Pesznecker, 1998)

While there was vocal support for the program, there were also those that argued in support of the administration's decision.

Robin Rose, a faculty member in the College of Forestry and the Faculty Senate President-Elect, wrote a response to Dr. Roberts' op-ed in *The Daily Barometer* arguing that there was silence from the campus community on the issue of DPD funding because "no one really believes in the 'dominant culture' theory or that DPD represents a significant path to take any longer." He went on to say that "[f]rankly, I have never once heard any particular group or individuals lend great support to the program. The silence must be 'discrimination fatigue,' which comes from having been preached to long enough on this subject on this campus" (Rose, 1995). On the afternoon of May 21, 1998, just one day after Rose's response was published, an open meeting of Oregon State students, faculty, and staff who were concerned about the defunding of the DPD Program was held. Students wrote a petition in support of the program complete with four action items for the institution to take (Xing et al., 2007, p. 11). The petition read:

> In 1993 the Difference, Power, and Discrimination (DPD) Program was founded to support the University's guidelines to 'free people's minds from ignorance, prejudice, and provincialism.' Currently, budget cuts have both jeopardized this program and the University's 'highest aspiration.' At a time that OSU is attempting to broaden its appeal to students of diverse backgrounds it is essential that the University honor its expressed commitment to educating students about the heterogenous world in which they will live and work.
>
> (*Student Petition in Support of the DPD Program*, 1998)

The four actions the administration was to take included providing funding: (a) comparable to the Writing Intensive Curriculum (WIC) program; (b) full support for a DPD director; (c) full support for the faculty seminars; and (d) "a public commitment by the administration to fund DPD on an ongoing basis" (*Student Petition in Support of the DPD Program*, 1998). Additionally, during this time period, a series of forums were held by the Associate Provost for Academic Affairs where the community expressed their support for the DPD program and the DPD program funding remained in limbo.

Once again, the combined actions of students, faculty, and staff were successful and on June 2, 1998 the Difference, Power, and Discrimination Program was awarded permanent funding by the institution. Not only did the Provost's office agree to fund the program, it funded the original proposal from April 1998 which included funding for an interim DPD Director, supplies and clerical expenses, and funds for running the faculty seminar and the accompanying stipends for faculty participants. During the following 1998–1999 academic year a full program evaluation of the DPD Program was conducted. During this evaluation, the DPD Program discovered that the Baccalaureate Core Committee had made changes to the DPD Criteria (Xing et al., 2007, p. 13). In the 1999–2000 academic year, the Faculty Senate formatted a DPD Task Force that was charged with assessing both components of the DPD Program – the faculty development program and the Baccalaureate Core requirement (Xing et al., 2007).

Finally, in 2002, permanent, reoccurring funding for the half-time Director of the Difference, Power, and Discrimination Program was secured. As of the 2018–2019, academic year 97, DPD courses are offered at Oregon State University and 137,431 students have taken a DPD course since the 1992–1993 academic year (Difference, Power, and Discrimination Program, 2018). Since its inception 28 years ago the DPD program remains a robust curricular approach to teaching issues of difference, power, and discrimination in higher education.

Conclusion

The rich history of the Difference, Power, and Discrimination program is made knowable through the institutional memories of people involved with the program over the past twenty-eight years and the archival materials that document these histories, making them, too, a part of the institution's memory.[3] The creation of the DPD Program began as a result of student organizing and was continued through the work of the Affirming Diversity Course Development Committee. The broader support of students, faculty, and staff held the institution accountable and forced it to take action in creating the DPD Program. In 1998 when the program faced elimination, this same coalition came together and used multiple avenues – personal conversations, letters of support, public outcry and debate, meetings, and petitions – to save the program from disappearing. Keeping the institutional memory of the origins and mission of the program enabled a vigorous defense of the value of the program. This kind of student organizing and coalition action with faculty and staff is not an anomaly in the history of Oregon State University, but rather a consistent legacy that is grown and adapted by new generations.

As a PhD candidate and graduate instructor of Women, Gender, and Sexuality Studies at Oregon State University who regularly teaches classes in the DPD category, I bring in the history of Oregon and Oregon State University when discussing the functions of systems of oppression with my students. They learn about the racial history of Oregon through readings such as Walidah Imarisha's *A Hidden History*, the history of student protests and bias incidents at Oregon State University through archival materials in partnership with the Special Collections and Archives Research Center, and the resources that currently exist on campus as a result of student action – such as the Cultural Resource Centers. For more on how to incorporate archival materials into courses, see Natalia Fernandez's "Collaborations between Professors and Archivists: Engaging Students with their Local Community History" and Natchee Barnd's "Scripting Change: The Social Justice Tour of Corvallis" chapters in this volume.

While Oregon State University has the specific history of the Difference, Power, and Discrimination Program, all institutions of higher education have their own histories with bias incidents, student activism, and institutional change. Below is a list of questions that faculty, staff, and administrators can use as a starting point to begin exploring their own institutional histories around these issues:

- What are the racial and gendered histories on your campus?
- What issues have students engaged in protest around? What time periods did these protests occur during?
- Are there programs, offices, or positions on your campus that were created as a result of student organizing?
- What is the state of student organizing on your campus today?
- What issues are most important to students?
- How can faculty, staff, and administrators use their institutional positions to support the work of student organizers?

Much institutional memory is lost or subsumed by the constant churning of institutional changes. It is easy for the histories of student organizing to be erased and forgotten until a present-day issue arises, and the cycle begins again. As faculty and staff who work in institutions of higher education, we can enable a deeper contextually-informed practice by learning our own institutional histories of student activism and coalitional organizing. In learning more about these histories at our institutions we can better understand how to conduct justice-based work and advocate for institutional changes without continually reinventing the wheel. Personal knowledge of institutional histories is one method of application, but certainly is not enough. Finding ways to bring institutional histories into our classrooms allows the sharing of institutional memory with students and for the possibility of creating new futures together.

Additional Resources

Readings

Ahmed, S. (2012). *On being included: Racism and diversity in institutional life*. Duke University Press.

Altbach, P. G., & Cohen, R. (1990). American student activism: The post-sixties transformation. *Journal of Higher Education, 61*(1), 32–49. https://doi.org/10.2307/1982033

Arellano, L., & Vue, R. (2019). Transforming campus racial climates: Examining discourses around student experiences of racial violence and institutional (in)action. *Journal of Diversity in Higher Education.* https://doi.org/10.1037/dhe0000122

Brown, O. G., Hinton, Kandace G., & Howard-Hamilton, Mary F. (2007). *Unleashing suppressed voices on college campuses: Diversity issues in higher education.* Peter Lang.

Denson, N., & Chang, M. J. (2009). Racial diversity matters: The impact of diversity-related student engagement and institutional context. *American Educational Research Journal, 46*(2), 322–353.

Hoffman, G. D., & Mitchell, T. D. (2016). Making diversity "everyone's business": A discourse analysis of institutional responses to student activism for equity and inclusion. *Journal of Diversity in Higher Education, 9*(3), 277–289. https://doi.org/10.1037/dhe0000037

Mcleod, J. (2011). Student voice and the politics of listening in higher education. *Critical Studies in Education, 52*(2), 179–189. https://doi.org/10.1080/17508487.2011.572830

Rhoads, R. A. (1998). Student protest and multicultural reform: Making sense of campus unrest in the 1990s. *The Journal of Higher Education, 69*(6), 621–646. https://doi.org/10.1080/00221546.1998.11780745

Rhoads, R. A. (2016). Student activism, diversity, and the struggle for a just society. *Journal of Diversity in Higher Education, 9*(3), 189–202. https://doi.org/10.1037/dhe0000039

Xing, J., Li, J., Roper, L., & Shaw, S. M. (Eds.). (2007). *Teaching for change: The difference, power, and discrimination model.* Lexington Books.

Notes

1 This number represents the number of domestic students of color. International student demographics based on race are not available.
2 The Oregon State University student newspaper was originally called *The Barometer* but later its name changed to *The Daily Barometer.*
3 My archival research on the Difference, Power, and Discrimination Program was supported through the Special Collections and Archives Research Center's Residential Scholar Program.

References

About | Oregon State University. (n.d.). Retrieved June 16, 2017, from https://oregonstate.edu/about

Affirming Diversity Course Development Committee. (1991a). *Affirming Diversity Course Development Committee minutes,* October 14, 1991 (Courtesy Difference, Power, and Discrimination (DPD) Program Records (RG 250)). Special Collections and Archives Research Center, Oregon State University Libraries, Corvallis, Oregon.

Affirming Diversity Course Development Committee. (1991b). *Affirming Diversity Course Development Committee minutes,* November 11, 1991 (Courtesy Difference, Power, and

Discrimination (DPD) Program Records (RG 250)). Special Collections and Archives Research Center, Oregon State University Libraries, Corvallis, Oregon.

Affirming Diversity Course Development Committee. (1991c). *Affirming Diversity Course Development Committee minutes*, November 25, 1991 (Courtesy Difference, Power, and Discrimination (DPD) Program Records (RG 250)). Special Collections and Archives Research Center, Oregon State University Libraries, Corvallis, Oregon.

Affirming Diversity Course Development Committee. (1991d). *Affirming Diversity Course Development Committee minutes*, December 9, 1991 (Courtesy Difference, Power, and Discrimination (DPD) Program Records (RG 250)). Special Collections and Archives Research Center, Oregon State University Libraries, Corvallis, Oregon.

Affirming Diversity Course Development Committee. (1992). *Affirming Diversity Course Development Committee minutes*, January 27, 1991 (Courtesy Difference, Power, and Discrimination (DPD) Program Records (RG 250)). Special Collections and Archives Research Center, Oregon State University Libraries, Corvallis, Oregon.

Armas, J., Ferrell, H., & Pope, J. (2015). President Ed Ray: Demand that OSU administrators listen to the voices of students of color. *Change.Org*. www.change.org/p/president-ed-ray-demand-that-osu-administrators-listen-to-the-voices-of-students-of-color

Bonnichsen, M. (1998, March 13). *Letter supporting DPD* [Personal communication].

Buccola, S. T. (1992). *"Diversity" courses: Blueprint for an illliberal education* (Courtesy Difference, Power, and Discrimination (DPD) Program Records (RG 250)). Faculty Forum Papers Oregon State University; Special Collections and Archives Research Center, Oregon State University Libraries, Corvallis, Oregon.

Concerned Student Leaders (1990). *Proposal to confront campus-wide discrimination* (Courtesy Difference, Power, and Discrimination (DPD) Program Records (RG 250)). Special Collections and Archives Research Center, Oregon State University Libraries, Corvallis, Oregon.

Foster, J., Lee, J., Nishihara, J., Roberts, L., Roberts, P., & Walker, A. (1998a, April 16). *DPD funding proposal* (Courtesy Difference, Power, and Discrimination (DPD) Program Records (RG 250)). Special Collections and Archives Research Center, Oregon State University Libraries, Corvallis, Oregon.

Foster, J., Lee, J., Nishihara, J., Roberts, L., Roberts, P., & Walker, A. (1998b, May 5). *Amended proposal J., Nishihara, J., Roberts, L., Ro* (Courtesy Difference, Power, and Discrimination (DPD) Program Records (RG 250)). Special Collections and Archives Research Center, Oregon State University Libraries, Corvallis, Oregon.

Gross, J. (1992). *Affirming Diversity Course Development Committee memo* (Courtesy Difference, Power, and Discrimination (DPD) Program Records (RG 250)). Special Collections and Archives Research Center, Oregon State University Libraries, Corvallis, Oregon.

Gross, J., Henderson, L., Lonergan, C., & Ford, S. (1999). *An assessment of the Difference, Power, and Discrimination Program* (Courtesy Difference, Power, and Discrimination (DPD) Program Records (RG 250)). Special Collections and Archives Research Center, Oregon State University Libraries, Corvallis, Oregon.

Hashimoto, A. (1998, May 13). *RE: Amended Proposal – Difference, Power, & Discrimination* [Personal communication]. (Courtesy Difference, Power, and Discrimination (DPD) Program Records (RG 250)). Special Collections and Archives Research Center, Oregon State University Libraries, Corvallis, Oregon.

Imarisha, W. (2013). A hidden history: A conversation project program reveals the stories and struggles of Oregon's African American communities. *Oregon Humanities*, 12–19.

Jaramillo, A. (1991). *Racism at Oregon State University: Findings of the President's Commission on Racism* (Courtesy Difference, Power, and Discrimination (DPD) Program Records (RG 250)). Special Collections and Archives Research Center, Oregon State University Libraries, Corvallis, Oregon.

Kaattari, I. M. (1991). *Oregon State University course, Initiation (DPD) Program* (Courtesy Difference, Power, and Discrimination (DPD) Program Records (RG 250)). Special Collections and Archives Research Center, Oregon State University Libraries, Corvallis, Oregon.

Marks, A. (1998, February 25). *DPD funding* [Personal communication]. (Courtesy Difference, Power, and Discrimination (DPD) Program Records (RG 250)). Special Collections and Archives Research Center, Oregon State University Libraries, Corvallis, Oregon.

Oregon Multicultural Archives, & Students of ALS 199 (2013). *Untold stories: Histories of students of color at Oregon State University, Campus Tour guidebook*. Oregon State University Libraries and Press.

Pesznecker, K. (1998). Difference, Power and Discrimination funding in limbo. *The Daily Barometer*, *1*, 6. Special Collections and Archives Research Center, Oregon State University Libraries, Corvallis, Oregon.

Rimel, A. (2015, November 16). OSU students discuss campus racism. *Corvallis Gazette Times*. Special Collections and Archives Research Center, Oregon State University Libraries, Corvallis, Oregon. http://www.gazettetimes.com/news/local/osu-students-discuss-campus-racism/article_48b1be95-6a41-5a5d-8864-7206107b972c.html.

Roberts, L. (1998a, February 23). *DPD funding* [Personal communication]. (Courtesy Difference, Power, and Discrimination (DPD) Program Records (RG 250)). Special Collections and Archives Research Center, Oregon State University Libraries, Corvallis, Oregon.

Roberts, L. (1998b, May 18). OSU must fund Difference, Power, and Discrimination program. *The Daily Barometer*, *4*. Special Collections and Archives Research Center, Oregon State University Libraries, Corvallis, Oregon.

Rose, R. (1995, May 20). DPD special collections and arc. *The Daily Barometer*, *4*. Special Collections and Archives Research Center, Oregon State University Libraries, Corvallis, Oregon.

Sayre, H. (1991). *Implementation of university diversity course* (Courtesy Difference, Power, and Discrimination (DPD) Program Records (RG 250)). Special Collections and Archives Research Center, Oregon State University Libraries, Corvallis, Oregon.

Student petition in support of the DPD Program (Courtesy Difference, Power, and Discrimination (DPD) Program Records (RG 250)). Special Collections and Archives Research Center, Oregon State University Libraries, Corvallis, Oregon.

Vanderpool, N. (1998, February 26). *DPD – continuation* [Personal communication]. (Courtesy Difference, Power, and Discrimination (DPD) Program Records (RG 250)). Special Collections and Archives Research Center, Oregon State University Libraries, Corvallis, Oregon.

Wilson, J. (2017, May 31). Portland's dark history of white supremacy. *The Guardian*. www.theguardian.com/us-news/2017/may/31/portland-white-supremacy-racism-train-stabbing-murder

Xing, J., Li, J., Roper, L., & Shaw, S. M. (Eds.). (2007). *Teaching for change: The Difference, Power, and Discrimination model*. Lexington Books.

2 Collaborations between Professors and Archivists

Engaging Students with their Local Community History

Natalia Fernández

Since 2014, the Difference, Power, and Discrimination (DPD) Program Academy has included a session in the Oregon State University (OSU) Special Collections and Archives Research Center (SCARC). The time in SCARC is an opportunity for DPD Academy participants to meet with an archivist and learn about the various ways archival materials can be incorporated into their public programing activities and courses. When professors and archivists collaborate to design instruction sessions and projects that engage students with history through archival materials, students can learn research skills with primary source documents, creatively share their knowledge, and, on a broader level, engage with their local community history. The projects shared in this chapter are examples of partnerships between three DPD participants and SCARC's curator of the Oregon Multicultural Archives (OMA) and OSU Queer Archives (OSQA). The three projects, including an event, an in-class activity, and an oral history project, offer a variety of ideas to inspire educators to reach out to their local archivists to develop archival collaborations of their own. In addition, to promote effective and fruitful partnerships, also included are lessons learned for successful collaborations between professors and archivists. The purpose of this chapter is for readers to learn about the various teaching collaborations that are possible with archivists and to inspire connections between faculty and local archivists.

Within the archival profession, there is a breadth and depth of literature pertaining to archival instruction. For archivists and special collections librarians, archival instruction is grounded in theory, is evidence-based, and continues to evolve with practice and assessment. We strive to use the most effective pedagogical strategies possible and develop appropriate learning objectives and activities for different audiences (Bahde et al., 2014). We emphasize various forms of knowledge in our teaching, including domain (subject) knowledge, an understanding of the topic being researched, and artifactual literacy, the ability to interpret and analyze primary sources. For us, "archival intelligence" encompasses the knowledge of archival principles, practices, and procedures; the development of effective search strategies to explore research questions; and an understanding of the relationship between primary sources and their surrogates (Yakel & Torres, 2003, p. 52).

DOI: 10.4324/9781003091998-3

In addition, many of us apply inquiry and object-based learning theories to "teach students how to think, not what to think" and we view our archives as "a research laboratory for the humanities" (Rockenbach, 2011, pp. 308, 301). Archivists conduct research studies that demonstrate the positive impact archival instruction can have on student learning, including critical thinking and research skills gained, as well as an increase in students' confidence levels to apply them (Daniels & Yakel, 2013; Krause, 2010). We document examples of student engagement through archival research assignments and term-long archivist/professor partnerships (Mitchell et al., 2012) as well as develop exercises focused on active learning and object-centered hands-on activities that "not only teach new knowledge and new skills, but also open students' eyes to a new way of thinking" (Bahde et al., 2014, p. xvii). In addition to the evolution of our instructional design, we continue to refine our teaching methods and activities through a number of techniques and models that evaluate students' skills learned through affective, cognitive, and behavioral assessment (Bahde & Smedberg, 2012).

Most recently, the archival profession developed and published "Guidelines for Primary Source Literacy" crafted by a joint Association of College and Research Libraries Rare Books and Manuscripts Section and Society of American Archivists task force (2018). Both professional organizations approved the Guidelines in 2018. The document includes explanations of four core concepts – analytical, ethical, theoretical, and practical – pertaining to the use of archival materials, a set of about two dozen learning objectives for primary source literacy, and appendices that include a glossary, annotated bibliography, and related resources. The Guidelines are not just for archivists and special collections librarians, but also for any teaching faculty who wish to identify the range of knowledge, skills, and abilities required to effectively use primary sources, as well as consider best practices for using these materials. In addition, to illustrate the application of the Guidelines for Primary Source Literacy, the Society of American Archivists created an open-ended series of case studies called "Case Studies on Teaching with Primary Sources" available online for both archivists and their potential collaborators to get ideas for archival activities and partnerships.

My Role as the Curator of the OMA and OSQA

I have been the curator of the Oregon Multicultural Archives, established in 2005, since 2010, and I co-founded the OSU Queer Archives with Professor Bradley Boovy in 2014. Both the OMA and OSQA are a part of the OSU SCARC. As the repository for and steward of the OSU Libraries' rare and unique materials, SCARC builds distinctive collections in its signature areas: natural resources, the history of science, university history, and Oregon's multicultural and LGBTQ+ communities. These collections encompass manuscripts, archives, rare books, oral histories, photographs, ephemera, audio and visual materials, and born digital records. As part of the university's land-grant mission, SCARC makes these resources available to the OSU community, Oregonians, and the larger community of scholars nationally and internationally. In my role, I support and enhance OSU's dedication to promote social progress and its mission as a land-grant institution serving Oregon's diverse communities.

My mission for the OMA and OSQA is to work in collaboration with Oregon's African American, Asian American, Latinx, Native American, and OSU's LGBTQ+ communities to support them in preserving their histories and sharing their stories. My work includes collection development, instruction, exhibit curation, and public programming. I joined the archival profession upon graduating the University of Arizona's Information Resources and Library Science (IMLS) graduate program. I chose to participate in the IMLS's Knowledge River Program, a program that focuses on community-based librarianship and partnerships with traditionally underserved communities. In my career as an archivist, I am dedicated to using social justice as a lens in my work. I sought out my position at OSU because I wanted to empower LGBTQ+ and communities of color to retain control of their histories, use the archives to highlight their impact on the past and present, and educate community members about their stories. While the OMA and OSQA are not community archives, I am inspired by the literature on community archiving and archivists that speaks to the importance of archival representation, autonomy, and community-based activism within communities (Bastian & Flinn, 2020).

I strive to be proactive in my role within the archival profession, to be an "activist archivist." I am continually inspired by the archival literature and discussions within the profession related to social justice. One of my favorite pieces is a 2010 lecture by the archivist Randall Jimerson titled "Archivists and the Call of Justice." In his lecture, Jimerson shares his ten principles for archivists responding to the call of justice. He expresses the need for archivists to recognize that neutrality is an illusion and that while archival records can symbolize healing and reconciliation, they can also support and perpetuate oppression. He states that archivists can participate in the cause of social justice through the materials they select for preservation and by opening the archives to diverse perspectives and multiple voices. To quote Jimerson (2010), but with switching out the words "archivist" and "archives" to "I" and "my" respectively, I use these statements to frame my work:

> [My] role unavoidably engages in politics. [My work can potentially] establish and reinforce power relationships in society. [Therefore, I] cannot remain neutral or passive ... [I] can become [an] active agent for change, in accordance with ... existing professional principles, by taking active steps to counter the biases of previous archival practices.
>
> (n.p.)

When read aloud, these ideas become declarations; they become statements made by an activist archivist. While I can make these statements, I must continuously think about how I can take action and make them a reality. Upon moving to Oregon, I learned that historically, both the state and OSU have had a tumultuous relationship with people of color and the LGBTQ+ communities. Past state and local laws excluded people of color from land ownership, prevented marriage between whites and those of other races and ethnic backgrounds, and discouraged immigration and permanent settlement by non-whites (Millner & Thompson, 2019). I believe learning about these histories can act as a method of reconciliation and a mechanism to move forward on a shared path toward social justice.

The Difference, Power, and Discrimination Program and my work with the OMA and OSQA have much in common. Both the DPD Program and the work I do strives to engage with OSU faculty across fields and disciplines to create inclusive curricula that address intersections of gender, race, class, sexual identity, age, ability, and other institutionalized systems of inequity and privilege in the United States. With my focus on documenting and sharing Oregon history, the DPD Program and I share the goal to focus on place-based learning to engage students with their local community histories. I practice place-based learning to provide a tangible and meaningful learning experience for students to connect to the archival content I share with them. For example, when I share stories of how past students of color – often the same age as my current students – were incredible activists who enacted social and policy changes on campus, they can see themselves in those stories. Alternatively, when I share stories of how Oregonian organizations like the Urban League of Portland and After 8 have advocated for and empowered African American and LGBTQ+ communities, the students can see social justice in action throughout history. My work also supports the DPD learning outcome to "explain how difference is socially constructed" (Difference, Power, and Discrimination Program, 2020) by recognizing that archives are socially constructed, by being proactive in my role as a curator to identify and fill gaps in the historical record, and by sharing these ideas with students through my archival instruction.

My Archival Instruction

Instruction is an important component of my position. Using materials from the OMA and OSQA, I teach students archival and information literacy research skills that enable them to effectively locate, evaluate, use, and in some cases, create primary sources within various disciplines. My focus as an instructor is to actively engage students in the scholarly process as well as share their research with their peers and the wider OSU community; an approach that reflects high impact practices. To further ensure impact, I collaborate with faculty to develop course-specific curricula. I design my instruction sessions with hands-on activities for students to learn what primary sources are, how to cite them, and of the significance of their preservation and accessibility.

I collaborate with professors in a variety of disciplines, on both the undergraduate and graduate level, to develop an archives session, assignment, or term-long project that showcases the experiences of people of color and LGBTQ+ communities in Oregon. I have been a guest lecturer in disciplines such as Ethnic Studies, History, Sociology, Spanish, and Women, Gender, & Sexuality Studies, as well as in the Honors College and First Year courses. I design students' visits to the archives based on the subject matter of the course, or with specific collection requests made by the professor. I strongly encourage professors to bring their classes to the archives so students can have the tangible experience of physically handling historical materials. However, if requested or more appropriate for the course, I offer the option of using digitized collections. My level of involvement in the course depends on the professor's overall learning outcomes and capacity to include the archives into their course. For some courses, the purpose of the archives visit is for the students to build archival awareness and set a foundation for their archival research skills. While there is no expectation the students will use the archives as a part of their course, the visit can complement class discussions on historical representation, intersectionality, and social justice issues. In other instances, the professor develops an archives-based writing assignment in which the students are required to use primary sources. In this case, I often meet one-on-one with the students to discuss their topics and develop a research plan. There are also courses in which I am embedded into a class project that typically results in a final product that becomes an addition to the archives and is made accessible to the public. Examples include exhibit curation, oral history projects, and the creation of history tour guidebooks. For these courses, the professor and I work closely together to develop timelines and expectations, schedule more class sessions in the archives as needed, and promote the students' work to the public.

Regardless of my level of involvement in a course, over the years I have developed a lesson plan for the students' first visit to the archives. An average instruction session for a class I teach includes a general introduction to archives, an explanation of primary sources, and information on how to conduct archival research. I devote a portion of the class time for students to explore archival materials I have pre-selected that match the themes and topics of the course. As part of the materials review, I have them complete a short worksheet to share their findings on the materials that most draw their interest. The students can choose to work in small groups, pairs, or independently. I conclude the session with time for a group discussion. Depending on the length of class time (50, 80, or 110 minutes), I adjust the length of my lecture and time allotted for reviewing the materials. After the session, I debrief with the professor either in-person or via email to assess how the class went and base changes for future sessions on my observations of the students' engagement as well as the professor's recommendations. While this is my typical approach, what I share in the three case studies in this chapter captures the specifics of how I adapt this approach in relation to my collaborations with courses taught by DPD participants.

As part of my instruction sessions, especially if the students have course assignments requiring the use of archival materials, I also share a number of practical and theoretical archival concepts. I talk about my collection development work, how I select materials and make them accessible, and more broadly, an archivist's role and power in shaping the historical record. To illustrate this, I often explain how the various collections I selected for their class session came to the archives. We discuss primary source bias and the need to analyze archival material with a critical lens, and I encourage students to consider not only the content represented in a collection, but to also think about the gaps and why they may exist – sometimes the silences, the voices not represented, speak volumes. Additionally, I acknowledge that archival research is challenging, and especially coming to an archive can be intimidating, but that archivists like me are here to support and guide them. I emphasize that archives are not just for historians, they are for everyone to use, and that there is a reciprocal nature to an archive – archivists collect and share content so it can be researched and brought to life by people just like them. Lastly, I express that archival research requires critical thinking, creativity, and original thought, and it can be very exciting to be the first to view a new collection or use a collection researched a dozen times before, but with their fresh and unique perspective.

The DPD Academy Participants' Visit to the Archives

My relationship with the DPD Program Academy began in 2014 when Professor Nana Osei-Kofi contacted me to arrange for the program participants to visit the archives. That spring term, Professor Natchee Barnd had just taught the course "Ethnohistory Methodology" in which the culminating work of the class was a student-led project to create a Social Justice Tour of Corvallis guidebook (for more information about his course, see Barnd in this volume). The guidebook featured sixteen local histories highlighting the experiences of people from traditionally marginalized communities who were a part of the OSU and Corvallis area communities. I had worked closely with Barnd prior to the course to brainstorm story ideas, and as part of the class, the students came to SCARC for a session on conducting archival research. The students used materials within the Oregon Multicultural Archives to write a number of the stories. Osei-Kofi arranged for the program participants to take the tour as part of the Academy. She hoped the tour would be a great jumping off point for faculty to think about how they could use the histories of OSU, as well as within the Corvallis community, to teach different topics in the area of difference, power, and discrimination as it relates to their specific disciplines. The goal of the DPD Academy participants' visit to the archives was to make participants aware of the wealth of resources available to them on campus for that very purpose.

Since that 2014 session, the DPD Academy participants have come to the archives annually as part of the Academy. While the exact details and length of the visit may change, the typical session takes place around the halfway point in the program and lasts about an hour and a half. Beginning in 2015, upon Osei-Kofi's request, I selected the article "Archives, records, and power: The making of modern memory" by Joan M. Schwartz and Terry Cook (2002), in which the authors talk about the power over memory and identity that archives have, for the participants to read. I ask participants to read it so they can begin to see the connections between the DPD Program and the work that I do as an archivist and instructor. The session with the DPD Academy participants is unlike any other archival instruction session I teach. My learning outcomes for the participants are for them to learn about the archives, but more importantly about my collaboration experiences with professors. In the archives reading room, I make available several selected instruction folders – my lesson plans, class syllabi, assignment information, examples of archival sources used, students' final assignments/products – laid out for participants to peruse. After a brief introduction to the archives and the types of materials we have, I give examples of the many ways in which I work with a variety of disciplines and share stories of my relationships and collaborative projects with professors. I also share examples of collaborations between professors and my colleagues whose areas of expertise differ from my own, so participants know there are others within SCARC with whom they can connect and collaborate.

During this session, I explain the valuable skills students can gain from conducting archival research and how the archives also benefit when students use our materials. The participants then have time to review the materials, ask questions, and share their ideas. I also make sure to explain to the participants what I (and my colleagues) need from them so we can collaborate successfully. My number one request is for professors to contact me prior to the start of the term. The more advance notice I have, the better we can plan our schedules and make sure that we have the information in the archives that they need. If we discuss that we do not have their topics represented in the archives, it means the class could potentially work to fill those gaps by adding content to the archives. Notably, in 2018, I added another component to the session that I will likely continue to incorporate in the future. Earlier that year, SCARC finally opened an instruction classroom so we now have an instruction space in addition to our reading room, which we used for instruction sessions for many years. Because of the availably of two rooms, just across the hall from one another, I used the instruction classroom to display archival materials from a variety of collections. This way, the participants receive both behind-the-scenes information on the types of archival instruction sessions and collaborations I offer, as well as an opportunity to engage in the student experience during one of my archival instruction sessions.

Over the course of five summers, 2014–2018, nearly 50 OSU faculty and staff have attended the DPD Academy archives session, and in that time, the relationship between the DPD Program and the archives has been mutually beneficial. For me, sharing with participants how they can incorporate archival materials as part of their courses is an opportunity to work on a programmatic level to effect change on OSU's curriculum. While I do not have exact numbers, anecdotally, I know that DPD Academy participants have worked with my colleagues and have conducted research in the archives. In addition, during the summer 2016, a participant noticed a gap in the representation of Indian Americans in the archives. He connected me with his daughter, a student at the University of Oregon, who conducted a set of eight interviews featuring twelve members of the Indian American community in Corvallis. Because of her project, we now have the Indian Americans in Corvallis, Oregon Oral History Collection as a part of the OMA. In terms of benefits to the participants, Osei-Kofi and I have talked about the impact of the archives session. Post the archives session, the DPD Academy participants have new knowledge, and a contact person, to facilitate processes for their students to become a part of creating history in the present through creative, innovative, and academically rigorous projects in collaboration with the archives. My relationship with the DPD Program has been incredibly fruitful; I have a growing list of potential collaborators and through continued collaborative endeavors, the OMA and OSQA will continue to grow.

Case Studies

During and after the DPD Academy participants' visit to the archives, I chat with professors about ideas they have for including archival materials into their public programing activities and classes, and in a few instances, these conversations lead to collaborative projects. The three case studies detailed in this chapter include an event, an instruction session featuring an in-class activity, and an oral history project resulting in a new collection for SCARC. These case studies reflect the transformative experiences of using and creating archival materials. The common themes of the studies include connections to place-based local histories and to the stories of people-of-color, at OSU and in Oregon, that help make the invisible visible. In all three collaborations, the relationship between the professor and me began with the DPD Academy visit to the archives, and each one reached out to me to begin planning our collaboration. Each case study includes the development of the collaboration, the collaboration itself, and the impact of the session. Additionally, I asked (and have included) my collaborators' perspectives on the collaboration.

Case Study 1

As part of the 35th annual Dr. Martin Luther King, Jr. Celebration in 2017, the OMA collaborated with OSU's Diversity & Cultural Engagement, University Housing and Dining Services, and the School of History, Philosophy, & Religion, to organize the event "Speaking Justice," a night of spoken word poetry by the OSU community and our feature artist, Too Black. Too Black is a spoken word poet based in Indianapolis, Indiana, who headlines venues throughout the country. He gives performances and teaches poetry workshops to empower young adults to think critically about issues of social justice. Prior to the performance, the OMA hosted the workshop "History of Race Relations at OSU" facilitated by Too Black.

I collaborated with DPD Academy participant and volume contributor Linda Marie Richards, an instructor in the School of History, Philosophy, & Religion, to organize and host the workshop. Richards had wanted to invite Too Black to OSU for some time and envisioned a workshop featuring archival materials from OMA collections. Richards reached out to Too Black to begin discussing the workshop's intended audience, content, and structure. Richards and I then met to discuss the logistics of the workshop and options for the archival materials he could use. We planned a workshop for OSU community members, with a focus on students. It would be an opportunity for Too Black and workshop participants to explore and use materials from the archives to create pieces of poetry to potentially share as part of the Speaking Justice event later that evening. We expressed to Too Black that we were open to the structure of the workshop, but that our goal was for participants to learn about Oregon's Black history through the stories documented within the materials in the archives. I spoke with Too Black over the phone and shared information with him regarding the OMA collections specific to Oregon's African American communities for him to review. Logistically, the workshop would take place in the archives reading room in the library the same day as the evening performance.

During Too Black's workshop facilitation, participants learned about the history of race relations at OSU and its connections to contemporary issues. In his presentation, "Today is Yesterday," Too Black shared his experiences from a then recent visit to South Africa. He connected it to an early 1980s protest and educational campaign led by the OSU African Students' Association in response to wrestling coach Dale Thomas' association with the South African wrestling community; the history of which is documented in the Ed Ferguson Oregon Anti-Apartheid Scrapbook. Professor Ed Ferguson, a specialist in African history, was a faculty member in the History Department from 1979 to 1991. He created and donated the scrapbook to the OMA; the scrapbook is comprised of newspaper clippings, correspondence, news releases, and some administrative documents.

Through Too Black's facilitation, workshop participants connected the anti-apartheid student activism that occurred locally on OSU's Corvallis campus to the international issue of the time period as well as to a number of contemporary issues: race relations at OSU today within the national context, what is currently occurring politically in South Africa, and the complex relationship between sports and politics. Too Black explained propaganda as well as counter-propaganda and how spoken-word poetry can be a form of counterpropaganda. Workshop participants reviewed selections from the scrapbook and wrote poems or created a form of art that represented counterpropaganda towards a particular social justice issue while tying the past to the present, the local to the international. When reflecting on the workshop, and the power of the participants engaging with local history, Richards wrote:

> The workshop was a powerful conductor of OSU and African American US history. For me, I could see how the participants were awed by the meaning of this injustice in a new way, how the hate and racial prejudice in South Africa was fed by white supremacy here and this thread of connection that ran thru these places.
> (L. Richards, personal communication, July 31, 2019)

Of the 20 participants, one participant performed as part of the evening's event. The performance took place in the campus Memorial Union Lounge with over 100 students, faculty/staff, and community members in attendance. During the open mic event, various performers, including one workshop participant, shared their spoken word poetry and expressed their personal social justice struggles. Too Black's performance included about a half dozen poems ranging in topics from apartheid and imperialism, to student debt, police killings of Black men, capitalism, and more.

Both Richards and I were pleased with the outcome of the workshop. We observed a high level of engagement by the participants in both the lecture and activity, and Too Black expressed how much he enjoyed his experience and his desire to return to OSU. To describe the transformative power of the workshop, Richards expressed:

> I think we all wanted to undo the history and to heal it in some way. The spoken word workshop was an intervention, its own act of 'artivism' to at least acknowledge this pain and see just a glimmer of the depths of what must be repaired for true equality.
> (L. Richards, personal communication, July 31, 2019)

Richards and I collaborated once again for another MLK Jr week event in January 2019. SCARC hosted the event for which over thirty people attended to hear Richards give a lecture featuring the histories of Indigenous Peoples and African Americans who were anti-nuclear weapons activists. A SCARC colleague and I selected archival documents from SCARC's History of Science and OMA collections for attendees to peruse after the lecture.

Case Study 2

In September 2017, after attending the DPD Academy, Deanna Lloyd, Instructor & Service-Learning Coordinator within the Sustainability Double-Degree Program in the Crop & Soil Science Department, contacted me. She expressed that she was intrigued by the possibility of having her students work on a project in collaboration with the OMA, specifically for her class "Agricultural and Environmental Predicaments: A Case Study Approach." Though it was not a DPD course, she was contemplating how to incorporate more multicultural awareness into the course and wanted to converse about potential collaboration opportunities.

The course focuses on an evaluation of agricultural and environmental problems with various topics as case studies. Lloyd asks the students to examine the course topics through the three pillars of sustainability: environmental, social, and economic; one of the topics covered is farm labor. She wanted to partner to create an activity that examines the importance and contribution of farm laborers in our country as well as the culture and policy around farm labor. My initial response was to offer the most relevant and accessible collection we had pertaining to farm labor in Oregon, the Braceros in Oregon Photograph Collection, a collection of 100 photographs from the 1940s. These photographs document the activities of Oregon's Bracero workers – their cultivation and harvesting work in the fields and orchards as well as the farm labor camps in which they lived. Most of the photographs were taken by OSU Extension staff members as part of a larger effort to document the various groups that contributed to alleviate the state's severe shortage of farm labor during World War II. The Braceros in Oregon Photograph Collection images are drawn from several archival collections and are available online as a digital collection. In addition, I strongly recommended she contact Professor Ron Mize within the School of Language, Culture and Society since he had recently developed and taught a course titled "Farmworker Justice Movements" and has written books about the Bracero Program. She did meet with him and found his knowledge on the subject matter to be very helpful; he recommended an article for her students to read that touched upon both current and historic labor perspectives (for more information about his course, see Mize's chapter in this volume). During our in-person meeting, we further discussed the goals for her course, and Lloyd determined that she would like to bring the class to the archives to view the Braceros images. I sent her two photo-based activities from a book called *Using Primary Sources: Hands-On Instructional Activities* (Bahde et al., 2014) and expressed that while they were not exact matches for what we discussed, they were designed for students to learn about visual literacy and we could take the elements we liked to create our activity. Lloyd's response was that she thought the photo-based lesson would be adaptable for her course. We met again to review a lesson plan Lloyd created for a group-based activity; I selected 20 photographs for the activity and created a PowerPoint presentation to accompany my short lecture, along with the activity directions. In late February 2018, Lloyd and 18 students came to the archives instruction classroom for an 80-minute session.

The four learning objectives for the session were to situate an image in its cultural, social and historical contexts; analyze historical photographs both objectively and subjectively; evaluate textual information accompanying images; and understand the historical context surrounding the Bracero Program. I had the room set up so that each of the classroom's four long tables had five photographs, along with each photo's contemporary metadata – title, date, description, county, and photographer. I provided gloves, pencils, and paper. During the first fifteen minutes of the session, I gave a brief lecture describing the Oregon Multicultural Archives, the work of archivists, as well as an explanation of what primary sources are, and more specifically how to "read" a photograph.

For the first of two activities, as a class we examined the same photo and completed a "write and pass" activity for students to describe the image both objectively and subjectively. The students passed the paper five times during the activity. Then we reviewed the observations made and perspectives of the image. We discussed the visual clues of the image itself as well as its accompanying metadata to make meaning of the photograph. The purpose of this activity was to demonstrate and model the group activity we planned for later in the session. I gave a brief overview of the Bracero Program's history and as well as the provenance of the photographs and asked, "Who might have produced these images and why?" I also shared various resources about the program – books, documentaries, other archives – for students to learn more if interested. As part of my lecture, I shared historic information about the intersections of race, gender, and class in the Bracero Program. Information such as the many interned Japanese Americans who owned or worked the farmland the Braceros worked; the lack of women in the Program, along with the reality that many families immigrated to the United States during and after the Program; and the specific socioeconomic recruitment of men conducted by and for the Program. I share this content to give an intersectional context to the collection of images and the history behind them, and to give voice to traditionally marginalized perspectives.

The bulk of the session was a twenty-five-minute activity in which groups of four to five students examined five different photographs. I selected and grouped the photographs to show a variety of images including labor, non-work-related activities, and the camp itself. The students analyzed each image both objectively and subjectively and evaluated the textual information accompanying the image. It was a "think, pair, share" activity for which each image had one sheet of paper for students to write their thoughts. They worked together to look for similar patterns and things that stood out to them. For the group discussion, one member of the group shared the information gathered. To conclude the session, we discussed the information gleaned and how it can affect our view of both historical and current events. Lloyd and I asked the students to compare images they see now in the media and their local environments to the Bracero images from over seventy years prior. We asked, "When comparing and contrasting these images of farm workers now, what has changed and what has remained the same?" and "Who was behind the lens then compared to now?" We asked them to think critically about farm labor imagery, the subjectivity of an image, how it is presented, and its purpose. Upon reflection on the impact the archives session had on the students, Lloyd shared that:

> The Bracero collection – and our activities analyzing the power, discrimination, and oppression perpetuated through those images – provides another set of perspectives and ideas for students to consider and analyze against their own. Having already discussed the Bracero Program and how the archival material demonstrated racial prejudice, students

appeared better able to discuss some of the DPD concepts highlighted [later in the course].

(D. Lloyd, personal communication, August 6, 2019)

Overall, the students were engaged in the session, and in the next academic year, Lloyd reached out to me again stating that she enjoyed the activities that we put together and was pleasantly surprised with the amount of positive feedback and level of enthusiasm she received about our activity. Lloyd expressed that the visit to the archives was a transformative experience for the students as it provided an "opportunity to expand on the social dimension of sustainability" and that she has "seen many students increase their awareness of social justice issues through this material" (D. Lloyd, personal communication, August 6, 2019). For our second collaboration, we kept the learning objectives and lesson plan. However, Lloyd decided the students should have more context about the Bracero Program and required them to read two articles and watch a documentary prior to the archives session. In addition, I received a request for an archives session from one of Lloyd's colleagues, Kelly Biedenweg, for her Fisheries and Wildlife course, "Multicultural Perspectives in Natural Resources," a class that explores multicultural influences on the development of natural resources in the American West; notably, it is a DPD course. With a much larger class of 70 students as well as a shorter class length, I modified the lesson plan and made printed copies of the photographs to bring to the course classroom. The learning objectives, however, remained the same, and I retained the activity for the students to analyze pre-selected sets of photographs. The session proceeded smoothly, and I hope to collaborate with both Lloyd and Biedenweg in the future.

Case Study 3

In 2019, I collaborated with DPD Academy participant Lucy Arellano on an oral history project for her graduate level course "History of Higher Education." The purpose of the course is to survey higher education in the U.S. across 200-plus years of history, with a specific emphasis on community colleges. The goal of the collaboration was for the graduate students to conduct oral history interviews with founding members of Oregon's community colleges, a history not broadly represented in the archival narrative. Arellano and I met to share information about the course, and for me to explain the logistics of incorporating an oral history project within a course. In the years prior, I collaborated with Professor Mina Carson and her "Lesbian and Gay Movements in Modern America" course for an oral history project to interview members of the local LGBTQIA communities. I shared my course lessons plans with Arellano, as well as the oral history collection to which students contribute the oral histories they conduct.

My work with students on oral history projects is always incredibly rewarding. For communities who have been traditionally marginalized in both the historical record and in historiography, oral histories can be a form of empowerment, a way in which community members can literally add their voice to the historical narrative. In addition, the process of a community sharing its stories can provide personal opportunities for self-reflection, an appreciation for the struggles endured, and a celebration of the community's accomplishments thus far. I share these concepts with students to frame their oral history projects and encourage them to think of oral history interviews as gifts. Oral histories can be a gift for both the interviewee who has the opportunity to share their stories and the interviewer who has the privilege to hear them, as well as the archives who then has the honor of preserving and making the stories accessible. With this framework especially, oral history projects can be transformative experience for students.

As part of the collaboration with Arellano's class, I met with the students for a two-hour oral history workshop. Prior to my visit, I gave the students a mini assignment to read the OHA Principles and Best Practices: Principles for Oral History and Best Practices for Oral History (Oral History Association, 2018) and to ask at least one question. In addition, I requested that each student listen to at least one interview from the OMA's *Multicultural Voices of Oregon* website (http://scarc.library.oregonstate.edu/omeka/exhibits/show/multiculturalvoices/main/) and make at least one comment, being something learned or a critique. Arellano emailed me the students' questions and comments the day before my visit so that I could incorporate the answers into my presentation. During my time with the students, I covered several topics, allowed for questions while presenting, and left time for follow-up questions at the end of the session. After introductions, I first described what archives are and shared information about my work with the OMA and OSQA, as well as SCARC. I gave an overview of oral histories – in theory and in practice – and reviewed the website I asked them to peruse. I shared my interview best practices and gave examples of lessons learned from oral history interviews I have conducted. Since one of the goals of the collaboration was to make the interviews accessible via the archives, I reviewed the consent form SCARC requires all interviewees to sign with the students. I engaged them in a discussion regarding developing interview questions and topics to ask the interviewees and reviewed the plan for the technology they were to use to conduct the interviews. To conclude, I shared an interview checklist for the students to use and explained my requirements for their assignment, which included the submission of the digital interview files, a signed consent form, and an interviewee bio as well as an interview summary. Upon reflection of the oral history workshop, Arellano expressed it "provided an avenue of motivation for [the students], realizing that their end products would end up memorialized in the archives" (L. Arellano, personal communication, August 5, 2019).

After my session, the thirteen students worked in pairs, with one group of three, to conduct interviews. Arellano determined the scope of the project; she decided that all the students had to select interviewees from community colleges in Oregon. She worked with the class to develop and finalize the interview questions, with the main goal of gathering stories pertaining to the community colleges' historical foundations. While it was not a requirement for the interviewees to agree to donate their interview to the archives, they were encouraged to do so. At the end of the term, the students submitted all the assignment requirements to Arellano, and she then shared the materials with me electronically. With the students' work, I created "The Oregon Higher Education Oral Histories Collection." All the interviewee biographies and interview summaries are a part of the collection, and the interviews themselves are accessible online to the public.

This collaboration was multifaceted in its benefits. With this oral history project, the students gained firsthand experience as scholars adding to the historical record; the oral history interviewees had the opportunity to share their stories; the archives created a new collection; and future scholars will benefit from now having these histories accessible to them for their research. From Arellano's perspective:

> the multiple components of the oral history project are what make it so engaging. Not only are students reading about the history of community colleges via the textbooks, but they also have a hand in shaping it. Through the process of setting up their interviews they also develop networking skills with college leaders, they practice qualitative methodologies, and they also learn to function within a group (and have support) of their peers. Ultimately it is my hope that students develop a deeper level of engagement and appreciation of history yet be critical of the perspective presented.
> (L. Arellano, personal communication, August 5, 2019)

Arellano intends to offer the course again, and we intend to continue our collaboration. Considering there are 17 community colleges – with over 60 campuses and centers throughout the state, there are still many stories to gather.

Lessons Learned about Collaborations

Through the three described case studies, as well as the many collaborations I have experienced during my career, I have developed a set of lessons learned for professors to consider when embarking upon an archives-based project. I also asked my collaborators for their perspectives on lessons learned when collaborating with an archivist and incorporated their responses in the list.

- Contact your university's archives, your local historical society, or a local community archives: Archivists know their collections best and can assist you to develop meaningful and relevant assignments appropriate for both undergraduate and graduate students.

- Build trust with one another: Trust is imperative with these types of projects. Thoroughly discuss your goals and determine if your teaching philosophies are a good match. Build trust so there is space for each person to make their best contribution to the collaboration.
- Discuss and plan the logistics of the collaboration: Take as much information to the beginning of the conversation as possible. With enough lead-time and multiple conversations, an archivist can nurture and curate the initial ideas of an instructor into what is realistic and doable.
- Discuss capacity: While many archivists' positions include teaching and engagement duties, some do not. Do not assume that all archivists will give the same amount of dedication to a collaborative project. There may be workload or institutional policy issues at play that may prevent a collaboration from occurring.
- Work with an archivist to build your network: Due to the nature of the work, archivists are connected to a variety of disciplines and can help you build new professional relationships.
- Connect with colleagues: If you have never conducted archival research before, connect with colleagues who have in order to gain their perspectives on using archival materials and working with archivists.
- Share your knowledge and learn from each other: Share literature that will help the archivist with whom you are collaborating understand your teaching methodologies and perspectives and ask for archival literature that they recommend.
- Be open to new ideas: An archivist may be able to provide recommendations and insight on how to structure an assignment, activity, or project that you would have never thought of to make the project a success.
- Conduct research ahead of time: Familiarize yourself with the archival material and learn the difficulties of the research process to be able to share them with your students.
- Design thoughtful assignments: Work together to develop activities to help students learn new skills and practice those skills in ways that lead to transformative experiences.
- Celebrate the research process, not just the product: Share the knowledge learned! If applicable, plan for a mechanism, print or online, to share students' work with local communities.

Upon reflection of her experience during her course's archives session, Deanna Lloyd expressed her thoughts on the power and depth of archival materials: "There is so much information contained within archival material – not only the image you see or the text you read, but also the context that surrounds it." Additionally, she added her thoughts on the impact our collaboration had on her teaching and the benefit of a collaborative project with an archivist stating:

Partnering with [an archivist] can lead to gaining insight into this depth [contained within archival material] ... to see how DPD concepts [are] represented in multiple ways through this material. Without that collaboration, I would not have been able to represent the material in a holistic way and create such an authentic and meaningful learning opportunity for my students.

(D. Lloyd, personal communication, August 6, 2019)

This is the type of experience I, and other archivists, hope will occur when collaborating with faculty!

Conclusion

In discussing the integration of primary sources into courses, archivist Barbara Rockenbach (2011) notes that faculty do not always realize the role archivists can play in helping them design opportunities for students to use archival materials that enhance their course learning objectives. It can be challenging for archivists, myself included, to promote the collaborative possibilities of our work especially with regard to instruction. The DPD Program goal to create inclusive curricula that address intersections of identities and institutionalized systems of inequity and privilege in the United States is complementary to my goal for the OMA and OSQA to act as resources for students and scholars to research and analyze those intersections and systems of inequity through primary source materials. Because of this shared goal, our partnership has been invaluable in enabling my ability to introduce faculty to my work. Not only are the DPD Academy participants' visits to the archives a rewarding experience for me, the collaborations with the participants are especially fruitful due to the participants' in-depth knowledge of social justice issues along with the frameworks they have with which to discuss them. As I continue in my role, I hope to develop my current partnerships and strive to create new collaboration opportunities with faculty. I look forward to hosting more DPD Academy participants in the archives and working with them to develop new ways to engage students with local community histories.

Additional Resources

Readings

Schwartz, J. M., & Cook, T. (Eds.). *Archival Science, 2*(1–4). (2002). A volume of Archival Science devoted to the theme "Archives, Records, and Power." Includes the article recommended for DPD participants to read: Schwartz, J. M. & Cook, T. (2002). Archives, records, and power: The making of modern memory. *Archival Science, 2*, 1–19.

Websites

Architecting Sustainable Futures (n.d.). *Recommendations for the Field*. https://architectingsustainablefutures.org/recommendation

Digital Public Library of America (2016, September 21). *10 Ways to Use the Primary Source Sets in Your Classroom*. https://dp.la/news/10-ways-to-use-the-primary-source-sets

Library of Congress (n.d.). *Teachers*. http://www.loc.gov/teachers/

National Archives (n.d.). *Educator Resources*. https://www.archives.gov/education

Oral History Association (2018, October). *OHA Principles and Best Practices: Principles for Oral History and Best Practices for Oral History*. https://www.oralhistory.org/principles-and-best-practices-revised-2018/

Society of American Archivists (2018, October 1). *Diversity and Inclusion Toolkits*. https://www2.archivists.org/advocacy/diversity-and-inclusion-toolkits

StoryCorps (2020). *StoryCorps*. https://storycorps.org/

Transforming Knowledge, Transforming Libraries (2020, May 1). Transforming Knowledge, Transforming Libraries Virtual Summit. https://sites.uci.edu/tktl/

U.S. Department of Arts and Culture (2015, March 8). *Story Circles*. https://usdac.us/hili-blog/storycircles

References

ACRL RBMS-SAA Joint Task Force on the Development of Guidelines for Primary Source Literacy (2018). *Guidelines for Primary Source Literacy*. www2.archivists.org/sites/all/files/GuidelinesForPrimarySourceLiteracy-June2018.pdf

Bahde, A., & Smedberg, H. (2012). Measuring the magic: Assessment in the special collections and archives classroom. *Journal of Rare Books, Manuscripts, and Cultural Heritage*, *13*(2), 152–174.

Bahde, A., Smedberg, H., & Taormina, M. (Eds.). (2014). *Using primary sources: Hands-on instructional exercises*. Libraries Unlimited.

Bastian, J. A., & Flinn, A. (2020). *Community archives, community spaces: Heritage, memory and identity*. London: Facet Publishing.

Daniels, M., & Yakel, E. (2013). Uncovering impact: The influence of archives on student learning. *The Journal of Academic Librarianship*, *39*, 414–422.

Difference, Power, and Discrimination Program (2020). *Proposing a DPD Course*. https://dpd.oregonstate.edu/proposing-dpd-course

Jimerson, R. (2010, January 27). *Archivists and the call of justice*. School of Library, Archival and Information Studies Colloquium Series, University of British Columbia. https://dx.doi.org/10.14288/1.0076588

Krause, M. (2010). Undergraduates in the archives: Using an assessment rubric to measure learning. *The American Archivist*, *73*(2), 507–534.

Millner, D., & Thompson, C. (Eds.). (2019). White supremacy & resistance [Special issue]. *Oregon Historical Quarterly*, *120*(4).

Mitchell, E., Seiden, P., & Taraba, S. (Eds.). (2012). *Past or portal? Enhancing undergraduate learning through special collections and archives*. Association of College and Research Libraries.

Rockenbach, B. (2011). Archives, undergraduates, and inquiry-based learning: Case studies from Yale University Library. *The American Archivist*, 74(1), 297–311.

Society of American Archivists (2020, April 10). Case studies on teaching with primary sources. www2.archivists.org/publications/epubs/Case-Studies-Teaching-With-Primary-Sources

Yakel, E., & Torres, D. (2003). AI: Archival intelligence and user expertise. *The American Archivist*, 66(1), 51–78.

3 Scripting Change

The Social Justice Tour of Corvallis

Natchee Blu Barnd

The Social Justice Tour of Corvallis has proven one of my most productive academic and personal engagements and serves as constant reminder of the profound potential of small acts undertaken with intentionality. The tour is founded on the transformative potential of intimacy that so readily shapes existence here at a Predominantly White Institution (PWI) nestled in a semi-rural but "liberal" college town. Yet, this tour has potential anywhere. The Social Justice Tour offers a model for scripting social and spatial change, and for intervening in dominant community or institutional politics and practices that further marginalize racialized, indigenous, and queer communities. It also testifies to the educational and community-building potential of weaving together research, critical pedagogy, and experiential learning with public engagement and the use of affect.

Like any tour, the Social Justice Tour of Corvallis delivers stories to an audience while traversing space. We move from place to place, sharing narratives about people, places, and events. Most of the stories share about our past, some focus on the present. Unlike most standard tours, however – which I describe in the next section – this tour invites new stories and storytelling practices, and consciously counters dominant and normative histories. Our bus-and-walking tour presents compelling local narratives, highlighting stories from marginalized individuals and communities based on race, class, gender, and sexuality. Most importantly, the tour is co-created by students, and thus produces real impact for student learning and empowerment, as well as community-building. Based on the feedback collected after our tours, this project also generates a uniquely galvanizing experience for the tour guests and larger public.

In the sections below I highlight several stories created by students (and one by the author) as examples of the narratives created, and the framework that helps give them community meaning and significance. In the first section, I describe this academic and community engagement project (the tour, and the class), and its origins. A quick second section provides sample stories to help visualize and "feel" how the tour works. Sections three and four provide the logistical and conceptual guidelines used to create the tour, with some suggestions for how others might re-create similar projects within their

DOI: 10.4324/9781003091998-4

communities or schools. In the fifth section I focus in on how the tour relies on critical practices of intimacy and speculative non-fiction storytelling to enhance learning and transform space. I conclude with some additional thoughts about how and why this project matters, as well as offering final words on how this framework could be taken up by those working within any higher education institution.

So, let's start the tour!

The Class and the Tour

Although I use the singular term, the Social Justice Tour of Corvallis actually refers to several unique creations. Since 2014, I have guided students in the creation and delivery of four distinct tours with four different cohorts of students (24 in total), with several subsequent offerings for each of those individual tours. We have collectively created 56 stories, and played a hand in the delivery of dozens of tour experiences, including one offered as a special edition "anthology" tour.

Students create the tour contents and develop delivery strategies as part of an Ethnic Studies class project focused on archival research methods. Each class initiates, completes, and delivers its tour within the limits of our 10-week quarter term – a truly blazing turn-around time. The final project (the tour) "concludes" when 30–50 invited guests come along to hear our stories, engage with/as community, and help us transform our local geographies (more about this later). As a final wrap-up, we frequently host a lunch debriefing to allow more sustained conversation and reflection, and for closer review of the tour booklet we create and deliver to each of our guests (see Figure 3.1).

In the academic catalog, the course responsible for the tour is designated as a combination undergraduate-graduate course, although the actual composition varies. In the most recent course offering, the class was composed of undergraduate, masters, and PhD students. The most important takeaway here is that it is designed for all levels and can operate effectively for such different students at the same time. In total, 21% of all enrolled students have been undergraduates. The last two course offerings saw that percentage rise to 38%, which indicates growing interest for undergraduates as they become aware of the course, and provides a great opportunity for undergraduate experience with a hands-on and more activist-oriented approach to research. While my pool of students taking an Ethnic Studies course is already more diverse than the average course, this class is uniquely diverse in its demographic and disciplinary composition. It enrolls at least 63% students of color at a PWI that enrolled 20–26% students of color between 2012–2019 and is heavily composed of students from numerous fields of study, including fisheries and wildlife, forestry, education, student affairs, and literature.

In terms of my own positionality, as the instructor for this course, I would highlight a few individual aspects. I am a first-generation college graduate who participated in a number of higher education pipeline programs,

Figure 3.1 Covers for Social Justice Tour of Corvallis #1 and #3 booklets: William Hartless (Kalapuya)[L], written by Gabe Sheoships; and Ruth Nomura [R], written by Kali Furman.
Images courtesy of Oregon Historical Society and Oregon State University's Special Collections and Archives Research Center (respectively)

including Upward Bound and the Educational Opportunity Program. I am a white-presenting cisgender and currently able-bodied male who comes from a multi-ethnic, multi-racial and indigenous, low-income family. I have lived in rural areas, on the reservation, and in suburban and urban locations. I was raised and cared for by Indigenous and non-Indigenous families and communities. These characteristics and my varied spatial experiences have shaped me as a person, and thus inform how I strive to synthesize research, teaching, and community engagement to reflect my interests in ethnic studies and cultural geography and in building with and for communities and marginalized students. Through the wisdoms of my various families, I strive to effectively center and validate my experiences and those of students from similar or

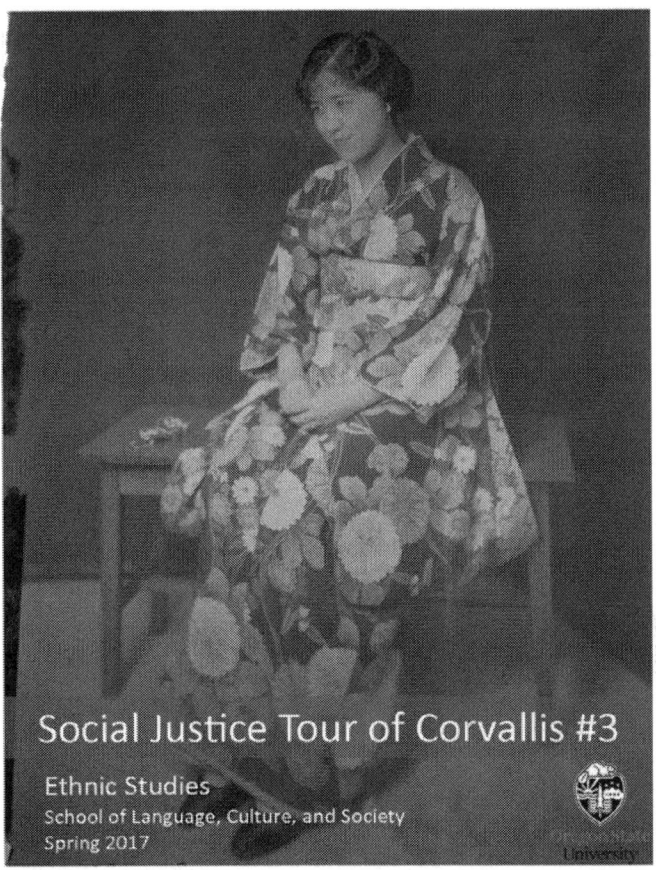

Figure 3.1 Cont.

related backgrounds, and to demonstrate how these serve as strengths for our research and creative processes.

The idea for the Social Justice Tour of Corvallis came after I had been on a handful of local, city-based tours. Sponsored by the city and the Chamber of Commerce, we puttered around in a recently acquired "trolley" – a bus with trolley façade – to see the Corvallis's historic homes and families. Standard fare, really. A gathering of almost entirely elders fascinated by "history." Excessive discussion of architectural styles and details. A healthy dose of corny local jokes. A few curated and largely celebratory stories about "important" past residents.

I like tours. I have been on many walking and history tours. I find the act of being in space with a story changes its reception and gives both the space and the story greater meaning and momentum. I also come from a background in indigenous teachings that remind us to pay attention to our relationships to the lands (and its peoples) wherever we find ourselves. So, I also prefer tours that help me with these kinds of spatial and cultural groundings. Yet, most walking tours are rather unsatisfactory. They tend to be uncomfortably voyeuristic; and even more troubling, to reinforce the dominant contours and mechanisms of power. In many ways, they tend toward stasis and un-reflectiveness. Toward relatively un-interrogated facts and ideas. Toward white people. White men. While they are sometimes "multicultural," they are rarely anti-racist. They blissfully swim in heteronormative and middle-class values. And settler colonialism. They tend avoid difficult topics or just shrug helplessly at past "discretions." In short, they present history as though it contains some sealed or unimpeachable meaning outside of our contemporary framings of past events and people.

When I was tasked with teaching an ethnohistory methodology class, I gained an opportunity to create my own tour. I wanted a way to create a truly engaging and all-encompassing experiential learning opportunity that allowed students to practice research methodologies and not just learn about them as a survey. In a completely separate line of thought, I was brainstorming about ways I could complicate the local city tours that celebrated city-founding and its founders. I considered how I might shift tour guests' attention away from supposed apolitical topics and architectural aesthetics. After sharing my interest in creating counter-tours with Bradley Boovy – one of this book's editors – he suggested I combine my interests in hands-on methodologies and creating a tour. It was one of those rare moments of personal and scholarly clarity.

From that moment, the classes have enrolled students who quickly and unexpectedly became voracious users of the archives (see Fernández's chapter in this volume for more on archival engagements). They transformed themselves into passionate storytellers, invested in their narratives and the process of fusing history, the present, affective techniques, and community-building experiences. From the first day of each course, the students directly practice techniques for collecting, analyzing, and incorporating community histories and highlighting the contested productions of geography, especially in relation to race and racism. As an applied research methods course, students immediately learn about and utilize archives (starting week 2), including both our university's special collections holdings and those of the local Benton County Historical Society. Students learn to review and analyze their findings, and then, gradually, determine what aspects will prove compelling for crafting a tour-ready narrative. They also seek out visual materials that add value to our high-quality printed guidebooks/scripts, and further inspire their stories. In the final weeks of the term (weeks 8–9) they conduct walkthroughs to problem-solve logistical challenges as we travel through the town, preparing to perfect the overall experience and generate the affective qualities we want to invoke or offer our guests.

We design our tours to last no more than two hours, making between four and seven stops including the initial starting and ending points (which are always on-campus). Each stop serves as the delivery site for two to four brief stories. Depending on the tour-stop locations, we may either walk small segments or simply board a rented yellow school bus to travel between sites (we also use accessible vans and identify more accessible routes, as needed). Every stop is intentionally selected to correspond spatially with at least one of the stories (also, see Figure 3.2).

Story Samples

Let me briefly share a couple examples to help illustrate how we most directly and consciously work to transform our cultural and social geographies, and how they are tied to location. During the first tour, we stood facing west toward the downtown post office. This post office is situated where a Chinese-run laundry once stood in 1906. At this location, with our speaker volume turned up to overcome the noise of traffic, Peter Bañuelos delivered his story (tour #1) about the near-fatal beating of "Old Tom" who worked and lived at that laundry facility, and outlined the horrifying lack of prosecution of his widely-known white assailant. Bañuelos skillfully takes on the persona and voice of a customer waiting for a haircut and listening to the assailant, Charles Carns, tell this story. Recounting the tale, Peter's disapproving character tells the audience (us) that the laundry worker:

> was saying something to Carns in his broken English and after some time Carns decided that enough was enough. No more dealing with that

Figure 3.2 Peter Bañuelos [L] and Luhui Whitebear [R] poised to deliver their stories during tour #1. They positioned themselves in front of an historic location for Peter's story about two African American women – Hannah and Eliza Gorman (mother and daughter) – who improbably built this home in 1856; a house that served as a domestic way station for later Black residents of Corvallis.
Photo courtesy of the author

non-English-speaking foreigner's nonsense, so he put his hands on Old Tom. Carns said it was Old Tom's fault for what had happened. I don't understand how that could be, but I continued to listen to the story. So as Carns tells it, the Chinaman didn't do anything except put up his hands in self-defense but Carns just kept at it—blow after blow to the Chinaman's head. Eventually, Old Tom lay still on the ground on Main Street. Apparently, Carns just walked away after that.

(Bañuelos, 2014)

That same downtown location allowed us to simply pivot the group's attention northward and toward a local pizza institution on the same street. Launching into her story immediately after Peter's conclusion, Luhui Whitebear painted a sobering picture of the daily and racially-structured challenges facing "Sunny" Jim Patton, an African American who lived in this predominantly white town in a predominantly white state during the early 1900s. Oregon was granted statehood in 1859, admitted as both a "free state" and yet one that also legally sanctioned the exclusion of African American settlement (Nokes, 2013). Framing this reality, Luhui starts by positioning Patton's business successes in the content of his local singularity and relative isolation.

Standing in a room full of faces not like your own causes an emptiness to crawl through you, especially when those faces represent a history of oppression to your people. Pushing through to reach a place of belonging takes a great deal of perseverance.

(Whitebear, 2014)

Whitebear explains that Patton worked as a shoeshine during the 1920s, his business literally and symbolically placed just outside the entryway, or the passing space between the street and the barbershop inside. Yet, he owned his business and equipment at "a time when black ownership of anything was unheard of." While acknowledging his measured success, Whitebear reminds us that Patton's story still tells us a great deal about "power whites held and the level of acceptance they practiced" in Corvallis.

In this moment of storytelling, our tour shifted the downtown space. We told buried stories about events and people historically linked to those locations, and we also began transforming the meaning of those geographies and our future relationships to them. A space previous seen as lacking any histories for people of color, for example, suddenly became alive with layers of experience and points of potential connection. Students and guests could locate those stories and embed those histories in the places where they had so often travelled before, but without maps of meaning that could speak to their own experiences, to the challenges and celebrations of their presence as well as their invisibilities in Corvallis. And we made this shift together, with a momentum of collective choice and remembering. To this day, I cannot approach that corner without recalling these stories and viscerally feeling that shift.

So, how do we choose stories and determine how to craft them in a way that does not simply reproduce simple conveyance of historical fact – as interesting as they may be? In other words, how do we make this project into something more than a potentially tiresome chronicle of past events that begin to lose force as they pile up and assemble into an indistinguishable or overwhelming mass? The key is the merger between narrative and history, and the explicit reliance on techniques of affect. The next section will discuss narrative and some of the other guiding techniques we use to create the tours. The subsequent section will then dive deeper into the use and importance of affect.

Logistical Guidelines

This model of storytelling illustrates that something as seemingly simple or mundane as a tour can facilitate learning, build community, and transform space. In part, I intentionally design the course to intertwine the best practices of engagement, research, community-building, retention, teaching, and learning (Koh, 2008). So, here I want to further explain some of the guidelines that I have used for this project, which can be useful for those who might be interested in adapting or "replicating" this sort of project elsewhere. There are two sets of important guidelines; one set logistical and one set based on principles. In this section, I present the logistical considerations that are helpful in making a social justice tour function smoothly. In the section following, I discuss the conceptual guidelines.

A tour such as this does require some resources. The bulk of the cost for the tour as I have it designed comes from the printing costs of the tour scripts/booklets. I opt for high quality paper, color, folding/spines. This choice serves several purposes. The booklet is intended, from the beginning, as an archival document. Because some of the images have reproduction restrictions, we do not produce digital ones. The booklets also work as cherished gifts for our audiences. They welcome the opportunity to revisit stories and gain clarity on something they perhaps missed or mis-heard, or share with others. The booklets hold wonderful photographs, art, and images that add further dimensions to the stories. The booklets also contain our list of sources, student information, thank you to our supporters and sponsors, and an introductory statement about the project. I always hold the booklets until the guests have completed the tour, so they can give the students their full attention, to hear the stories as they were intended to be delivered. The booklets also serve a powerful "marketing" purpose. They provide potential supporters a tangible outcome that they can see and touch, which makes them more likely to offer critical support, especially in the form of funding.

While the tour requires resources to start, I have also found (at least at my institution) that some decisions generate interest in supporting the project, including financial support. Each tour is documented with photography, and sometimes with print media or video. Our first tour was featured on the front page of the local paper's Sunday edition, a powerful reminder of the community engagement and impact, and for generating awareness of the project and our degree program. Together with the booklet, these offer some "tangible" outcomes that make it easier for other to support the project. Since we invite guests, many of the tours usually include at least a subset of strategic invitations that may result in further support, extended "publicity," increased student interest, and other kinds of support. The bulk of the guest list remains comprised of student invitations and other colleagues who I know will support the students and generally appreciate the tour.

The class and tour alone would no doubt have generated attention on its own, yet partnering directly with the Difference, Power, & Discrimination (DPD) program – and at one point with another parallel grant-funded seminar program, ADVANCE – has greatly expanded its audience and impact. The summer seminars have exposed dozens of faculty, staff, and administrators to the tour. The partnership with DPD creates an opportunity for this project and this model of cultural and spatial engagement to reach people in fields and places I was unlikely to reach; STEM fields, administration posts, individuals working at our satellite campuses, and those from the local community college. With this relatively easy partnership model, the tour has extended its potential to make meaningful change on my campus and in our local community.

Conceptual Guidelines

Beyond the *structure* of creating, funding, and sharing this project, there are also several vital principles I use in the design, creation, and delivery that allow this project to produce meaningful and even crucial outcomes. I lay out seven principles here, and follow up with special treatment for one additional pair of principles (affect and speculative non-fiction) in the final section before concluding.

The principles here include:

- Use a fully *hands-on learning* approach.
- Trust *critical pedagogy* techniques that center student learning.
- Create (or reveal the) *meaningful stakes* in the project.
- Tackle *knowledge production and collaboration* together.
- Embrace the need to take on *current and personal issues* of social justice.
- Foster the *connections between research and creativity*.
- *Link story to geography, or place.*

One of the most important design features is the hands-on approach and workshop-like use of class time. Our turning point often proves to be the moment students fully realize that they have creative license; when they finally see an avenue for their contributions and the need for the stories to be simultaneously personal, historically rooted, and yet overtly applicable to our current lives. They suddenly feel empowered to craft their narratives and grab full ownership over the project. These transformations take place through the class collaboration, as we workshop our ideas, our stories, our research techniques, and our performative concepts. As then-masters student Gabe Sheoships reflects,

> One thing I felt worked well was the class discussion, and editing of each individual narrative. I got a lot of feedback, and with the small class size, it was easy to make your voice heard. [The work was] serious, but we were allowed to be creative at the same time.
> (G. Shoeships, personal communication, June 9, 2014)

In the class setting, we use a critical pedagogy that puts the tools in the hands of the student and asks them to learn by usage, and to develop their skills and their projects by seeking guidance where needed. When we are in the classroom, our time is dedicated to sharing, feedback, active brainstorming, collaborative visioning, and constructive critique. Most of our "in-class" time, however, is not spent in a classroom. From the first day, we take a tour. Within in the first three weeks we have spent most of our time directly in the archives, examining materials and exploring possible stories. The next few weeks are spent revising stories, practicing and giving feedback, and tracking down archival details and finding visual supplements. As the term moves toward the end, we shift toward refining our techniques, crafting an experiential opportunity for our guests, and honing our delivery.

The stakes of this project are high. Students know they will be delivering their project to an audience of their peers, faculty, university staff and administrators, and community members (sometimes up to 50 in total). As the project grows, the students also find themselves responding to the "legacy" of previous tours and classes; sometimes even using that as inspiration for creating the "best tour yet." All of these principles of project and class design generate internal motivations that allow me to serve more as mentor-guide-cheerleader than director-instructor, which reflects my preferred teaching and learning style anyway.

Importantly, this approach changes how students understand knowledge production and collaboration. Any story can be told if it can be shaped convincingly and if it can fit within our agreed upon frame of social justice. While we center archival research and materials, we actively engage with current issues and personal interests that will drive the needed passion and collaborative investments. We mirror that approach and lean into the value of affect and building connections through story and storytelling. To the students' surprise, this approach also changes their relationship to research and the university, as well as their perceptions of their current place of residence. Their projects are suddenly more meaningful. They feel the full weight of effective and appropriate representations as well as their newly-recognized responsibilities as researchers.

The relationship between research and creativity prove vital for this project. It is also key to a more participatory and meaningful learning experience. We embrace the fuzzy line between fact and fiction, and use that fluidity and ambiguity in order to tell stories that could not be told without creative license. In this way, the student stories often defy what is otherwise an uncooperative and incomplete archive, and thus can more effectively center themes that open up larger social and spatial issues. Thus, the stories represent speaking out the "narrative possibilities" and not just the facts of the archives, which will always be inadequate for marginalized communities (Crew & Simons, 1991).

We take this approach to the project because, as the students learn through course readings and discussion, history is only relevant as reflection of the present – and here we drew inspiration from the work of Michel-Rolph Trouillot (1995). Our guests quickly grasp our intentions, and express appreciation for how we take what could easily be a dull historical recitation and make it a vibrant and current point of contention and consideration. A tenured faculty member in the Liberals Arts (and another author in this volume), who has generously attended several versions of the tour, directly lauds the students for their ability to make those contemporary links so clear in their writings and for the audience. In his reflections, he explains that "what stuck with me from the social justice tours I've attended … is how the students deeply understand Corvallis history not as distant, disconnected, and unrelated to the present but very much the latter" (R. Mize, personal communication, June 14, 2019).

The Social Justice Tour of Corvallis provides a reintroduction to our college town and extends awareness of often hidden communities and experiences. The tour helps physically anchor stories to places that will be commonly and regularly traversed again in the future. When participants walk by or enter a building where one of our stories occurred (or was shared), the newly formed memory of the tour is triggered. A faculty member in Literature exclaimed as much, noting that "the tour was a fun, moving and engaging way to re-frame the city and community in which I have lived for the past six years" (A. Ribero, personal communication, June 26, 2019). Another literature faculty member, observed how the tour

> profoundly changed how I see the place where I live and work because it helped me to understand Corvallis as a place of historical and on-going struggle rather than a quiet, complacent town that has and will always be made by and for middle-class white families.
> (E. Sheehan, personal communication, June 16, 2019)

An engineer who attended the DPD seminar similarly found the localized narratives enhanced their understanding of social justice beyond abstractions or distant geographic or historic locations. They shared that "although I'd heard about the ubiquity of systems of power and oppression, it was the Social Justice Tour that really helped me see how those systems are here with us in our home" (D. Monfort, personal communication, June 17, 2019). These audience reflections reveal the principles I introduced above becoming tangible precisely because each of the stories are generated through these principles. For the rest of this section, I offer story selections and student reflections that result from the intricate convergence of all (or many of) these principles as they are manifested more concretely.

In the second tour, Allen Dean created a compelling dialogue based on several 1890's paychecks we found at the Benton County Historical Society. Oregon State College (now University) had issued these checks to a handful of Chinese workers. Although we did not know the nature of the work (more than likely manual), Allen saw how the checks highlighted both their invisible labor and cultural dismissal. Many of the checks were issued to pseudo-names like "John Chinaman." Using a first-person literary approach, he sets up a scene that describes how the mundane experience of collecting a paycheck can signal a series of events infused with ethnocentrism, discrimination, and racism.

> The college officer called out to the line of dormitory workers. Someone nudged me forward, it was my turn to speak with the man at the counter.
> "Name?" he asked.
> "Zhang Liu," I responded.
> "What? I'm just going to write down John," the man shook his head as he wrote.
> "No, my name is…"
> "John Chinaman. I like it! Much easier to say and makes sense. Here you go!"
> He handed me the check. I looked down and saw he'd written "John Chinaman" as my name. I noticed the others in line were irritated that I had taken any longer than required, so I took the check for John Chinaman and left.
>
> (Dean, 2016)

Allen's story reflected his experiences working closely with international students (who boost the university budget but do not always find easy or meaningful inclusion), and study abroad programs. He resonated with how the dismissal scripted directly onto those checks still reflected the experiences of contemporary international students who almost invariably create names in English for themselves to avoid tensions; or those domestic students with "non-standard" names that likewise experience daily reminders that their cultural or racial identities are marked as difficult or suspect.

In a few cases, students feel emboldened enough to create original autobiographical narratives which create a unique, new primary document aimed at shaping the future archives and simultaneously confronting their own difficult or meaningful individual experiences in Corvallis and/or at Oregon State University. Consider Jasmine Brown's first-hand story about her unwelcome challenges as a Black woman in forestry and her related critiques of institutional commitments to diversity, delivered directly in front of the forestry building (see Figure 3.3).

We opened tour #4 with her story, called "Dear Black Girls." Describing her experiences as the lone Black graduate student in Forestry and the failures of the official processes to resolve her complaints of tokenism and dismissals, she states:

> I would be lying to say that there have been no systemic and institutional barriers in my way...
>
> My mere existence in the College of Forestry today serves as an act of resistance.
>
> *This is me breaking my silence and sharing my truth.* I am well prepared for any possible repercussions of breaking my silence, as the College of Forestry has already tried getting rid of me twice. Having my character continuously besmirched by the College encouraged me to co-found the Women of Color Caucus... *This is me documenting an intersectional history that is currently not recognized or discussed.*

Figure 3.3 Jasmine Brown [center] delivers the powerful opening story for Social Justice Tour of Corvallis #4, describing her experiences as the lone Black graduate student in the College of Forestry. Fellow classmates and tour creators, Adrianna Marlen [L] and Amanda Ekabutr [R], prepare to perform call-and-response elements within Jasmine's story.

Photo courtesy of the author

A final note for any black girl reading this:
For I know
what happens to
successful Black girls in the College of Forestry
who want to be themselves and pave their own paths
Dear Black girls,
your magic might not be welcomed everywhere.
That is no reason for you to dim your light
Shine a light on your experiences
Shine a light on everything they never wanted you to talk about
Be as magical as you'd like

(Brown, 2019)

Telling these stories and listening to these stories in community creates new geographies and spaces of memory that are clearly needed and powerful. The specific stories may not always be predictable, since there are many that remain untold and in need of recovery, but the act of speaking them into space and into community allows for the space to be transformed. The spaces transform in the way needed for the students, and in ways unexpected by the audience; but because of the earnestness, tend to be generously accepted and understood. Through the stories, the burden of an intimate place like our small college town can be lifted and the benefit of that intimacy can be instead redirected and affirmed in a way most did not even realize was necessary, or possible. In Jasmine's story, she is speaking out about the most intimate structure that shapes her student life, and doing it precisely where she experienced her "barriers" and felt muted. Instead, with a community gathered in support, she used the moment and the space for "breaking [her] silence and sharing [her] truth."

The content and the structure of the tour provide a unique opportunity to create space together across several scales. At the smallest scales, the individual students in the class find themselves changed by their individual learning process. As undergraduate student Diana Santiago reflects,

> My favorite part of this class was the end, when we shared the stories we found and the new stories we created with everyone. I also enjoyed seeing the process everyone went through creating their stories and the fact that we were able to bond as a class throughout this process was something I wouldn't have expected.
>
> (D. Santiago, personal communication, June 14, 2019)

Together, the students create a unique community of peers with whom they collaborate and grow in ways that they direct, but do so in response to a meaningful opportunity with potentially longstanding impact.

Eddie Rodriguez, a graduate student with tour #4, observed that his research and storytelling work extended beyond the classroom. He found strength in the fact that his "experiences within Ethnohistory Methodology provided [him] the opportunity to engage with [his] community in a deeper level" (E. Rodriguez, personal communication, June 14, 2019). Likewise, when we gather for the tours, the community circle widens to include friends, family, colleagues, and the broader communities. One administrative staff member reflected how "it was beautiful to see the passion of these students, and the support and camaraderie and love of the whole group on the tour" (P. Johnson, personal communication, June 14, 2019). A faculty member well-versed in experiential learning "loved the student-researched narratives and voices at the center of it all" (A. Schwartz, personal communication, June 17, 2019). Our archival librarian (and another author in this collection), who has direct engagement with the early process and creation of the tour, as well as insight into the content of the original materials, points out that she was "deeply moved by how [the students] interwove their personal stories into the narratives, thus bringing the archival stories even more meaning and impact for present day audiences" (N. Fernandez, personal communication, June 17, 2019).

Kali Furman, one of the students that created tour #3 – and one of the editors for this volume – reminded me of this impact during a recent workshop. She insisted that the class/tour "fundamentally changed [her] relationship to Oregon State University" (K. Furman, personal communication, June 26, 2019). As she put it: "how I think about this place and every space that I walk through is different because I have taken [the] class and participated in the creation of this tour" (K. Furman, personal communication, June 26, 2019). A faculty member in public policy and engaged in work on natural resource policies, was highly impacted by Tami Gann's story (tour #3, see Figure 3.4) about the deep natural history of the Willamette River, and marveled at how the tour "allowed [her] to experience Corvallis is new ways," while also being given the tools to consider that the "the river has stories!" (A. Spalding, personal communication, June 15, 2019; Gann, 2019). An administrator with teaching and community education duties reflected on their experience more generally, thinking "aloud" about how our institution can use this type of locally-based learning more effectively. After the tour they found themselves "sitting with the power and impact of place-based pedagogy as a particularly effective and congruent form of social justice education" (J. Kenney, personal communication, June 13, 2019).

Next, I turn attention to two principles in need of some level of special differentiation. The principles of affect and of using speculative non-fiction are probably less expected for those familiar with general techniques for student engagement, critical pedagogy, social justice education, and applied research. Each, however, has proven crucial to the power and the success of this project.

Embracing Affect and Speculative Non-Fiction

Affect can loosely be characterized as a bodily engagement with and sometimes emotional interface with the world (Johnson 2018; Gregg & Seigworth, 2010). This is important for a number of reasons, including the need to attend

Figure 3.4 Guests and fellow classmates brave the weather during social justice tour #3 to hear Tami Gann's story about settler colonialism in the Willamette Valley. The tour group gathered near a cluster of canoe sculptures created by artists from the Confederated Tribes of Grand Ronde. Tami's previous story spoke from the perspective of the Willamette River looking across it's millennia of existence and change.
Photo courtesy of the author

to a holistic approach to learning and community-building as well as the psychologically and emotionally charged nature of working in areas of social justice or (sometimes) just coming from oppressed, marginalized, and colonized communities. In addition, the supposed split between rational or intellectual thinking and emotion-centered processing has been challenged as over-simplified or false. The binary of rationality-emotion is often a power-laden means for disenfranchising alternative modes of knowledge production or for simply dismissing critiques of power as irrational, subjective, and non-neutral (Lakoff, 2010). We have also seen that appeals to emotion are often far more effective and commonplace than appeals to logic or "facts" which are always interpreted through a variety of pre-established lenses and frames that have gathered affective (and unconscious) force.

The core of speculative non-fiction is writing a reasonable or even probable story based on the limited evidence on hand while still centered on historical data and "facts" (Walker, 2013). This technique is critical when information gaps need to be filled, or where composite stories can actually help provide contextual framing. This approach is most effective when dealing with the shared experiences generated by particular social identity categories (race, gender, sexuality), as well as with more broadly shared traits like jealousy, anger, or love. To maintain a sense of narrative fidelity, the speculative aspect is always acknowledged and directly framed as viable techniques in both the creativity and in research method.

So, let's consider some examples. For tour #2, Miwa Tokunaga, an international graduate student from Japan, presents a story about former Oregon State University student Ray Yasui, from inside the Benton Hotel lobby. She sets the tone in several important ways. She introduces the important Yasui family and explains her framing concept of "shigata ga nai," a Japanese phrase roughly meaning "it cannot be helped."

Then, she pauses, and bows.

Drawing on her cultural protocols, which are also directly relevant to her story, Miwa links herself to the narrative and signals to the audience a crucial transition in voice. With her next words, she performs as Ray Yasui recounting his experiences at the university, and then lamenting his brother Kay's suicide in 1931: "My name is Tsuyoshi and my English name is Ray.... [i]f you choose to fight every single fight, you won't last.... [m]y brother, Kay, he fought and got stuck. I couldn't tell exactly what he was feeling, but this poem taught me how much he was struggling" (Tokunaga, 2016). Miwa then reads a portion of Kay's poem about racialization and his struggles with discrimination (here excerpted):

> You call me Jap
> And boast, saying you yourself are American
> ...
> You insult and torment
> You say you are my superior
> ...
> I, too, claim this land as my birthplace.
> As much American as you,
> I, too,
> Am American.
>   (Yasui, 1931)

Kay Yasui's poem strategically references Langston Hughes' famous 1926 poem (*I, Too*) about anti-Black racism and belonging (Hughes, 1926). In using this piece, Miwa also generates her story precisely as a new wave of "I, Too" social media campaigns rages across U.S. universities, starting with UCLA and spreading to institutions like Harvard and Oregon State University. Miwa also unfolds her story amidst national discussions about internment camps and Muslim registries. Her juxtaposition reminds us that these discussion points of internment and racial/ethnic registries find quick resistance from many contemporary Japanese Americans who easily recall their families' racially targeted internment during the 1940s.

So, here we see a powerful example of a student presenting a speculative non-fiction story using historically based archival materials and connecting contemporary issues of racism and the ongoing tensions of inclusion/exclusion. Ray Yasui attended our university nearly a century before, but through Miwa's retelling his story including her use of affect, the concerns of Hughes' landmark poem, and current events, it all came together in one seamless and impactful narrative.

That year, for the first time, I also created a story for the tour along with the students. Paired with Miwa's story about Ray Yasui, my story addressed some newly gathered data on a previous story and turned attention to how different uses of archives and different sets of questions changes the processes of history-making and story-building. Extending Luhui Whitebear's work on "Sunny" Jim Patton during the tour #1, I updated our audience about the Corvallis Boot Blacks, a handful of "unknown" Black men who worked in Corvallis in the 1920s and 1930s. Before collecting this information, Patton had often been tagged as the only Black person in town during that era (Barnd, 2016b). Standing in the Benton Hotel precisely where many of these men worked shining shoes, I offered a reflection on what we can find in archives and how we can engage research values, asking

> What else of their stories can we uncover? How many more stories are not accounted for? How can we better recover the lineage of the Corvallis boot blacks and the mostly forgotten African Americans that have lived here since the mid-1800s?
>
> (Barnd, 2016b)

Drawing on the poignancy of not knowing their stories and being forced to sit with their silence and erased experiences, I created a list of their names, and places of origin. I simply read each out loud. The simplicity of the "story" reversed or perhaps challenged the power of knowledge and focused on creating affective connections to the archives, trying to reclaim a space normally seen as dry, distant, and stoically exclusionary.

By being earnestly engaged with the same project and taking on the same tasks, the students also saw my own process of research and creation developing just as it unfolded for them. I sought out feedback during class workshop time just as they did. I edited and adjusted according to their guidance. They also saw firsthand how I crafted a unique and highly speculative, but compelling story out of minimal bits of archival information. I created my story only because it moved me, just as I encouraged them to find their emotional link and point of passion for each story.

The instructor's openness, even encouragement of, many forms of storytelling repeatedly proves another vital element for success. Students invariably reflect on their class experience by noting their appreciation of being allowed many ways of telling stories and being encouraged to both use techniques comfortable to them as well as to try new techniques that push their growth. In the previous student story examples, I share models that use standard historical narrative voice, personal-as-political strategies, personification of non-humans (the river), and interweaving politics of past and present. Although each strategy uses a great deal of creative force, poetic forms have also proven empowering and flexible in how students make connections between themselves and their archival research efforts. Poetry also offers a nice variation in the tour delivery as audience members appreciate the sliding across genres and styles.

Consider, Jason Tena-Enarnacion's poem about the first Indigenous (Siletz) students at Oregon State University (see Figure 3.5). Jason responsibly crafts their experiences (both documented and speculative) into a relevant contemporary narrative. In this case, we are rewarded with a (here excerpted) poem written by a mixed-race, Indigenous student who openly ponders the 19th century experience of previous mixed Indigenous students at this same institution. He tackles the weight of assimilation and how it comes to impact Indigenous students, sometimes even pressing down most forcefully from within one's own family.

> The Collins brothers of Oregon State University
>   Did George the Indian Agent let them hear storytelling
>   From their grandmother and grandfather Shellhead
>   Did he mourn the death of his son's mother as a husband or as an Indian Agent?
>   Did he teach his sons her life…or try to erase her from their memory
>   James, Benjamin, and William
>   The 1880s is so far, yet so close
>
>   (Tena-Encarnacion, 2016)

Figure 3.5 Jason Tena-Encarnacion [standing] delivers his poem about the Collins brothers (Siletz tribal member) near Avery Park, named after the town's founder and first European American settler, Joseph Avery.
Photo courtesy of the author

This kind of personalized and emotionally mature storytelling strategy is possible because in my classes and during the tours, I introduce the work of the Social Justice Tour as engaging in speculative non-fiction. We use this technique as a way of opening possibilities when the archives are limited or uncooperative. Many of our stories are based on the smallest snippets of archival findings. While this does not allow for robust historical accounting, it does allow us to extend and more thoughtfully contemplate narratives that have been neglected, hidden, or erased. This approach of making reasonable and openly speculative narratives pushes back against archives that would otherwise continue to deny substance and presence to those without institutional documentation. In Jason's poem and storytelling, he draws upon limited archival data, extrapolates on the likely tensions in the lives of young men in an often-unforgiving white supremacist and settler colonial context, and links that reality to his own experiences of similar tensions. While a speculative non-fiction approach does not feign historical accuracy of the story itself, we do embrace the affective and instigating stakes created by telling it. His story thus brings their experience back to the forefront, and asks us to genuinely consider their lives, as well as to ask why their story (and many more like it) is opaque in the first place.

Conclusion

My interest in creating the ethnohistory methodology course and offering the Social justice Tour of Corvallis was aimed at showing what happens when social justice concerns stand at the center of teaching, learning, research, community-building, and public engagement. As an unexpected bonus, the tour also ever-so-slightly transformed the town for many of those living and working there. The Social Justice Tour helps make several interventions. It helps change relationships with the space of the university and town. It allows students and guests to create new kinds of space. It makes visible, and better reflects, a broader and diverse range of student experiences and communities. It develops student skills through research, community engagement, and deliberate use of affect and speculative non-fiction.

Few academic endeavors I am involved with receive these kinds of outcomes and achieve this kind of holistic success. In an earlier publication, I shared my reflections and early assessments of the tour concept, concluding that "using projects such as these are exceptionally successful and worthwhile well in excess of the admittedly extra labor required" (Barnd, 2016a, p. 220). At that time this was still a relatively unproven claim given the possibility that my measures of success could have resulted from an anomalous set of factors and outcomes. I was convinced, however, that the way we tackled difficult topics in social justice was effective and meaningful to the students. Students clearly poured in their hearts and souls in a way I had not seen before. They told personalized stories and created much needed narratives that spoke from deep within their personal lives. Their responses to the course design and project idea clearly reflected geographer Chris Merrett's (2004) pedagogical challenge: "Teachers can either offer an uncritical, 'neutral' education that supports the status quo or choose to empower students to question dominant ideas, possibly leading to social change" (p. 93). In this context, perhaps the most important social change began in the classroom as the students found their voices, told their stories, and expressed their desires for newly scripted spaces where they could live and thrive. And they did it together; *with* one another and *for* one another, in a genuinely collaborative and self-empowering way.

Since the first tour and that previous reflection, I have taught the course three additional times and guided two dozen students in the creation of four distinctive tours (in 2014, 2016, 2017, and 2019). Some minor elements change, but the tour and the learning experience is steady. Students always rise to the challenge. They understand that their words and their vision will be shared with others. They know their contributions and voices will be added to the archives, which will be richer than they found it because of their effort and intentionality. They come to find a unique pride in their work that I find so often missing in many other courses that I teach.

In some ways, this is by design. Yet it certainly exceeds the intentions of the original design. What began as a solution to the question of how best to teach a new methods class has become a tool for reshaping space and crafting belonging for students of color, Indigenous students, and queer students within a semi-rural, largely white community and from within a PWI. The Social Justice Tour of Corvallis has become a well-known project familiar to the college deans and university president, to local media, and researchers using our campus and local county archives. It has fundamentally shaped my understanding of engaged and experiential learning.

Lastly, I want to suggest that any reader of this chapter could begin a similar project. Any school or community organization could create a locally centered tour with similar success. Anyone with access to a local archives can begin the process of searching for and creating stories. I have included below some additional resources pulled from the course reading list. These readings provide both critical framings and sometimes models for how to think about the creation and experiences of tours. They also provide some accessible tips for how to engage with archival materials and archival institutions themselves. I also recommend beginning with a simple goal: find stories that speak to people's interests and identities. Allow creativity to shape the storytelling, rather than being confined by the inevitable limits of the archives. Fill in the gaps when the stories are incomplete, and be honest about the strategies and limitations. Most importantly, work together and work toward a community-focused purpose and sharing.

Additional Resources

Readings

Barber, R., & Berdan, F. (1998). *The emperor's mirror: Understanding cultures through primary sources.* University of Arizona Press.

Bendiner-Viani, G. (2012). Layered SPURA: Spurring conversations through visual urbanism. *Radical History Review, 114,* 206–215.

Dickey, J. (2012). Historic Milwaukee walking tour. *The Public Historian, 34*(4), 71–77.

Flores, R. (2008). The Alamo: Myth, public history, and the politics of inclusion. In D.J. Walkowitz, & L.M. Knauer (Eds.), *Contested histories in public space: Memory, race, and nation* (pp. 122–135). Duke University Press.

Gregg, M., & G. Seigworth. (2010). *The affect theory reader.* Duke University Press.

Hall, S. (1996). The West and the rest: Discourse and power. In S. Hall, D. Held, D. Hubert, & K. Thompson (Eds.), *Modernity: An introduction to modern societies* (pp. 165–173). Blackwell.

Johnson, E.L. (2018). *Cultural memory, memorials, and reparative writing.* Palgrave Pilot.

Le Corbusier. (1987). *The city of to-morrow and its planning.* Dover Publications.

Marcuse, P. (1997). Walls of fear. In N. Ellin (Ed.), *Architecture of fear* (pp. 104–114). Princeton University Press.

Pulido, L, Barraclough, L., & Cheng, W. (2012). *A people's guide to Los Angeles.* University of California Press.

Solnit, R. (2001). *Wanderlust: A history of walking.* Penguin Books.

Stanley, M. (2012). Third ward neighborhood self-guided walking tour. *The Public Historian 34*(4), 85–88.

Walker, M.S.N. (2013). *Bending genre: Essays on creative nonfiction.* Bloomsbury Academic.

Websites

Movers and Shakers NYC. www.moversandshakersnyc.com/
Dear Visitor. www.dearvisitor.app/

References

Bañuelos, P. (2014). *Old Tom and Chinese laundries. Social justice tour of Corvallis.* Oregon Multicultural Communities Research Collection (MSS OMCRC), Oregon State University Special Collections and Archives Research Center, Corvallis, Oregon.

Barnd, N.B. (2016a). Constructing a social justice tour: Pedagogy, race, and student learning through geography. *Journal of Geography, 115*(5), 221–223.

Barnd, N.B. (2016b). *The Legacy of the Corvallis boot blacks. Social justice tour of Corvallis #3.* Oregon Multicultural Communities Research Collection (MSS OMCRC), Oregon State University Special Collections and Archives Research Center, Corvallis, Oregon.

Brown, J. (2019). *Dear Black girls. Social justice tour of Corvallis #4.* Oregon Multicultural Communities Research Collection (MSS OMCRC), Oregon State University Special Collections and Archives Research Center, Corvallis, Oregon.

Crew, S., & Simons, J.E. (1991). Locating authenticity: Fragments of a dialogue. In I. Karp, & S.D. Lavine (Eds.), *Exhibiting cultures: The poetics and politics of museum display* (pp. 159–175). Smithsonian Institution Press.

Dean, A. (2016). *Bank checks. Social justice tour of Corvallis II*. Oregon Multicultural Communities Research Collection (MSS OMCRC), Oregon State University Special Collections and Archives Research Center, Corvallis, Oregon.

Hughes, L. (1926). *The weary blues*. Knopf.

Kuh, G.D. (2008). *High-Impact Educational Practices: What They Are, Who Has Access to Them, and Why They Matter*. Association of American Colleges and Universities.

Lakoff, G. (2010). Why it matters how we frame the environment. *Environmental Communication 4*(1), 70–81.

Merrett, C. (2004). Social justice: What is it? Why teach it? *Journal of Geography 103*(3), 93–101.

Nokes, R.G. (2013). *Breaking chains: Slavery on trial in the Oregon Territory*. Oregon State University Press.

Tena-Encarnacion, J. (2019). *Collins brothers. Social justice tour of Corvallis II*. Oregon Multicultural Communities Research Collection (MSS OMCRC), Oregon State University Special Collections and Archives Research Center, Corvallis, Oregon.

Trouillot, M. (1995). *Silencing the past: Power and the production of history*. Beacon Press.

Tokunaga, M. (2016). *Ray Yasui. Social justice tour of Corvallis*. Oregon Multicultural Communities Research Collection (MSS OMCRC), Oregon State University Special Collections and Archives Research Center, Corvallis, Oregon.

Whitebear, L. (2014). *Sunny Jim Patton. Social justice tour of Corvallis*. Oregon Multicultural Communities Research Collection (MSS OMCRC), Oregon State University Special Collections and Archives Research Center, Corvallis, Oregon.

Yasui, K. (1931). Untitled. In L. Kessler (Ed.), *Stubborn twig: Three generations in the life of a Japanese American family* (p. 122). Oregon State University Press.

Section 2
Frameworks for Transformative Pedagogies

4 Universal Design for Instruction and Institutional Change
A Case Study

Stephanie Jenkins and Martha Smith

This chapter introduces Universal Design for Instruction (UDI) and presents a case study in a cross-unit collaboration between UDI advocates at a public research university. We offer two first-person narrative accounts – a tenure-track faculty member and a Director of Disability Access Services – outlining the success of our partnership. We describe the history of our combined efforts to promote UDI at Oregon State University and create accessible learning experiences beyond the requirements of legal compliance, including obstacles to our collaboration. Using our experience partnering to organize accessible pedagogy workshops, advocate for UDI at all levels of OSU, and partnering with OSU's Difference, Power, and Discrimination program, we offer suggestions, exercises, and examples for incorporating UDI, combatting academic ableism, and advocating for institutional change.

Across the Great Divide: Who are We?

In this section, we describe each of the co-author's backgrounds, positions, and perspectives on our collaboration. Because we were unable to find any literature outlining a cross-unit partnership similar to ours, we use a narrative method to document how our paths crossed and relationship unfolded. We do so with the hopes that other faculty and DS providers will think outside the narrow boundaries of their job descriptions to establish productive, transformative coalitions for change. We also hope to demonstrate the value of our cross-unit partnership, which lies outside the traditional boundaries of our job descriptions, will encourage university administrators and decision-makers to recognize, reward, and nourish similar alliances at their institutions.

Martha

While I was an undergraduate student studying biology, there was a great deal of research being done regarding teaching chimpanzees and gorillas sign language. I started taking sign language with the intent to do graduate research related to language acquisition with chimpanzees. Once I started learning sign language I was enthralled by the language and the culture of the Deaf community. I became

DOI: 10.4324/9781003091998-6

a sign language interpreter and that became my entry into the world of disability and disability culture. I am a white woman who does not experience a disability. My entire adult life I have been working in and with the disability community. This expands over 30 years and across multiple countries. Over those 30 years my knowledge of disability rights, ableism and my place in those conversations have changed substantially. I, hopefully, am no longer the all-knowing fixer, the know-it-all with the all the answers. Rather, I hope that I am able to conduct myself as an impassioned ally, a good listener, and good collaborator. I try to make sure that the most important voices are those of individuals with disabilities themselves. Most recently, I have worked as a Disability Services Director at three different Oregon institutions of Higher Education. The first was a small regional State institution with the largest number and percentage of deaf students at a college in the state. Additionally, I worked at the state's only health sciences higher education institution. While there I worked with faculty and clinical staff regarding how to make clinical sites and rotations accessible to students with disabilities often using UD as the guiding principles. I also worked at an Oregon state agency working with employees with disabilities and providing access and accommodations in diverse work environments. Currently, I am the director of Disability Access Services at the state's Land-Grant University (over 30,000 students at multiple sites including a very robust online environment).

Stephanie

I am a tenure-track associate professor of philosophy at Oregon State University, where I have worked since 2012. I am a white woman who experiences disabilities that are intermittently apparent and poorly understood. In addition to holding a dual PhD in Philosophy and Women's Studies, I conduct teaching and research in the field of Disability Studies. I teach "Introduction to Disability Studies" and serve as co-founding member and coordinator of the OSU Disability Network, a collective of faculty, staff, and students interested in promoting a Disability Studies curriculum and accessibility on our campus. I am passionate about developing innovative and accessible learning opportunities for students at all stages of their careers.

My interest in Disability Studies developed in graduate school after reading Susan Wendell's (1996) *Rejected Body*. Her account of disability through a critical re-reading of the history of Philosophy was a unique – and affirming – account of my home discipline. For most of my life, I have struggled with chronic illness. Like many women with severe pain, medical professionals treated me like a modern-day hysteric; for years, countless doctors dismissed my symptoms as psychosomatic manifestations of stress and depression. At the same time, I benefited from (and continue to do so) class privilege, as my education and access to health insurance enabled me to navigate complex medical institutions, visit multiple specialists, and finally obtain a rare diagnosis. Because I am white, medical providers took my pain more seriously and were more likely to view my persistent questions as effective self-advocacy, rather than signs of a "difficult" patient. As a student, I felt the burden of disability stigma and thought I had to hide my impairments from my professors and peers; I feared my fatigue, pain, and failure to fit the typical image of a sick person, would mark me as a less serious student. This concern was not without merit, of course, as the existence and effects of ableism in higher education are well-documented (Dolmage, 2017; Hutcheon & Wolbring, 2012; Price, 2011). Discovering and throwing myself into Disability Studies transformed my relationship to my chronic illness and pain. When I began my teaching career, I vowed to make my classroom as accessible as possible to all students and to always believe students' accounts of their impairments. My lived experience with disability informs how I organize, deliver, and evaluate course content and I actively solicit feedback from my students regarding ways to make my classes more accessible.

Academic Ableism in Undergraduate Education

Ableism, or the systemic privileging of bodies and minds judged to be normal and healthy, is ubiquitous in the United States. Academia is no exception; it was borne out of, preserves, and replicates disability discrimination, oppression, and prejudice. Disability Studies scholars have rigorously documented the numerous effects of ableism on higher education. Jay Dolmage calls this "academic ableism," claiming that "academia exhibits and perpetuates a form of structural ableism" (2017, p. 53). In this section, we address three components of academic ableism that we find most relevant to our partnership and argument.

First and foremost, universities are centers for knowledge creation, disciplinary training, and education. We initiate students into knowledge frameworks that assign negative value to disability and, as Jay Dolmage and others have argued, have a eugenic past and aims. "Higher" education is, after all, in contrast to "lower" education such as asylums and schools for the "feebleminded" and deaf (Dolmage, 2017, p. 3, 49; Berger, 2015; Carlson, 2015; Price, 2011). Despite the recent advances in the growing field of Disability Studies, most undergraduate teaching about disability focuses on what Fiona Kumari Campbell terms the "negative ontology" – or, simply stated, the "badness" – of disability (2015, p. 109). In other words, disability is something to be cured, eradicated, and pitied. For example, in Stephanie's field of philosophy, the lives of disabled individuals are often devalued in thought experiments, compared to non-human animals, or presented as obstacles to health and progress (Carlson, 2010). More directly, biomedical fields such as psychology, pharmacology, bioengineering, and other sciences train future medical professionals to diagnose, avoid, and eliminate disability (Scully, 2008). This approach objectifies disability as Other, ignores and erases the experiences of people with disabilities, and perpetuates disability stigma.

Second, faculty are not immune from ableist beliefs, habits, and practices. They are hired for their content expertise, not their knowledge of disability or accessibility. Regardless of disciplinary background, individual instructors bring their preconceptions about disability and ability into the classroom (Lombardi & Lalor, 2017; Price, 2011). Faculty may assume students with disabilities are faking their impairments, seeking unfair advantages over their peers, or making excuses for failure to meet a deadline or inferior performance.

Third, the physical, social, and intellectual space of educational environments are produced through and by academic ableism. Our very professional ideas of how students demonstrate their commitment to education and successful learning outcomes themselves are infused with academic ableism. Course design reflects the values of the society it inhabits. While instructors alone do not create social categories, we play an essential role in setting pedagogical environments and establishing academic norms that replicate and amplify the social realities they help create. Instructional methods, assignment requirements, and course delivery are matters of design. As designed physical, social, and pedagogical environments, they are produced through and by power relations of academic institutions and the society at large. In other words, classroom design itself is a power relation. Like our built environments, course design is not value-neutral but, rather, is produced by and through power relations. Ableism pervades the design of syllabi, course expectations, assignment design and more. How instructors design and deliver courses actively conditions and frames the academic assumptions, habits, and practices that students and colleagues hold regarding what content should be taught and how.

Disability Services providers have not been immune to academic ableism either. Disability Services, from a legally required perspective, first came into play in higher education in 1979 with the passage of Section 504 of the Rehabilitation Act (Madaus, 2011). Access to higher education relied heavily on the medical model of disability (Fine & Asch, 2000). In this model the person with the disability is the "problem." If the person can be provided accommodations that "fix' their disability, then access is achievable. In this model professionals, most of whom do not experience a disability, make the decisions. This includes, doctors, teachers, rehabilitation specialists, social workers, and disability services offices. As a result, disability services offices have been in the "power" position to determine if a student is disabled enough to warrant receiving accommodations. Additionally, disability services professionals determine if an accommodation request is reasonable. As many disability services professionals do not experience disabilities themselves, they are determining whether a student may or may not be successful based on their potentially ableist views.

For these reasons and other, Dolmage (2017) argues "few cultural institutions do a better or more comprehensive job of promoting ableism" (p. 7). But if universities are unusually effective promoters of academic ableism, they present influential and momentous opportunities for transformation. In the following sections, we argue that UDI initiatives and strategized cross-unit collaborations are a needed response to academic ableism.

What is Universal Design for Instruction?

Universal Design (UD) was first introduced as a concept in architectural design. Ron Mace at the Center for Universal Design at North Carolina State University (1985) created the concept of UD. He created seven principles with the idea that UD was a way to make buildings and products more accessible to everyone. The design features were built in from the beginning. As a result, designing with access in mind was part of the entire process not an afterthought. These UD features can be seen in items as diverse as automatic doors, scissors that can be used by left or righted handed individuals, and the "undo" button on your computer are just a few examples. Through his work Mace was able to demonstrate the artificial distinctions that architectural and product design can create, or through UD help to eliminate. Why build steps when ramps work for everyone? The person doing the designing holds a great deal of control and power regarding the design features. As a result, those who have been in power are able to create buildings and products that benefit, or can be easily used, by those in power. As a result, those with less power are literally physically left out in the rain. Lack of physical accessibility impacts access to education, jobs and other benefits of living in a community for many people, including those with disabilities. If you can't get in the restaurant, how do you interact in the community? If you can't read the sign how do you know if you are doing something wrong or not? If you can't cut the paper how do you create a collage with your other classmates? Resistance to change which involves shifting power dynamics does not come easily.

In the early 2000s, higher education began to look at how to apply UD within the educational environment. The Office of Postsecondary Education in the U.S. Department of Education provided grants to institutions of higher education to explore how to bring UD into the higher education environment. Through these grants many projects popped up across the country to explore how to support students with disabilities in higher education through UD as well as projects that focused on how to bring faculty in higher education on board to begin to use UD in the teaching and learning environment.

UDI applies the architectural concept of Universal Design to learning environments, course materials, and curriculum development. UDI does not replace the formal accommodations process, but rather refers to the principles and practices that strive to create a flexible, inclusive environment for diverse students. Moving beyond a one-size-fits-all learning model, UDI prioritizes flexible curricular materials, assignments, and presentation formats. UDI steps away from solely relying on providing accommodations for or increasing access to students with disabilities to providing a more equitable and accessible educational environment for the entirety of the diverse student population.

Using the seven principles from the work of Ron Mace at the Center for Universal Design at North Carolina State University (1985) which were used as a way to address inaccessible environments, Scott and McGuire (2003) developed two additional principles to help bring UD into the higher education environment. These nine principles can be used as a starting point for how to think about approaching UDI when modifying or developing curriculum.

The seven principles are:

1 Equitable use: The design is useful and marketable to people with diverse abilities.
2 Flexibility in use: The design accommodates a wide range of individual preferences and abilities.
3 Simple and intuitive: Use of the design is easy to understand, regardless of the user's experience, knowledge, language skills, or current concentration level.
4 Perceptible information: The design communicates necessary information effectively to the user, regardless of ambient conditions or the user's sensory abilities.
5 Tolerance for error: The design minimizes hazards and adverse consequences of accidental or unintended actions.
6 Low physical effort: The design can be used efficiently and comfortably and with a minimum of fatigue.
7 Size and space for approach and use: Appropriate size and space is provided for approach, reach, manipulation, and use regardless of the user's body size, posture, or mobility.

(The Center for Universal Design, 1997, n.p.)

Scott, McGuire, and Foley add two additional principles for Universal Design for Instruction:

1 A community of learners: The instructional environment promotes interaction and communication among students and between student and faculty.
2 Instructional climate: Instruction is designed to be welcoming and inclusive. High expectations are espoused for all students.

(Scott et al., 2003, p. 44)

UDI is essential for advancing equity, inclusion, and diversity on college campuses. UDI interventions support students with disabilities by directly contributing to the creation of more inclusive classrooms. According to the World Health Organization (2011), people with disabilities constitute the largest minority group across the globe; around 15% of the world's population lives with a disability. Furthermore, addressing the needs of students living with disability is especially important in the state of Oregon, as 23% of adult Oregonians have a disability according to the Oregon Office on Disability and Health (2013).

According the National Center for Education Statistics, 19.4% of all college students experience some kind of disability. Of those 3% will disclose their disability to ask for accommodations. The reasons for not disclosing are varied including students: not needing an accommodation, not seeing themselves as a person with a disability, not wanting to deal with the "hassle" of working through a disability services office, and having other reasons. At OSU, one in 30 OSU students disclose a disability (in 2018–19 OSU Disability Access Services worked with over 1306 students who disclosed their disabilities), according to OSU Disability Access Services (2019). The number of students with disabilities that OSU serves has more than doubled over the past ten years.

In addition to serving students with disabilities, UDI principles and practices foster inclusive, supportive learning environments for English for Speakers of Other Languages (ESOL) students. It is a way to provide transformative curriculum that enables all students to see themselves as active participants in the classroom (concrete or online) and through the coursework. As Thomas Tobin (2019) says "UD = Access for everyone. No matter why. No matter who. No matter where."

Obstacles to Collaboration

Martha

Practitioners in disability services have been working with the concepts of UD since the late 90s and early 2000s. The struggle has been getting faculty on board. It has been a challenge to shift their mindset. Most faculty see the barrier to access as being the student's disability. As a result, the responsibility for providing or creating access falls on the student to adapt to the situation as best as possible and to disability services to provide accommodations to the individual student. The shift is getting faculty to see that the greater barrier is caused by how curriculum is developed and how faculty choose to teach or present their information to the class. The "aha" moment comes when faculty realize that UD is not just about including students with disabilities, but about including all students.

UD is about retention and support for students who traditionally have been excluded from higher education because the teaching and learning expectations have been narrow and conform to a "one size sits all" philosophy. UD allows more students to be welcomed into the higher education environment. This perspective also challenges the traditional norms of higher education and how faculty create and teach their classes. It is a shift in power dynamics. Disability Services (DS) providers are asking faculty to recognize that disability does not solely reside in the person experiencing the disability, but actually exists as a result of the way the educational environment is created to systematically exclude individuals with disabilities (Asch & Fine, 1988). UD requires faculty to accept the role they have played in creating non-accessible learning environments and curriculum that has excluded a wide array of students. It means faculty must acknowledge and accept their role in changing the current system. They cannot rely solely on Disability Services, in the case of students with disabilities, to fix the environment for them.

DS providers and faculty approach the classroom from different perspectives. Faculty often do not trust DS offices. They see us as meddlers and as people trying to tell them what they can and cannot do in their courses/classroom. DS folks often see the courses and the classroom as a place full of barriers that they need to fix. If faculty would just think about how they *do* their courses everything would be so much easier. DS see themselves as allies for students with disabilities, the faculty and the university as a whole. We are the great facilitators to make the orchestra and each piece in it (student, faculty, peers, etc.) perform at their best when no obstacles exist.

Initially doing UD in the classroom can take more work not less so it can be a hard sell. What helps is when a conversation can take place around faculty seeing DS as partners in creating an environment that supports the faculty's goals for the course as well seeing the benefits to all students. Using UDI can provide faculty with: a new-found sense of academic freedom; the ability to think in new ways about how to teach and assess student learning; offer the ability to determine competency for students in new ways; and give flexibility that not all students will need to show "competency" by doing exactly the same task.

UDI allows faculty to be creative and challenged in how they view learning and demonstrating how competency in a subject matter takes place. DS and faculty coming together can put students at the center of the discussion while entertaining the idea that there are multiple ways to demonstrate competency, in the same class. This approach provides opportunities for choice, creativity and an openness to think beyond the constraints of the curriculum that we have imposed upon ourselves.

Demonstrating UD and including faculty in the conversation has been a challenge. Finding a champion can make all the difference and can come in very unexpected ways. For me, Martha, every conversation with a faculty member is an opportunity to learn about their class and course. I explain that I ask a lot of questions so that I can better understand what they are trying to achieve and how best to support the student and the faculty to be successful. It was one of these conversations Stephanie and I had that lead to our partnership.

Stephanie

Like most faculty, I learned to teach by example; because most of my philosophy professors taught through discussion and lecture, this is the model I first used in my own classrooms. For the same reason, I assessed learning primarily through in-class participation and argumentative essays. Thinking critically about UDI and collaborating with Martha to implement it within my classrooms has been one of the most influential and transformative experiences of my academic career (see also Pitcher and Martinez, this volume). Working together has changed my understanding of what is possible within the classroom, making my teaching and research more accessible for my students and also myself. Yet, our innovative partnership almost didn't happen, because working with Martha violated nearly every piece of (well-intentioned) professional advice offered to me as an early career scholar.

In my first experience with a disability service provider I was a graduate student instructor. A student requested an electronic copy of our textbook to accommodate a brain injury. I referred her to our DS office, but the office was backlogged and the accommodations would not be approved in time for our class. I reached out to the publisher who refused to provide access without a formal accommodation. The advice I received boiled down to: don't make exceptions for a single student, especially one without proper documentation. They might be faking it. I was heartbroken to learn that I could not help this student, because, at the time, I was also a student who needed accommodations and could not provide adequate documentation due to mis- and under-diagnosis of my complicated and misunderstood chronic illnesses.

From the student perspective, the legal process for requesting accommodations can be intimidating, foreign, and inadequate. As a consequence of DS' strained relationships with faculty and students, accommodations for disability are often handled on an ad hoc, informal basis through requests for exceptions and extensions between individual faculty and students. At several points in my graduate training, I considered dropping out of my program for health reasons. I was also forced to take a medical leave of absence because, at the time, I did not know I had a legal right to request accessibility interventions. I completed my undergraduate and graduate education due to the generous flexibility and good faith of my mentors. I am now that faculty member.

Faculty often have polemical relationships with disability service providers. Required trainings and accommodations are additional stresses on our valuable and limited time. They can be perceived as encroachments on academic freedom. For these reasons, it can seem "easier" and less time consuming to circumvent DS officials and make decisions regarding individual student accommodations as they arise (or, even worse, to simply say "no" to access requests).

The common, well-meaning career advice that discouraged me and other early career scholars from working too closely with DS, included:

1 Focus on your research. Faculty collaborations with DS only count as service and no one has ever been denied tenure because they did too little service.
2 Minimize the time you spend on teaching. Stay out of the DS accommodation process, because no one student should take up much of your time.
3 Disability service providers only care about legal liability and are not committed to UD as a social justice framework. DS providers function as access gatekeepers and are cogs in the academic ableism machine.

Before beginning my position and in my early years at OSU, I was encouraged to carefully limit the amount of time spent on teaching tasks and individual students. I perceived DS units, as a result of this advice, to be in an adversarial relationship with academic units. In short, my main takeaway was the devaluation of social justice work in higher education and, in particular, the tenure and promotion process. In certain contexts, this is important advice, especially to a newly hired faculty member. At the same time, this advice makes UDI interventions seem optional, rather than essential to effective and socially just teaching. As a result, instructors, including myself, spend less time on tasks like creating accessible PDFs, syllabi, and lecture materials. Collaborating with DS providers like Martha, at best was deemed to be a waste of my time and, at worst, risked violations of academic freedom in the classroom.

Coming together to support students through UDI: Martha and Stephanie

Faculty collaborations with DS providers are rare, even–although perhaps surprisingly–among scholars in Disability Studies (Oslund, 2015). Despite the obstacles to our collaboration, we met through the OSU Disability Network. In 2012, a working group of OSU faculty, staff, and students was created to assess the viability of a Disability Studies undergraduate certificate. Since then, the group has evolved to organize and host a number of events and workshops to promote disability studies research, accessible curriculum development, and inclusive pedagogical practices. While the group has made significant advancements, its success has been limited by its small size and the lack of institutional enforcement to promote changes we recommend. In order for UDI to really take ahold across the university there needs to be training and policies at every level. In other words, instructors who do not specialize in Disability Studies need to be invested in resisting academic ableism and working to create accessible spaces and learning environments.

In our experience, convincing faculty who do not specialize in Disability Studies or experience their own disabilities in the value of UDI requires direct testimony from students who benefit from accessibility interventions. Additionally, accounts from faculty advocates who have experimented with UDI successfully and can report disciplinary-specific strategies and outcomes are an essential persuasive component. Such student and faculty perspectives can be communicated and amplified in faculty training sessions that afford instructors dedicated time and resources for acquiring UDI competency. These trainings must recognize and have direct input from students with a variety of experiences to "test out" how accessible pedagogies might work or impact particular groups such as student veterans, first-generation students, students with a variety of disabilities, socio-economic differences, single parents, LBGTQ students, students of color, etc.

It is often difficult to enact policies or training university wide. Universities are siloed. Faculty time, energy, and attention are limited. There are different departments to address the needs of different student groups and not often can one person represent all those perspectives effectively. Policies are written with the "average or traditional" student in mind. Policies become embedded and can be hard to change. However, small steps can be taken and their cumulative effects can snowball into substantial and long-lasting interventions.

For several years we were both invited independently to the OSU Difference, Power, and Discrimination Program Summer Academy to present information to faculty in the program. Martha presented an introduction to UDI that covered how to apply it to course development and teaching. Overall, she focused on the concept of what an accessible classroom might entail. Each time she presented, she would give ideas about how to apply UDI principles and would ask faculty for suggestions to add to her list. In these sessions, this dialogue would uncover examples of UDI practices faculty were already implementing, without realizing that they were doing so. Separately, Stephanie presented introductions to the field of Disability Studies during the DPD Academy. Faculty were interested in learning about the scholarship and teaching resources, but the material was not always relevant to the courses they were teaching. Additionally, merely adding Disability Studies concepts or readings to a class doesn't make it accessible; resisting academic ableism with UDI demands modifications to how instructors design, prepare, deliver, and assess courses.

After Stephanie and Martha connected, we were able to present to the Difference, Power, and Discrimination (DPD) cohort in 2018 together. What a fabulous and transformative experience! Martha was able to provide the background on UD and Stephanie was able to provide the faculty perspective. We provided case studies from Stephanie's implementation of UDI in her classroom and fielded questions together at the end of our session. According to Martha, Stephanie was able to give leverage to her faculty colleagues that she cannot do alone as a DS provider. According to Stephanie, Martha's input on pedagogical challenges she faced in the philosophy classroom have made her a better instructor and advocate for UDI. Together as a team, we were able to move beyond the introduction of keywords and concepts to demystifying UDI and providing clear starting points for other faculty to promote accessibility in their course designs and deliveries.

UDI is not an endpoint, checklist, or individual accommodation but rather a pedagogical praxis. The design in UD, as Dolmage (2005) notes, is intended as a verb, not a noun, because it is a dynamic process of "negotiation and collaboration" (Overview) and "mode of becoming" (p. 115). Additionally, as Aimi Hamraie (2013) argues UD is a "form of activism" (n. p.). In the following section, we offer five actions as case studies for implementing UDI that faculty at other postsecondary institutions can implement. The provided actions are not intended as one-size-fits-all solutions. We hope they offer instructors springboards for rethinking learning environments and catalysts for innovative and accessible pedagogy. Most importantly, we hope they demonstrate the inaccuracy of the widespread assumption that instructors should not make exceptions for individual students. Instead, access requests from students can be access opportunities for transforming classroom expectations and outcomes in ways that benefit all students and instructors.

Action #1: Demonstrating Active Commitment to UDI

Include a personal accessibility statement, in addition to the required DS language from your institution within your syllabi. For example, here is the brief statement Stephanie includes:

> I am committed to implementing the principles of Universal Design for Instruction in our classroom. If there is anything I can do to make our course materials, lectures, assignments, or environment more accessible to you, please let me know. I will try to incorporate these requests, if possible.

Explain what UDI is and why it is important to students when you go over syllabi at the beginning of the term. Solicit feedback from students about how to make your instruction more accessible and follow-through on requests when possible. Consider offering extra credit to students who make suggestions for improving accessibility that are more in-line with UDI principles than the original course design. These measures actively demonstrate that you consider disability to be part of human diversity that should be represented in the classroom; it combats academic ableism and disability stigma, while setting the tone for a respectful learning environment.

Action #2: Rethinking Assignments

One way to make undergraduate education more accessible is to critically assess and, when possible, revise course assignments and assessments. The following example assignment revision demonstrates one concrete outcome of our partnership in Stephanie's PHL 360 classroom. The course is a special online section on the philosophy of art and music. The course enrolls approximately fifteen students each summer term. The original course assignments were writing-heavy, as is typical for an upper-level Philosophy course.

The original assignment required students to write weekly argumentative essays responding to the reading assignments. Students without previous experience in Philosophy and especially students taking the class for whom English was not their first language routinely struggled with these weekly papers. Because Stephanie initially viewed more frequent, short papers as an "easier" alternative to one long final term paper, she faulted students' inability to meet course requirements for their poor grades. When a student requested an informal accessibility accommodation related to the assignment, Stephanie approached Martha for feedback. Martha pushed Stephanie to clarify the purpose of the assignment and to think about ways students could demonstrate their engagement with the reading through other means. Why, she asked, is an argumentative paper using academic language necessary to achieve course objectives? Could they be met another way? This dialogue challenged Stephanie to create more specific expectations and instructions for the assignment. Here is the final revised assignment:

PHL 360: Conceptual Tool assignment
  Instructions
  Over the course of the term, through this assignment, you will create your own conceptual tool kit from your assigned readings. Each week, you will identify one "tool" – or idea – from the assigned reading that you think is interesting, important, and/or relevant. Each week, your entry must identify and describe the following components of your chosen conceptual tool:

1 **What**: Identify the conceptual tool that you've chosen.
2 **Define**: What is it? Summarize the most important details of this idea, in your own words. (Approximately one paragraph)
3 **Where**: Where did you find it? Provide a brief quotation from the assigned reading that explains the conceptual tool, as evidence supporting your definition in #2. Provide an in-text citation.
4 **Why**: Why is this idea significant? Explain in your own words. (Approximately one paragraph)
5 **Respond**: Briefly respond to your idea. (Approximately one paragraph) Some suggested starting points:
   a Why do you find it helpful?
   b Can you think of an example?
   c Do you have a question or concern about it?

  Points Possible 50
  Rubric
  0–10: Conceptual tool is clearly identified
  0–10: Definition is provided and clearly paraphrased
  0–10: Quotation, with in-text citation, from assigned reading is provided to support definition
  0–10: Explanation of conceptual tool's significance is clear
  0–10: Student response extends conceptual tool beyond summary of material

From a UDI perspective, this revised assignment demonstrates flexibility in use, because it accommodates a relatively wide range of student abilities. It is also an example of simple and intuitive efforts, because the directions more clearly explain what is expected. Finally, there is also tolerance for error, because at the end of the term, students' lowest grades will be dropped.

Action #3: Rethinking Academic Requirements

Stephanie regularly teaches an introductory existential philosophy course, "The Meaning of Existence," as one of her large lecture courses (50–75 students). It is one of her most popular offerings, drawing students excited to discuss topics central to being human such as time, freedom, and authenticity. Because death and suicide are necessary and unavoidable topics in any adequate survey of existentialism, Stephanie begins the term with a content warning. However, she was finding a disproportionate number of students approaching her at the end of the term to notify her of mental health obstacles to attending class. Attendance and in-class assignments are a significant portion of course requirements; infrequent class attendance, if severe enough, could result in failure of the class.

Stephanie consulted with Martha, because she was dissatisfied with the options available from academic units. Would it be fair to waive the attendance requirement for a student who did not have a formal disability accommodation for flexible attendance? Martha challenged Stephanie to understand the purpose of requiring attendance. Through their dialogue, Stephanie realized that she was requiring attendance, in part, because she thought she *had* to do so. Attendance was required in all of her courses at the undergraduate and graduate level, so she received this pedagogical habit through disciplinary norms. Attendance is one of the ways students demonstrate serious engagement with course content. Why, Martha asked, does a student have to attend class to meet the course objectives listed in the syllabus? For Stephanie, the answer was that the material covered in class is essential. Additionally, she worried that not requiring attendance sets students up to fail; introductory philosophy can seem deceptively easy and she wanted to set students up to be successful on the midterm and final exams. But, yes, she conceded, it is possible for a student to miss classes or even, perhaps, to never attend class and still meet the course objectives.

Stephanie's discussions with Martha led her to build aspects of what DS providers term "flexible attendance" into her courses. Instead of including "in-class participation" as a percentage of students' final grades, Stephanie has revised all of her courses to include a "course engagement" requirement. Moving beyond the model of a student attentively raising their hand to ask a well-phrased question as evidence of the model for valuable interaction with course material, this UDI-informed alternative rewards and recognizes diverse modes of representing, expressing, and engaging in the classroom. Some examples include: attending office hours or outside class events, submitting questions or examples via email or the online class discussion board, offering feedback via notecards distributed in class, participating via in-class responseware (e.g., Top Hat or TurningPoint) and sharing art works, songs, news articles, or other case studies that relate to course material. Course engagement, rather than or as participation, implements flexibility in use because it offers students choices regarding how they will interact with their instructor and peers. It also reflects tolerance for error, as it permits variation in individual learning pace, communication, and attendance.

Action #4: Promote Community Building and Institutional Change

The siloing of academic institutions preserves academic ableism; community building is a vital antidote to academic ableism, as cross-unit collaborations are essential to developing campus-wide support for UDI and curriculum transformation (Finn et al., 2015). The fight for accessibility will not be won by a lone instructor and no single DS provider will institute a flawless UDI curriculum. Rather, institutional change requires building creative coalitions between faculty, staff, and students who share the common goal of creating accessible learning environments. At Oregon State University, our story for planting the seeds of UDI began with the OSU Disability Network, but its success – or failure – hinges on recruiting widespread campus support, as well as institutional resources, for accessibility initiatives. As other units join our cause, including Disability Access Services, Equal Opportunity and Access, and Ecampus, the impact and reach of our efforts expand.

Revamping curriculum and course materials, especially in early phases, is a time and energy consuming process. While DS staff can assist instructors by providing UDI resources and consultation about problems and solutions, faculty ultimately have to make decisions about how to modify course design and invest the hours in implementing those changes. Workshops like OSU's DPD program provide faculty with the necessary time, support, and resources to put their UDI ideas into action, as well as essential peer support, expert guidance, and community of action. The partnerships that form within faculty learning communities like the DPD Academy can become powerful advocates for institutional changes necessary for combatting academic ableism by implementing accessibility measures and reforming instructional policies across campus.

University-wide polices that address how materials are purchased or ordered are needed. Books – including any supplemental materials such as publisher websites – should not be assigned or ordered if they are not accessible. Additionally, it is important to make UDI resources available to all instructors. Individual departments can create internal guidance for faculty to use around UDI. Faculty will need to use and follow guidelines when creating new courses, while expectations should be created for revising established courses to include UDI over a period of time. Additionally, departments can create internal UDI teams. Designated leaders would become the teachers for their colleagues around UDI application in department courses. Regular meetings of these faculty learning communities would serve as further opportunities to develop, share, and teach in accordance with UDI principles. (In their 2018 book, *Reach Everyone, Teach Everyone Universal Design for Learning in Higher Education,* Tobin and Behling provide multiple examples of ways to bring UDI to teaching faculty.)

Action #5: Take One Step

The greatest impact for all students, and especially students with disabilities, around improving course access comes from putting UDI principles into action in the classroom. UDI interventions can range from small tweaks to existing course materials to major revisions of a curriculum. If you are an instructor, commit to one to three UDI revisions a term. Ensure that all aspects of a new curriculum are accessible. Ask yourself: "Have I made my class, my course, my activities, my curriculum accessible to as many of my students as possible no matter why, no matter where, no matter what?" DS professionals should engage in one-on-one conversations with faculty that helps them spark UDI ideas. Instead of asking "Is this assignment really needed?" or "What accommodation can Disability Services provide?", ask: "What it is you want your students to show competency in in your course? How does the assignment accomplish that? Are there other ways a student could show you that they are competent in the material?"

As we have emphasized, UDI is a pedagogical practice that requires on-going commitment and negotiation; it cannot be reduced to a clear-cut "to do" list. Using the nine principles of UDI, we offer some ideas to get you started:

Some Ideas to Get you Started

Equitable Use

- Use only captioned videos. Use only appropriately captioned content from the internet (Note: Not all captions are created equal. Turn off the volume and watch/read the captions. If it doesn't make sense the captions are not good).
- Provide an open-house for all students to visit a lab prior to the first meeting (this enables all students to get a better understanding of the lab environment. For those needing accommodations this may help the student to determine what or if any accommodations are needed in that particular lab environment).
- Open all Learning Management System (LMS) such as Canvas or Blackboard modules at the beginning of the term. This allows all learners access to information to better prepare and to manage their time more efficiently. For those that need more time as an accommodation or who may need to manage a chronic health conditions this gives more control in their ability to do just that.
- Require all students stay for the entire exam regardless of when they finish. The student has already set aside the whole exam time; this limits the amount of disruption of students coming and going.

Flexibility in Use

- Allow students to show competency in a variety of ways: tests, speech, create a game, project, song, etc. This allows students the ability to use their strengths to really demonstrate their knowledge of the material instead of relying on standard measures that don't always accurately capture learners' competency.
- Allow students to choose between working in groups or alone. This autonomy allows students to choose the social environment in which they work the best.
- Use the accessibility tools within your LMS.

Simple and Intuitive

- Be attentive to how you create your syllabus:
  - Is it organized intuitively?
  - Is it easy to find due dates for assignments and big-ticket items (tests, papers, projects)?
  - Is it easy to find what are the expectations for each assignment, project, test, etc.?
  - Is it easy to find out what each component of the class is worth?
  - Is there contact information?
  - Do you use multiple ways to identify information (Words, bolding, underline, symbols, etc.)?
  - Do you use color to communicate content? If using different colors as a way to identify information, always use a second method as well (i.e. bold, underline, etc.). For those who are blind or colorblind, differentiating through color is not accessible.
- Make sure instructions for papers, projects and assignments are easy and simple to follow.
- Make sure your LMS course set up is easy to navigate:
  - What about students who have never used this system before?
  - What about students who need to follow information in a linear way?
  - What about students who jump around to find information?
  - Is the same information found in multiple places within the Canvas site?

Perceptible Information

- Create information in accessible PDF formats.
- Assign curriculum products that are accessible (including supplemental study materials and websites for students).
- Make sure there are multiple ways to access the information you are presenting either through an online class or an in-person class. Are you presenting the information in multiple ways, including visual, auditory, and hands-on formats?
- Do you use references that are only pertinent to certain parts of the country or only to U.S. students (Talking about Monopoly, The Game of Life, "Friends", and "Game of Thrones")? If you use cultural references, humor, and/or cartoons, make that information accessible to all learners of diverse abilities and cultural backgrounds (e.g., international students, students with learning disabilities, etc.).

Tolerance for error

- Throw out the lowest test or assignment score.
- Provide opportunities for extra credit points.

- Give credit for multiple drafts of a paper, allowing students to earn incremental points.
- Allow flexibility in your attendance requirements. All students receive a "free" day of their choosing to not be present.

Low Physical Effort

- Pay attention to the layout of the room.
    - Will there be movement required around the room?
    - Can everyone equally access tables, whiteboards, outlets, etc.?
- If physical activities are required in the course are there alternatives?
    - Could a field trip be made more accessible using a Go-Pro camera for the parts not physically accessible?
    - Could a student do activities online if not in the field?
- Make sure your LMS course page set up is easy to navigate
    - What about students who have never used this system before?
    - What about students who need to follow information in a linear way?
    - What about students who jump around to find information?
    - Is the same information found in multiple places within the Canvas site?

Size and Space for Approach and Use

- In lab settings, are there options for both high tables and low tables.
- Is the equipment available at different levels?
- Is safety equipment available at different levels (eye wash, shower pull, etc.).
- How will a service dog be accommodated in the lab?

A Community of Learners

- Provide examples of previous good work by other students.
- Teach students how to work in a team
    - Explain (verbally and in writing) the different roles and expectations of group members. Most students don't know how to make an effective group work for group projects.

Instructional Climate

- Think about the environment you are creating for all students.
- Are there multiple means of engagement?
- Is information clearly explained in the syllabus?

- Do you offer multiple ways for students to engage with you outside of class time?
- Offer an open house to your lab. In this way, all students have an opportunity to see how the lab is set up (lighting, tables, equipment, etc.) before the first meeting.

Conclusion

The story of our unlikely collaboration is far from over; we intend to continue fighting academic ableism and promoting UDI at OSU. In the years that we have collaborated, we have both learned the importance of flexibility and keeping an open mind when implementing UDI in the classroom. Rather that treating UDI as an obstacle to effective teaching or problematic exceptions for individual students, we challenge instructors to implement innovative and accessible course design, delivery, and assessment. At the same time, we call for university administrators to nurture faculty learning communities and UDI trainings necessary to support and encourage this vital yet time-intensive work. Specifically, we have argued the importance of demonstrating commitment to UDI, rethinking assignments, rethinking requirements, promoting community building and institutional change, and taking one step. Perhaps most importantly, we hope the narrative of our partnership inspires faculty and DS providers to work outside the narrow confines of their units and job descriptions and come together to transform higher education for the benefit of all students.

Building partnerships across institutional silos is something with which every university struggles. Additionally, all universities in the United States employ DS providers, instructors with disabilities, and faculty with interests in Disability Studies. While this chapter has focused on our unique partnership, transformative alliances are possible; there are Stephanies and Marthas at your university. This chapter shows how colleagues and professionals from different areas within postsecondary education can collaborate towards better access and engagement for all students. These partnerships can occur across any institutional areas/boundaries. It just takes two people willing to take the risk and trust to work together on improving outcomes for students (see also Pitcher and Martinez, this volume). Yet, as we have argued, such transformative cross-unit collaborations are more likely to form and persist when this work is recognized, sustained, and valued beyond faculty's regular service requirements. We have offered the narrative and outcomes of our partnership as a roadmap for incorporating UDI, combatting academic ableism, and advocating for institutional change at OSU and beyond.

Additional Resources

Accessible Syllabus (2015). *Accessible syllabus.* www.accessiblesyllabus.com
Boston College Center for Teaching Excellence (2015). *UDL explainer* [Video]. YouTube. www.youtube.com/watch?t=5&v=W_fUmt_D2pY

CAST, Inc. (2020). *UDL on campus.* http://udloncampus.cast.org/home

The Center for Universal Design in Education (2020). *Overview.* www.washington.edu/doit/programs/center-universal-design-education/overview

Council of Ontario Universities (2017). *Accessible campus teaching tips.* www.accessiblecampus.ca/tools-resources/educators-tool-kit/teaching-tips/

DO-IT University of Washington (2020). *DO-IT videos.* www.washington.edu/doit/programs/accesscollege/faculty-room/resources-faculty/do-it-videos

Dolmage, J. (2015). *Welcome to Universal Design: Places to start.* http://universaldesignideas.pbworks.com/w/page/97590854/FrontPage

Hamraie, A. (2020). *Accessible teaching in the time of COVID-19.* www.mapping-access.com/blog-1/2020/3/10/accessible-teaching-in-the-time-of-covid-19

Harvard Graduate School of Education (2020). *Universal Design for Learning stories.* https://www.gse.harvard.edu/news-tags/universal-design-learning

Humber Center for Teaching and Learning (2019). *Universal Design of Learning in higher education* [Video]. YouTube. www.youtube.com/watch?v=VwA8cQ2xA9o

National Center on Universal Design for Learning (2020). *About Universal Design for Learning.* www.udlcenter.org/aboutudl

Ohio State University Office of Distance Education and eLearning *UDL and accessibility perspectives.* https://u.osu.edu/personas/

Seattle Central College (2011). *Universal Design* [Video]. YouTube. www.youtube.com/watch?v=4FE1CLS7i3k

References

Asch, A., & Fine, M. (1988). Introduction: beyond pedestals. In M. Fine, & A. Asch (Eds.), *Women with disabilities: Essays in psychology, culture, and politics* (pp. 1–37). Temple University Press.

Berger, J. (2015). Uncommon schools: Institutionalizing deafness in early-nineteenth-century America. In S. Tremain (Ed.), *Foucault and the government of disability* (Enlarged and revised edition) (pp. 153–171). University of Michigan Press.

Campbell, F. K. (2015). Legislating disability: Negative ontologies and the government of legal identities. In S. Tremain (Ed.), *Foucault and the government of disability* (Enlarged and revised edition) (pp. 108–130). University of Michigan Press.

Carlson, L. (2010). *The faces of intellectual disability: Philosophical reflections.* Indiana University Press.

Carlson, L. (2015). Docile bodies, docile Minds: Foucauldian reflections on mental retardation. In S. Tremain (Ed.), *Foucault and the government of disability* (Enlarged and revised edition) (pp. 133–152). University of Michigan Press.

Dolmage, J. (2005). Disability studies pedagogy, usability and universal design. *Disability Studies Quarterly, 25*(4). https://dsq-sds.org/article/view/627/804

Dolmage, J. (2017). *Academic ableism: Disability and higher education.* University of Michigan Press.

Fine, M., & Asch, A. (2000). Disability beyond stigma: Social interaction, discrimination, and activism. In M. Adams, W. J. Blumenfeld, R. Castaneda, H. W. Hackman, M. L. Peters, & X. Zuniga (Eds.), *Readings for diversity and social justice* (pp. 330–339). Routledge.

Finn, D., Getzel, E., Asselin, S., & Reilly, V. (2015). Implementing universal design: Collaborations across campus. In S. Burgstahler, & M. Young (Eds.), *Universal Design in higher education: From principles to practice* (pp. 267–268). Harvard Education Press.

Fox, J., Hatfield, J., & Collins, T. (2003). Developing the Curriculum Transformation and Disability (CTAD) workshop model. In J. Higbee (Ed.), *Curriculum transformation and disability: Implementing Universal Design in higher education* (pp. 23–39). Center for Research on Developmental Education and Urban Literacy.

Hamraie, A. (2013). Designing collective access: A feminist disability theory of Universal Design. *Disability Studies Quarterly, 33*(4). https://dsq-sds.org/article/view/3871/3411

Hutcheon, E. & Wolbring, G. (2012). Voices of "disabled" post-secondary students: Examining higher education "disability" policy using an ableism Lens. *Journal of Diversity in Higher Education, 5*(1), 39–49.

Johnson, D., & Fox, J. (2003). Creating curb cuts in the classroom: Adapting universal design principles to education. In J. Higbee (Ed.), *Curriculum transformation and disability: Implementing Universal Design in higher education* (pp. 7–21). Center for Research on Developmental Education and Urban Literacy.

Kalivoda, K., & Totty, M. (2003). Disability services as a resource: Advancing Universal Design. In J. Higbee (Ed.), *Curriculum transformation and disability: Implementing Universal Design in higher education* (pp. 187–201). Center for Research on Developmental Education and Urban Literacy.

Krebs, E. (2019). Baccalaureates or burdens? Complicating "reasonable accommodations" for American college students with disabilities. *Disability Studies Quarterly, 39*(3). https://dsq-sds.org/article/view/6557/5413

Lombardi, A. R., & Lalor, A. R. (2017). Faculty and administrator knowledge and attitudes regarding disability. In E. Kim, & K. C. Aquino (Eds.), *Disability as diversity in higher education: Policies and practices to enhance student success* (pp. 107–121). Routledge, Taylor & Francis Group.

Madaus, J. W. (2011). The history of disability services in higher education. *New Directions for Higher Education, 2011*(154), 5–15.

Oregon Office on Disability and Health (2013). *Disability in Oregon: 2013 annual report on the health of Oregonians with disabilities.* Institute on Development & Disability, Oregon Health & Science University.

Oslund, C. (2015). Disability studies, sisability services: Would addressing the gap in professional communication impact implementation of the ADA? *Disability Studies Quarterly, 35*(3). https://dsq-sds.org/article/view/4946

OSU Disability Access Services (2019). *Raw data review from internal database.*

Pearson, H., & Boskovich, L. (2019). Problematizing disability disclosure in higher education: Shifting towards a liberating humanizing intersectional framework. *Disability Studies Quarterly, 39*(1). https://dsq-sds.org/article/view/6001

Price, M. (2011). *Mad at school: Rhetorics of mental disability and academic life.* University of Michigan Press.

Scott, S., McGuire, J., & Foley, T. (2003). Universal Design for Instruction: A framework for anticipating and responding to disability and other diverse learning needs in the college classroom. *Equity & Excellence in Education, 36*(1), 40–49.

Scott, S., Loewen, G., & Funckes, C. (2003). Implementing Universal Design in higher education: Moving beyond the built environment. *Journal on Postsecondary Education and Disability, 16*(2), 78–89.

Scully, J. L. (2008). *Disability bioethics: Moral bodies, moral difference.* Rowman & Littlefield.

The Center for Universal Design (1997). *The Principles of Universal Design, Version 2.0*. Raleigh: North Carolina State University.

Tobin, T. (2019, January 31). *Universal Design for Learning: The hidden chapters* [Webinar]. https://www.3playmedia.com/resources/recorded-webinars/wbn-01-31-2019-udl/.

Tobin, T., Behling, K. (2018). *Reach everyone, teach everyone: Universal Design for Learning in higher education*. West Virginia University Press.

Wendell, S. (1996). *The rejected body*. Routledge.

Wilson, J. D. (2017). Reimagining disability and inclusive education through Universal Design for Learning. *Disability Studies Quarterly*, *37*(2). https://dsq-sds.org/article/view/5417/4650

World Health Organization & World Bank (Eds.). (2011). *World report on disability*. World Health Organization.

5 Critical Pedagogy Online
Opportunities and Challenges in Social Justice Education

Jenny N. Myers

Technology is not neutral, nor is the Western educational model it is used to export. Both are products of historical and political contexts reflecting dominant culture values. Western notions of progress underpin the assumption that online courses open doors for more learners. English is the predominant language of the Internet, and the majority of online content originates in industrialized nations, further compelling "people of marginalized cultures to assimilate Western epistemologies and ideological discourses" (Smith & Ayers, 2006, pp. 406–407). Research also suggests that the digital divide continues to gatekeep information access, disproportionately impacting communities that are minoritized based on race, language, disability status, and socio-economic status (Domingue, 2016).

When I was asked to design an online course for the Difference, Power, and Discrimination program, I was humbled by the complexity of this terrain and the incongruences I perceived between online education and my pedagogical commitments. "Educational technologies," Audrey Watters (2018) observes, are "embedded in educational institutions; they're entwined with the histories and the practices of schooling. Even the technologies that are imagined to 'disrupt' institutions and revolutionize teaching and learning are inescapably bound to cultural expectations" (p. xii). The transition from campus to online classroom requires that faculty working to decolonize the academy confront these tensions and grapple with our role in systems that can replicate homogenizing and oppressive practices. This chapter provides an overview of my effort to address these challenges, designing and facilitating a social sustainability course through the Oregon State University (OSU) Ecampus program.

My approach to this work is shaped by my positionality as a white, cis-gender, middle class, temporarily able-bodied, heterosexual woman. My perspective is further influenced by my disciplinary commitments in sustainability education, which center experiential learning and interdisciplinary, collaborative approaches to knowledge production. I am also influenced by my role as an instructor in an academic program without tenure lines at a large, predominately white research institution with a nationally-ranked online education program.

DOI: 10.4324/9781003091998-7

After participating in OSU's Difference, Power, and Discrimination (DPD) Academy, I redeveloped a 400-level Ecampus course called Social Dimensions of Sustainability. The course spotlights U.S. case studies to illuminate the synergies between environmental and social justice movements and illustrate the root causes of environmental racism; varied responses to community activism; and the disparate public health and economic impacts of issues including toxics exposure, food and farming practices, and climate change. Students interpret and apply their learning about systems of oppression, institutional power, and intersectionality through asynchronous discussions with peers and reflective writing assignments. In addition to the DPD course learning outcomes, students learn to:

- problematize the Euro-centric cultural narratives that shaped U.S. environmentalism, compare them to minoritized environmental histories, and critique the mainstream environmental movement;
- describe how political and cultural marginalization produce disproportionate environmental risks for minoritized populations in the U.S.; and
- critique efforts within the sustainability movement to model social dimensions of sustainability.

As this volume illustrates, in designing this course I joined a community of faculty from across the disciplinary spectrum who are implementing strategies to address the needs of all learners we meet in our classrooms. The process enabled me to confront my assumptions about online education, and I discovered strategies in this rapidly-evolving field to facilitate student learning in creative, engaging, and culturally-sensitive ways. I worked with OSU Ecampus instructional designers to experiment with course design strategies and found that many of the techniques shared in this volume can readily be adapted for online courses (see for example, Clough's and Maldonado's chapters in this volume). I've learned that while faculty shouldn't rely on a static suite of best practices, there are a variety of ways to deliver effective social justice education online through intentional course design, content selection, and facilitation techniques that decenter the instructor and enable power sharing in the online classroom (Morris & Stommel, 2018). Below I present a brief overview of the demographic landscape of online learning, followed by an overview of the pedagogical strategies I experiment with in the Social Dimensions of Sustainability course.

Demographic Landscape

As of 2015, 95% of public degree-granting institutions in the U.S. with over 5,000 students were offering online courses (Allen & Seaman, 2015). While significant numbers of campus-based students take online courses, online programs also serve different learners than campus-based programs. Distance students are often working professionals, active members of the military, and parents

(Radford, 2011). The asynchronous, self-paced nature of online learning eases pressures for adult learners who are juggling multiple responsibilities. It also allows greater flexibility for students with disabilities who may have physical or mental health considerations that impact their participation in face-to-face classrooms (Accessible Campus Action Alliance, 2020; Kirby, 2020; Kotera et al., 2019).

Online enrollment at Oregon State University during the 2018–2019 academic year included 24,959 students, 39% (9,752) of whom were exclusively distance students. Oregon residents account for 24% of Ecampus' distance students, with students enrolled in all 50 states and 50 countries throughout the world. OSU is a predominantly white institution, and the reported racial breakdown of our online learners reflects the ongoing legacies of Oregon's problematic racial history: 8.5% are Hispanic-identified students, 6.5% identify as African American, 6.5% identify as Asian American, and 67% identify as White. International student enrollment accounts for less than 3% of Ecampus students. Gender data indicate that the Ecampus population is made up of 55% female-identifying students and 45% male-identifying, an exact reverse of our campus binary ratios. Enrollment data for non-binary-identifying students is not yet available. Approximately 17% of distance students are first-generation students, and 9% are in the military or are military spouses or dependents. Of the 945 distance students who responded to a survey conducted in 2018, 68% work full-time and an additional 18% work part-time while attending OSU. Of the respondents, 6% are single parents and 27% reported that they are raising children with a partner. The average age of distance students enrolled in OSU's Ecampus program is 31 (Oregon State University Ecampus, n.d., para. 1).

Humanizing the Online Classroom

As these demographic trends indicate, faculty have a responsibility to design courses that address diverse learners whose needs may be very different from the needs of students we teach face-to-face. Effective online courses begin with a design to foster a welcoming classroom environment that allows all community members to engage as real people, countering the perceived anonymity of the computer screen. Having an authentic online presence, and interacting with other real people, is a key factor in student success in any online course and essential for social justice pedagogy. As bell hooks (1994) observes, "As a classroom community, our capacity to generate excitement is deeply affected by our interest in one another, in hearing one another's voices, in recognizing one another's presence" (p. 8). Establishing learning communities in online classrooms directly supports students who learn best through relationships and students with integrated learning styles who understand education as a collective endeavor (Ke & Chávez, 2013). What's more, carefully designed spaces allow students to take risks and venture outside of their comfort zones, laying the groundwork for transformative learning.

There are a variety of tools to facilitate authentic relationship building online. In the Social Dimensions of Sustainability course, I set the tone by establishing my own presence, introducing myself with an autobiographical video on the classroom homepage. I make my commitment to decolonizing pedagogy clear from the start, sharing my pronouns and beginning the video with a land acknowledgement to recognize that despite our disparate locations, our class is facilitated by Oregon State University's physical presence on colonized land. I then describe the personal and professional journey that brought me to the course, accented by photographs, so students can develop a sense of who I am before opening course content. From there, I maintain a presence in the course by engaging regularly in discussion forums, posting video announcements, narrating PowerPoints and video lectures, and providing consistent, personal feedback on student work. Instructor presence is particularly critical in online discussion forums to monitor for and address problematic content and offer course corrections when discussions go awry.

Designing spaces for students to interact with each other is just as important as instructor presence and can be facilitated using a variety of strategies and technological tools. The Social Dimensions of Sustainability course begins with a low-risk video introduction to start the community building process. In large enrollment courses, I assign students to discussion groups of five to ten students so they can interact with a manageable-sized cohort, switching groups half-way through the term so they can share ideas with different peers. After introducing themselves, students watch Jay Smooth's *How I Learned to Stop Worrying and Love Discussing Race* (TEDx Talks, 2011) and read the Interaction Institute for Social Change's (2014) "Heartset and Mindset for Adversarial Versus Deep Listening and Norms for Listening as an Ally." As a whole group, we then establish group norms through a facilitated discussion.

To maximize flexibility and student choice, I offer students the option to respond to most discussion prompts via video, audio recordings, or written posts. Adding video assignments to my courses has truly transformed my experience as an online instructor; while research suggests that online presence is key to student satisfaction and success (Hunt, 2018), I would argue that faculty reap comparable rewards. I now get to know students in their homes, their offices, and in their cars. I meet students' children and pets when they bound unexpectedly into video frames. This minor shift in my course design has provided an avenue to develop the kinds of relationships with students I feared would be lost in the online arena – relationships that shape and motivate my teaching – and I respond to them with more care and authenticity than I did when our connections were formed solely through written interactions.

I recommend prompting students to consider their responsibilities in co-creating classroom spaces from home. I include a statement in my syllabus and discussion boards requesting that students check their physical surroundings before they hit record:

> In this course, our classroom discussions take place in videos filmed in our private spaces. It is important that we are all aware of the messages we are sending, and the impacts they may have on others, when positioning ourselves in front of a camera for a video that will be part of our classroom learning environment. Please think about what is in the frame (on your walls, etc.) when recording videos to ensure that we are maintaining a safe and positive environment for everyone to learn.
>
> (Myers, 2020, pp. 4–5)

It is important not to make assumptions about students' prior knowledge and skills with technology and to provide clear instructions for any assignment that requires technical skill (Peralta Community College District, 2019). This is particularly important in courses for first-year students or students new to online learning. Invite students to privately self-disclose if they are new to online learning or unfamiliar with the tools used in the course so you can provide additional guidance and encouragement to support their success (Dolan et al., 2017). Learning to use the technologies I require students to use has strengthened my ability to provide this type of personal support.

It is also crucial to recognize that some students prefer the privacy afforded by impersonal online interactions. For some, it is the driver behind their decision to enroll in distance programs. Students may have important (sometimes legally-protected) reasons to maintain a degree of anonymity. It is critical to consider the needs of all learners when designing courses and allow for ample choice in assignments so students control how much personal information they disclose. Some students decide to post audio-only recordings so we still have a chance to interact personally while maintaining their needs for privacy.

Decentering the Instructor-as-Expert

As discussed by Bradley Boovy and Nana Osei-Kofi (this volume), faculty have a responsibility to reflect on our positionality in the classroom and how we are perceived and interpreted by our students. Decentering ourselves and creating conditions for co-learning are fundamental strategies in social justice education. As Sean Michael Morris and Jesse Stommel (2018) write:

> The instructor's own social location must be included in the narrative of the classroom so that there is a chance to decenter it. If we do not speak up about our own power—if we don't do more than simply concede the podium or the center of the room—we have done too little to undo that power. Then, our presence is an elephant in the room; our social location the litmus for all social locations. A silent authority silences without ever saying a word.
>
> (pp. 118–119)

With intention, this narrative can be challenged in online spaces more readily than traditional classrooms where faculty are often positioned at the front of the room, on a stage, or behind a podium. I often draw attention to the power dynamics built into the design of campus classrooms but rarely find opportunities in large-enrollment courses to decenter myself physically. In online classrooms, the physical cues that shape our perceptions of power and authority are largely absent. The online environment allows us to center student knowledge, as well as expertise from members of minoritized communities, intentionally positioning ourselves as guides and facilitators of learning instead of experts conferring knowledge to a passively receptive audience.

In the Social Dimensions of Sustainability course, students conduct independent research and introduce new material in weekly discussions. Peer-to-peer learning is facilitated through discussion assignments where students present narrated PowerPoint presentations on case studies to illustrate weekly course themes. Midway through the course, students collaborate with their discussion group members to create a multimedia timeline (discussed in detail below) showcasing perspectives that have been neglected or silenced in the Euro-centric histories of the U.S. environmental movement. As my teaching evolves, I see further opportunities to decenter myself and design spaces that foster collaborative learning with more student-generated content, dialogical engagement through video peer reviews, and extended discussion threads to enable on-going conversations over the course of the term. Allowing for flexibility in assignment formatting also provides students the autonomy to shape the course to best suit their learning styles. Some faculty even co-construct their course syllabus with students as the term progresses (Morris & Stommel, 2018).

The work of disrupting power dynamics in any classroom is an on-going practice. It requires a critical examination of the ways instructor identities influence teaching and the ways pedagogical choices serve to reinforce or dismantle power structures. This work requires investments of time and care during all stages of course design and facilitation. Creating more equitable power dynamics remains a significant challenge in an institutional climate where many online instructors do not have the freedom to change their course content or lack institutional support for course redevelopment (Allen & Seaman, 2015; Straumsheim, 2015).

Content Integration: Centering Knowledge from Frontline Communities

As I work to decenter myself in online classrooms, I can also design curricula that center voices from communities that have long been excluded from formal academic knowledge production systems. With the important caveat noted above that the English language dominates the Internet and most online content is produced in industrialized nations, to a degree, virtual classrooms have the potential to make access to diverse content and sources of knowledge the norm. Online blogs, films, YouTube videos, TEDx Talks, and music can easily be embedded or linked on course content pages. Open Educational Resources play a role in easing textbook costs for students, and having access to learning materials from day 1 of the course removes barriers for students who rely on financial aid disbursements that come after the term begins. What's more, utilizing a variety of online content like blogs, videos, and music provides an opportunity for students to engage with different content formats, providing the flexibility to meet individualized learning needs (Center for Applied Special Technology [CAST], 2019).

In the Social Dimensions of Sustainability course, students learn from people on the frontlines of social sustainability movements, the communities most impacted by inequities and leading the work for change. We read hooks' (2011) reflections on African Americans' complex relationships with nature. We watch a talk by Shelton Johnson, a ranger in Yosemite National Park who inspires connections between African American communities and the park, retelling stories of the Buffalo Soldiers who served there at the turn of the 20th century (Chicago Humanities Festival, 2013). We listen to a conversation between National Park Ranger Alex Carr Johnson and Loren Othon of the Seattle Office for Civil Rights at OUT for Sustainability's Fab Planet Summit discussing efforts to queer the environmental movement (Out4S, 2016). We learn about the role of allies in climate justice work from Women of Color Speak Out (2016) and from Dolores Huerta in solidarity with Sioux protestors at Standing Rock (Teton Productions, 2016).

First-person accounts and case studies help make the theory about social constructs, institutional bias, and systems of oppression more tangible. The conversation in the course about institutional bias starts with an example close to home: we read a letter from the Oregon State University (formerly Oregon State College) School of Forestry rejecting a female applicant in 1957. The letter outlines the reasons the program has never admitted "girls," including the fact that "the number of jobs that are available for a woman in forestry are limited entirely to clerical type of jobs" (Oregon State University, 2018a, p. 1). Students compose a response, identifying explicit examples of institutional bias in the letter and suggesting reforms the school could implement to remove barriers for women.

In another assignment, we read a post by blogger CrippledScholar. Kim Sauder (2016) writes about a viral Twitter discussion calling out Whole Foods for selling peeled oranges in plastic containers, exposing the invisibility of disability in the debate. This assignment brings attention to the ways sustainability efforts often reproduce dominant assumptions and underscores the importance of recognizing privilege and positionality in efforts to address environmental problems. Students with backgrounds in environmental fields often report that Sauder's (2016) piece is one of the most eye-opening in the course. One student reflected:

> When I first saw the tweet about peeled oranges being sold in plastic packaging at Whole Foods, I reacted like many people, labeling the

practice as wasteful and unfriendly to the environment. My background of working for a waste management service formed my reaction to this. Kim Sauder (2016), on the other hand, saw that tweet and began to think about how helpful a product like that is for people with disabilities. Living with limited hand dexterity formed her reaction to this issue. Whole Foods ended up pulling the product from shelves and, if I were the employee at Whole Foods who had to make that decision, I would have done the same thing. Because of my background, I probably wouldn't have thought about this product's usefulness among those with disabilities, who make up about 15% of the world's population and who "often encounter discrimination and exclusion on a daily basis" (United Nations, n.d.). While my decision would have beneficially impacted the environmental dimension of sustainability, I would have inadvertently ignored the social dimension of sustainability that Sauder would have argued to prioritize over the environmental dimension. Sauder, through her article and through her interaction with the tweet was able to help others understand the importance of considering the needs of a non-dominant group and was able to advance social sustainability in the process. Although our different backgrounds caused us to react differently to this product, if Sauder and I were able to come together to solve this issue, we might have been able to create a solution that benefited both the environmental and social dimensions of sustainability.

Another student responded:

I found the article When Accessibility Gets Labeled Wasteful by Kim Sauder especially interesting and informative in this week's content. When I first saw the tweet that she talks about in her article, I was shocked and disappointed in the wasteful packaging that was being used by Whole Foods. Kim completely changed my perspective on the issue, she saw the packaging as an advantage for her since she has limited hand dexterity. It really made me realize the privilege I have when I labeled the packaging "wasteful." Since I do not have a disability, I didn't recognize the benefits someone like Kim saw in the "wasteful" packaging. This article really helped me put perspective into perspective, and I think it can be related to a lot of other issues regarding diversity.... A more inclusive community that takes diverse needs into consideration creates more resilience in regards to social sustainability.

Near the end of the course, we discuss strategies for allyship following guidance from members of minoritized communities outlined in course readings and videos. One student reflected:

Being a strong ally is something that has been important to me and it is something I am constantly reevaluating, in order to be better. I think that

Ahsante the Artist (2017) gives a really concise but insightful way of approaching being an ally. One thing she touched on is the difference between "speaking up" and "speaking for," I think this distinction demonstrates how an ally ought to support those who are being marginalized. I think that being an ally often requires you to make yourself smaller, to push attention away from yourself in order to allow the voices of the marginalized to be heard. When you "speak up," you echo their voice and make it louder. When you "speak for" you override their voice and it gets lost.... For an ally, amplifying the voices of those who are marginalized and making it stronger should be the goal. In the article by Alfred (2018) part of what is said an ally should do is "embrace the discomfort." I think this is an important reminder for an ally, you simply cannot be comfortable and expect to change anything. You cannot call yourself an ally to those who are struggling without struggling yourself. Discomfort comes from reducing your position, by making your voice smaller and rejecting the systems of power that have led to marginalization. You have to be comfortable with discomfort.

The examples above illustrate how course content can drive learning in online classrooms, with faculty who curate content and offer questions to support critical reflection serving as facilitators. As an educator committed to anti-racist and decolonizing pedagogy, providing content that allows students to learn directly from members of minoritized communities is a priority.

Transformative Learning Online: Simulating Institutional Discrimination

Educators create spaces for students to 'rock the boat' and challenge their inherited assumptions (Morris & Stommel, 2018). Instructor questions can guide student thinking and provide context as they re-interpret their worldviews with new knowledge and understandings. In an effort to design an opportunity for transformative learning in Social Dimensions of Sustainability, I took inspiration from Sharyn Clough's (this volume) exercise to illuminate themes of cognitive bias and structural injustice, which Clough modeled during the DPD Academy. Her lesson, derived from Sandra Lawrence's (1998) in-class art exercise, invites students to design and judge each other's mobiles after one team is allocated fewer supplies than the others. To design a collaborative online exercise with built-in inequities, I worked with Ecampus Instructional Designer Chris Lindberg to manipulate the technological features of the instructional platform to simulate discriminatory conditions.

In the assignment, groups of four or five students are responsible for creating biographical profiles showcasing perspectives from individuals whose voices have been neglected in the cannon of U.S. environmental thought. The majority of the class is required to submit text and a photo or video to illustrate the people they profile, which I then upload to a multimedia timeline designed for the course. I randomly select one group of students and provide them a truncated version of the instructions without the multimedia requirement. I also limit that group to text-entry submissions so they are unable to include photos or video files with their submissions. After I upload everyone's contributions to the timeline, students submit critiques of each other's work and nominate profiles for extra credit based on criteria that include how well they creatively illustrate the person's work. The following week, I explain that the assignment was designed with built-in institutional inequities and we discuss the experience as a class. The reflection prompt reads as follows:

If you were a member of the group that faced structural discrimination in this assignment:

1   What was your reaction when you reviewed the timeline and saw your peers' posts with photos and videos compared to your own?
2   Last week, what was your perspective on the criteria used to award extra credit, including requirements to "clearly illustrate" and "creatively demonstrate" your person's work?
3   Does your awareness of the structural inequity you worked within change your perception of the criteria?

If you were a member of a group that benefited from the structural bias:

1   Share any judgements you made about the quality of your peers' posts when you viewed the biographies without photos or videos.
2   Did it cross your mind that your peers may not have been given the same information about the assignment that you received?
3   Does this new information change the way you would evaluate their contributions?

At the end of the week, everyone replies to these prompts:

1   Compare the parallels you can draw from this experience with an example of institutional discrimination faced by minoritized communities. Using examples from this week's material, describe ways that institutional rules were/are biased.
2   Reflect critically on the ways the consequences, both material (ex. access to a loan to buy a home in a "good" neighborhood, access to quality schools, etc.) and perceptual (ex. stereotypes or judgements made about groups of people because of their circumstances) are unfair.

The addition of this experiential element produces excellent evidence of students' learning. Responses to the assignment are candid and demonstrate a level of synthesis and self-reflection that I don't often see in prior assignments. Their responses hit on a variety of relevant themes. Students in the group that have inadequate direction often describe self-doubt upon comparing their submissions to their peers'. One student reflected, "I was quite disturbed when I saw the other posts. I felt I had completely missed something. I did not feel there was a chance our group would receive extra credit." Another student responded:

> I was part of the group that faced built-in institutional inequalities. The information about submitting a photo or video did not show up on our assignment. My first reaction when I noticed that other groups had pictures and videos was that I needed to find a link to submit a photo to make my assignment have an equal chance at gaining extra credit. After looking, I did not see a link and so I figured that my group had made a mistake.

This student reported that they had judged themselves for not going above and beyond the assignment instructions as they assumed others had:

> My reaction to reviewing the timeline posts from my peers with photos and videos was of surprise. I didn't remember seeing any requirement that I had to add anything else. After double checking the guidelines I had of the assignment, I just assumed my classmates were doing something extra, and I started to feel a little frustrated about my personal life situation and the time I have available to do things, etc. Even though I followed the directions I felt like I hadn't done enough to my post because everyone else included something. After reading the requirements on extra credit, I did feel like it was a bit unfair.... The material consequences of not having all the information available for the assignment could result in a lower grade, even though I would have been following directions.... I only had my own lens to perceive the other work through, and to be honest, I was a little worried. I was hoping I'd be part of the group that got picked so that I could make up what I might have been marked down for on my assignment not being up to the same standards as the others. I could easily see myself thinking I would have to work twice as hard in order to get a good enough grade.

When students report that they were self-critical and look back to see if they misread the instructions, we also discuss the power dynamics the activity exposes. Thus far, none of the students have contacted me after comparing their submissions to their classmates' to see if there was a technical problem or ask if I made a mistake.

Students in the groups that receive an advantage because of the inequity are often forthright about assumptions they made about their peers' effort and the impact that the opportunity to reflect on their judgements has in the broader context of the course. One student wrote:

I had perceived my peers' work as lower quality work due to the lack of photos and videos that made the posts less engaging and less interesting. I was curious why and began making some assumptions about the students who contributed. I imagined that the students (who were faced with institutional bias) simply disregarded instructions or had no intention of producing quality work by fulfilling all instructed requirements. It did not cross my mind that my peers were given separate instructions. This new information that has come to light does alter my perception on the students who worked on the posts. Given the same instructions and opportunity, I believe they would have contributed just as well as the rest of the class.

Another reflected:

It's so interesting that this was all a setup, because I was wondering why there were a few posts without pictures. My immediate thought was how these people blatantly missed the instruction about having to add multimedia components to the timeline post. And those judgements steered me away from choosing any of the posts in my top three. It never for a second crossed my mind that my peers had been given different instructions or had a lack of resources available to them. It actually made me feel a lot better about my own post, because regardless of the quality of writing or deep analysis, at least I was able to follow directions! Really interesting to go back and look upon my past judgements like that. I think this new information would absolutely change how I judged my peers' posts.

This student compared the experience to lessons learned about the history and legacies of redlining:

My peers and I had an advantage over the other group with less information. The circumstances of the advantages and disadvantages of this exercise can be related to the circumstances between whites and blacks when institutional bias was carried out using redlining. In our case it was a chance for a good grade; in terms of redlining, the advantages and disadvantages determine one's opportunity to get a house in a good neighborhood. I was a part of the privileged group. I had access to the resources and the instruction to do well on this assignment; redlining made it so that white people had access to resources such as subsidies, low-interest mortgages, guaranteed housing, and opportunities to live in good neighborhoods (Gross, 2017). On the other side of the spectrum, the group not given the opportunity for extra credit can be related to a degree of what blacks faced in a redlined housing market. Redlining made the house buying process more difficult by considering black neighborhoods "too risky" to ensure [sic] along with segregation of communities (Gross, 2017). The decision to classify their neighborhoods as too risky limits the individual families' opportunities to find the best home in the best areas for their families.... In a sense, my classmates and I experienced, to a degree, what it was like.

This student reflected on their own privilege:

> Learning about communities that have been underprivileged for generations when it comes to the ability to advance social classes kind of struck a chord for me. Growing up, I was always taught that if I could dream it and worked hard enough, I could accomplish anything. That is because I never faced any obstacles such as institutional discrimination. I am playing with a full deck of cards.

As this assignment illustrates, online courses can be platforms for critical social justice pedagogy. Adopting my teaching style using the technological tools available has stretched my thinking about online education and the possibilities to challenge dominant pedagogical narratives. As I have demonstrated, creative, personalized engagement is possible, and with simple modifications, instructors can build authentic relationships with students we never meet face-to-face. As a final offering, I highlight a few additional resources to support the development of online courses that address the needs of all learners.

Additional Resources for Online Course Design and Evaluation

Stephanie Jenkins and Martha Smith (this volume) introduce strategies for applying Universal Design for Instruction frameworks in social justice education courses. Many of their techniques are transferable to the online environment and are an excellent place to start addressing the needs of diverse learners through intentional course design. Another tool for maximizing online course accessibility is the Universal Design for Instruction Guidelines from the Center for Applied Special Technology (CAST), which outlines succinct guidelines for moving Universal Design principles beyond ability-based considerations.

Design principles for accessibility should be a baseline for online course design. Developing a critical online pedagogy also requires that we design culturally responsive courses. CAST (2019) suggests that faculty use affective strategies to create courses that are inclusive across culture and learning style to encourage learner buy-in and motivation, maximize student choice, and offer clear explanations of the course's relevance and value.

Faculty interested in assessing their course design can also use the Online Equity Rubric developed by the Peralta Community College District (2019). This tool enables course evaluation based on criteria including how well the course supports student access to technology and academic support services; how effectively the course demonstrates a commitment to diversity, equity, and inclusion; and whether teaching faculty address their own biases and positionality in the classroom.

Systemic Challenges

It is clear that online pedagogy, like any educational engagement, must be a reflective practice, with educators continuously examining our positionality and power as facilitators of students' learning. I have been fortunate to work with colleagues from Oregon State University's Ecampus program who are actively advancing inclusivity in our online curricula through faculty trainings and instructional design while acknowledging that, like the rest of OSU, "We have work to do" (Oregon State University, 2018b, para. 1).

It is essential to note, however, that adopting many of the strategies outlined in this chapter will be easier for some faculty than others, depending upon the identities we hold, as well as our positions within our institutions. For example, I noted that humanizing the online classroom can be achieved by posting personal videos that make us visible to students as real people. The risks associated with this level of authenticity are higher for some faculty than others. Decades of research demonstrates bias in student evaluations of teaching based on race, gender, and other social categories. These biases impact faculty teaching online courses as well as face-to-face. For example, Lillian MacNell and her colleagues (2015) conducted a study of perceived gender identity of online instructors and found that students ranked instructors they perceived as female significantly lower than those they thought were male.

Similarly, strategies to decenter the authority of the instructor can also influence students' perceptions of faculty expertise and legitimacy. These risks are inherent in transformative pedagogy and not particular to online education, but when used in combination with other recommendations such as humanizing instructor presence and centering expertise and knowledge from outside the academy, faculty of color and non-male presenting faculty are more vulnerable. To meet affective learning goals that enable students to have critical conversations about social justice issues and encourage innovative approaches to online teaching, institutions must address the bias in student evaluations of teaching and their role in the promotion and tenure process.

For these and other reasons, many remain skeptical that the opportunities presented by online learning outweigh the costs. According to Elaine Allen and Jeff Seaman (2015) leaders of public universities acknowledge that online course development takes more time than face-to-face instruction. They report that the need for faculty training in design, facilitation, and technological skills required for effective online instruction remains unmet, and that faculty continue to question the "value and legitimacy of online education" (Allen & Scaman, 2015, p. 21). These factors are significant, coupled with the trend that online instruction is often delegated to adjuncts who often have little control over the content in the courses they are assigned to teach (Straumsheim, 2015). Despite these challenges, distance learning remains central to many institutions' strategic visions, with 70.8% of leaders from U.S. degree-granting institutions reporting that "online education is critical to the long-term strategy of my institution" (Allen & Seaman, 2015, p. 15).

Lessons Learned

Designing and facilitating an online social sustainability course for the Difference, Power, and Discrimination program has allowed me to confront my assumptions about online education as a modality for transformative learning. I am inspired by the authentic relationships I have built with students despite the distance. I have developed new skills and adapted my teaching strategies, all the while maintaining my commitments to social justice pedagogy. In a climate changing world, these strategies, and the technologies that mediate them, will play an essential role facilitating the exchange of ideas without the carbon footprint incurred through travel.

However, we must continue to challenge the narrative that online learning is an equalizing force nationally and globally, with awareness of both the digital divide and the colonizing risks of exporting Western pedagogical paradigms. Online social justice courses must be crafted with attention to the vulnerabilities of students and faculty who are members of non-dominant groups within the academy. It is essential that faculty have access to the training, tools, and time required to develop online classrooms that model university commitments to diversity, equity, and inclusion. With care, distance courses have the potential to connect students in learning communities, provide spaces to share their ideas and experiences, and to reframe knowledge production to help build more just, sustainable communities. I am by no means expertly traversing this path, but rather embracing the discomfort, following advice my students gleaned from communities on the frontlines of environmental and social justice movements. As with any effort in critical pedagogy, the work is ongoing.

Acknowledgements

I am grateful to the students in Social Dimensions of Sustainability who have shared this learning journey and allowed me to share their perspectives here. Many thanks to my colleagues at OSU Ecampus, particularly Chris Lindberg, Sarah Brabham, Dorothy Loftin, Kyle Whitehouse, Katherine McAlvage, and Nadia Jaramillo Cherrez for providing training, resources, and support at all stages of this project. Thanks, too, to the colleagues who have provided feedback, inspiration, and resources to strengthen my course design, including members of the 2018–2019 DPD Academy, the contributors to this volume, Miguel Arellano Sanchez, Deanna Lloyd, and Kim Townsend.

Additional Resources

Readings

Baker, R., Dee, T., Evans, B., & John, J. (2018, March). *Bias in online classes: Evidence from a field experiment.* Stanford Center for Education Policy Analysis. http://cepa.stanford.edu/wp18-03

Bradshaw, A. C. (2017). Critical pedagogy and educational technology. In A. D. Benson, R. Joseph, & J. L. Moore (Eds.), *Culture, learning, and technology: Research and practice* (pp. 8–27). Routledge.

Dillon, L., & Sze, J. (2018). Equality in the air we breathe: Police violence, pollution, and the politics of sustainability. In J. Sze (Ed.), *Sustainability: Approaches to environmental justice and social power* (pp. 246–270). New York University Press.

Dolan, J., Kain, K., Reilly, J., & Bansal, G. (2017). How do you build community and foster engagement in online courses? *New Directions for Teaching and Learning, 151*, 45–60. https://doi.org/10.1002/tl.20248

Ke, F., & Chávez, A.F. (2013). *Web-based teaching and learning across culture and age.* Springer.

Morris, S. M., & Stommel, J. (2018). *An urgency of teachers: The work of critical digital pedagogy.* Hybrid Pedagogy, Inc. https://criticaldigitalpedagogy.pressbooks.com/

Oblinger, D. (2014, September 14). Designed to engage. *EDUCAUSE Review 49*(5). https://er.educause.edu/articles/2014/9/designed-to-engage

Phirangee, K., & Malec, A. (2017). Othering in online learning: an examination of social presence, identity, and sense of community. *Distance Education, 38*(2), 160–172. https://doi.org/10.1080/01587919.2017.1322457

Websites

Center for Applied Special Technology (CAST). (2020). *Universal design for learning guidelines.* www.cast.org/our-work/about-udl.html#.XUiyyHt7mM9

Peralta Community College District. (2019, May). *Peralta online equity rubric.* https://web.peralta.edu/de/peralta-online-equity-initiative/equity/

References

Allen, I. E., & Seaman, J. (2015). *Grade level: Tracking online education in the United States.* Babson Survey Research Group and Quahog Research Group, LLC. http://onlinelearningsurvey.com/reports/gradelevel.pdf.

Center for Applied Special Technology (CAST). (2020). *Universal design for learning guidelines.* www.cast.org/our-work/about-udl.html#.XUiyyHt7mM9

Chicago Humanities Festival. (2013, February 7). *Shelton Johnson: The best idea America ever had* [Video]. YouTube. https://www.youtube.com/watch?v=S28x3MtDc3s

Domingue, A. D. (2016). Online and blended pedagogy in social justice education. In M. Adams, & L. A. Bell (Eds.), *Teaching for diversity and social justice* (pp. 369–396). Routledge.

Dolan, J., Kain, K., Reilly, J., & Bansal, G. (2017). How do you build community and foster engagement in online courses? *New Directions for Teaching and Learning, 151*, 45–60. https://doi.org/10.1002/tl.20248

hooks, b. (1994). *Teaching to transgress: Education as the practice of freedom.* Routledge.

hooks, b. (2011). earthbound: on solid ground. In A. H. Deming, & L. E. Savoy (Eds.), *Colors of nature: Culture, identity, and the natural world* (pp. 184–187). Milkweed Editions.

Hunt, A. N. (2018). Pedagogical techniques for creating a community of inquiry in online learning environments. In M. L. Kozimor-King, & J. Chin, (Eds.), *Learning from each other: Refining the practice of teaching in higher education* (pp. 27–39). University of California Press.

Interaction Institute for Social Change (2014) *Excerpt from the workshop: Facilitative leadership for social change.* Interaction Institute for Social Change. http://interactioninstitute.org/wp-content/uploads/2016/11/Listening-as-an-ally-page.pdf.

Ke, F., & Chávez, A.F. (2013). *Web-based teaching and learning across culture and age.* Springer.

Kotera, Y., Green, P., Hutchinson, L., Shaw, P., Bowskill, N., & Cockerill, V. (2019). Towards another kind of borderlessness: Online students with disabilities. *Distance Education, 40*(2), 170–186. https://doi.org/10.1080/01587919.2019.1600369

Lawrence, S. (1998). Unveiling positions of privilege: A hands-on approach to understanding racism. *Teaching of Psychology, 25*(3), 198–200. https://doi.org/10.1207/s15328023top2503_8

MacNell, L., Driscoll, A., & Hunt, A. N. (2015). What's in a name: Exposing gender bias in student ratings of teaching. *Innovative Higher Education, 40*(4), 291–303. https://doi.org/10.1007/s10755-10014-9313-9314

Morris, S. M., & Stommel, J. (2018). *An urgency of teachers: The work of critical digital pedagogy.* Hybrid Pedagogy, Inc. https://criticaldigitalpedagogy.pressbooks.com/

Myers, J. (2020). *Sustainability assessment* [Syllabus]. Sustainability Double Degree Program, Oregon State University.

Oregon State University (2018a). *Oregon State College School of Forestry letter* [Unpublished letter]. Search Advocate Program.

Oregon State University (2018b). *We have work to do.* Office of Institutional Diversity. https://diversity.oregonstate.edu/we-have-work-to-do.

Oregon State University Ecampus (n.d.). *Module 2 overview: Who are OSU's 9,752 exclusively online students?* Posted in Inclusive Teaching Online ORG 8096 classroom, archived at http://canvas.oregonstate.edu

Out4S (2016). *Intersectionality* [Audio recording]. Soundcloud. https://soundcloud.com/out4s/intersectionality

Peralta Community College District (2019, May). *Peralta Online Equity Rubric.* https://web.peralta.edu/de/peralta-online-equity-initiative/equity/

Radford, A. W. (2011). *Undergraduate Enrollment in Distance Education Courses and Degree Programs.* U.S. Department of Education. https://nces.ed.gov/pubs2012/2012154.pdf

Sauder, K. (2016, March 4). When accessibility gets labeled wasteful. *Crippled Scholar.* https://crippledscholar.com/2016/03/04/when-accessibility-gets-labeled-wasteful/.

Smith, D. R., & Ayers, D. F. (2006). Culturally responsive pedagogy and online learning: Implications for the globalized community college. *Community College Journal of Research & Practice, 30*(5/6), 401–415. https://doi.org/10.1080/10668920500442125

Straumsheim, C. (2015, November 12). *Supporting online adjuncts.* Inside Higher Ed. https://www.insidehighered.com/news/2015/11/12/study-explores-hiring-and-managing-practices-online-adjunct-faculty-members

TEDx Talks (2011, Nov. 15). *TEDxHampshireCollege - Jay Smooth - How I learned to stop worrying and love discussing race* [Video]. YouTube. www.youtube.com/watch?v=MbdxeFcQtaU

Teton Productions (2016). *Dolores Huerta – Standing Rock* [Video]. Vimeo. https://vimeo.com/197346960

Women of Color Speak Out (2016, May 9). *WoCSO: Break Free PNW, Allyship* [Video]. YouTube. www.youtube.com/watch?v=NWm-yMJO72c

Watters, A. (2018). Foreword. In S. M. Morris, & J. Stommel, *An urgency of teachers: The work of critical digital pedagogy*. Hybrid Pedagogy, Inc. https://criticaldigitalpedagogy.pressbooks.com/

6 Peace Literacy, Cognitive Bias, and Structural Injustice

Sharyn Clough

This essay is organized around an in-class art exercise designed by Sandra Lawrence (1998) as an experiential accompaniment to Peggy McIntosh's essay "White Privilege and Male Privilege" (1988). Especially for white feminist scholars like me learning and teaching about anti-racist feminism, McIntosh's essay provided a starting point for talking with students about the ways that racism, sexism, and other intersecting forms of oppression are not only attitudes held by individuals, but are also social forces instantiated in the conventions, cultural expectations, historical practices, and institutions that structure, prop-up, and constrain our imaginations, hopes, and lived realities. Her essay helped remind me that the ubiquity of these structural components of injustice makes them hard to recognize precisely because they are everywhere. The structural components of injustice are like water to fish, and oxygen to us. And I would add here that I mean "us" to refer to everyone. While structurally unjust advantages are especially invisible to those of us who benefit from them, even those of us negatively impacted by unjust structural arrangements can have internalized to some extent the fact of the unjust restrictions as normal, natural, and unchanging (hooks, 2003), a point I return to in the discussion of cognitive biases in the third section of the essay.

Lawrence's art exercise disrupts the normalcy and inviibility of structural injustice by reproducing it in a way that makes it recognizable and tangible. In the fourth section, I discuss the set-up for the exercise as I have used it in my face-to-face classes (see Myers in this volume for a discussion of how to set it up for online classes). Briefly, the exercise involves an art project where students are challenged to design and construct a mobile – Marcel Duchamp's name for Alexander Calder's kinetic sculptures of colored geometric shapes. The mobiles designed by the students are simple structures using wire clothing hangers. The students are tasked with using their mobiles to illustrate some feature of structural injustice discussed in class. In the version of the exercise that I have developed, the students then judge each other's mobiles based on criteria supplied ahead of time by the students. Students have 45 minutes and can use only the supplies given to them. I tell them there will be a prize. What I don't tell them, and what most students don't notice, is that the art supplies needed to make their mobiles have not been uniformly distributed. The

DOI: 10.4324/9781003091998-8

disparity in distribution of supplies is usually reflected in the quality of their creations and in the judgments the students make about whose creations best meet the criteria. Once debriefed, their judgments of each other's work in the contest provide rich opportunities for discussion of structural injustice generally. Ultimately, there is no prize, except for the opportunity for discussion afforded by the exercise. Usually, though not always, that is prize enough.

I have used this exercise for the past 20 years in my introductory philosophy classes when I teach about the relationship between knowledge, knowers, and structural injustice. I have added my own layer to the lessons of structural injustice illustrated in the exercise, by situating the exercise against a backdrop of research on cognitive biases and the way that biases, while held by individuals, can inform and be informed by broad structures of unearned, inequitably distributed advantage and power. For one thing, as I explain in terms of the art exercise, our biases can affect our ability even to *notice* structural inequities, let alone see those inequities as unjust.

More recently I have begun to weave the structural and cognitive discussions together within the context of a new framework called Peace Literacy, designed by Paul K. Chappell (2017, 2015, 2012). For Chappell, peace–at the individual, community, and global level–involves three elements. The first is an accurate understanding of the world and our place in it. This element is an invitation to continue the research with which we as educators for structural justice and peace are engaged, with some reminders about elements that might get neglected or need more emphasis. For example, in addition to requiring an accurate understanding of structural injustice and cognitive biases, Peace Literacy requires an accurate understanding of our shared psychological needs, such as self-worth and belonging, as well as an accurate understanding of the ways that injustice and biases interact both to mask our ability to see those needs in others, and to recognize when trauma has become tangled in those needs, often with predictably negative results. I am only newly coming to appreciate the importance of understanding these latter phenomena. The second element is a positive set of skills and habits (hence peace *literacy*), such as listening, perspective-taking, and seeking clarification. The need for these skills might be obvious, but learning these skills is still difficult. We need to learn and practice these skills if we are to build the kind of strong communities required to dismantle structural injustice. The third and final element is the development of a number of capacities, such as empathy, conscience, imagination, and hope – capacities designed to help us use the new skills strategically and effectively (Chappell, 2012). Structural injustice properly evokes our moral outrage, and working for positive change, can be at times exhausting and frustrating. Developing all three elements of peace helps provide us with energy and sustenance to keep us from sinking into cynicism and despair.

This conceptual positioning of peace, not only as a call to more accurately understand social injustice, psychological needs, and trauma, but also as the set of positive skills and habits Chappell proposes, has a number of critical implications.

It helps us see our cognitive biases, for example, not so much as intrinsic features of our individual identities or personalities, but as a set of negative habits that we have learned and practiced, habits that reinforce and are reinforced by broad structural patterns, social conventions, cultural expectations, historical practices, and institutions. One of the many reasons that working to end structural injustice is so difficult is that it involves the active avoidance of the cognitive habits and shortcuts to which we have all been enculturated systemically by the structures within which we are educated formally and informally over a lifetime (Eisner, 1979), and the substituting and practice of new cognitive habits and skills, often with little support or training. The more we can recognize how our own thinking inevitably becomes entrenched in the very systems we are trying to resist, the more empathy we can have for ourselves and others caught in the same systems. The more empathy we can generate, the more we can fuel the imagination and hope we can bring to bear on solutions, the more energy we'll have for exercising our conscience, increasing our ability both to make more accurate diagnoses of the injustices against which we struggle and to develop new habits and practices. Increasing our literacy in peace requires:

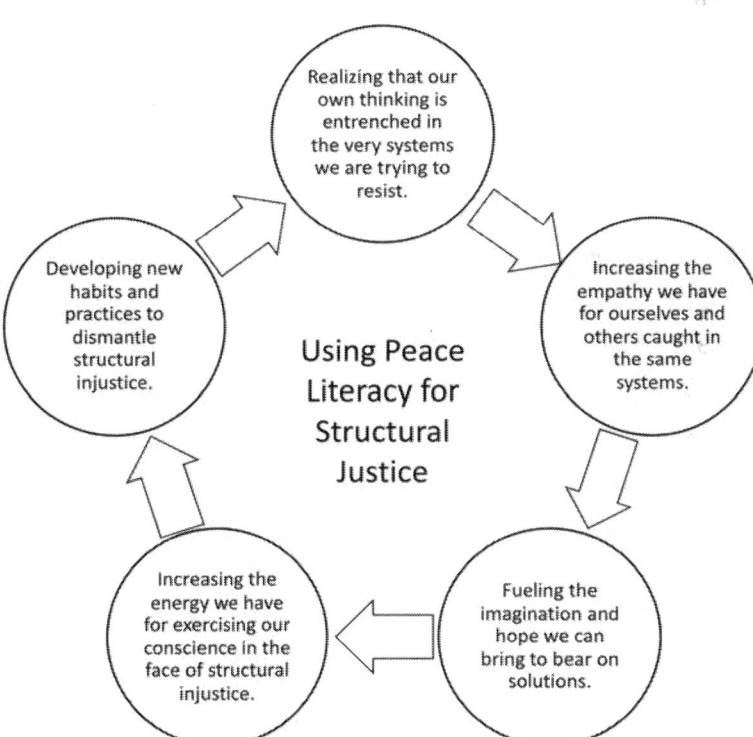

Figure 6.1 Using Peace Literacy for Structural Justice

Importantly, this call to develop Peace Literacy is not offered as a demand for civility if such a demand would also mean suppressing moral outrage, passively acquiescing in oppression, or placating rather than holding accountable those who perpetrate injustice. On the contrary, Peace Literacy involves developing a more accurate understanding of injustice and its various and complex histories and manifestations; as well as developing, in addition to empathy and hope, a capacity for *conscience*. There is no way to do this well that will avoid moral outrage, and much that will instead provoke it. Indeed, moral outrage can function in a number of helpful ways (Cherry & Flanagan, 2018). Moral outrage can be alertive (Matheis, 2019); it is a kind of distress that can orient those who experience and express it to the existence of oppression and other forms of patterned harm to which ameliorative efforts ought properly be directed. It can be cathartic when oppressed peoples long told to be patient and passive instead give voice to their moral outrage. It can be transformational when that moral outrage then provokes direct action in the service of structural justice (Lorde, 1997). What is critical to note here is that while the process of becoming more literate in peace is compatible with and can in some cases encourage moral outrage, Peace Literacy is designed to help those engaged in its learning express that moral outrage in strategically effective ways that can endure as long-term habits for positive structural change, and discourage the expression of moral outrage that turns to violence, retaliation, socially corrosive political factioning, etc.

The Rev. Dr. Martin Luther King (1998) provides a model here. He expressed his moral outrage in response to racial injustice in a calculated, disciplined strategy of nonviolent direct action. In order to dismantle structural injustice, call people to account for their participation in injustice, and decide carefully and fairly on the conditions of that accountability, moral outrage alone is not enough – we need an effective strategy. The overarching thesis for this essay is that Peace Literacy provides teachers and students with the strategic understanding, skills, and capacities needed to learn about and work to dismantle structural injustice.

The balance of the essay has four sections. The first focuses on Peace Literacy, followed by a section on cognitive biases, and a section on the art exercise. A brief conclusion reinforces the relationship between Peace Literacy and pedagogy for structural justice.

Peace Literacy as Phronesis

My philosophical research and teaching are informed by the American pragmatist tradition (think John Dewey and Jane Addams), which views knowledge, and the study of knowledge, as a practical and problem-oriented affair. Rather than arising out of abstract thought-experiments, this pragmatist view arises out of the everyday experiences of embodied knowers, in social conditions that are often unjust and in need of melioration (McHugh, 2015). There is little in the way of pragmatist philosophy as I am describing it here that can be done well solely from an armchair (full disclosure: I am currently sitting in an armchair).

This pragmatist focus is in line with a centuries-old tradition beginning with Aristotle's emphasis on phronesis – sometimes translated as prudence or practical wisdom (Pagan, 2008). Viewing wisdom as a practice rather than a product, pragmatists argue that knowing well requires the build-up of habits, which in turn requires experience, which reinforces the habits, and so on. Accordingly, wisdom isn't something we have, it's something we do, embodied, in social relations, in the world, defined and constrained by particular and often unjust social conditions. Recently I've joined forces with public philosopher Paul K. Chappell in the study of a new conception of phronesis: Peace Literacy.

Peace Literacy as Accurate Understanding

On Chappell's view, to be literate in peace requires not only an accurate understanding of cognitive biases, structural injustices, and the rationalizations that support and are supported by biases and injustice, but also new understandings of, for example, our shared human needs and the practical wisdom best suited to help individuals and communities meet those needs (Chappell, forthcoming). Upending Maslow's hierarchy, Chappell shows that in addition to our physical needs for food and shelter, we need to meet a number of very basic *non-physical* needs such as belonging, purpose, and self-worth. Work for structural justice has often focused on the fair and just distribution of material goods to satisfy physical needs. This is as it should be – people suffer terribly from material poverty and those of us who work for social justice, especially from a position of material privilege, need to work to end that suffering. However, we need also to more accurately understand and attend better than we have to helping end the suffering that is caused when non-physical needs for belonging, purpose, and self-worth are not met, or not met in healthy ways – not least because the kinds of problems arising from this kind of suffering often play a causal role in maintaining the structures that *cause* material poverty (Chappell, forthcoming).

Being literate in peace involves understanding how racism, sexism, and other forms of structural injustice mask our ability to see that humans not only share basic needs for food, shelter, and safety, we also share non-physical needs for belonging, purpose, and self-worth; the mechanisms and practices of injustice keep us from seeing more fully these crucial elements of our common humanity.

Peace Literacy also requires a more accurate understanding of the psychological effects of trauma, positioning trauma centrally in discussions of our non-physical needs, and providing a vocabulary for describing the predictable effects of trauma as it tangles and disrupts our attempts to meet these needs in ourselves and others (Chappell, forthcoming). Like many of you, and many of our students, I was drawn to work for structural justice when the trauma I experienced in my family home led me to explore feminist accounts of the gendered and racialized patterns of violence of which my own experience with my father's violence was merely a painful data point. Growing up in Canada, racial politics centered around indigeneity and colonization, some of the devastating effects of which were meted out on the bodies and minds of Indigenous children adopted into families of European heritage. My adopted brother did not survive this experiment. Those of us who did survive, experience the kinds of emotional precarity that make survival an accomplishment and a burden by turns. As Chappell tells his own story of trauma (e.g., Chappell, 2015) it is both unique and familiar all at once. He is multi-racial and growing up in Alabama he experienced racial alienation and bullying at school. He also survived trauma from a violent upbringing – his father served in Korea and Vietnam and brought his war trauma home. After graduating from West Point in 2002, Chappell served overseas in Kuwait, and Iraq. Chappell left the U.S. Army as a Captain in 2009. He researches trauma extensively and his Peace Literacy framework is dedicated to overcoming trauma by helping all of us become as well-trained in fighting for structural justice and waging peace as soldiers are in waging war. It is a pedagogy for *Soldiers of Peace*, to use Gandhi's (1958) phrase.

Peace Literacy as a Skillset

In addition to more accurately understanding our shared human needs for belonging, purpose, and self-worth, and the tangles of trauma that keep us from meeting those needs in healthful ways, peace also involves articulating and practicing a set of basic peace skills so that they can become habituated into a new kind of phronesis. Some of these skills are familiar (listening with empathy, perspective-taking, cultivating calm, and seeking clarification), but some are less familiar (recognizing aggression in ourselves and others as a distress response) (Chappell, 2017). It is not without some irony that Chappell notes that he learned many of these skills when he studied at West Point and served in the U.S. military. It turns out that if you are sending a group of trained killers, armed to the teeth, into circumstances where they are going to be physically uncomfortable, anxious, and at times terrified, then it is ideal to have trained them to listen to each other with empathy and stay calm. Of course, the military has many ideals that aren't put into practice. Still the ideals are often recognized as *requiring* practice.

Many of us working for structural justice assume that by virtue of our goals we should just somehow *excel* at these skills without any practice at all. But most of us were not trained in these skills. Well, I wasn't, anyway. And my students struggle as well. It is one thing to read about phronesis from Aristotle, it is another to actively practice it, and practice it in the explicit service of peace. And even for those of us who did have active training in these skills, it was probably hit and miss. What if instead we formalized it in our teaching and teacher training? And not just as ideals but in practice? Imagine what we could accomplish if we did.

Peace Literacy as Capacity Development

Finally, the Peace Literacy framework articulates a set of capacities – empathy, conscience, hope, curiosity, imagination, language, discipline, reason, and appreciation – that must be developed for our skills and habits to be effective (Chappell, 2012). Many of these capacities arise naturally in most children, but for these capacities to become habitual elements of phronesis they need to be cultivated by social institutions such as families and schools. Unfortunately, there is much in our social learning that not only fails to build these capacities but actively suppresses them. Public education in the USA does not focus on all or even many of these capacities. The capacities of language, and (some elements of) discipline and reason get attention in public education, but without the development of other capacities, like empathy, hope, and conscience, our strength in language, reason, and discipline can become unbalanced. We need to strengthen in tandem all the "muscles of our humanity," to use Chappell's phrase (2012, p. xvii).

Gandhi and Rev. Dr. MLK Jr. recognized the importance of viewing peace as a skill set arising through the development of muscles of practical wisdom such as empathy, conscience, and discipline. Gandhi noted the importance of his own military training and service and called those who wielded the weapons of nonviolence *Soldiers of Peace* (Chappell, 2017). King worked with James Lawson to discipline and train a community of direct-action strategists with the peace skills needed to organize and participate in nonviolent interventions such as the Lunch Counter Sit-Ins. But most of us did not get an education that would develop our capacity for empathy, conscience, or hope, nor did we learn peace skills, so we shouldn't be surprised when we find ourselves struggling with the requisite practices and/or doubting the feasibility of turning them into lifelong habits in ourselves and our communities.

In *Soldiers of Peace*, Chappell asks readers to imagine sending a bunch of kids out to play a basketball game, except none of them know how to play basketball. It would be chaos. But we wouldn't be surprised. We don't expect kids to just know how to play basketball. Importantly, when we saw them floundering on the court, we wouldn't weep for humanity and despair. We'd teach the kids how to play basketball! We'd teach them an accurate understanding of the rules of the game, we'd teach them some skills to build a strong team, and we'd help them build particular muscles and capacities to play well. Similarly, when we look around at the pain, suffering, and injustice in our communities, we shouldn't feel hopelessness or despair. It takes know-how, skills, capacity development, and lots and lots of practice to live well and work for justice, in community with others.

When you consider our lack of literacy in peace, and the depths of our collective vulnerability, trauma, and fear, it is astonishing that we have lasted this long. Humans are amazing when you think about it. There is a lot to work with here. More to the point, as we attend carefully to changes in climate, political and otherwise, both in the USA and around the globe, we can see all too clearly what will happen if we don't do this work.

My partnership with Chappell involves changing policy and attitudes in order to encourage education in Peace Literacy, from K-12, through to higher education and adult education. Broadening and deepening the scope of educational models in Social Emotional Learning, we design curriculum to help students build peace skills and capacities, to teach them about their nonphysical needs for belonging, purpose, and self-worth, and how to meet those needs in healthful ways. I want to pause to note that if you are compelled by anything you read here, it would be great to have you on the team (to access more info about our Peace Literacy curriculum, I've included a link under "Additional Resources").

Peace Literacy Review

To increase our Peace Literacy, we need to develop a more accurate understanding not only of structural injustice, but also of our human needs and vulnerabilities that we often ignore; we need to learn some peace skills that most of us don't have; and we need to develop more evenly our capacities or metaphorical muscles, balancing our well-honed muscles of language and reason with our often less-well developed muscles of empathy, appreciation, hope, and conscience. Even though all of these capacities or muscles develop naturally, without training they become weaker through lack of use. Finally, we need lots and lots of practice. Increasing our literacy in peace requires:

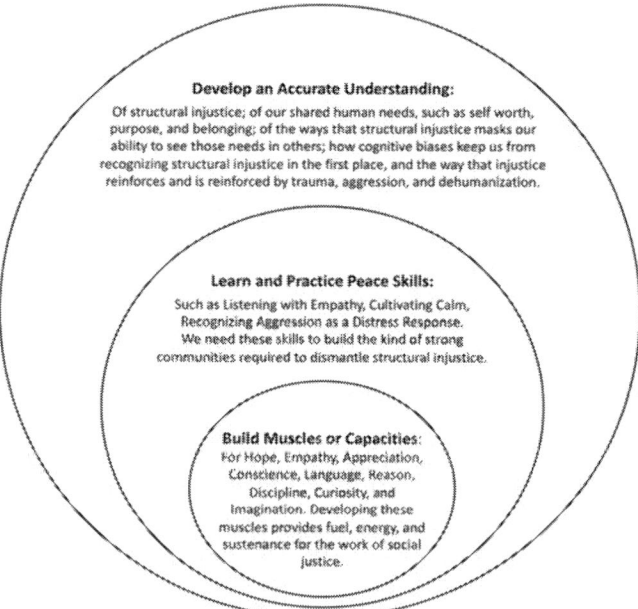

Figure 6.2 Requirements for Increasing Peace Literacy

Before I started work on Peace Literacy, most of my philosophy teaching around structural injustice focused on helping students develop an accurate diagnostic understanding of these structures, how they developed, and what it is about the structures that made them unjust. In addition to philosophical clarity around the relevant concepts, my work to help students gain a more accurate understanding of structural injustice involved helping them gain a more accurate understanding of history, sociology, and economics, including a careful examination of statistics on criminal justice, the social determinants of health, mortgage lending, fair pay, and the historical factors that affect how those statistical patterns shift over time, or don't. As I explain further in the next section, providing an accurate understanding of the psychology of cognitive biases has also proved to be helpful. Teaching this material helps students build their capacities for language and reason. In addition, having them take seriously unfamiliar viewpoints and perspectives, helps them strengthen their capacity for empathy and imagination.

Keeping Peace Literacy in view, I have more recently tried to expand the scope of topics around which I want students to develop a more accurate understanding, including helping them understand: (a) our shared nonphysical needs; (b) the ubiquity of trauma; (c) the depth of our shared human vulnerability; (d) our shared human need for trust; and (e) our unremitting shared human desire to be loved and understood. Academic philosophy, and perhaps academia more generally, does not take these needs very seriously, yet when I invite students to think about what weighs on them most and keeps them from concentrating on their studies and instead glued to their phones, it is usually a longing for connection, self-worth, and community. I should note here, that acknowledging human vulnerability generally, requires acknowledging my own in particular, which routinely makes me feel uncomfortable. Fortunately, peace skills and capacities around empathy and compassion for myself as well as my students helps make the teaching of this material go more smoothly, and it gives me an excuse to exercise my muscles of hope and appreciation. These latter two muscles had become atrophied from years of cynicism. I can no longer afford cynicism. Humans, non-human animals, and the planet on which we all live can no longer afford cynicism.

In the next two sections of this chapter I model a Peace Literacy approach to discussions of cognitive biases and the in-class art exercise I use to show students how certain biases are informed by and reinforce structural injustice, often functioning to keep us from detecting that injustice in the first place.

Cognitive Biases

In very general terms, I explain to students that biases are cognitive habits that humans use to make decisions under conditions of uncertainty (i.e., most of the time). Our capacity for biased thinking is enormous, and the literature on cognitive biases is similarly vast. I find Benson's cognitive bias "cheat sheet" to be a helpful guide (Benson, 2016). He organizes over 100 cognitive biases into four main contexts, according to the conditions under which those biases are primed: (1) when we have too much information; (2) when we do not have access to enough meaning or context; (3) when we need to make decisions quickly; and (4) when we need to remember data easily. Many biases fall into more than one of these categories. Importantly, not all cognitive biases are related to structural injustice, though for purposes of a philosophy class dedicated to understanding the relationship between knowledge, structural hierarchies, and social position, I explain that these are the biases on which we will be focusing.

Because the class is an introduction to philosophy, students have typically not self-selected for exposure to content discussing structural injustice. But even if they had, we all know that discussions of these kinds of injustice trigger discomfort (for a discussion of this problem see Lawrence (1998), as well as other chapters in this volume, especially Boovy and Osei-Kofi). At the very least, identifying the determinative power of social and structural forces over which students have little to no control can be demoralizing, and (further) disruptive of their sense that the world is fair. Additionally, as a pragmatist approach to social epistemology reminds us, students are embodied knowers with idiosyncratic histories, living and studying under unjust social conditions, all of which create differences between them, and they will bring those differences to the class. These differences matter, and students benefit from Peace Literacy skills that help encourage understanding of differences and similarities, alike. For example, while we all share needs for self-worth, purpose, and belonging, these needs can be prioritized and expressed differently under different social conditions. Students who are unfairly marginalized by the particular social forces under discussion in any given class period will have their own reasons for being uncomfortable discussing the details, and those who are newly learning ways in which they are unfairly privileged by these same forces have to struggle with guilt and defensiveness. For these reasons, I tend to hold off on discussions of this material until mid-way through the term, when the classroom has had a chance to become a community space with some substantial and persistent level of trust developed between me and the students, if not between each of the students themselves. Often the classes are too big, and the terms are too short, for this latter kind of trust to develop. This work, under these conditions, is always fraught and requires skillful management. I don't always succeed. Let me rephrase, there is success in every attempt. There are always lessons to be learned. Breathe.

So. Cognitive biases. The biases exploited by systemic injustices that then lead to further prejudices and in turn further structural injustice can best be explained by appeal to the vast amount of data available to us at any one time—in order to make sense of any of it, we must first ignore much of it, and that which we do attend to, we come very early on to chunk into categories or schemas for easier and quicker processing of new instances. I have students read contemporary philosopher Tamar Gendler (2011) for her clear exposition of cognitive biases and the energy required to circumvent them – note the empathy and understanding of her presentation:

> Categorization and stereotyping are tools used by finite minds to operate effectively in an overwhelmingly complex environment. ... [t]he world is complicated, our cognitive resources are limited, and classifying objects into groups allows us to proceed effectively in an environment teeming with overwhelming detail.
>
> (pp. 38–39)

At its most basic, language learning involves identifying and sorting individual items into relevant categories. For English language-learners a number of typical and rudimentary categories develop early on: all small four-legged furry creatures are called "dogs"; all adults with short hair are called "men." Overgeneralizations on the part of young language learners require patience and gentle correction from short-haired women and cats. The writers of Sesame Street sought to help young language learners out with a memorable song: "One of These Things is Not like the Other." I sometimes have students sing this song. It helps everyone relax. More on why we might want to relax and minimize anxiety in these discussions, below.

For schemas or categories to function, we have to develop stereotypes based on the feature that all the things in the category must share for membership in the category. Having in mind a stereotype helps us sort new items into the right group, even or especially when we have incomplete information about the new items (this is the second priming condition for cognitive biases discussed by Benson, above). Stereotyping has the unfortunate epistemic effect of minimizing between group similarities and maximizing within group similarities. When our stereotypes are about people, formed in the contexts of systematic and structural injustice, based on arbitrary embodied markers such as "sex" and "race," then things go badly quickly.

In addition to stereotypes, attribution errors too can lead to, and be reinforced by, structural injustice. The Fundamental Attribution Error (FAE) for example, involves the tendency when offering causal explanations for other people's behaviors, to over-attribute the causal role of personality traits over which individuals are thought to exert some control, while downplaying situational, contextual, and sometimes structural explanations understood to be beyond individual control (for a classic discussion of the Fundamental Attribution Error, see Ross, 1977).

The students typically commit the FAE in their explanations for why some groups perform so poorly in the art exercise. They make attributions of internal, dispositional features–the students in those groups were lazy or made bad decisions about time management – unaware that there were broader structural inequalities at work. They could of course have looked around and registered the inequities in the distribution of art supplies. But they usually don't. Cognitive biases keep us from recognizing what is often in front of our faces.

The flipside of the FAE is the "Self-Serving" bias (Heider, 1958). Especially when explaining the causes of negative outcomes in our own lives, we over attribute external forces beyond our control; when explaining our successes, we over-attribute internal forces within our control. In his paper on the

"Ultimate Attribution Error" Thomas Pettigrew (1979) combined this group of attribution errors together to explain how prejudice can be reinforced: "when prejudiced people perceive what they regard as a negative act by an outgroup member, they will more than others attribute it dispositionally, often as genetically determined, in comparison to the same act by an ingroup member" (p. 461). All of these attribution errors reinforce and are reinforced by "Just World" biases, revealing of our need to believe that the world is a rational place where people get what they deserve (Pettigrew, 1979). Further reinforcing these are "Confirmation biases" that lead us to notice data that supports views we already hold and ignore data that conflicts. All of these biases can lead to victim-blaming.

Taking seriously that cognitive biases are habits developed to handle epistemic uncertainties, means that cognitive biases will be primed and exacerbated by stress and anxiety. I explain to students that they will find themselves having any number of biases activated when we study stereotyping and structural injustice. Gendler (2011) reminds us that simply being made aware of a stereotype, even if we disagree with it, can prime our biased cognitive associations, and working against those associations takes incredible effort. No one wants to sound racist or sexist, so everyone gets anxious and stressed in class periods where we are discussing racism and sexism, which means we have to work even harder to avoid the racist, sexist cognitive shortcuts with which we are habituated, which makes everything worse.

While I don't endorse all of Gendler's conclusions, her main lesson is well-taken and worth emphasizing: If we are trying to learn about and work around our biases, then this is going to cost us in terms of cognitive energy. And as I noted at the outset, "us" is everyone. Because these biases are reinforced by structural injustice, *everyone* has them, even folks who are subjects of that bias. I often share with students a story about the first time I heard a woman's voice come over the PA of a commercial airliner introducing herself not as the flight attendant who would be bringing beverages around once we reached cruising altitude, but as the captain announcing that we had reached cruising altitude. My first reaction was terror. Because obviously women can't be pilots and we were all going to die. Did I say I was on my way to a feminist philosophy conference when this happened? I was. Within a millisecond I was laughing at myself. Still. There it was. I share this admission with students as a call to compassion for ourselves and others when trying to do the difficult work of subverting our cognitive associations. We have some deeply entrenched habits. But we can, with practice, acquire new and better habits.

The unconscious level at which these cognitive associations can have their most pernicious effects has led to a whole new industry around the conceptualization and detection of biases that work implicitly – i.e., prejudicial stereotypes that we do not consciously endorse but which affect our decision-making none-the-less. I usually take one of the many free online Implicit Bias tests the night before we discuss this material (Harvard has the most well researched version of the test and I have put a link to it in "Additional Resources"). The last time I did this, I got a typical result: "Your data suggest a strong automatic association between weapons and African American faces compared to European American faces." Sigh. It is worth noting and not surprising that in the USA, Black folks are just as likely to get this result on tests of implicit bias. Of course, while the results are often equivalent for Black and white folks, the societal implications are not. We must also be careful not to take the unconscious element of these biases to mean we are not responsible for working against them, especially those of us who benefit from the structural injustices that these biases both produce and perpetuate. Too often, discussions of implicit or unconscious biases end with their detection, as if having detected the biases in ourselves, we feel our work is done. In fact, it has just begun. (For a critical examination of the way that tests of implicit bias can function to perpetuate racism, see Tate and Page (2018).)

On the day of the in-class art exercise, I begin with a variety of video clips to illustrate the cognitive biases around which the students will be designing their mobiles. No video is timeless or appropriate for all contexts, but a current favorite of mine is a two-minute piece produced for a 2016 UK campaign to combat gender stereotypes (Redraw The Balance, 2016, link in "Additional Resources"). In the video, young children in a class are asked to draw an air-force pilot, a surgeon, and a fire-fighter. Of 61 drawings only five depicted women. Then the kids get a chance to meet in real life an air-force pilot, a surgeon, and a firefighter. All are women of course. At first the kids wonder if the women are just playing dress-up. Their mouths hang open in shock and awe. It is remarkable. And again, it's from 2016.

It is worth noting that in this clip the schoolteachers are careful to use gender-non-specific language in describing the three vocations. Still the sexist effects persist. I remind students that changing our language is a necessary, but not sufficient, step on the path to social justice. Habits are hard to break. But not as hard as we may feel or think.

To illustrate the Fundamental Attribution Error, I show a clip from a 2000 *Comedy Central* stand-up routine by Greg Giraldo (2000) discussing problems faced by the unhoused; Giraldo uses the term "homeless" which activists are trying to move away now from to remind us that people living without shelter often have homes and communities. In this clip Giraldo reports hearing a passer-by yell at an unhoused man that he should stop being so lazy and get a job. Giraldo then notes that the unhoused man was wearing his underpants outside his pants, and imagines that the man's resume is unlikely to be up-to-date. Giraldo's observation corrects the FAE made by the passer-by. Giraldo moves the causal attribution of the unhoused man's misfortune from a dispositional attribute within the man's control (laziness) to something situational and outside his control (mental illness). Giraldo's presentation here is funny, humble, and compassionate. In another section of the comedy special he talks about immigration and prejudice against Latinx immigrants in particular (Giraldo self-identifies as Hispanic). I don't endorse his entire hour-long special, but these two sections are almost pitch perfect. Giraldo was born the same year I was (1965). He got his JD from Harvard but he decided stand-up comedy was where his heart was, so he left law. He struggled with anxiety and depression all his life and self-medicated with drugs and alcohol. He died in 2010 of an overdose at the age of 45. I tell students all of this. It feels important that they know it. Successful people struggle. Trauma and addiction are ubiquitous. Empathy. Breathe.

I explain to students that individual cognitive biases such as the FAE scale up, contribute to, and are reinforced by massive structural injustices based on racism and sexism, and the intersection of these as well as other systems of oppression like ableism and homophobia. I remind them that these social forces are based on identity abstractions – no one is ever just a woman, or just a white person, or just a lesbian – we need these abstractions to analyze the unjust social forces at work, but we also need to remember that we have artificially abstracted these identities out from a myriad of details – more cognitive shortcuts – and we have to be careful not to reify the abstractions. And, of course, a number of these identity abstractions are also indirectly inferred, and we are often wrong in our inferences! We are all of us complex individuals who experience unfair advantage along any number of social axes and we can use these experiences to strengthen our empathy. Breathe.

In-class Art Exercise

At this point in the term, even if the students have a sense of community in the classroom, the discussions of racist and sexist cognitive biases have usually had the effect of making everyone nervous. Beginning this particular class period with videos and humor helps put the students a little more at ease, as does the introduction of an art exercise. The use of art as a pedagogical device makes a welcome change of pace for the students (see Osei-Kofi, 2013 for a discussion of the importance of art in pedagogical contexts).

Method for the Art Exercise

- Ahead of time, sort brown paper gift bags containing the art supplies.
- Depending on the size of your class, fill one or two of the bags with extremely limited supplies:

    A wire hanger, three white recipe cards, three pieces of one-foot long pieces of string, and two pencils. That's it.

- The rest of the bags need to look roughly the same from the outside as the bags with limited supplies, even though the rest of the bags contain more supplies:

    A wire hanger, six white recipe cards, six larger sheets of colored paper, a ball of colored string or yarn, a pair of scissors, a glue stick, and a pack of colored felt pens.

- In class, after you watch the videos, be sure to highlight the brilliance with which Giraldo handles the FAE, especially in terms of the unhoused man (foreshadowing!).

- After sorting students into groups (no more than four or five, no fewer than three), tell them that each group will be getting a wire hanger and some art supplies to make a mobile that illustrates some feature of structural injustice discussed in the videos or our class reading.
- Also tell them that they will only have 45 mins to make their mobiles (I have found that 35–40 mins is the bare minimum needed for students to produce something with which they are happy).
- Explain that at the end of the time period they will each vote on which mobile is the best, based on criteria they all chose as a group, and that there will be a prize.
- Show them a photo of Alexander Calder holding up one of his original mini-mobiles (I've put a link to my favorite photo in "Additional Resources" – make sure that "colorful" is among the criteria chosen for the mobiles; ditto for "original."
- Tell them that they can only use the supplies in their giftbags – so no dipping into their backpacks (even for the students with the more generously distributed supply bags, the exercise should present a challenge in terms of time, creativity, and sharing of the single pair of scissors and one glue stick with members of the group).

In the 20 years that I have been doing this exercise, only two students have ever asked whether they are all getting the same supplies. At these times I have simply replied, "This is America, The Land of Equal Opportunity! Everyone has a chance to succeed." Given that "original" is one of the criteria, I tell them to make sure they keep their desks close together in their groups so that competing groups can't copy their ideas. But everyone can of course see everyone's work, and everyone's supplies. But most of them don't. This is key. They are busy competing for a mystery prize. They are excited.

My classes tend to be predominantly though not exclusively white, owing primarily to the whiteness of the institutions at which I have taught (and teach), and secondarily, though not insignificantly, to the whiteness of the discipline of philosophy. People identified as women make up not quite half of most of my classes. These patterns affect how I distribute the art supplies. I tend to give the worst supplies to groups of students who identify as white and/or have made clear in class that they have access to privilege through their social economic status. I don't want this exercise to reinscribe structural disadvantages for students I know already to be struggling. In a very few instances, the groups with severely limited supplies will pull off an incredibly creative mobile and win the contest; sometimes the groups who have every material advantage don't get their acts together in time and produce a mediocre mobile. You can discuss these unusual circumstances (and why they are unusual) in the debriefing period.

As students begin their work, watch for the groups who have limited supplies. As these groups of students get frustrated by the lack of scissors and glue, they often start to look around at what the other groups have. If you see them notice the disparity in the distribution of the supplies, head over and debrief them quietly. Tell them immediately, and then at the end, tell everyone, that this has been an experiment for which there are three hypotheses that in 20 years have never failed to be confirmed:

Hypotheses for the Art Exercise

1. The only students who will notice the arbitrary inequity of the distribution are those who have been disadvantaged by the distribution.
2. Students who have been advantaged by the distribution will not notice the arbitrary inequity of the distribution.
3. When it comes time to judge the quality of the mobiles, students from the advantaged groups are likely to commit the FAE; attributing the sorry state of the mobiles made by the disadvantaged groups to laziness, poor use of time, or unwise decision-making (why did they choose not to use any color when color was a criterion?!). See if you can get someone to confess this error in their own thinking. (Here is where you will discover what kind of trust you have built up in the room.) You might then ask students to reflect on ways that this cognitive error contributes to systemic injustice, by keeping them from recognizing the injustice in the first place. Be sure to draw parallels between the unjust distribution of the art supplies, and the structural injustices in the U.S. that link property taxes to K-12 school quality, SAT prep, and college preparedness more generally.

At the end of the class we discuss how the skills of perspective taking and seeking clarification can disrupt the Fundamental Attribution Error. After the art competition is over, I hang the student mobiles around the room and keep them up for the remainder of the term. They serve as a visual reminder that I often reference in later lectures. The lessons of the exercise can sometimes take a while to sink in. People coming to terms with their ignorance generally lack the focus needed to take seriously someone else's suffering. Empathy and patience become even more important here. Students make clear in conversation that they remember who was in what group, and who made which mobile. They report talking about this exercise with their families and friends. They write about it in their papers. Maybe they also remember something about the history of philosophy. Maybe we should change our learning outcomes. Of course, we should change our learning outcomes.

Conclusion: Educating for Peace

I have come to use Peace Literacy as an aspirational frame for my philosophy teaching, both in terms of content and pedagogy – it guides my teaching for accurate understanding about structural injustice and strategies for dismantling it, for developing phronesis through peace skills, and for developing deeper, richer capacities, not only for language and reason, but also empathy, curiosity, hope, imagination, and conscience. Philosophical topics concerning the cognitive habits and practices that bias our judgments about who can know and what counts as knowledge, and how those biased habits and practices inform and are informed by often unjust social and structural conditions – the teaching of each and all of these topics are enriched through the use of Peace Literacy content and pedagogy.

I focused on the art exercise as an example of the critical link between the development of Peace Literacy and the struggle against structural injustice. In the art exercise, inaccurate appeals to moral failings like laziness are both caused by and contribute to structural injustice for the under-supplied student groups who typically perform poorly in the exercise. Working for structural justice is intimately linked to having a more accurate understanding, in this case a more accurate understanding of the causal attributions of others' misfortune. Gaining this understanding requires peace skills like listening, perspective taking, and seeking clarification, which in turn is linked to the development of our capacity for empathy, conscience, curiosity, and reason.

I have shared in this essay my work using Peace Literacy in the service of justice, primarily though not exclusively, through teaching about cognitive biases, and the importance for each of us as individuals in unlearning the cognitive biases that keep us from recognizing *in*justice. But Peace Literacy helps remind us that while both our negative cognitive biases and our positive peace skills and habits of mind are learned by us as individuals, we individuals are part of communities that reinforce and are reinforced by broad structural patterns, social conventions, cultural expectations, historical practices, and institutions. Peace Literacy helps us identify the structural, social, and relational conditions that help create the communities within which breaking old habits is easier and building new positive skills more likely. It takes accurate understanding, skill building, and the development of capacities, and lots and lots of practice to live in peace, in community, with others. There is work to be done and it takes training and support to do it well.

Acknowledgements

For helpful commentary and support, I am grateful to the editors, to Paul K. Chappell, to my co-contributors, especially Qwo-Li Driskill and Marta Maldonado, to Christian Matheis, and to Anne Gillies.

Additional Resources

Audiovisuals

Huntley, M. (Director). (2006). *Redraw the balance* [Film]. MullenLowe Group. www.campaignlive.co.uk/article/gender-stereotyping-laid-bare-childrens-drawings-charity-campaign/1387345

Giraldo, G. (2000, August 8). *Comedy Central presents* [TV Series]. Comedy Central. https://www.cc.com/episodes/p0j6eq/comedy-central-presents-greg-giraldo-season-3-ep-10

Websites

Benson, B. (2016, September 1). *Cognitive bias cheat sheet*. Medium. https://medium.com/better-humans/cognitive-bias-cheat-sheet-55a472476b18

Olsen, A. (2018, August 3). *21 facts about Alexander Calder*. Sothebys. www.sothebys.com/en/articles/21-facts-about-alexander-calder

Clough, Sharyn, et al. (2017). *Peace Literacy curriculum*. Peace Literacy. www.peaceliteracy.org/curriculum

Greenwald, T., Benaji, M., & Nozek, B. (2011). *Implicit Bias Test*. Project Implicit. https://www.projectimplicit.net/

References

Boovy, B., & Osei-Kofi, N. (2020). Teaching about race in the DPD classroom. In N. Osei-Kofi, B. Boovy, & K. Furman (Eds.), *Approaches to social justice education: Equity and access in the college classroom* (pp. 189–204). Routledge.

Chappell, P. K. (2012). *Peaceful revolution*. Easton Studio Press.

Chappell, P. K. (2015). *The cosmic ocean*. Prospecta Press.

Chappell, P. K. (2017). *Soldiers of peace*. Easton Studio Press.

Chappell, P. K. (Forthcoming). A new peace paradigm: Our human needs and the tangles of trauma. Excerpted from *The transcendent mystery* (excerpt available for download at peaceliteracy.org).

Cherry, M., & Flanagan, O. (2018). *The moral psychology of anger*. Lanham MD: Rowman and Littlefield.

Eisner, E. W. (1979). *The educational imagination: On the design and evaluation of school programs*. Macmillan.

Gandhi, M. (1958). Speech at Victoria Hall, Geneva, December 10, 1931. In *Collected works* vol. *54* (pp. 415–421). Publications Division, Ministry of Information and Broadcasting, Government of India.

Gendler, T. (2011). On the epistemic costs of implicit bias. *Philosophical Studies, 156*, 33–63. https://doi.org/10.1007/s11098-011-9801-7

Heider, F. (1958). *The psychology of interpersonal relations*. Wiley.

hooks, b. (2003). *Teaching community: A pedagogy of hope*. Routledge.

Jones, E. E., & Harris, V. A. (1967). The attribution of attitudes. *Journal of Experimental Social Psychology, 3*(1), 1–24.

King, M. L.Jr. (1998). *The autobiography of Martin Luther King, Jr*. Warner Books.

Lorde, A. (1997). The uses of anger. *Women's Studies Quarterly, 25*(1/2), 278–285.

Lawrence, S. M. (1998). Unveiling positions of privilege: A hands-on approach to understanding racism. *Teaching of Psychology, 25*(3), 198. https://doi.org/10.1207/s15328023top2503_8

Matheis, C. (2019, July 18–23). *Nobody (a phenomenological hunch)* [Paper presentation]. Society for Philosophy in the Contemporary World 26th Annual Meeting, University of Central Arkansas, Conway, AR, United States.

McHugh, N. (2015). *The limits of knowledge: Generating pragmatist feminist cases for situated knowing*. SUNY.

McIntosh, P. (1988). White privilege and male privilege: A personal account of coming to see correspondences through work in Women's Studies. Working Paper 189, Wellesley Centers for Women, Wellesley, MA, United States.

Miller, J. G. (1984). Culture and the development of everyday social explanation. *Journal of Personality and Social Psychology*, *46*(5), 961. https://doi.org/10.1037/0022-3514.46.5.961

Osei-Kofi, N. (2013). The emancipatory potential of Arts-Based Research for social justice. *Equity & Excellence in Education*, *46*(1), 135–149. https://doi.org/10.1080/10665684.2013.750202

Pagan, N. (2008). Configuring the moral self: Aristotle and Dewey. *Foundations of Science*, *13*(3/4), 239–250. https://doi.org/10.1007/s10699-008-9137-8

Pettigrew, T. F. (1979) The ultimate attribution error: Extending Allport's cognitive analysis of prejudice. *Personality and Social Psychology Bulletin*, *5*(4), 461–476.

Ross, L. (1977). The intuitive psychologist and his shortcomings: Distortions in the attribution process. *Advances in Experimental Social Psychology*, *10*, 173–220.

Tate, S. A., & Page, D. (2018). Whiteliness and institutional racism: Hiding behind (un)conscious bias. *Ethics & Education*, *13*(1), 141–155. https://doi.org/10.1080/17449642.2018.1428718

7 From Here to There

Educating for Wholeness

Erich N. Pitcher and Charlene C. Martinez

> Love and justice are not two. Without inner change, there can be no outer change. Without collective change, no change matters.
>
> Reverend angel Kyodo Williams, Radical Dharma

How can we achieve the twin goals of wholeness and justice within higher education? In response to this question, we engaged in a series of iterative dialogues–both spoken and written–to develop a set of theories and practices that bring about greater wholeness and justice. Through our friendship, solidarity work, and collegial relationship, it became evident we have a shared commitment to achieving the goals of justice and wholeness within higher education. Our shared desire for wholeness emanates from the disjuncture that we both feel as we move across academic and student affairs spaces. Through our dialogues, we identified a key lever in the twin goals of justice and wholeness. Namely, sentipensante pedagogy as a framework to achieve wholeness in social justice education specifically, and higher education more broadly. How we enter this conversation about justice and wholeness and from what subject position matters. As such, we each explore our subject positions in relation to the theories and practices.

About Us

Charlene

Over the course of nearly two decades, my professional roles in student and multicultural affairs span five campuses, ranging from a large public land-grant to small liberal arts colleges. I have also served in roles within cultural resource centers and across a broad spectrum of experiential learning organizations in student affairs. In my early professional years, I quickly realized I needed to strengthen my abilities to hold space for emotions and all of the complexities that students bring with them, especially in doing social justice work. I discovered the intimate connection between healing work and nurturing change agents. I would spend countless hours on the couches of student service centers processing with students how they experienced microaggressions as a result of

DOI: 10.4324/9781003091998-9

their minoritized identities or helping them make meaning of their lived experiences in higher education. These precious moments brought a clarity to what I had intuitively gathered: in order for students to uncover their purpose they had to do critical internal work of unpacking how they have come to understand themselves and the world surrounding their belief systems. This would often involve the pain of the past and understanding the resilience and assets they had a result of their cultural communities (Yosso, 2005).

Regardless of the position that I hold, I identify as an educator, and also a healer and cultural organizer. My work weaves together creative methods and social justice education. I also infuse ethnic studies and the liberal arts into my practice, transgressing normative frames as a student affairs practitioner. My graduate degree in Education, with an emphasis in Multicultural Counseling, provided me tools for understanding how everyone brought up in this imperfect world requires healing. Part of this process revealed that in uncovering and accessing my own stories, I gained strength to be able to support students in navigating their own. Kip Fulbeck, an arts professor and mentor in undergrad, nurtured within me the importance of telling my story of growing up mixed heritage through the arts. Unknowingly, creativity and self-exploration would become a core value in how I guide, mentor, and support students, and it is now embedded into student service praxis.

As an Asian-Latinx American cis-woman at Oregon State University, a Predominantly White Institution (PWI) in a (recently) historically white region, I am required to do mental and emotional gymnastics on a regular basis. In spite of the hurdles and nuances of doing social justice work with my social identities – often being the only person of color in the room – I am relentless in my commitment to grow as a practitioner. While I am aware of the ways I have targeted group memberships, I have grown in my ability to do critical work in my privileged identities. I take seriously the ways in which I have power in class, educational status, national origin, and sexuality. From my early college years as a student until now, I continue to challenge myself to lean into the discomfort of the ways in which the power I have impacts others. This is an imperfect process.

A powerful moment of growth came when I coordinated and instructed the Arts and Social Justice Living Learning Community (ASJLLC) that we will further talk about in this chapter. In creating gender-inclusive housing for first-year students, I encountered having to do homework when it came to variance in gender identity and ensuring that students had a safer place to reside while at the university. While being an advocate for creating gender inclusive housing often took going against the grain at the university and stretched my comfort zone in having challenging conversations with colleagues, it ultimately changed systems and processes on behalf of students. Through the process I remain grateful to others who have held space for me when giving critical feedback, allowing me to process how I can show up better. This story demonstrates how I do my work in higher education. In alignment with community organizers and activist scholars, I believe that changing the world requires the critical work of changing ourselves (Jahoda & Woolard, 2019). In this chapter, I offer stories and reflections which I hope will empower faculty committed to social change work to do the same.

Erich

At the time of writing this chapter, I was an academic affairs educator serving as the Program Lead and Instructor for Adult and Higher Education at the College of Education at Oregon State University. My educational background and much of my professional experiences are within higher education and student affairs. My most recent appointment allowed me to develop my capacities as an advisor/femmetor (femme mentor), in which I take a holistic approach to support student wellness. As I have iterated in my advising practice, I have begun to ask students about their basic needs, become attuned to the emotional lives of students, and consider the ways that I need to adjust my teaching and advising practices to better support wholeness for students. This approach is quite different from much of the mentoring and advising I received, which was far more cold, distant, and transactional. I also had to learn to practice vulnerability as I am not a person who is oriented in a socially open way. I recognized that my teaching demanded some level of vulnerability from students and, as such, that I should at least be willing to share tender parts of my story with students. It still makes me anxious to talk about my feelings and stories in front of students.

Through my academic appointment I enjoy deep partnerships with my student affairs colleagues. I am also responsible for the preparation of student affairs and higher education leaders through my teaching and advising. In fact, my wholeness and thriving is deeply connected to my relationships and connections with educators and students who are struggling for wholeness and justice. Additionally, I approach my educational work as a justice-minded organizer. I am uninterested in neoliberal forms of diversity work. I am focused on justice. Further, within my classroom, office, and meetings, I focus my energy on how to be more fully present, to be present for others, and to practice my own wholeness.

In terms of my social location, I am white, middle class, highly educated, queer and trans educator. My whiteness allows me to navigate Oregon State University with ease. My ongoing work with other white folks around our racism often feels incomplete and stunted by the historical and contemporary contexts of Oregon as a racist white utopia. My adherence to white cultural norms and patterns of communication have currency within the university. As I continue to unlearn white ways of being, particularly around affect, this is where my healing and wholeness journey continues to lead me.

Even as I diverge from gender norms, I am mostly viewed as an authority and inherently respectable. As a gender non-conforming educator, I routinely experience sideways glances. People who have only spoken to me over the phone are confused about whether to call me sir or ma'am. People who come to my office to meet me in-person are confused by the pairing of a masculine name and a feminine gender presentation. There is a good bit of vulnerability for me in attempting to show up authentically at work within my social location. In many ways, I use my weirdness (gender or otherwise) and midwestern friendliness to ease some of the intensity of my personality.

My experiences within student affairs are shaped by the social locations I am describing here. In particular, my work with my co-author and co-conspirator is rooted in our mutual interest in working in solidarity with each other around our marginalized and dominant social group memberships. For example, I have worked with Charlene in several contexts regarding issues of race, including a research project about multiraciality. We have also collaborated about how to support gender non-conforming students in higher education.

Throughout this essay, we pose questions and offer answers to guide us and the reader towards theories and practices that achieve the goals of wholeness and justice. We draw on examples from the Arts and Social Justice Living Learning Community to demonstrate theories and practices that further justice and wholeness.

On Wholeness

ERICH: Charlene, what does wholeness mean to you?
CHARLENE: For me wholeness is the ability to feel fully present to one's self, one's community, and the world. Wholeness allows us to know our power and exercise our agency. Wholeness allows us to exhale and breathe deeply without anticipation of future anxiety or the remnants of past trauma.
ERICH: So, what is the opposite of wholeness?
CHARLENE: The opposite of wholeness is not brokenness or a lack of suffering, but unattended to damage.
ERICH: It seems to me that with the work we take up in this chapter, we are particularly concerned with the kinds of damage that marginalized students and educators face.
CHARLENE: What do you mean by damage?
ERICH: Damage comes in the form of living within systems of oppression, including, but not limited to, racism, sexism, classism, ableism, heterosexism, and cisgenderism.
CHARLENE: I agree. I believe the damage comes from being undervalued and unseen within educational spaces. Damage comes from witnessing violence and abuse, being subject to violence, and perpetuating violence. Damage comes through the generations as intergenerational trauma (Bombay et al., 2009; Graff, 2014; Sangalang & Vang, 2017; Sigal & Weinfeld, 1989).

We both view damage as something that prevents us – students and educators – from being present with ourselves through internalized oppression and dominance (Sensoy & DiAngelo, 2017). Damage prevents us from being able to meaningfully connect with others. Damage prevents us from feeling a sense of connection and community for which we are hard wired (Lieberman, 2013). Without adequate attention, the damage marginalized students and educators live with will ultimately negatively shape educational experiences. Further, without addressing this damage by creating spaces for healing and wholeness, educators run the risk of graduating students with ongoing unaddressed damage at best and, at worst, further damaging students. As such, we see sentipensante pedagogy as a critical framework for both curricular and co-curricular learning. We focus on sentipensante pedagogy to get from here (damaged, disconnected, not belonging) to there (wholeness, connected, belonging).

On Sentipensante

ERICH: Charlene, what do you think Laura Rendón (2009) means by sentipensante pedagogy?

CHARLENE: I understand sentipensante pedagogy as a teaching/learning practice that centers non-dominant knowledge systems towards wholeness creating possibilities for liberation of the self and communities.

ERICH: In other words, sentipensante asks teachers and learners to bridge between intuition/sensing and intellectualism/thinking to support students in more deeply knowing themselves and the world. How we each connected to sentipensante also matters.

CHARLENE: I learned about sentipensante from a Latinx faculty member at Sacramento State around the time that Laura Rendón published *Sentipensante Pedagogy: Educating for Wholeness, Social Justice and Liberation*. This faculty member reflected back to me that her leadership style as the Director of a Multicultural Center incorporated multiple modalities and ways of knowing that was inclusive of a critical lens, yet highly empathetic to the needs of historically under-represented communities, students and staff alike. During that time, I understood sentipensante as an overarching framework that helped to reconcile the impacts of neoliberal administrative decision-making processes on historically under-represented communities. The community center I co-created with students, staff, and faculty was a representation of the culture that sentipensante has the ability to foster. Namely, the staff were trained to be critical and caring, and to hold space for big vision around culture change on campus towards facilitating greatness. In this space student leaders grew to unapologetically tell their stories through art and community building. However, this did not mean that it was a space immune to conflict or having difficult conversations. The community center ethos embodied thinking and sensing pedagogies that brought community members to change campus culture to become more aware of power, privilege, and oppression in our everyday actions.

ERICH: I longed for sentipensante well before knowing the word. While I was working on my master's degree, I also worked at a church as a social justice programs coordinator. There was a sense of disconnection and discomfort I felt as I moved across the two spaces of church life and the university. Within my master's degree program, which focused so intensely on my cognitive and leadership capacities, I yearned for a more intuitive, sensing, spiritual rootedness. Within my church life, which focused on my and other congregants' spiritual lives and sense of purpose in the world, I yearned for a more theoretically and cognitively grounded approach. It was not until my doctoral education that I began to understand that what I yearned for in my master's program and church life respectively could be intertwined. I read *Sentipensante Pedagogy* in my teaching and learning doctoral seminar. It was then that I understood that the spiritual groundedness I felt in church could be matched with the cognitive experience I had in graduate school. Sentipensante to me means that my whole self can be brought to educational spaces and that in so doing, there will be room for my healing, the healing of others, and potentially the healing of the world.

A Refashioned Dream of Teaching and Learning

Moving from our individual entry points into sentipensante, we turn to Laura Rendón (2009), who articulated the vision of Sentipensante Pedagogy as "a refashioned dream of teaching and learning ... based on wholeness, harmony, social justice, and liberation" (p. 132). Sentipensante is an educational practice that bridges between Western and non-Western ways of knowing, intuition and intellect, and formal knowledge and inherited wisdom (Rendón, 2009). The word sentipensante loosely translates into thinking/sensing (Rendón, 2009). An approach like sentipensante is necessary if we are to educate towards wholeness. Additionally, strengthening the capacity for emotional intelligence beginning with faculty is an essential component to creating holistic environments for student learning (Rendón, 2009).

Having said this, sentipensante is not merely a pedagogical strategy, rather it is a belief system and a way of teaching which integrates multiple ways of knowing, sensing and thinking domains, social change, and contemplative practices (Rendón, 2009). In fact, Rendón (2009) cautions that this framework must be met with enthusiasm and a willingness from its practitioners to engage in building capacity for contemplative practice and emotion-centered work. Further she notes that:

> Sentipensante Pedagogy is not for every professor or for every student. A unitive, harmonious pedagogy is very challenging to prepare for and to implement. A significant amount of preparation is required from the instructor. Professors will need professional development in the uses of contemplative practice and the design of a relationship-centered

classroom based on caring, trust, support, and validation. In addition, educators will need assistance with the development and incorporation of a curriculum that is inclusive of multicultural perspectives and worldviews and that is focused on social justice. A professor must be willing to take risks and to deal with emotions and tensions that often arise in class. Also important is the professor's openness and willingness to engage in self-reflexivity and in the politically risky behavior to do things differently in the face of institutional resistance.

(p. 136)

ERICH: What does this quote mean for those who want to do work that is aligned with sentipensante pedagogy?

CHARLENE: Dealing with emotions and tensions that arise from understanding issues of power is part of the process of dialogue, and for many, not a typical part of academic or student-affairs training. Negotiating the difficult reality of managing emotions is also complex, especially when teaching in a historically white region and institution. My training in multicultural counseling helped me to realize that healing at the individual and group levels is an integral part of equity and inclusion work. This is why I have also gravitated toward critical studies disciplines which rely upon embodied knowledges, storytelling, and meaning making from holistic places. Yet, even in these disciplines teaching the content of social justice does not mean that professors are equipped to deal with the classroom dynamics of racism, sexism, or classism as they appear in real time.

CHARLENE: What about for you Erich?

ERICH: One invitation that sentipensante pedagogy offers is emotion-centered work. I had to work really hard to even be able to name my own feelings and to talk about them openly. I am still practicing how to access my emotions when dynamics of racism, classism, or sexism become evident in my or other's behavior. A decade ago, I was not yet ready to implement sentipensante pedagogy, I still needed to do a great deal of healing to be whole enough to consider approaching teaching and learning in this way. In addition to the challenges I face/d in connecting with my emotions, I need/ed to grow my capacity to engage contemplative practices. As I described earlier, I worked in a church and this allowed me to develop tools for ritual, reflection, and contemplation. Additionally, I have followed healing justice work that helps me to better understand what healing might look like for social justice advocates.

How to Get from Here to There

The National Conference on Race and Ethnicity in American Higher Education (NCORE) brings together higher education leaders across the U.S. to address the resurgence of racist incidents in higher education. We met at the conference in 2019 and had a dialog about our chapter and our approach to praxis of wholeness and justice. Through our dialog, we realized that individual commitments to wholeness and justice need to make connections across divisional lines to be effective. We first explore the way we did this and then provide an example of how deep connection and relationships can build programs that advance justice and bring about more wholeness. We sought to support one another as whole people because we know that deep, connective relationships allow both parties to grow.

CHARLENE: How has my work in student affairs influenced your work? Does it feel like I helped you grow in any particular sphere? Student Affairs or Academic Affairs?

ERICH: It's both for me, actually ... I understand Student Affairs differently because I can see the way that you've interpreted what this practice is in a way that I did not have models for. I had not seen the kind of work that you were doing within the cultural centers anyplace else, particularly the arts-based pieces. I started integrating it into my pedagogy almost immediately. Your use of journey maps is an example. I do a modification of that activity where I ask students to do a journey map based on a theory. They put themselves into the student development theories through their own journey maps and use their story to navigate through. I probably would not be teaching student development theory that way if we hadn't worked together. So, in that way, my Student Affairs practice changed, but then it also changed my Academic Affairs practice to start to engage art and story. I don't think I would have gotten through the past experience without you, and I'm thankful for that. That was a tough time in my life. Knowing that I had you mattered. That you saw me, that you understood, mattered. It really mattered. [Erich is crying]

CHARLENE: I think we helped each other. I know you helped me through that time, and I think the stories and the art that we were doing with the students helped us stabilize ourselves as well because it gave us hope during a challenging time. We knew we needed to be better, and we needed to be more whole. We saw the students going through the same thing. They had the questions around wholeness and enoughness and politics among groups. There was never a denial of the magic that happened when people connected at a soul level and shared their stories and got some sense of clarity. Then, they put that back into their work in their classrooms. They developed courage and bravery in places that other people didn't even know that they had in them. They surprised themselves as they became facilitators of story circles and developed their voice through the practice of their own storytelling. They emerged as change makers in their respective disciplines and within their communities... with that particular cohort, we saw them becoming recognized leaders among their peers. That is such an incredible inspiration to know that the affinity-based work, the community-based work, the heart-work that we were doing with each other cultivated student leadership. They saw that we were also real people going tough times. We infused creative methods to express our realities and find ways of being in our bodies more authentically. I believe this created a container among the group of students to develop resonance, heal, and thrive. Two years after the program ended, the affinity generated within that cohort lives on through community calls as they continue to support each other. While this particular story took place in the co-curricular realm, it is important to realize that you never know what will plant the seed for transformation in learners. The arts-based healing and storytelling practices are now ones that the individuals of the cohort are taking into their respective communities in Oregon from the medical field to the rural community organizing and beyond.

What we revealed in this portion of our dialog is the importance of coming to understand the emotional-spiritual-cognitive dimensions of our work. Without our connectivity and commitment to trying on new tools in our practice we would not have been able to iterate, learn, and grow. As educators of social justice education, it is imperative that we find community or people who are open to experimental design and the process of vulnerability. Next we turn to specific examples that we hope exemplify the aforementioned.

Praxis Example: The Arts and Social Justice Living Learning Community

The living learning community project emerged from conversations from both academic and student affairs at Oregon State University. When professors Qwo-Li Driskill (Queer Studies) and Natchee Barnd (Ethnic Studies), and student affairs practitioners, Jeff Kenney (Diversity & Cultural Engagement) and Ben Mederios (University Housing & Dining Services) engaged in the initial brainstorm, they were hopeful about the prospect of student exposure and exploration of social justice concepts and disciplines through creative methods. An indirect goal of the project was to bolster enrollments in Ethnic Studies, Women, Gender, and Sexuality Studies, and/or Queer Studies majors. After the idea of the project came to fruition, I (Charlene) coordinated the effort from the ground up serving as a convener and the instructor for the student seminars.

Many of the first-year students who started in ASJLLC attribute their retention and involvement at the university to their early experiences in the courses. The majority of students who engaged with an aspect of the program became student leaders in the cultural resource centers on campus, student activists, community organizers, and have graduated with a purpose of changing the world in positive ways. Students also found that early exposure to critical studies fields in social justice allowed them to find affinity in their classrooms or gave them rationale to keep pursuing those disciplines, especially if they had not entered as a major or minor in Ethnic, Queer, or Women, Gender, and Sexuality Studies.

The ASJLLC story matters because it is an example of a social justice education program extending past the classroom and into the residential experience and contributed to many students' sense of self-efficacy and belonging. For the most part, students entered the program with a desire to care for the world in some way. Many of their passions were connected to their emerging gender identities, understanding of their social locations, and questions about social issues that deeply mattered to them. In their first quarter and first year at the university the students began to tackle difficult topics of power and privilege by centering their own positionalities and expressing their views through art. The ASJLLC became a microcosm of what is possible when we partner across divisional lines, focus on deep relationship building of which supporting each other as whole people matters as much as developing a program.

An example of some of the work that students engaged in through ASJLLC includes a project where they created emojis, as representations of how they were feeling in the moment. This important and humanizing exercise allowed the class to land on common ground and to build empathy for each other's conditions and experiences. It was also fun and engaging and students grew to look forward to it at the beginning of every class. Over the course of the ten weeks students would have a collection of their emojis over the quarter. The opportunity to reflect and connect with themselves and each other became a critical element of the classroom experience. This exercise had an added element: it allowed for the identification of unmet basic needs and provided an opportunity to refer students to much needed resources.

The reflection time carved out at the beginning of the class enabled intentional time and opportunity for students to ground themselves. Students were invited to share their emojis and how they were doing. As an additional prompt, students were encouraged to consider what, if anything, was preventing them from being fully present and what they would need to "leave at the door" in order to more fully come into the present moment to be prepared and engage in the course.

Both the use of emotions and identification of unmet basic needs reflects sentipensante in asking students to account for their emotional lives and the conditions under which they are living. For first-year students and transfer students, acclimating to the university can take an emotional and mental toll. These exercises allowed for a more holistic integration as they were able to process their transition stories and emerging identities in a place that created possibilities for connection.

Story Circles

Another example of our praxis is the utilization of different forms of art practices as a critical site for first-year students to share their lived experiences and to creatively process their stories/experiences of belonging and not belonging. To support their processing, we have utilized a Story Circles format to support storytelling, building empathy, and meaning making among their peers. Story Circles (USDAC, 2015) come from several traditions that engage the power of story to build connection and empathy between groups of people (e.g., Aguirre, 2000; Beverley, 2004; Corntassel, 2009; StoryCenter. org). Story Circles have three benefits: (a) to develop one's narrative, (b) to nurture connections to community, and (c) to practice deep listening. Story Circles require both thinking and sensing, in keeping with sentipensante.

The basic idea is that groups of five to seven sit in a circle and tell a story based on a shared prompt, in this case about belonging or not belonging. The storytelling is timed to ensure equal airtime. There is no cross-talk or feedback given. Everyone thanks the storyteller and takes a collective breath between stories. So simple, and yet so transformative. The art then led into exhibition and open mic after the presidential election of 45 that illuminated their fears, frustrations, and hope for the future.

Praxis Example: Arts-based Projects as Praxis

Our final intervention relates to the importance of emotion-center work and emotional intelligence within the context of student and academic affairs partnerships. If a group of educators is unwilling to engage in the difficult work of unearthing systems of oppression and facing the brutal realities of the injustices we see in society, then these partnerships will continue to maintain the status quo of society and educational practices that exacerbate injustice.

As an instructor and mentor, I (Charlene) learned that many times students are looking for an environment to explore their identities and experiences. Most importantly, we need to remember that most humans desire to be seen and valued. Generating assignments which infuse creativity, reflection, and critical studies allows students to engage in challenging content through entry points which are welcoming (the arts) and salient (their own stories or stories of their communities). Arts-based projects can also be used as way to bring contemplative practice to educational spaces. In this section, we reflect on examples which illuminate how the arts can be utilized in curricular and co-curricular transformative learning for social justice education.

Students within the Arts and Social Justice Living Learning Community (ASJLLC) addressed critical issues like race, class, gender, and sexuality by exploring their social locations and histories through creative practice. It allowed them to express themselves through poetry, writing, or film. The assignments themselves encouraged students to connect with issues around their own racial or gender identities that were alive for them. Weekly assignments instructed students to pair art mediums of their interest, including visual arts, literary arts, theater, and music with a social justice issue area that was meaningful to them. The final project became a showcase of their best pieces, allowing the campus community to learn from their stories and growth. ASJLLC graduating seniors and alumni attributed some of their earliest memories of feeling a sense of belonging on campus to some of the arts-based assignments they completed in those seminars.

These reflective exercises through the arts allowed students to gain confidence, find strength, and resilience through their narratives combined with history and social issues. In the end, some students chose to talk about personal stories of struggle and resilience, others spoke about global and systemic issues. It was an honor and privilege to witness students finding their voices and passions about issues surrounding food insecurity, familial connections to the prison system, or navigating their gender non-conforming and multiracial identities. The final project brought together community members, administrators, family members, and various affinity groups. There was mutual admiration between the student storytellers of the course and the audience. The presentations moved people in ways the students had not anticipated and gave them motivation to continue their journeys as changemakers even after the course concluded.

The Healing Card project originated from the group of peer educators who became principle facilitators for Story Circles. Integrating creativity as a form of expression and meaning- making can support wholeness and healing and can also be used in the co-curricular realm. At the end of each Story Circle, after reflecting on their own and the stories they heard, facilitators invited participants to generate a word and corresponding image to support their healing process (Martinez, 2019). Images were then utilized to develop a deck of Healing Cards with reflection questions on the backside of the cards. Cards included words and art such as: writing, community, balance, belonging, nourish, freedom, growth, courage, overcome, and self-care. Each card corresponds to a story a participant told or heard.

Upon seeing and holding the full deck of cards and reflecting about the corresponding stories, student leaders developed pride in what they were able to co-create based off of storytelling, reflection, and art. While the Healing Card project started at the university it has gained momentum in the regional community. At a Portland Art Museum gathering of K-12 teachers of all disciplines, participants were inspired by the Story Circles and Healing Card project that they wanted to learn how to facilitate the exercises and recreate in their own versions in their classrooms. As a part of the process, they enjoyed generating a Healing Card deck of their own. Some of the teachers left the workshop saying that the experience was restorative and reenergizing. Two women of color teachers said that they were grateful for a moment to center their own healing, and that the exercise was timely and necessary for them to keep going.

What we have come to realize, through our shared commitments, is that it is our job to co-create opportunities for students to be able to develop a sense of wholeness by wrestling with difficult topics of injustice and oppression with a sense of purpose and hope. There are few places in academia that allow students to experiment with difficult topics through creative means. By intentionally carving out exercises and assignments which allow students to be seen and validated through their own stories, we open the possibility of new social justice leaders to emerge.

The Capacity for Contemplative Practice

As described earlier, sentipensante, and the types of facilitating the types of activities we have shared thus far, are not for all educators necessarily. Part of what makes sentipensante not for everyone is an individual educator's ability to hold what will come up especially if emotions, personal and community histories, and inherited traumas become an important part of the learning experience. Part of the ability to hold all that will or could come up, is having gone into these kinds of places with one's self and/or in community with others. As Malcolm X stated, "You can't teach what you don't know, and you can't lead where you won't go" (cited in Howard et al., 2016). What is required of sentipensante-informed educators is the desire to continue to engage in ongoing self-work and personal transformation. hooks described the importance of self-work elsewhere as engaged pedagogy (hooks, 1994). Part of how one deepens into the work of sentipensante is through contemplative practice and reflection on one's own story, as well as empathy building and perspective taking. In our dialog, we focused specifically on breathing, meditation, and slowing down as critical interventions that allow us to access the bridging work and meaningful partnership we seek to create in the world.

CHARLENE: Social justice educator Shakti Butler is someone who models this in an outstanding way. She often begins her talks by slowing the energy in the room down so that people can breathe. She does this by simple grounding herself and breathing deeply. She then invites the audience to breath. She spends the first five minutes, sometimes longer, breathing with the audience. This allows people to get present with what is happening in their bodies and offers a moment for introspection. She does this because she knows the content of her talk or videos will touch on some pretty intense social justice topics. And the intensity of the topic needs to be met with an appropriate energy level for people to sit with the discomfort of those topics.

Moments like these are gifts and can often be overlooked. While activities like these may seem small and insignificant, they can fundamentally offer moments of connection that are not found in classrooms or in higher education in general. In watching Shakti over the years, she is deliberate in inviting opportunities for people to connect their mind, body, and soul before talking about potentially triggering topics. I think that is a beautiful lesson: account for basic human needs when teaching about sensitive issues.

ERICH: I'm really relating with what you're saying. One of the things that I do before I go into a classroom or a workshop is I clear my schedule for about 30 minutes to an hour before I'm supposed to be at the thing. I make sure that I put a block on my calendar so that I'm not checking email and eating and whatever other thing I feel like I need to attend to before I go to my scheduled appointments. I really try to connect with my breath and say, "What's on top for me today? What could I let go of so that I can be present in this room right now?"

ERICH: I value this mindfulness and this connecting with breath and making sure I had some water and some food. Even if things are really hard in my world, I know I need to do that in order to show up and also have a meaningful check-in for the students to do the same. Taking breaths together. What's on top of folks? Where are they at today? What are they bringing with them into this space? Can they let go of that thing for a little bit so that we could do this learning together? Or does it need to be about that thing?

CHARLENE: I think this last piece about emotional intelligence, is not just vacant from Academic Affairs. It can also be vacant from practitioners in Student Affairs. The process of desensitization is unfortunately due to how our capitalistic world operates. I think that's why anxiety and depression are increasing because people don't have an ability to be whole in many spaces. Sometimes, we just need to stop everything and go, "What are we really doing here?" Do we need to have another conversation that's going to be super rigid or are we going to actually walk the talk around serving our students and meeting them where they are by actually talking about hard things? Re-centering our values is an everyday act, we must take a moment to remember that we convey our values through our behaviors and actions. Building capacity for emotional intelligence must become a regular and intentional practice.

Conclusion

At the outset of this chapter, we stated that we experience disjuncture as educators as we move across student affairs and academic affairs spaces. More specifically, we are both drawn towards spaces that allow us to do justice work and to experience wholeness. We both agree that it is not enough for us to teach about power, privilege, and oppression without thinking about the social locations and conditions from which our students are entering the conversation. Without thinking about the holistic dimensions of our students, we miss a crucial part of the project of moving our societies toward just and empathy-driven worlds. Educators need to engage empathy to support students in becoming change agents and to understand that every person needs an affirming entry point to that work. Inherent within justice-oriented spaces are the need to talk about our emotions and our stories. We have also introduced creative expression as another important tool in this conversation. Practices that have the potential to disrupt a sense of disconnection within classrooms, communities, and social justice efforts. As we reflect together on the importance of educating for wholeness, it is clear that we need each other. In this case, "we" includes us as authors, you as readers, but also practitioners and students who can be transformed by the power of connection and community. Our concern is that if we do not educate towards wholeness, we will continue to fail our students. Failing our students will be especially damaging if we espouse to develop change agents yet refuse to consider the ways in which empathy and sensing knowledges can improve our capacities to change the world. In other words, when we discount the affective domain and fail to meaningfully integrate the emotional responses to social justice curriculum and lived experiences of our students within a traditionally heady space like classrooms, we are staying here and not going there.

In order to become stronger teachers and facilitators of justice-oriented classrooms, faculty ought to consider not only the benefits to students derived from sentipensante pedagogy, in particular the importance of reflexivity, but also the importance of such approaches as they/we teach against the grain of normative expectations within higher education (Rendón, 2009; Shahjahan, 2005). Given the rates of anxiety and depression growing among Generation Z, with nearly two-thirds of college seniors surveyed reporting occasionally or frequently feeling depressed during the past year, we collectively need to reimagine how and where we connect with students (Seemiller & Grace, 2019). Additionally, connection and community serve as buffers for individuals experiencing depression and anxiety; as such, strong student and academic affairs partnerships could play an important role in better supporting the health and well-being of students (Wei et al., 2010; Woodford et al., 2015).

While sensing and thinking pedagogies may not be for every faculty member, we believe it is essential to consider the repercussions to the souls of students if classrooms continue to operate in disconnected ways. This is not to say that every instructor should become just like a student affairs practitioner; however, thinking creatively about how and where students are allowed to bring their whole selves into the conversations that occur in classrooms should be a priority for all faculty. While this may not be the traditional format of a student and academic affairs partnership, building the capacity of instructors to support integrative experiences should be a priority for all within higher education. In light of all that we have shared in this chapter, we conclude with a call to educators bracing against injustice, who intuitively know that what is happening in their work context is wrong, to breathe, to connect with yourself, and to connect with colleagues who will link arms with you to do justice-oriented work.

Additional Resources

Readings

brown, a. m. (2017). *Emergent strategy: Shaping change, changing worlds*. AK Press.

Chung. L. C., & Rendón, L. I. (2018). Education for wholeness in the intersections. *Diversity & Democracy, 21*(1), 8–12.

Hill, P. S. (2017). Let my story speak for me: Story circles as a pedagogical tool. In Behrman, C., Lyons, B., Hill, P., Slowiak, J., Webb, D., & Dreussi, A. S. (Eds.), *The Akron story circle project: Rethinking race in classroom and community* (pp. 51–75). The University of Akron Press.

Martinez, C. C. (2019). Story Circles, changing culture, and deepening leadership. *New Directions for Student Leadership, 163*, 57–71. https://doi.org/10.1002/yd.20347

Rendón, L. (2009). *Sentipensante (sensing/thinking) pedagogy: Educating for wholeness, social justice and liberation.* Stylus Publishing, LLC.

Treleaven, D. A., & Britton, W. (2018). *Trauma-sensitive mindfulness: Practices for safe and transformative healing*, 1st ed. W.W Norton.

Websites

Anaissie, T., Cary, V., Clifford, D., Malarkey, T., & Wise, S. (2017, March 14). *Liberatory design cards.* https://dschool.stanford.edu/resources/liberatory-design-cards

Asian American Literary Review. (2017, January 13). *Asian American tarot: A mental health project.* https://www.kickstarter.com/projects/1750978990/asian-american-tarot-a-mental-health-project

CMind: The Center for Contemplative Mind in Society (n.d.). www.contemplativemind.org/

Creative Reaction Lab *Equity-centered community design (ECCD)*.www.creativereactionlab.com/our-approach

Integrated Learning for Social Change (2018, May 1). *Healing cards.* https://see.oregonstate.edu/healing-cards

Jahoda, S., & Woolard, C. (2019). *Making and being.* https://makingandbeing.com/

The Circle Way (n.d.). *Meaningful check-in questions*.www.thecircleway.net/articles/2016/12/27/questions-for-check-ins

U.S. Department of Arts & Culture (n.d.). *Revolution of values.* https://usdac.us/takeaction

U.S. Department of Arts & Culture (2015). *Story circles.* https://usdac.us/storycircles

References

Aguirre, Jr., A. (2000). Academic storytelling: A critical race theory story of affirmative action. *Sociological Perspectives, 43*(2), 319–339.

Beverley, J. (2004). *Testimonio: On the politics of truth.* University of Minnesota Press.

Bombay, A., Matheson, K., & Anisman, H. (2009). Intergenerational trauma: Convergence of multiple processes among First Nations peoples in Canada. *International Journal of Indigenous Health, 5*(3), 6–47.

Corntassel, J. (2009). Indigenous storytelling, truth-telling, and community approaches to reconciliation. *ESC: English Studies in Canada, 35*(1), 137–159.

Graff, G. (2014). The intergenerational trauma of slavery and its aftermath. *The Journal of Psychohistory, 41*(3), 181–197.

hooks, b. (1994). *Teaching to transgress: Education as the practice of freedom.* Routledge.

Howard, T. C., Tunstall, J., & Flennaugh, T. K. (2016). *Expanding college access for urban youth: What schools and colleges can do.* Teachers College Press.

Jahoda, S., & Woolard, C. (2019). *Making and being*. Pioneer Works Press.

Lieberman, M. D. (2013). *Social: Why our brains are wired to connect*. Crown Publisher.

Rendón, L. (2009). *Sentipensante (sensing/thinking) pedagogy: Educating for wholeness, social justice and liberation*. Stylus Publishing, LLC.

Sangalang, C. C., & Vang, C. (2017). Intergenerational trauma in refugee families: A systematic review. *Journal of Immigrant and Minority Health, 19*(3), 745–754.

Seemiller, C., & Grace, M. (2019). *Generation Z: A century in the making*. Routledge.

Sensoy, Ö., & DiAngelo, R. J. (2017). *Is everyone really equal?: An introduction to key concepts in social justice education*, 2nd ed. Teachers College Press.

Shahjahan, R. A. (2005). Spirituality in the academy: Reclaiming from the margins and evoking a transformative way of knowing the world. *International Journal of Qualitative Studies in Education, 18*(6), 685–711.

Sigal, J. J., & Weinfeld, M. (1989). *Trauma and rebirth: Intergenerational effects of the Holocaust*. Praeger Press.

US Department of Arts and Culture. (2015). *Story circles*. https://usdac.us/storycircles

Woodford, M. R., Kulick, A., & Atteberry, B. (2015). Protective factors, campus climate, and health outcomes among sexual minority college students. *Journal of Diversity in Higher Education, 8*(2), 73–87. https://doi.org/10.1037/a0038552

Wei, M., Liao, K. Y. H., Chao, R. C. L., Mallinckrodt, B., Tsai, P. C., & Botello-Zamarron, R. (2010). Minority stress, perceived bicultural competence, and depressive symptoms among ethnic minority college students. *Journal of Counseling Psychology, 57*(4), 411–422.

Yosso, T. (2005). Whose culture has capital? A critical race theory discussion of community cultural wealth. *Race, Ethnicity and Education, 8*(1), 69–91.

Section 3
Destabilizing Dominant Narratives

8 "The Tree of Anger"

Queer and Trans Studies in the Difference, Power, and Discrimination Program at Oregon State University

H. Rakes and Qwo-Li Driskill

In writing about the necessity of understanding the ways multiple forms of oppression are experienced by queer women of color, Audre Lorde (1973) writes in her poem "Who Said it was Simple," "There are so many roots to the tree of anger/that sometimes the branches shatter/before they bear" (p. 39). As two scholars and teachers in Queer and Trans Studies that experience multiple – though different – systems of power and control, we read Lorde's metaphor of the "tree of anger" as the embodied experience, and logical response, to lives conditioned by intersecting forms of oppression. We read the "shattering" of the branches as those moments in which the possibilities of resistance and transformation are broken before anger can be put into "use." In her pivotal essay, "The Uses of Anger: Women Responding to Racism" published in *Sister Outsider*, Lorde (1984a) writes:

> (A)nger expressed and translated into action in the service of our vision and our future is a liberating and strengthening act of clarification, for it is in the painful process of this translation that we identify who are our allies with whom we have grave differences, and who are our genuine enemies. Anger is loaded with information and energy.
>
> (p. 127)

Anger, when put into use to end systemic oppression, has the possibility of bearing fruit for our collective liberation.

Queer Studies and Trans Studies are integral to teaching issues of power and oppression, particularly when centered on queer and trans people of color critiques. Understanding Lorde's metaphor of oppression located in the "tree of anger," and within a national context of rising racism, transphobia, homophobia, and misogyny, this chapter narrates the work of developing queer and trans studies courses and curriculum in Queer Studies at Oregon State University. We centralize the entwined relationship to racialization and colonization and argue for pedagogies and curriculum that enable us to uproot the multiple roots of "the tree of anger" and take seriously Lorde's (1973) calls to put anger to transformative use towards bearing the fruit of collective liberation rather than allowing the "branches" to "shatter/before they bear" (p. 39).

We write this chapter as two colleagues who teach and research in the areas of Queer Studies and Trans Studies, both with somewhat complex class backgrounds and some shared relationships to trauma. This chapter will give a detailed overview of the queer and trans studies curriculum in the Queer Studies Program at Oregon State University and its relationship to the Difference, Power, and Discrimination program (DPD) at OSU, and will also highlight collaborative work that bolsters our programming. The tree of anger has so many roots, so much under the ground that isn't usually seen. We understand that Queer and Trans Studies have their own oppressive roots, their own erasures of cis and trans people of color, and their own stories of themselves as fields that reinforce hegemonic settler whiteness, cisness, and abledness. We envision this chapter as a call to those teaching in Queer and Trans Studies and related fields to center the experiences and analyses of people of color in their curriculum. The Queer Studies curriculum at OSU may provide a model for other queer studies programs to create curriculum that intentionally disrupts these erasures by centering queer and trans people of color.

We begin critically engaging the histories and hegemonies of queer theory and trans studies, and then explicitly focus on the role of Queer Studies in DPD with a brief history of Queer Studies at OSU, including the hiring process for our own job positions.[1] Then we each talk about our personal and identity backgrounds. In these sections when we are speaking to our own respective experiences, we've included our name before the section and use the first-person "I." In all other places we use "we" as we have so far in the introduction. After situating ourselves and our backgrounds, we discuss OSU's Ecampus Queer Studies minor as an important and unique part of our program, then address the OSU Queer Archives project that provides a collaborative model of intersectional queer studies research and resources for queer and trans histories for our communities at OSU and beyond. In the final sections of the chapter, we offer examples of OSU Queer Studies-specific curriculum and programming that transforms the fields of Queer and Trans Studies.

Re-Narrating Queer and Trans Studies

Canonical formations of Queer Studies and Queer Theory, as well as Trans Studies and Trans Theory, tend to narrate their history as focusing on white experiences, identities, struggles, and modes of resistance, even while the work and activism of queer and trans people of color have always been central to "the field(s)." Even within what could be called "canons" of queer and trans theory, people of color have been present and central from the beginning. In the pivotal moments of coining the term "Queer Theory" – Teresa De Lauretis's organizing of the UC Santa Cruz 1990 Conference, "Queer Theory: A Working Conference on Lesbian and Gay Sexualities," and De Lauretis's introduction to the 1991 special issue of *differences: A Journal of Feminist Cultural Studies* – which discusses the conference – explicitly places the work of queer women of color as central to questions of theorizing "lesbian and gay" (at the time) identities. People of color were part of the original conference, and three of the eight essays in the special issue are by people of color. De Lauretis explicitly discusses race as a central concern and names whiteness, rather than allow it to remain invisible. She specifically cites Barbara Smith, Audre Lorde, Alice Walker, Ann Allen Shockley, Jewelle Gomez, Carla Trujillo, Emma Pérez, Samuel Delany, Gloria Anzaldúa, Cherríe Moraga, and others. In her discussion of work by people of color she writes:

> The differences made by race … argue for the necessity to examine, question, or contest the usefulness and/or the limitations of current discourses on lesbian and gay sexualities.… Those differences urge the reframing of the questions of queer theory from different perspectives, histories, experiences, and in different terms.
> (De Lauretis, 1991, p. x)

While people of color, and discussions of race's relationship with gender and sexuality, were central to these original articulations of "queer theory," white-dominated concerns quickly shifted the terms of debate and scholarship. As David M. Halperin (2003) argues (without naming whiteness as a central driving force),

> The moment that the scandalous formula "queer theory" was uttered … it became the name of an already established school of theory, as if it constituted a set of specific doctrines, a singular, substantive perspective on the world, a particular theorization of human experience, equivalent in that respect to psychoanalytic or Marxist theory.
> (p. 340)

He further points out:

> Queer theory … had to be invented after the fact, to supply the demand it had evoked.… All of this would be merely amusing, if the hegemony of queer theory hadn't had the … effect of portraying all previous work in lesbian and gay studies as under-theorized … and … radically narrowed the scope of queer studies.
> (p. 341)

Queer theory, and hegemonic queer studies, in this particular genealogical formation, remains a white-dominated project encumbered by debates in U.S. scholarship in the 1990s (in particular) pushing back on "identity politics" and "essentialism" in ways that ignored and silenced the lived material realities of people of color, broadly, and queer/trans people of color in particular. As E. Patrick Johnson (2010) argues, in specifically naming the racism of hegemonic queer theory, white-dominated queer studies deploys accusations of "essentialism" at the very moments in which people of color attempt to intervene into racist formulations of gender and sexuality.

Trans Studies, in the process of field formation, has likewise rooted itself in white-centered histories where people of color are often present, but the frameworks, commitments, and visions of people of color are not centralized.[2] Having multiple courses dedicated to trans studies, as well as several that have "queer and trans" in the title and central to the curriculum, means that OSU Queer Studies is unique among similar programs, centering QTPOC curriculum in both dedicated courses and across the curriculum. Our trans-focused curriculum is distinct, particularly in its formulation of racism and colonialism as central concerns to trans studies and identities.[3]

While the multiple roots of the "tree of anger" were originally acknowledged as central within the formation of the fields of queer and trans studies, and the pivotal work of queer women of color – including their already-existing calls for attention to racism's intersections with gender, sexuality, and class – white hegemonic formations of queer studies were unable to answer the calls from Lorde and others to make use of anger, and – instead – largely ignored the multiple roots of the tree of anger, allowing the possibilities of radical transformation to "shatter" before bearing the possibilities of deeper social change. As an explicit way of intentionally centralizing the roots to this tree, Queer Studies at Oregon State University is designed to understand those roots by centralizing the theories, scholarship, and experiences of queer and trans people of color and is informed by the lived experiences of multiply marginalized faculty and students.

History and Background of Queer Studies at OSU

Queer Studies at Oregon State University is a nested program within Women, Gender, and Sexuality Studies. The program was started by Patti Duncan through the creation of a "QS" prefix within the university catalog system in order to begin creating a distinct institutional identity for Queer Studies. At the time, Duncan was the Coordinator for the Women, Gender, and Sexuality Studies Program and taught the first course in Queer Studies, "Introduction to Queer Studies," which has a particular focus on the intersections of racism, homophobia, transphobia, and sexism.

Qwo-Li

I was hired to further develop and launch Queer Studies at OSU through a Provost's Initiative cluster hire throughout the university to help advance issues of "diversity" on campus, and as the Coordinator of Queer Studies, I created the undergraduate minor – including the original syllabi for most of our courses – as well as the master's and doctoral-level minors in Queer Studies. Since 2015, I have been the Director of Graduate Studies, which includes teaching professional development and mentoring Graduate Teaching Assistants (GTAs). I emphasize Indigenous kinship values, specifically drawing on Daniel Heath Justice's (2018) four questions of critical kinship, urging our students to reflect on what it means to be good kin to one another and to support each other rather than compete with each other as they are encouraged to do by settler capitalism and by many academic institutions. In my role as DGS, I have also insisted along with colleagues that we fully fund our graduate students, and, so far, we've been able to maintain that commitment, with the exception of students already employed by OSU who have tuition discounted as a result, and are not allowed to accept additional tuition funding. This commitment helps foster a shared experience of GTA duties and a sense of belonging, and discourages graduate students from feeling like they have to compete with each other for funding to meet their basic needs. Further, because our GTAs teach the majority of our program's DPD courses, the commitments we make to them as faculty and mentors not only align with our values and political commitments, but also support the important work of teaching in DPD.

As a program that, from the beginning, was started by queer and trans people of color, Queer Studies at OSU has always centered queer and trans people of color critiques as central to its curriculum, and as an originator of the Queer Studies curriculum, I specifically created courses and a program that focuses on queer and trans people of color. Queer Studies as a larger field has remained centered on white experiences, modes of analysis, and modes of production that queer and trans people of color have always pushed against and resisted.

H.

When I was hired for the second designated QS faculty position, the job ad was clearly not for a "diversity hire" in the sense that departments and programs that are hegemonically white will advertise for marginalized or interdisciplinary areas of research focus, often under pressure from their Colleges or broader units, in order to attract nonwhite faculty. I highlight this both because it was an ethical and political commitment of mine that I didn't apply for those jobs, because however flawed that process might be, I believe there need to be more tenure-track faculty of color, and to further emphasize the commitments of the program from its very beginning. In the case of OSU's Queer Studies and WGSS programs, it was clear that there was already a racially diverse faculty, that women of color feminisms and queer of color critiques were areas of focus for the core of the faculty, and that trans studies and disability studies were already being taught, but there was need for continued commitment to these areas through hiring an assistant professor.

Our Personal Backgrounds

Qwo-Li

I come to this work as a multiracial, light-skinned, non-citizen (unenrolled) Cherokee person also of Black, Irish, Lenape, Lumbee, and Osage ancestries who identifies as *asegi aquadanto* ("strange-hearted"), or Two-Spirit, as well as queer and trans. I am also someone with several disabilities, both physical and psychological, many of them as a result of recurrent physical and emotional trauma, and someone who – while now solidly middle-class (though with the major disruptions to public universities due to lack of state funding, perhaps not so solidly) – grew up in poverty, but with formally educated parents, both of whom were teachers, though my mother retired from teaching before I was born and was a daycare provider in my early childhood.

My activist background is in both rural Colorado and in Seattle, where I was part of queer and trans organizing. My graduate-level academic training is in Rhetoric & Writing – specifically in Cultural Rhetorics – and Whole Systems Design (an interdisciplinary field that brings together holism, systems theory, and design concepts), where my work focused on Indigenous writing, theater, and story as a tool to create decolonial coalitions. My undergraduate degree was in Interdisciplinary Studies, where I brought together what had been a major in Musical Theatre with minors in Women's Studies and Africana Studies to create a specific degree program I called "Social Transformation and the Arts" after becoming deeply disillusioned by my theater training while perusing activist projects on and off campus as well as in my studies. I am also a poet, and continue to do work in performance and performance studies. My life-experiences and embodied reality as a multiracial Indigenous activist and as a Two-Spirit/Queer/Trans person with disabilities deeply inform my practice as a teacher and curriculum designer, particularly my commitments to scholarship and the classroom as places of transformation and activism.

H.

I enter this work as a white, transmasculine and nonbinary queer person and first-generation college+ student. While my background is middle class and I'm currently middle class, I experienced certain forms of scarcity growing up because of my parents' prior experiences of poverty as a trauma. I identify as crip-proximate because while I have my own trauma and chronic pain and these are impairments at times, my race and class privilege (especially access to good healthcare including mental healthcare), and current employment significantly buffer me from what is disabling for so many. I understand disability as an assemblage that doesn't exist in isolation from other intersections of who we are. I've also learned a great deal from disability activists and scholars and want to be in community with those who've experienced the shift in consciousness that a disability justice politics entails.

My training is in philosophy, and while my graduate program was a "continental" philosophy program, rather than the sometimes more conservative "analytic" philosophy that dominates the U.S. settler state context, it was a program that has retrenched its "European" (French, German, and Ancient Greek) philosophy claims to legitimacy. When I started there, the faculty was more racially diverse and their projects were far more diverse than they had ever been (they had never been at all until recently) and this changed dramatically in the time I was there and shortly after. My dissertation director, Namita Goswami, was hired to teach and research in postcolonial feminisms and then was punished with a tenure denial for doing so *too well*. This was also my most direct organizing and activism experience. While I was a part of queer transformative justice initiatives in my communities in Chicago, a lot of my early experience with confronting institutions came directly though my collaborative work with others to fight my own program and university. As a first-generation college student with little prior knowledge or understanding of graduate work, at first I didn't know that in academia I could even hope to be a part of this radical and transformative work of queer studies and trans studies that centers people of color. What I learned in graduate school was that I could not survive in my initial discipline and more importantly I didn't want to, so I sought out the learning and experience I would need to find a home in a program like ours.

Beyond an Additive Approach

Because of erasure and/or tokenization of race and colonization within queer studies, and white queer/trans movements broadly, Qwo-Li consciously designed Queer Studies within theoretical and activist frameworks that center racialized and Indigenous peoples. During the development of the Queer Studies minor, they very consciously designed syllabi and curriculum that centered queer women of color feminisms, using the work of these writers, activists, and scholars to frame what Queer Studies is. For instance, in Introduction to Queer Studies, we use Audre Lorde and Gloria Anzaldúa as foundational thinkers and writers in understanding gender and sexuality as forms of power and control dependent on formations of race (and vice versa). Further, the curriculum is designed so that Indigenous peoples' scholarship and activism are "always-already" part of the work of queer studies, including a specific course, "Indigenous Queer and Two-Spirit Studies." Even when Indigenous people, and (other) racialized people are not mentioned in course titles such as Introduction to Queer Studies, the curriculum itself centers on discussions of racism and colonization.

At a predominantly white university, these frameworks and course content can be usefully disconcerting for white LGBTQ+ students who unconsciously believe that these courses will reflect and confirm white gender and sexual identities. As Bradley Boovy and Nana Osei-Kofi discuss in this volume, white students at a historically white institution often have not been in a position to have to interrogate their own racial privilege, and this includes white students who often assume that Queer Studies courses will focus on white experiences and identities. Our courses intentionally disrupt the idea that queer/trans identities and struggles are white, where people of color exist as "spice, seasoning that can liven up the dull dish that is mainstream white culture" (hooks, 1991, p. 21). The misuse of Crenshaw's (1989) coinage of "intersectionality" often leads students (and faculty and activists, for that matter) to perceive gender and sexuality as "white" and "neutral" until "intersected" with race. Drawing on Emma Pérez's (1999) critique of Chicano studies approaches that move from a masculinist formula of "Chicano" to "Some Chican*os* are also women, Chicanas" (p. 22), we see a similar formula in Queer/Trans Studies, and students' perceptions of LGBTQ+ identities and issues are white but acknowledges that "LGBTQ+ people are also people of color." The curricular work of our program is to disrupt this formula by imagining a more radical, Indigenous and people-of-color centered, understanding of Queer Studies that embraces the multiple roots of oppression and the generative uses of anger about those roots towards transformation.

Queer Studies at Oregon State University Ecampus

As of the authoring of this chapter, OSU has one of the only Queer Studies Ecampus degrees – if not *the* only – including a significant post-baccalaureate student population. At least one of our current "postbacc" students is a university professor. Our QS Ecampus program often attracts nontraditional students, and many of our Ecampus students are doing various forms of activism where they are located. For Queer and Trans students, sometimes our Ecampus community is the sole source of queer/trans community for them.

The creation, development, and continuation of the Ecampus QS minor is due in large part to the contributions of Michael Floyd, MSW, an Instructor since 2013, who also taught one of the first sections of Introduction to Queer Studies on campus in Fall 2013. Before, during, and after their official role as Program Development Coordinator for the Queer Studies Minor on Ecampus from 2016–18, they have developed, revised, or created the original design for over a dozen courses. The original courses they designed include "QS/WGSS 321: Queer Pop Culture" and "QS/WGSS 362: Serving LGBTQ + Communities." Their credentials and experience in Social Work, and their training and activism for LGBTQ+ elders, have been important for building and furthering a curriculum that emphasizes the relationship between theory and practice and centers queer and trans people of color.

OSU Queer Archives (OSQA)

Collaborative work between a WGSS/QS professor and an Oregon Multicultural Librarian has resulted in the Oregon State Queer Archives (OSQA). Beginning in 2014, archivist Natalia María Fernández and faculty member Dr. Bradley Boovy have centered community-based relationships and culled existing multicultural archives to produce an archival project that seeks intersectional LGBTQQIA stories rather than a hegemonic archive that reifies privileged (white, middle class, English-speaking, cisgender) experiences of queerness. In their article explaining the OSQA project, "Co-Founding a Queer Archives: A Collaboration Between and Archivist and a Professor," Fernández and Boovy (2017) indicate three main points to their mission:

- fostering intersectional community activism across and providing opportunities for students' engagement and activism;
- resisting erasure of queer and trans narratives; and
- positioning the collection as a space to imagine alternative futures for LGBTQQIA communities and people.

(n.p.)

These points dovetail with the DPD objectives outlined in the Introduction to this volume and the collaborative emphasis of the work "can serve as a model for a sustainable approach to collaboratively developing and maintaining a Queer Archives initiative within a higher education setting" (Fernández & Boovy, 2017, n.p.). The OSQA project has also worked with two paid student interns who respectively bridged their own academic thesis work with the OSQA and collaborated with the Eena Haws Native American Longhouse, one of our campus cultural enters, to create an event for Native American Heritage Month.[4]

Structure of Syllabi

The QS Courses were developed with the intent of moving students from the personal to the political and from theory to practice. In Introduction to Queer Studies, for example, students begin with an autobiographical "Theory in the Flesh" project, in order to situate themselves within personal experiences and reflection. They then move to a Media Analysis, designed to go beyond autobiographical work and into an analysis of constructions of power. The final project asks students to engage in research around a topic of their choice and develop something that can be implemented outside of the classroom. The course assignments, then, are intentionally recursive: they begin with the personal, spiral outwards towards the analytical, and finally spiral further outward into specific projects focused on creating interventions outside of the classroom.

Theory in the Flesh Project

Qwo-Li

The first major project in Introduction to Queer Studies is "Autobiography: Theory in the Flesh," which asks students to briefly (three to four, double-spaced pages) tell an autobiographical story. It is based on Gloria Anzaldúa and Cherríe Moraga's (1981) theorization of "Theory in the Flesh" from *This Bridge Called My Back*:

> A theory in the flesh means one where the physical realities of our lives – our skin color, the land or concrete we grew up on, our sexual longings – all fuse to create a politic born out of necessity. Here, we attempt to bridge the contradictions in our experience.... We do this bridging by naming our selves and by telling our stories in our own words.
>
> (p. 23)

This assignment takes place within the first three to four weeks of a ten-week quarter system, specifically to root the students in their own experiences, enable them to tell their own stories, and develop an analysis of systems of power. *This Bridge Called My Back* is taught during the first three weeks of the term, along with supplemental essays and the film *The Question of Equality: Out Rage '69* (Dong, 1995), and in Week 4 the course moves into reading Audre Lorde's (1984b) *Sister Outsider*.

The assignment asks students to not only situate themselves within, but also reflect on, their personal experiences within the social constructions of gender and sexuality as they intersect with other forms of power and control:

> With particular attention to gender and sexuality (which are never separate from other social locations), this project asks that you create "theory in the flesh" through a short autobiographical essay. The purpose of this project is to ask you to situate and reflect on the ways you have come to understand, or have understood in the past, issues of sexuality, gender, race, class, disability, and other social categories. (How did/do you know what you know?) It is also to ask you to discuss how "the physical realities of our lives…all fuse to create a politic born out of necessity."
>
> While "theory in the flesh" does ask us to take risks, this project doesn't need to disclose any information about your life that you don't wish to disclose. This project isn't about who can tell the most upsetting story. Rather, this project asks you to use your personal experiences as a way to create theories of social transformation.
>
> (Driskill, 2020)

The assignment description also gives students ideas for how they might approach the project:

> You might ask yourself:
>
> - What was I taught – through words or actions – about gender/sexuality/race/class/disability growing up? How did this impact me?
> - What do I experience on a daily basis because of my social locations?
> - How can the world change? What is my vision of social transformation?
> - What is left out of discussions for social justice that my personal experiences tell me need to be addressed?
> - How is my understanding of gender/sexuality informed by cultural, class, geographical, religious, and other backgrounds/experiences?
>
> (Driskill, 2020, n.p.)

The grading rubric for the assignment intentionally asks students to demonstrate a personal understanding of issues of Difference, Power, and Discrimination through their own lenses, and ensures that students will discuss gender and sexuality in relationship with other intersecting forms of power:

A 4.0 portfolio will:

- Discuss how *your* experiences were/are constructed by systems of power.
- Relate your personal experiences to larger social justice issues.
- Address sexuality and gender in relationship to other social locations.
- Be thoroughly proofread and edited.

(Driskill, 2020, n.p.)

It's important to note that we have no genre expectations here – this assignment can be written in any genre, or mixed genres, in any ways the students would like, as long as it clearly meets the expectations of the assignment. The purpose of this assignment is not to have students create a piece of writing in Standard American Academic English, but instead to really think about what their relationships are to systems of power, how it is they've come to understand gender and sexuality – specifically their own – in relationship to other social locations.

Even while this is an autobiographical project, part of the openness of this assignment is to allow students who identify as straight and/or cis, as well as students who may not be ready to disclose queer and/or trans identities to their classmates (or anyone else), a way of reflecting on how systems of power have shaped their understandings of gender and sexuality broadly. It also means that white queer/trans students cannot simply talk about their sexual and gender identities as existing in a racially "neutral" (white) vacuum, but are asked to situate this discussion within realities of race, class, disability, citizenship, and religious background.

As part of the scaffolding of the course and as a pedagogical practice, every class period I ask students to write for five to ten minutes based on a prompt, sometimes based on the readings, and sometimes based on an exercise I learned from Alabama Creek poet and scholar Janet McAdams, which asks students to write a list of ten things (ten types of wind, ten things that are blue, etc.) and use eight of them in a freewrite. I then give the opportunity for students to share both their lists (if we've written them) and their freewrite. We don't workshop or comment on these poems/short prose pieces in this course. My purposes for this exercise are multifold:

1. to create a specific opening ritual to the class that allows students to get into a new headspace and transition from whatever happened outside of the classroom;
2. to allow students to create and share their own stories in a fairly low-stakes writing activity;
3. to provide the opportunity for students to hear from and learn about each other as part of a community-building exercise; and
4. to provide invention activities for the writing of course projects, including their "Theory in the Flesh" project.

After introducing students to the "Theory of the Flesh" project and after they've been assigned to read the first half of *This Bridge Called My Back*, I read Nellie Wong's "While I Was Growing Up" aloud at the beginning of class, using it as a writing prompt for the opening writing activity by asking students to write for ten minutes on a piece of writing that starts with the line "While I was growing up." After student volunteers have read their freewrites aloud, I point out to them that they've all started drafting their first projects.

The "Theory in the Flesh" project prepares students for the readings, and conversations that will take place throughout the term, and sets them up for the final project, as well as the entirety of the Queer Studies curriculum at OSU. It helps them begin to look closely at the "roots to the tree of anger" and imagine how we might create and pursue different presents and futures.

Final Project in Queer Theories

H.

I teach Queer Theories every spring term. Already in the title of the course, the plurality and intersectionality of queer *theories* is indicated, marking it differently from "Queer Theory" courses and as an area of inquiry. The readings center queer and trans people-of- color and queer-of-color critique as a methodology as coined by Roderick Ferguson in *Aberrations in Black*. The presumed whiteness of queer theories is challenged from the beginning and throughout. When students reach the final paper, then, they are prepared to tackle the challenge of writing a textual analysis paper that stages their own queer theories methodology. I give them a range of options within this open-ended project: from generating a thesis and arguing for a queer theories methodology that bridges two of the authors and texts from the course to more creatively assembling their own methodology from at least two authors in the course. The assignment builds on weekly close reading assignments they have completed throughout the term, which emphasizes the attentiveness and care that are required not just for understanding theory texts but specifically for understanding intersectional approaches that center queer and trans people of color and disability studies analysis. This attentiveness and care is often fueled by our collective anger. We allow the branches to bear that anger out rather than shatter, and the final project is a shaping and reshaping of critiques of what angers us as queer people, as trans people, as anti-racist white people like myself, as Indigenous and Black people, and people of color. Members of the class are required to do the recentering work – focusing on queer and trans people of color – in their own final paper project, whether it is more so constellating the ideas of theorists we've read in the course or has more of their own novel approach based in their knowledge of those works.

Disability Studies and Crip Theories Curriculum and Programming

H.

In Queer Theories and all of my courses, I engage disability studies and crip theories as modes of analysis. Adding key texts that treat disability intersectionally and facilitating discussions that frame core texts that don't directly name disability, I resist the whiteness of disability studies and crip theory and encourage students to interrogate ableism and its interlocking with other oppressions. We follow the branches of the tree of anger, understanding mainstream queer and trans studies as inherently marginalizing people with disabilities, and understanding mainstream queer and trans studies and disability studies as marginalizing people of color. We work against this mainstreaming and marginalizing as we try to uproot the roots of the tree of anger.

I am also part of the OSU Disability Network, and in Fall 2018 I worked with the group to bring disability studies scholar Liat Ben-Moshe to campus to give her talk, "Why Prisons Are Not the New Asylums," and to meet with undergraduate and graduate students as well as faculty and staff (see also Jenkins and Smith in this volume). In addition, I'm developing a new course on Crip Feminisms that will likely be an upper level undergraduate and graduate course.

Conclusion

This chapter has sought to uproot the roots of the "tree of anger." Challenging Queer Studies and Trans Studies to center race and colonialism and to reject the hegemonies that emerge even as interdisciplinary fields may still think of themselves as new. We urge those in these fields to engage in this de-centering and re-narrating work. As we look back at how a Queer Studies program was created and highlight the work that has made it possible, we look to a future that was always uncertain given the realities of settler colonial university settings. We hold the anger and fear of our students, our own anger and sadness and fatigue where the roots of the tree of anger don't seem to budge. We also know that the work of queer and trans studies when grounded in an intentionally intersectional, queer/trans people-of-color approach – does disrupt the root systems of power. We hold the hopes and dreams of our students, and our collective imaginings of what we can make together out of what we have already made together. It is through this work that we are able to see the tree of anger bear the fruit of resistance.

Additional Resources

Readings

Anzaldúa, G. (2012). *Borderlands/La frontera: The new mestiza*, (4th ed). Aunt Lute.

Clare, E. (2015). *Exile and pride: Disability, queerness, and liberation (Reissue edition)*. Duke University Press Books.

Clare, E. (2017). *Brilliant imperfection: Grappling with cure*. Duke University Press Books.

Cohen, C. (1997). *Punks, bulldaggers, and welfare queens: The radical potential of queer politics? GLQ, 3*(4), 437–465. https://doi.org/10.1215/10642684-3-4-437

Driskill, Q., Finley, C., Gilley, B. J., & Morgensen, S.L. (Eds.). (2011). *Queer indigenous studies: Critical interventions in theory, politics, and literature*. University of Arizona Press.

Driskill, Q., Justice, D. H., Miranda, D.A., & Tatonetti, L. (Eds.). (2011). *Sovereign erotics: A collection of two-spirit literature*. University of Arizona Press Press.

Ferguson, R. A. (2004). *Aberrations in black: Toward a queer of color critique*. University of Minnesota Press.

Incite! Women of Color Against Violence (2006). *Color of violence: The Incite! anthology*. South End Press.

Mock, J. (2014). *Redefining realness: My path to womanhood, identity, love & so much more*. Atria Books.

Stanley, E. A., & Smith, N. (2015). *Captive genders: Trans embodiment and the prison industrial complex, expanded 2nd ed*. AK Press.

Sueyoshi, A. (2019). Redefining higher education: Reflections on queer ethnic studies. *Ethnic Studies Review, 42*(2), 225–231. https://doi.org/10.1525/esr.2019.42.2.225

Willis, M. M. (2017). *Outside the xy: Queer black and brown masculinity, a bklyn boihood anthology*. Riverdale Avenue Books.

Websites

The Audre Lorde Project https://alp.org/
CLAGS: The Center for LGBTQ Studies https://clags.org/

Notes

1 There is a larger, and longer, history of LGBTQ+ content being taught at Oregon State University, as well as a deep relationship between both Queer Studies/WGSS at OSU and our campus's Women's and Gender Center, Pride Center, and other Cultural Resource Centers (CRCs) that is outside of the scope of this particular essay, but deserve further attention and documentation.

2 For further specific critique of this, see Treva E., Green, K.M., Richardson, M. & Snorton C. R. (Eds). (2017). The Issue of blackness. *Transgender Studies Quarterly, 4*(2).

3 Our transgender-focused courses include QS/WGSS 364: Transgender Politics, QS/WGSS 472/572: Indigenous Queer and Two-Sprit Studies, QS/WGSS 473/573: Transgender Lives and QS/WGSS 477/577: Queer/Trans People of Color Arts & Activism.

4 Eena Haws Native American Longhouse is directed by Dr. Luhui Whitebear, a graduate of the PhD program in WGSS at Oregon State University, who was also the first doctoral-level minor in Queer Studies at OSU to complete the degree.

References

Crenshaw, K. (1989). Demarginalizing the intersection of race and sex: A black feminist critique of antidiscrimination doctrine, feminist theory and antiracist politics. *University of Chicago Legal Forum, 1989*(1), 139–167. http://chicagounbound.uchicago.edu/uclf/vol1989/iss1/8

De Lauretis, T. (1991). Queer theory: Lesbian and gay sexualities. *differences: A Journal of Feminist Cultural Studies, 3*(2), iii–xviii.

Dong, A. (Director). (1995). *The question of equality: Out rage '69* [Film]. Testing the limits & Independent television service.

Driskill, Q. (2020). *Portfolio #1: Theory in the Flesh* [Assignment Description]. Corvallis, OR: Queer Studies, Oregon State University.

Fernández, N. M., & Boovy, B. (2017). Co-Founding a queer archives: A collaboration between an archivist and a professor. *Archival Practice, 3*(0). http://libjournal.uncg.edu/ap/article/view/1365

Halperin, D. M. (2003). The normalization of queer theory. *Journal of Homosexuality, 45*(2–4), 339–343. https://doi.org/10.1300/J082v45n02_17

hooks, b. (1992). *Black looks: Race and representation*. Routledge.

Johnson, E. P. (2010). "Quare" studies, or (almost) everything I know about queer studies I learned from my grandmother. *Text and Performance Quarterly, 21*(1), 1–25. https://doi.org/10.1080/10462930128119

Justice, D. H. (2018). *Why indigenous literatures matter*. Wilfrid Laurier University Press.

Lorde, A. (1973). *From a land where other people live* (1st ed). Broadside Lotus Press.

Lorde, A. (1984a). The uses of anger: Women responding to racism. *Sister outsider: essays and speeches*. Crossing Press.

Lorde, A. (1984b). *Sister outsider: essays and speeches*. Crossing Press.

Moraga, C., & Anzaldúa, G. (Eds). (2015). *This bridge called my back: Writings by radical women of color* (4th edition.). State University of New York SUNY Press.

Pérez, E. (1999). *The decolonial imaginary: Writing Chicanas into history*. Indiana University Press.

Treva, E., Green, K.M., Richardson, M., & Snorton, C. R. (Eds.). (2017). The issue of blackness. *Transgender Studies Quarterly, 4*(2).

9 Reflections on Race/Ethnicity, Gender, and Labor in the Latinx Studies Classroom

Marta María Maldonado

> "How can unlearning be a fundamental reorganization of power?"
> Nashwa Khan, June 21, 2016, briarpatch.

In all likelihood, readers are familiar with the idea that *learning* often requires *unlearning*. In effect, the idea of unlearning is ubiquitous within a wide range of contexts, from pedagogy to psychological practice, to business and marketing. The crux of the idea of unlearning is that, to imagine and access new possibilities, we must let go of the blinders and restrictions imposed by old ways of knowing. Unlearning is a prerequisite for creativity and innovation. In this chapter, I center a specific kind of unlearning – a critical unlearning that is primarily concerned with situating learners, knowledge production, and knowledge sharing within their broader sociopolitical context. I discuss some ways in which I've aimed to foster unlearning of dominant ideologies in introductory level Latinx-focused DPD courses. I describe some exercises I use to encourage students to notice, interrupt, and interrogate how race, class, and gender – connected and mutually shaping as they are – have shaped and continuously shape our thoughts, actions, and emotions. Rather than a simple intellectual exercise, such unlearning ultimately aims to inform interventions for social justice, and to help learners envision paths to actively pursue positive social transformation individually and collectively.

I begin by describing two sets of *pedagogical challenges* I have encountered in teaching these courses: First, I discuss challenges associated with teaching Latinx Studies (LS from here on) at a predominantly white university. Second, I share some of the challenges I have faced in trying to get students to think of *work* and *the economy* as simultaneously racialized and gendered institutions and processes, and to see worker struggles as integral or relevant to their lives. I begin by discussing challenges because I feel that they reflect how the dominant ideologies that I seek to disrupt through my teaching show up in the classroom. They are symptoms of that which needs disruption. Following my discussion of each set of challenges, I share some exercises I have used in an effort to address them. A word of warning: I am one of those teachers for whom coming up with creative assignments is not always easy. These exercises are not fully mine. That is, I didn't entirely create them. Several are my adaptations of and developments

DOI: 10.4324/9781003091998-12

Figure 9.0 "Unlearn Racism"-lit sign on foot bridge.
Photo by Joe Brusky, via Flickr

upon ideas or exercises I have seen in various printed and online teaching resources over the years. Also, the degree of success I have had accomplishing the goals I describe here through these exercises varies with each group of students. I share the activities here also as a way to share my own pedagogical journey, my thoughts in progress and attempts to create spaces for students to stop and think critically, my efforts to interrupt and denormalize dominant ideologies and discourses in students' minds. I invite you to consider, use, critique, and tweak them as you see fit. It is my conviction that the honest sharing of our pedagogical journeys, our notes, tools, successes and failures, and lessons learned, is necessary to advance critical pedagogy as a collective intellectual and political project.

A few words about the assumptions and frameworks that inform my pedagogy. From a critical feminist standpoint, I consider the relational and the affective as integral to learning situations. Hence, I see acknowledging and grappling with the relational and emotional aspects of subject matter *and* teacher-student interactions as necessary components of a critical, socially transformative pedagogy. I'm also guided by the premise that teaching and learning are *always already racialized social situations*. They are also gendered, classed, and imbued with all kinds of relations of power. But explicit attention to *racial content* is crucial in my pedagogical practice for several reasons. For one, in the contemporary United States, where an ideology of color blindness is dominant, racism is maintained and reproduced, to a great extent, through its denial. That is, racist outcomes persist largely through our pretense that social arrangements and situations have nothing to do with race (Bonilla-Silva, 2001; 2017). Also, I teach LS as part of an Ethnic Studies curriculum, among whose central goals is to provide students with the tools to understand how race has shaped and continues to shape life in the United States. So, *race, racialization,* and *racism* are central analytics in the courses I teach. Furthermore, I start from the assumption that students and teachers are racialized subjects. Like everyone else, we live racialized lives, and experience and interpret racialized situations and relationships *practically* and *emotionally* on a quotidian basis (Denzin, 1984). Institutions of higher education and classrooms are also *always* racialized spaces. We do not *insert* race into this or that aspect of academic life; race is already there. Although this might seem a truism from the perspective of scholars of race and Ethnic Studies, everyday academic discourses and practices typically obfuscate this fact, with deleterious consequences for minoritized groups. Anchored in such an understanding, the type of liberatory pedagogy I seek to practice through interruption and denormalization aims to make the invisible visible, to help students uncover and recognize the ways in which race shapes what they know, or what they think they know, their day-to-day lives in the university and beyond, and even their own emotions.

Teaching Latinx Studies at a PWI: The Challenges

My own ethnoracial positionality and that of my students bespeaks the first set of challenges (and admittedly, opportunities) I have faced in teaching Latinx Studies at a predominantly white institution. Ethnoracial markers seem to be especially salient or significant in my interaction with students in LS courses. The majority, or many, of my students are white (what the U.S. Census would refer to as *non-Hispanic White*). I also have in my classrooms a good share of Latinx students of different national origins, racial groups, and citizenship and immigration statuses. I am a brown Latina. My body, my accent, get me read as such in most U.S. contexts – the classroom included. It has been my experience that this fact matters, that it affects how different students interact with me, how they receive what I have to say. Being a Latina who teaches about Latinx histories and politics in academic spaces where whiteness is normative actually places me in an interesting quagmire. On the one hand, dominant homogenizing rhetorics about the vastly diverse groups subsumed under the panethnic label "Latina/o/x" suggest to students that Latinx people share *the same* stakes and allegiances. In many students' minds, especially white students, I bring to the classroom a bias that favors an imagined (homogeneous, monolithic) Latinx agenda. This bias, students imagine, entails a number of presumed commitments, including notably, a pro-immigration stance (because many students believe incorrectly that most or all Latinxs are immigrants) and further, a support of "illegal immigration."[1] Because the topics of immigration and "illegality"[2] are constantly at the center of public debate in the U.S., fueled by an ongoing barrage of racialized, dehumanizing media representations of Latinxs and the U.S.-Mexico border – or what Otto Santa Ana (2002) has called, representations of a "brown tide rising" – many of my non-Latinx students arrive in the classroom with strong, emotionally-charged opinions about these topics. It is quite difficult to disabuse them of these "opinions," and of what they think they know, and for them to consider the complexity and even humanity of Latinx and immigrant perspectives and experiences. Likewise, because dominant racialized narratives tend to treat Latinxs as forever foreign, outside the physical and symbolic borders of the imagined U.S. nation (Chavez, 2008; Santa Ana, 2002; Oboler, 1997), and due to an "us vs. them" mentality common among many students, the centering of Latinx perspectives in Latinx Studies, and exhortations to consider U.S.-Latin America relations critically, are often interpreted by students as additional elements of the teacher's "Latinx (anti-U.S.) bias" (or as one student mentioned on a course evaluation, "she doesn't present the U.S. perspective").

Earlier, I alluded both to challenges and opportunities associated with positionality. Being a Latina professor seems to afford me a useful entry point with some students. Some white students have a genuine curiosity for understanding Latinx experiences, and see the fact that they have seldom, if ever, had Latinx teachers as a loss. Those students are always full of questions and are often eager to have conversations in and out of the classroom. I am Puerto Rican, and while the specificity of my simultaneously national and ethnoracial location may or may not be immediately apparent or always of interest to white students (many seem satisfied with locating me simply as a Latina professor), my Latinx students often want to know more, they want to know what "sort" of Latina I am, they want to know where I am from. Most Latinx students in my courses have been Mexican or Central American, and I don't look or sound exactly familiar to them. Therefore, every new term, Latinx students will ask me directly where I am from if I don't self-disclose this information. In effect, our distinct Latinx national and cultural identities and histories provide some of the content of my interactions with Latinx students in and out of the classroom, and also affect the sense of distance or connection some Latinx students seem to chart between us. Likewise, I have encountered more than a handful of Latinx students who have told me that I am the first Latina teacher they have ever had. For some, I am the first Latina teacher they have had in their entire life, including their K-12 education. For these students, having a Latina professor (independently of my particular national origin) seems a momentous thing, which enables them to see themselves differently within the university and the classroom. From what several of these students have shared in conversations in my office, a sense of connectedness with the teacher and a corresponding implicit validation of their experience *as Latinx* people motivates them to participate in classroom conversations differently, more fully, with a sense that they have something important to contribute.

Another set of challenges related to teaching LS courses at a PWI has to do with why students take these courses. At the beginning of each term, I ask students why they enrolled in the course. Many students, especially white students, report candidly that they are there to fulfill general education requirements. While some of these students might also be interested in the substance of the course, many are not. They might or might not see themselves as connected to course substance or perceive Latinx conditions and experiences as relevant to their own lives. Further, many come from STEM fields or other disciplinary areas across campus in which routine advising and curricular practices suggest to students that courses focused on the experiences of historically marginalized groups, and/or which are concerned with structural inequities and social justice are only tangential to their academic interests – hurdles they need to overcome to complete their degree. As William Robinson (2018) writes,

> [the] turn to STEM areas devoid of any critical social content seduces millions of young people with the promise of a viable niche in the capitalist labor market and both dazzles and depoliticizes them with the allure of technological glitz.
>
> (p. 35)

Some such students don't take these DPD courses seriously, feel that they should be able to obtain "an easy A," and that they should not have to invest too much time or energy, relative to courses in their primary areas of academic focus. All of this has ideological underpinnings – it is symptomatic of the neoliberal embrace within higher education, and of the routine differential valuing of knowledge areas based on their ability to produce revenue and to serve the needs of the capitalist market (for a discussion of the impacts of neoliberalism on faculty, students, and critical knowledge production in universities, see Maldonado & Guenther, 2019).

Finally, as I alluded to in this chapter's introduction, there are the challenges associated with engaging race and ethnicity explicitly in a predominantly white space. On the one hand, by the time students get to my introductory LS courses, they might or might not have taken courses that give them language and tools to begin thinking critically about the racialized content of their own lives. They have also likely learned dominant narratives about race, and as racialized subjects, developed particular thoughts and emotions connected to their location in the racialized social structure. Emotions especially run deep when it comes to issues of race. Students experience an array of emotions when thinking and engaging questions and histories of race: confusion, sadness, anger, guilt, are perhaps the most common, but there are many more. Knowing how to guide students, helping them acknowledge, understand, and manage those emotions, is one of the most difficult tasks one faces in teaching about race, as is learning to manage one's own emotions in the classroom. Following is a discussion of several tools I've used to begin addressing these various challenges.

The Tools: Positionality and Social Situatedness

Processes of learning and unlearning happen differently and at different speeds for students from different social and cultural locations. Since my goal is to get students to unlearn dominant ideologies, I start from the Althusserian premise that ideology interpellates individuals as concrete subjects (Althusser, 1972) not only as individuals, but also as gendered, classed, and racialized subjects. In an effort to address some of the recurrent challenges discussed in the previous section, I spend the first several weeks of each term getting to know students, and inviting them through class exercises, discussions, and assignments to reflect on their own selves and lives, as individuals embedded in social structures. From there, my next step is to "push" them to think about themselves in relation to (familiar and unfamiliar) "others." The *Identity Exercises* (Figures 9.1 and 9.2) are examples of how I have done this.

I usually use the Identity Exercise in Figure 9.1 during the first week of the term. In class, I ask students the question, what is identity? I write their responses on the board and, as a class, we use them to synthesize a definition and some aspects or characteristics of identity. I further prompt them to consider whether one's identity ever changes. What aspects of identity might change and why, and which ones are more enduring or permanent? I then ask the class, is identity important? Why or why not? We typically are having a very animated discussion by then. Most everyone seems comfortable talking about identity in these general terms. Once we've had the chance to discuss at some length, I draw my name on the board and draft a version of my identity chart. The "Facing History and Ourselves" website (facinghistory.org) has a very useful video that explains identity charts. A simple template to get students started is also available at the "Learning for Justice" (formerly "Teaching Tolerance" website (learningforjustice.org). I write things on my chart like, "professor," "sociologist," "daughter," and, "friend." Sometimes I change some of the things I write, move them in the chart, or erase them. For example, I might write, "dog lover," or "baseball lover" but change where the words are placed (closer or farther from the center, where my name is). I might write, "Puerto Rican," and then change it to, "Latina," and then add, "American." And so on and so forth. While I work on my chart, students watch. I want them to see my process. I want them to note where I pause, what I write, what I change, what I move. I don't say anything until I'm done. I then explain to students that this is called an identity chart, and that this is my chart. I ask them to take a good look at it. And I give them the assignment of creating their own (Figure 9.1, Step 2) and bringing it to the next class. Some students take pictures of my chart with their phones or take notes. At the next class meeting they work in pairs to share and discuss their charts. I ask them to discuss how they decided what to include, whether they're sure

---

Identity Exercise

1. Identity can be thought of as our answer to the question: "who am I?" How do YOU answer this question? What categories do you consider when thinking about who you are? (for example, your role in your family, your membership in various groups?)

2. Based on your answers above, create your identity chart, as modeled in class. (You will be sharing your identity chart with peers, so do not include information that you want to remain private.)

Figure 9.1 Identity Exercise

they included *all* aspects of their identity, or if some aspects might be missing, why and how the various aspects of identity they noted in their chart are important to them, and how their daily lives – what they do day-to-day – is shaped or determined by aspects of their identity. Students are usually very engaged and seem happy to share with each other stories about the aspects of identity they chose to share. I usually follow this discussion with an introductory conversation on the concept of "Latinidades," (usually students have also been assigned a reading – Frances Aparicio's work has been helpful on this particular topic (see for example, Aparicio, 2007). I explain that a vast array of identities exists among Latinx people, like they exist for all ethnoracial groups. And that there are as many diverse experiences among Latinx people as there are identities. At the end of that class period, I ask students to prepare for the next class by completing the "Diverse Identities and Experiences Assignment" (see Figure 9.2).

In our discussion of this second exercise, I point out that students who identify as Latinx and students who identify as non-Latinx share some identities and aspects of experience, for example, being university students, or of a particular gender identity. One of my goals here is to get students to think about points of nearness or similarity of experience (perhaps even solidarity) across ethnoracial groups. I want to interrupt the perceived totality of boundaries – in fact, borders – across ethnoracial lines, and to encourage students to find points of convergence, of shared humanity. I often remind students of this early conversation later in the term, if/when, in discussion, students engage alienating or dehumanizing narratives about Latinx people or immigrants. Likewise, discussion of this second exercise allows us to begin considering the ways in which identities are not purely individual, but also social and cultural. We discuss how institutions and "society" define us in ways that might or might not align with our definitions of ourselves, but which still have consequences for us. I turn the focus to the nation-state and immigration policy as examples of social and institutional actors that shape Latinx identity and experience, defining people as citizens or non-citizens, authorized or unauthorized. I ask students to work on a third assignment. They are asked to identify three examples from news media of representations of Latinx people. Discussion focuses on how popular culture and media create ideas of who Latinxs are, which might or might not align with actual Latinx identities and experiences. And we discuss the consequences of these imposed identities.

Starting critical learning and unlearning processes with students' own identities and experiences accomplishes several things. First, it enables students to locate themselves in relation to what they are learning. In so doing, it lets them know that it is valid (in fact, it is necessary) to start learning from exactly where they are, and who they are; what is known offers an experiential anchor and a vantage point from which to think about connections and disconnections between them and the rest of the world. Next, it is a useful place to begin exploring human histories, perspectives, and experiences as multiple and complex, even at the most micro level. Last, the self is a manageable site

Diverse Identities and Experiences Assignment

The purposes of this assignment are:

- to help you reflect on the fact that we all have *multiple* identities, that is, our identities have multiple aspects
- to help you think of the ways in which identity is not purely individual, but also shaped by cultural and social factors.

Rationale (or why this assignment?):

Reflecting on your own identities, and on how these are connected to your life experiences can be a useful entry point as we begin to explore diverse Latinx identities and experiences, and how these are shaped by social and cultural forces. Independently of whether you identify as a Latinx person, chances are you will find that you share some aspects of identity and/or experiences with Latinx people. You will also become aware of differences in identities and experiences, including different opportunities and obstacles due to social and cultural factors. This assignment connects with course learning outcome # 2: "Identify the factors that lead to diverse Latinx identities and experiences..."

Instructions:

For your previous assignment, you created an identity chart that named different aspects of your own identity. For this assignment, you will:

1. Pick **three** aspects of your identity from the chart you developed that are most important or salient to you.
2. For each of the **three** aspects of your identity, respond to the following questions:
    a. Why is this aspect of your identity important to you?
    b. In what ways does this aspect of your identity shape your daily life? What do you do in your daily life because you have this identity?
    c. What are some positive or rewarding things you associate with this identity? What are some challenges or difficult things associated with this identity?
    d. In what ways is this aspect of your identity about membership in or connection to a group or a category of people?
    e. If you do not identify as Latinx, answer prompt i, below. If you do identify as Latinx, answer prompt ii, below.
        i. is this aspect of your identity one that you imagine some Latinx individuals might also share? Why or why not? Would the experiences associated with this aspect of your identity be different for a Latinx person? Why or why not?
        ii. is this aspect of your identity one that you imagine some non-Latinx individuals might also share? Why or why not? Would the experiences associated with this aspect of your identity be different for a non-Latinx person? Why or why not?

Figure 9.2 Diverse Identities and Experiences Assignment

to begin taking stock of our embeddedness in institutions and social structures. Thinking about our own identity and experiences, we can begin to see ourselves in social context (as people interacting within families, communities, schools, nation states, and so on).

To interrupt notions of objectivity that many students adhere to unquestioningly, and to open conversation on the reasons why, before my course, most students have not learned that Latinx history has long been integral to U.S. history, early each term we have a discussion on "bias" and multiple perspectives in history. I tell them that yes, I, their teacher, am biased, and so is everybody. I encourage them to identify their own biases. We talk about where our biases come from (lived experience, social location, institutions we interact with, and so on), and I have them work in small groups to discuss different types of biases, as well as whether bias is necessarily a bad thing and whether some biases might be better informed than others. This makes for animated discussion early in the term, but as the course progresses, some white students seem to revert to the perception that the decentering of dominant U.S. narratives about Latinxs, and the centering of Latinx perspectives (definitional of LS) is somehow unbalanced. Notions of balance and objectivity are especially inculcated into students in the sciences. While critiques of such scientific premises are not new, most students trained in the sciences are not as steeped in the critiques as they are in the embrace of these ideas. And the tendency is for them to have a difficult time imagining other ways of thinking. So, they resist. Throughout the term, I use every opportunity to provoke discussion on the ways much of what we are sold as purportedly objective isn't really so.

I use the prompt in Figure 9.3 to provide them an opportunity to reflect in writing on questions of bias and history, to ask themselves what they know, how they know it, and what they might *not* know about Latinx histories and experiences, and why. Following this essay, we have a discussion of how certain versions of historical events become official and others get obfuscated, obliterated, or simply left out of the historical record, and with what consequences.

Because emotions are such an integral dimension of lived experience, including with the racialized dimension of our lives, I aim to create spaces for students to routinely tune into and acknowledge their emotions, and to see them as a potential source of meaning. In the words of Janine Young Kim (2016), "(w)ithout engaging in the complex and sometimes messy world of racial emotions, we cannot cultivate the desire for otherness, the feeling of equality" (p. 499). Recently, I have used an online discussion forum to get students to think and converse with each other about their own emotions regarding our ongoing conversations on race/ethnicity (Figure 9.4). The perceived "distance" that an online forum provides versus a face-to-face conversation seems to make students more comfortable and willing to share their thoughts (and their emotions) with each other as they arise.

Teaching about (Racialized and Gendered) Work: The Challenges

The topic of work is central in introductory LS courses for multiple reasons. First, jobs are one key factor driving migration from Latin America to the United States.[3] Latinx workers (both immigrant and U.S.-born) have long

> **Reflective Essay: History**
>
> We are often taught sanitized, uncomplicated versions of history, which suggest that there are no other possible interpretations, that everybody agrees "this is how things were," or "this is how things happened," and "this is what it means." Interestingly, nations tend to portray themselves favorably in their own historical accounts. But history is rarely, if ever, a straight forward, single account; it is rather complex, rich, and often full of contention and contradiction. A critical approach to history (and to History, with capital h) demands that we ask questions such as, whose (hi)story is being told? Who is telling the (hi)story? Whose perspectives, concerns, experiences might be missing and why? What specific investments and biases shape the telling of this history? What did/do different historical actors have to lose in the telling of this story in this particular way? With these ideas and questions in mind, write a 5-page essay (typed, 11-point font, double-spaced, 1-inch margins on all sides) in response to the following:
>
> * Discuss how the above applies to your own experience learning about world and US history. What are some of the major historical storylines you have learned to date? Where and how did you pick these up? What impact did they have on you and on others around you? How did these stories shape your identity or your thinking?
>
> * Now focus specifically on what you have (or what you feel you have not) learned about the US relationship with Latin America and about Latinxs in the United States. What historical storylines have you learned about Latin America, about Latinxs, and about Latinx immigration to date (before this class)? How might a critical approach to history help you expand your thinking on Latinxs in relation to US history?
>
> * What might be some consequences of ignoring, forgetting, "erasing," or misrepresenting certain histories? How can we do, as critical thinkers and students of history, to shed the historical blinders that are often imposed on us? What tools do we have at our disposal to obtain a richer, more complete understanding of our history?

Figure 9.3 Reflective Essay: History

> **Online Discussion Forum: Emotions and Race**
>
> We closed our last class with the recognition that emotions are an important factor shaping people's comfort level talking about race. Post your thoughts about what emotions might get in the way of honest and fruitful conversations about race, and how. Then respond to at least one post by a peer. Try your hardest to be both honest and respectful in your post and responses.

Figure 9.4 Online Discussion Forum: Emotions and Race

been and continue to be integral to the functioning of the U.S. economy and to U.S. labor history, and constitute a growing share of the U.S. labor force. Also, an instrumentalizing notion of Latinxs as "always already laborers" (Maldonado, 2017) is prevalent within the U.S. imaginary, and imbricates U.S. cultural and political discourses. From the get-go, students have a good sense of the types of occupations and jobs wherein Latinx workers are concentrated. When asked why they think Latinxs are, as they rightly identify, overrepresented in the bottom rungs of the U.S. economy, they explain it as the result of a lack of educational and linguistic capital. Of course, this is only part of the picture: the parts of the picture students usually miss are those that have to do with the demand side of labor, the ways in which capital and the state work together to *produce* the conditions that keep Latinx people in these jobs and in precarious economic conditions. In the words of Alejandro Canales (2007),

> In the context of economic deregulation and labor flexibility, modernization generates and reproduces its own forms of poverty and precariousness. Individuals' social vulnerability as members of social, demographic, and cultural minorities based on gender, ethnicity and migration ceases to be a factor that exposes them to possible economic exclusion and becomes a prerequisite for their inclusion.
>
> (p. 75)

Relatedly, students have not necessarily considered the ways in which the routine placement of Latinxs within the U.S. labor queue is enabled through simultaneously gendered and racialized processes. Even when they themselves are easily able to list, off the top of their head, jobs where women are highly concentrated, and jobs where Latinxs are the majority of workers, and they note that those jobs tend not to be as prestigious or as well remunerated as other jobs, I can sense their skepticism and resistance when I mention that indeed, jobs in the United States are heavily segmented and segregated along both gender and racial lines. Their comments when we have these discussions suggest that these trends must result from a type of self-selection: men and women tend to be interested in different types of jobs, and in the case of Latinxs, for the trend to change, they simply need to get an education and learn English. So, my pedagogical challenge is twofold: First, I have to get students to consider ways the economy is shaped by factors other than human capital and individual workers' motivation. And, second, I need to get them to consider the ways jobs are to a large extent, gendered and racialized *by design* – that is, I want to help them recognize how, as a society, we routinely attribute gendered and racialized characteristics to skills and jobs – and that, indeed, we come to *think* of and *value* jobs in terms of their bearers and their place within U.S. racialized and gendered hierarchies.

A third challenge I've encountered when teaching about work in LS courses has to do with students' seeming detachment from and disinterest in the politics of labor, and the extent to which they subscribe to the idea that it is important for workers to organize and protect or defend their rights as workers. Many of my students report working part-time while in college, and some work full time. Yet, surprisingly, many hold negative views of unions. By the time they get to my classroom, they have picked up two notions: (1) that a university education will land them jobs where they won't have to worry about job conditions or worker rights, and (2) that employers will do right by workers without the need for worker organizing.

Tools: The Racialized and Gendered World of Work (That We Are ALL In)

I use the exercise in Figure 9.5 to get students to begin thinking about the world of work in which we are all immersed. They work on these exercises individually and then discuss them in groups. The first step of the exercise gets them to think about the characteristics of jobs and occupations, independently of who workers are. It gets them to think about what employers offer workers, and how this might shape who they aim to recruit for the work. It is also useful in getting them to think about upward mobility as something that is not available to all workers. Sometimes they still presume that people can get an education while they're working low-end jobs and can move up the economic ladder in that way. But in discussions we can interrogate how feasible that actually is by talking about schedules, employers' expectations, and lack of flexibility in low-wage jobs. Students are able to identify good and bad jobs readily. Occasionally, someone will want to avoid discussion of material conditions and talk about a good job as one that allows one to make an honest living, or that is fulfilling, but usually it is fairly easy to make the point that the material conditions of a job are part of what might or might not make a job desirable or fulfilling.

Understanding the dual US labor market

Individual Brainstorm: Hand out a sheet of a paper to each student. At the top of the sheet on one side have students write the words "good jobs." At the top of the page on the other side, have them write the words "bad jobs." Then have them respond to the following questions for each side, in as much detail as possible:

* What makes a job good/bad?
* What are the characteristics of good/bad jobs? (Again, address each, good jobs and bad jobs, on separate sides of the blank sheet.)
* What are the requirements for landing a good/bad job?
* What are some examples of good/bad jobs?
* What protections/assurances are in place for workers in these jobs?

Group Discussion: Have students share their answers and take notes on the board. Probe for areas that might be missing in students' accounts. Examples for good jobs: require more and higher credentials, tend to be well-paid, allow for mobility in the workplace, variety of benefits (health, visual, dental, retirement, etc) and perks available to workers, flexibility in schedule and work arrangements, stability, autonomy, ease and clarity in the method of payment (workers know when they'll be paid, how much, and how, they don't have to travel to some inconvenient location to retrieve their payment, might even have their wages deposited into their bank account), regular paychecks, workplaces and work are regulated (what is regulated in different types of work, by whom, and what are the mechanisms for enforcement--for example, health and safety, breaks, sexual harassment, etc.) Examples for bad jobs: Seasonal, part-time, unstable/contingent, lower wages, hours/pay are inconsistent, no overtime, workers have little flexibility and autonomy, jobs are unregulated, tend to be informal, no benefits, work environment may be inhospitable or physically taxing. Do we tend to think of particular groups as better fit for these jobs? Think of examples of good jobs and bad jobs and whose images come to mind for the people filling these jobs (think of gender, race/ethnicity, language skill, level of education, other markers of life and identity).

Figure 9.5 Understanding the Dual U.S. Labor Market

The exercise in Figure 9.6 is one I developed more recently in response to my perception that students do not see worker organizing as personally relevant. I envision it as a prompt for a research paper and personal reflection. However, I have not yet used it in my LS-focused courses because its aim is to get students to think about the workplaces they hope to join. I also wonder to what extent students in introductory level courses would be able to undertake the research it requires. I am considering using it in more advanced courses, or perhaps courses with a focus on work/labor. I share it here for others who teach in these areas and might wish to use it as a starting point to engage students in thinking about their own work lives.

Concluding Thoughts

In this chapter I have shared some of the most recurrent pedagogical challenges I have encountered teaching introductory Latinx Studies DPD courses at a PWI. I've also shared some of the theoretical and analytical frameworks through which I make sense of my own work as a teacher and a handful of tools I use to engage students who enroll in those courses in critical unlearning to prompt reflection about their/our embeddedness in hierarchical social structures. In the course of writing this chapter, and in conversation with colleagues from my own university who teach DPD courses, or are otherwise involved with the DPD Program, I am reminded that critical pedagogy is a collective effort, a transformative project that spans across disciplinary fields and that calls for community building and knowledge sharing among those committed to social justice. This collective effort can only be sustained on the basis of collective ingenuity and labor: it requires sharing tactics and strategies–trials, errors, and successes – but also the emotional

---

Exploring Specific Work Contexts and Labor Struggles

1. What types of workplaces, occupations, and jobs exist in your field of interest? Map them out. How do various occupations jobs rank in a relative hierarchy of prestige, wages, and conditions?

2. Can you identify patterns of gender or ethnic/racial segregation of occupations or jobs related to your field of interest? If so, how do wages and conditions and overall notions of prestige compare for jobs with different concentrations of men and women, and/or different ethnoracial groups? Are there racialized or gendered perceptions "out there" of workers or certain jobs in your area of interest?

3. What connections are there between primary and secondary sector jobs in your area?

4. Do some research on labor history in your area: What major gains have workers in occupations/jobs in your field/area experienced regarding work conditions? How were these accomplished (e.g. legislation or policy change, union work, other types of organizing?)

5. Is there a history of union activity/activism in occupations/jobs related to your area of interest? What forms of organizing, if any, have been enacted?

6. What particular obstacles do workers in occupations/jobs related to your area of interest face in their struggle for better wages and job conditions? What challenges exist?

Figure 9.6 Exploring Specific Work Contexts and Labor Struggles

content of our work, and intentional reflection on our subjectivities and how they are implicated in what knowledge is produced and how. Of course, more than ever, it requires that we uphold the question, *knowledge for what end?* The existence of institutional mechanisms such as the DPD Program enables and encourages such collective approaches to teaching for positive social transformation. As neoliberalism becomes ever more entrenched in higher education spaces, the work of DPD and the collective commitment to critical pedagogy must respond in kind.

I hope this chapter and the DPD volume that contains it get taken as an invitation for further conversations on pedagogy and the role of social justice education across institutional and disciplinary contexts. I hope to remain in conversation with the wide range of actors who support student learning across campus.

Additional resources

Audiovisual

Courtney, H. (Director) (2003). *Los trabajadores/The workers* [Film]. New Day Films/Independent Lens/ Corporation for Public Broadcasting (CPB).

Hernandez, C. (Director) (2019). *Building the American dream* [Documentary]. Panda Bear Films.

Lears, R., & Blotnik R. (Directors and Producers) (2014). *The hand that feeds* [Documentary]. Jubilee Films.

NPR (February 23, 2014). Latino workers at risk. *Latino USA*. National Public Radio. www.npr.org/2014/02/28/280773324/latino-workers-at-risk

Prado, A. (Director and Producer) (2005). *Maid in America* [Documentary]. Impacto Films.

Readings

Catanzarite, L., & Aguilera, M. (2002). Working with co-ethnics: Earnings penalties for Latino immigrants at Latino jobsites. *Social Problems 49*(1), 101–127.

Chavez, L. (2013). *The Latino threat: Constructing immigrants, citizens, and the nation (2nd ed.).* Stanford University Press.

Massey, D. (2014). The racialization of Latinos in the United States. In Bucerius, S., & Tonry, M. (Eds.), *The Oxford handbook of ethnicity, crime, and immigration* (pp. 21–40). Oxford University Press.

Waldinger, R., & Lichter, M. (2003). *How the other half works: Immigration and the social organization of labor.* University of California Press.

Web Pages

Teaching Tolerance (2011). *Ten myths about immigration: Debunk the misinformation students bring to school – and help them think for themselves.* Teaching Tolerance. www.tolerance.org/magazine/spring-2011/ten-myths-about-immigration

Time Magazine (March 12, 2015). How Mexican immigration to the U.S. has evolved. A post in collaboration with The John W. Kluge Center at the Library of Congress. https://time.com/3742067/history-mexican-immigration/

Notes

1 I strongly discourage the use of this language by my students, as it dehumanizes and vilifies the populations to which it refers, in addition to being technically inaccurate.
2 I present "legality" and "illegality" to students as sociopolitical categories. Our focus is on how they get produced and reproduced and with what consequences.
3 The factors that explain continued immigration from Latin America to the United States and Latin@ incorporation into the U.S. economy are, of course, multiple and complex. Economic restructuring, wage differentials between sending countries and the United States, immigration policies, social networks, employer recruitment and State-led economic development initiatives have all been major driving forces. Also, immigration from particular Latin American countries has slowed down at points, responding to changes in the U.S. economy.

References

Althusser, L. (1972). Ideology and ideological state apparatuses. In *Lenin and Philosophy and other essays*. Monthly Review Press, 79–87.
Aparicio, F. (2007). (Re)constructing latinidad: The challenge of latina/o studies. In Flores, J. & Rosaldo, R. (Eds.) *Companion to Latina/o Studies* (pp. 35–48). Blackwell Publishing.
Bonilla-Silva, E. (2001). *White supremacy and racism in the post-civil rights era*. Lynne Rienner.
Bonilla-Silva, E. (2018). *Racism without racists: Color-blind racism and the persistence of racial inequality in America* (5th edition). Rowman and Littlefield.
Bonilla-Silva, E. (2019). Feeling race: Theorizing the racial economy of emotions. *American Sociological Review*, *84*(1), 1–25.
Brusky, J. (2012). *Unlearn Racism 4* [Photograph]. Flickr. www.flickr.com/photos/40969298@N05/9339142359/in/album-72157634744584303/
Canales, A. (2007). Inclusion and segregation: The incorporation of Latin American immigrants into the U.S. labor market. *Latin American Perspectives 34*(1), 73–82.
Chavez, L. (2008). *The Latino threat: Constructing immigrants, citizens, and the nation*. Stanford University Press.
Denzin, N. K. (1984). *On understanding emotion*. Jossey-Bass Inc.
Facing History and Ourselves (2020). www.facinghistory.org
Kim, J. Y. (2016). Racial emotions and the feeling of equality. *University of Colorado Law Review 87*(2): 437–500.
Maldonado, M. M. (2017). Not just laborers: Latina/o claims of belonging in the U.S. heartland. In Valerio-Jiménez O., Vaquera-Vásquez S., & Fox C. (Eds.), *Latina/o midwest reader* (pp. 102–120). University of Illinois Press.
Maldonado, M. M., & Guenther K. M. (2019). Introduction: Critical mobilities in the neoliberal university. *Feminist Formations, Special Issue on Critical Feminist Exits*, *31*(1), vii–xxiii.
Oboler, S. (1997). So far from God, so close to the United States: The roots of Hispanic homogenization. In Romero, M., Hondagneu-Sotelo, P., & Ortiz, V. (Eds.), *Challenging fronteras* (pp. 31–54). Routledge.

Pew Research Center (2019). Race in America 2019. www.pewsocialtrends.org/2019/04/09/the-role-of-race-and-ethnicity-in-americans-personal-lives/

Robinson, W. I. (2018). *Into the tempest: Essays on the new global capitalism.* Haymarket Books.

Santa Ana, O. (2002). *Brown tide rising: Metaphors of Latinos in contemporary American public discourse.* University of Texas Press.

Learning for Justice (2021). www.learningforjustice.org/

10 Talking About Class

Allison L. Hurst

The Importance of Adding Class to the Discussion

As I originally wrote this chapter, in the summer of 2019, my Facebook feed had blown up over a *Washington Post* op-ed by then presidential candidate Bernie Sanders in which he argued, "the straightest path to racial equality is through the one percent."[1] Many of my friends are partial to Sanders, so the shares were mostly approving, with some fierce opposition from many of my female friends, still raw from Clinton's 2016 loss and who were happy to see Kamala Harris emerging as a frontrunner. I know who my friends are on Facebook tells you a lot about me, and I want to start this chapter with this level of honesty. I am a white woman of Generation X, who was raised working class, carries a lot of student debt, and still struggles with the privileges of being a tenured professor. I cannot *unsee* class. It is everywhere before me, which is probably why I, and others like me, found Sanders so appealing.

One of the responses on my feed came from an anarchist friend who linked to Keeanga-Yamahtta Taylor, a professor of African American Studies at Princeton and frequent contributor to the Leftist journal *Jacobin*. Dr. Taylor appeared tickled that Sanders quoted her in his op-ed, "There is no race without class in this country." This proposition may seem relatively uncontroversial, but it is not. For decades conversations about class were used to silence conversations about race. It is similar to how the response of "blue lives matter" was an attempt (by many, if not all of its users) to shut down "Black lives matter" protests. For those aware of this history, Sanders' commitment to talking about class to talk about race may appear to be just another attempt at diverting attention away from serious social issues, like reparations, that other candidates (e.g., Kamala Harris) foreground in their campaign speeches. I would argue, however, that both Dr. Taylor and Senator Sanders have it right, although it is very important to also keep this history of diversion in mind.

The levels of economic inequality we currently experience are largely unprecedented and a serious threat to both our democracy and the lives of ourselves and other creatures on this planet. Keeping silent about class does not make class go away; it merely confuses many issues, including racialized ones. Class is not merely about who has what and who doesn't but about how we think about other people – how we put them into hierarchies of power. If we don't talk about how we do this, we can get stuck pointing out problems and finding people to blame who may not have any power to make changes. Abstractions are good in theory, but less helpful on the ground. We are all part of this system of classification, and our positions in this system are going to affect what we see and how we talk about what we see. To give a specific example, consider the issue of "white privilege." A real problem, yes. But what happens so often when we introduce our white students to this concept? Many resist it. Some out of bad faith and others because many white people have assumed that racism is a problem mostly resolved in the U.S. Others resist it because they have not really felt privileged in their (white) communities, because they and their families have been at the bottom of the social order. If we could acknowledge this, talk about it, we would be more successful in getting those students to understand how they can be both relatively disadvantaged economically and relatively privileged racially. Their parents may work multiple jobs that don't pay well, but they are less likely to be shot by the police at a traffic stop. Further, adding class to the discussion here can help form stronger alliances, as students come to understand what they have in common as well as what operates to separate them. In other words, talking about class is going to help us build those necessary alliances between Black, Brown, and white people. Strategically, obfuscating class has always helped the racists win.

In this chapter, I lay out some of the ways I have talked about class in my teaching. For purposes of brevity, I am foregrounding class here, but this does not mean that these discussions should ever take place in a vacuum. Other identities, but particularly racialized identities, are integral to the conversation, as I hope this introduction has demonstrated. I have indicated places and spaces where integration of these identities into the exercises may be most productive, but others will probably have much to add. After all, I am also hampered by my own social position as a White woman, and I am sure there are more ways to make a discussion of class truly intersectional. I recommend reading this chapter alongside other chapters in this volume, and I particularly recommend those by Maldonado and Mize. Before getting to the exercises, however, I want to lay the ground by asking us all to think about who "we" refers to in our teaching, and among our students.

Laying the Ground: Who is "We"?

A few years ago, I began changing the pronouns I use when teaching students about the founders of sociological theory. Marx, Weber, and Durkheim each formulated their theories around problems and issues that emerged with the advent of industrial capitalism in Europe. In place of small, local communities centered on subsistence production, an entire new system of urbanization, inequality, and commodity production rose up, threatening to dismantle traditional norms and beliefs. Both Marx and Weber focused on the novelty of "formally free labor," something that is now a largely taken-for-granted fact of life. I used to explain this to students by saying, "capitalism created a system where some owned the means of production and others had to sell their labor (go to work) in order to get money to buy things they needed." I now say, "capitalism created a system where *we* go to work and sell our labor to buy things." It is a subtle difference, but it has opened up an entire new vista on teaching. Sometimes I will say, 'well, maybe there are a few capitalists in class but most of us are workers." As I teach at a large public university, I have yet to have a student tell me they actually are able to survive without having to work. This subtle shift has personalized the material for many students, bringing it closer to home. When students use "they" to explain the proletariat, I often gently suggest that they replace *they* with *we*. I see the lights go on.

Of course, in Marx's formulation, there are the capitalists and the workers, the bourgeoisie and the proletariat. It is easy to belong to and teach to the 99%. It is a little more difficult to get students to understand the subtler, but, I would argue, incredibly important differences of class that operate to advantage some, disadvantage others, and distinguish all of us to each other within that large 99%. There is the difference between the working class and the middle class, for example, and between those of us with college-educated parents and those first in our family to go to college. In Oregon, where I teach, there is often a powerful distinction felt and made between those raised in "rural" communities versus those from suburban or metropolitan areas. Often these geographic distinctions overlay class distinctions (particularly that between an educated professional-managerial class who lives in major cities and a more traditional middle-class who lives in the country). Other times, racial differences are read as class differences. These readings can be wide of the mark, of course.

I am aware that my students come from various locations in social space, but also aware that one of the ways that class works in the U.S. today is to ignore that fact. Instead, we (and here I mean both those who work in academia and those who have the power to make pronouncements about the social world, such as those working in media) pretend it doesn't exist, read it as something else (e.g., "rural"), or mischaracterize it as race. There is an unspoken "we" operating here, where everyone is the same, and that same collective is middle-class (and white). So, I talk about class a lot. And I am always careful with the pronouns I use, beyond even using a collective we to talk about us as proletarian workers. I am particularly careful when talking about "working class/middle class" identifications. Too often, the working class is othered as "they," while the middle class is assumed to be the norm, what "we" who are speaking are. I purposely upend this, and I tell my students I am doing it. As with using *we* to mean "all of us who work for a living," I use *we* to refer to the working class, because I myself am from the working class. I was raised working class and identify as a "working-class academic," a hybrid, because my loyalties and my culture cannot be uprooted or altered within a single lifetime.

Being attuned to how we refer to collectives is a good first step in talking (and thinking) about class. Once you are so attuned, it is amazing how often you will find yourself rethinking and problematizing the readings you provide your students. For example, I recently read an article by a fellow sociologist, David Riesman, writing in the 1950s. It was a good article, comparing an industrialized postwar American society with agrarian 19th century life. But in the comparison lay a buried but insidious collective we statement. He pointed out that the (19th century) protagonist in a Henry James novel spent his summer loafing around, while *we spend our summers in busy activity*. He then argued that *we have forgotten to live like gentlemen*. Now, I must emphasize in case you did not already pick up on it, that the character in the James novel was indeed a white "gentleman," who not only had his summers off but who worked the rest of the year only when he wished, having the ability to rely solely on income from inherited property. If I were a white middle-class college student today, particularly a white male-identifying student, and I was provided this text, I would indeed think, "Wow, back in the day we had summers off! Look at us engage in the rat race now!" If I were a student of color, or even more specifically a Latinx student whose family included migrant workers, I might feel even more isolated from the conversation, as I would understand this person was clearly not ever talking about my family. In contrast, most white middle-class students, and even many white working-class students, would have *identified* with the James character, because Riesman suggested they do so. Riesman identified himself with the hero of the story and then pulled in his readers to do the same. We (teachers) should be much more careful about who we use "we" to refer to, especially in front of our students.

Classroom Exercises

Being attuned to collective we statements is an important first step when talking about class. It is difficult to ask students to interrogate their own class positions without first being aware of how easily we silence talk about class, agglomerating experiences into a common collective or set of shared understandings (e.g., "millennials rely on their parents too much!" "students these days are too involved with social media," "when you go on Spring Break, remember to be safe!"). In case you didn't pick up on that, much of what has been said about millennials and college students refers to the experience of (mostly white) middle-class young adults, and may be wholly untrue for first-generation college students, non-traditional college students, and many students of color. I once had a student tell me that she was afraid to speak in a class about rural poverty, because the perspective was always about "those people" who lived in trailer parks. Because she grew up living in a trailer park, she felt alienated (actually, more like crushed) hearing the conversations around her.

There are several exercises I have developed over the years to help students talk about class. *All students*, not just students who grow up in trailer parks or inner cities. Again, it is important to displace that collective middle-class we. If you retain it, and simply add "voices from the margins," you are not going to get it right. Although I have not yet been able to realize my dream of instituting a Class Studies Curriculum, I have been fortunate to teach several courses on various aspects of class, class identity, and class formation. In this section, I want to discuss three exercises that lie on a continuum from the most general and generic to the most personal and concrete. Most recently, these were used in a DPD-inspired experimental course titled *Class: Systems, Meanings, and Applications*, with both undergraduate and graduate students.

Mapping Exercise

The first exercise asks students to work in groups to map the current class structure of the U.S.[2] I first get them talking about what they think distinguishes class groups – is it money (income or wealth)? Is it education? Is it occupation? Is it race, immigration status, nationality, religion? Over the many years I have done this exercise, about three-quarters of all groups use education as the primary indicator of class status, drawing the line between those with and without a college degree. This is what many pollsters do, as it is an easy line to draw. What happens in those group discussions, however, is that some students challenge this choice. They begin thinking through how income is related to education, and how sometimes it is not so clear that more education means more money (they often bring up the two college "dropouts" here – Bill Gates and Mark Zuckerberg). More interesting to me, however, are the times that groups come up with something completely different in their mapping – one group that included a lot of students in the Crime & Justice Track, drew a line between those that had been caught up in the criminal justice system and those who had not. They then went on to explain all the ways the former were marked, by race, by educational status, by neighborhood, by sex. The first step of this exercise then, coming up with the divisions used to distinguish classes, can really push students to think about the connections between social categories, groups, and power.

After the students have conceptualized the division, I ask them to map them onto the U.S. population, I ask them to "take a guess" at the proportional magnitude of these classes (as well as to clearly identify each class by name). If, for example, they define the working class as not having a college degree – what percentage of [Americans] fall into this category? Each map must include a specific *number* of *named* classes – some groups will have as few as two classes (e.g., named "rich" and "poor") while others groups may end up with six or eight (e.g., poor, lower class, working poor, working class, lower middle class, etc.). This is another area where group members challenge each other. They may be in agreement that education matters most, but how does that play out in the number of classes? Are those without a high school degree distinguishable from those with one? If income (or wealth) is the big divider, where does one draw the line and how many lines should be drawn? I usually have one group who defines class in such a way that there are too many levels to count, like a ladder of mobility. They tend to use small increments of income, but then get confused if they try to link these up to other divisions, such as education.

Once each group has created a pictorial representation of the class structure, complete with descriptions and percentages, I ask them to present and explain their map to the rest of the class. In a large class, there will be many similarities but also usually one or two total surprises, which makes for a great discussion. Because class is a moving target (more on this later), I am careful not to make judgments or pronouncements about what class really is, although I will help out by providing data on actual percentages (e.g., one-third of Americans have a college degree; more than half of American families make less than $45,000 a year). This data often surprises them, and can make them rethink their named divisions. In my mind, a successful conclusion to this exercise is (a) an appreciation of the complexity of naming and mapping class divisions: and (b) an awareness that the mapping of classes is itself a form of social power. Of course, on a more basic level, it is also a success if students learn that there is much more poverty and inequality in [American] society than they may have grown up expecting. This helps more privileged students situate their privilege and less privileged students recognize their averageness. In the grand scheme of American class society, "those" people are more likely to be the wealthy than the poor.

Writing about Family Trajectories: Bringing it Home

The second exercise is more personal, although it hews to the line of identifying and analyzing social and structural forces (rather than individual beliefs, values, and experiences). In this way, it operates as a bridge between the wholly impersonal structural mapping of society and the third exercise, which takes students into their own beliefs and practices. The second exercise calls for students to describe the class trajectory of their families and their own educational experiences. This is not shared with anyone but me, and I tell the students that I take what they say in great confidence. "Outing" students before they are ready to share can cause students to shut down. This is as true for the third-generation college student who grew up in a mansion as the student from rural Oregon who grew up in a home without running water. Because the exercise is *not* shared with others in class, it is a relatively safe place for students to explore privilege and harm. I find it is important to keep this second exercise, a bridge between the abstract and the shared personal, anonymous so that students can be as honest as possible with themselves and find an encouraging and non-judgmental listener (me). There are both apparent and covert stigmas associated with class, both as privilege and its obverse. One not used to this area may be surprised at what seemingly innocuous statement or question can bring up a torrent of fierce emotional responses. For example, I once had a student break down in tears when she confessed that her biggest embarrassment in life was her mother's home.

Prompted by a series of readings on class and education (e.g., the unequal funding of public K-12 schools; differential classroom teaching styles related to class, race, and gender; parental involvement in students' schooling; differential aspirations and connections to labor markets), students grapple with identifying the social forces that both assisted and placed limits on their educational trajectories. By thinking about this alongside the class trajectories of their families, they can compare and contrast the impact of education on their own paths relative to other forms of advancement. This is also a great exercise to help middle-class students, especially white middle-class students, articulate and discuss their own class and racial privileges. They may discover that their parents or grandparents' generation was the first to break the college/professional barrier and think about how their own paths have been smoothed over by theirs (and gain sympathy for classmates who are experiencing what their parents or grandparents did before).

Although these biographies are not shared openly with others in class, I do reserve a class period to talk about them generally and to allow students to share things they are comfortable sharing with others. They come to that class, I find, very curious to learn about others' experiences. Depending on the number of students in class, I may disclose that five or six students are the first in their families to go to college. Even though these students are not named, they may feel more at ease knowing they are not alone. Unlike race, which is often visibly marked so that students of color have nowhere to hide in a predominantly white classroom, working-class students (and very wealthy students, too) can appear to blend in, and this is particularly so for white students in these groups. Displacing one collective we away from "we are all middle class here" is another way of opening up the classroom to diverse experiences and expectations. After this exercise, I have seen students be more aware of how the use of blanket statements might operate, given the diversity of experiences and social locations actually in operation in their classroom.

Talking about Class: Opening Up in a Focus Group

The third exercise builds on the previous two and asks students to work in groups and really get personal, although once again it does this in a way that is respectful of students' privacy concerns. This exercise only works if there has been some ground prepared in previous coursework, and students feel they can both open up to others without being judged *and also have the power to remain silent.* One of the practical skills that we try to develop in sociology is the ability to conduct focus groups. A focus group is a demographically diverse small group whose reactions or responses to a series of questions (or, in some cases, a campaign or product) are used to generate knowledge about the subject of those questions. Focus groups are best confined to six to eight persons, with (ideally) two focus group moderators, so multiple groups will be necessary in large classes.

In order to get the students to be personal about class with other students, I frame this discussion as professional training in how to conduct a focus group.

I explain the ethical requirements of conducting a focus group, including the necessity of confidentiality and empathetic non-judgmental responses. I allow students to opt out in the same way that in the real world a focus group participant always has the option to not answer a question they find too intrusive. To prepare for the focus group, students are given several short and deeply reflective accounts of people located in different class positions. These accounts are diverse and include intersectional struggles (e.g., Kirby Moss explaining how being middle-class and Black affects his interviews with "poor whites"). Here are some questions I have used for the focus group exercise:

1 Did any of the readings resonate with you, in terms of similarities (or differences)? Do you share the experience of any of the authors?
2 Is it hard (or easy) to talk about class? *Why does this make you uncomfortable?*
3 When did you first hear the words "working class"? "middle class"? Was this about someone else, yourself, or someone you knew well? *Do you remember learning any lessons about class? (impolite to talk/ask about?)*
4 Let's talk a little bit about intersectionality. How does your own class identity relate to other identities that are important to you? What is most important to you in terms of how you see yourself? *How important is class identity compared to these other identities?*
5 *Anything else you want to add?*

Asking these questions in the context of a focus group exercise allows for empathetic sharing in a professional setting. Students are prompted to listen deeply and non-judgmentally. They learn to share their stories in what I have worked hard to cultivate as a relatively safe setting, with the assumption that there is something useful to be learned about the ways we experience and talk about class. Often, the question about intersectionality brings out dimensions of race, religion, and geography that students have used (they realize) to talk about class. Having the chance to reflect about the intersections of these identity strands and how they are sometimes used to obviate the necessity of confronting class privilege directly has proven very useful. Note that the focus group questions are fairly simple and that the list is quite short. This is important so that students do not end up answering in short yes/no responses so that they can move on to the next question. If one of the questions elicits thirty minutes of responses, that is all the better for the impact of the exercise. When the focus group concludes, we spend time debriefing (a) what we learned about class and (b) what we learned about the process of talking about class. If done well, students are excited at this point, and a little bit in awe at their own ability to dig deeply in a professional manner.

Why Not to Do the "Privilege Walk"

For all the reasons discussed above (generating empathetic understanding, enabling students to remain silent when necessary, asking questions in a professional manner in order to understand a phenomenon and its impact on people), I am strongly opposed to the privilege walk, an exercise that I have encountered in almost every setting in which people try to "add class" to a larger discussion of privilege. I have seen the privilege walk used at conferences as part of panelist presentations, in workshops, and in the classroom. In almost every case, there was simply not enough preparation for its use, with the result that privileged participants learned to recognize their privilege only at the expense of those less privileged. Let me briefly explain the privilege walk for those readers unacquainted with it. Participants are asked to line up, at an equal point in space. A moderator reads statements about class privilege aloud. For each statement with which the participant agrees, he or she moves forward a step (or more). The statements include such things as, "I had my own bedroom as a child," or "I attended a private high school," or "My family often took vacations abroad." By the end of the reading of the statements, the most privileged students will be standing at the front of the space, and the least privileged will be standing at or near the starting point. The moderator then asks those in the front to look around and recognize their privilege.

One can imagine how this might reinforce class shame (and anger!) but let me provide one example. I attended a panel on educational inequalities. One of the panelists asked us all to line up for an "instructive exercise." My heart sank, as I realized what this was going to entail. In a bid to be inclusive, the graduate student who was assisting with the conference setup and technical logistics was encouraged to participate. She was one of the only people of color in the room, and the only non-faculty person, and, as I knew from a previous conversation with her, the first person in her family to go to college. She was very excited to be helping out at this conference and saw herself as a professional, like the rest of us. Well, at the end of the exercise, it was she and I standing near the starting line, with everyone else seemingly miles ahead of us. While the moderator was pleased at how she visually conveyed the privilege of those at the front, I saw the young woman's eyes fill with confusion and shame. She ducked her head when we returned to our seats and mentally (in my opinion) checked out. That is why I do not ever do the walk of privilege exercise, despite its ability to visually depict privilege in a stark and recognizable way. That woman's confusion and shame is the reason I spend so much time developing a rapport with students and treating each of their stories and sets of belief with care and respect.

For those readers who disagree with me, and who are adamant that students should be shocked into recognizing their privilege, I suggest an anonymous (paper-based) version instead. Give students the list of privileges and allow them to take it home and check those that apply to them. Have them return these to you without any identifying personal information (like names). Ask them to keep a copy. Tally the responses and report them to the class, allowing students to compare their answers to the class average, low score, and high score. It won't have the same visual kick of seeing how far ahead of everyone else you stand, but neither will that visual kick come at the expense of the students hovering near the starting line.

What It Means to be a Working-Class Academic

I want to conclude this chapter with my own thoughts about where I stand on that privilege line. But first I need to relate what I know and have come to believe about class from a sociologist's perspective. Class is not like several of the other major identities used to differentiate and privilege some over others (e.g., race, gender, age). What we make of skin pigmentation, biological sex, or the physical states of our bodies is a social construct, but there is some basic physical reality on which these social constructs are based. This makes arguing with people about them a bit different than arguing about class. Class is purely abstraction. Classes may be denoted physically, by race and sex and any number of other factors, but it itself is purely and wholly a social construct. What makes a class a class is that "each member of the same class is more likely than any member" of another class to have been confronted with the situations most frequent for the members of that class (Bourdieu, 1977, p. 85). Classes are sometimes made by reference to race, gender, and even age (as in a society where elders receive better quarters and food and hold all the power). Class only exists *to the extent* that it classifies – that some are given more resources than others, a greater chance of living a long life, an easier life overall. *We need not be a class (nor a racialized nor a gendered) society*. Indeed, humans have spent most of their time on the planet unclassed; it has only really been in the past 10,000 years or so that human society differentiated itself by task and distribution of resources. This means that talking about class is itself a deeply political enterprise. "The word 'class' will never be a neutral word so long as there are classes: the question of the existence or non-existence of classes is a stake in struggle between the classes" (Bourdieu, 1993, p. 21).

I grew up relatively poor, the daughter of teen parents who struggled throughout my childhood to find a purchase in American society. They have done so now, and I can perhaps attribute their success not only to my parents' unflagging hard work but also to our relatively privileged space as a white family in a deeply racist society. The wounds of my childhood nevertheless run deep in me, and they have motivated most of my adult actions, both professionally and personally. To provide just one more quote from my favorite theorist, a man who also ended up in life in a much better position than his childhood prepared him for, "the position one takes on the question of classes depends on the position one occupies in the class structure" (Bourdieu, 1993, p. 57). As someone who has moved out of the working class and into the middle class, I am deeply aware of the impact of class and the privileges that belonging to the middle class affords. Although I carry a great deal of student loan debt, I no longer hold that paralyzing fear that I would be homeless, incarcerated, or dead at an early age that I held for the first three-quarters of my life. I am still outraged that my brothers and sisters (metaphorically and literally) struggle so much to receive half of what my current colleagues hold so easily and seemingly without recognition. I know what it means to live without expectations, to literally have no faith in the future and its possibilities. I cringe when I hear reports of (supposedly average, but always privileged) people who do this or that when I know that objectively these averages fail to represent the majority of Americans.

I spent many years grappling with the cultural and psychological dislocations I incurred as a result of becoming educated. In graduate school, I turned away from the study I was pursuing (international intellectual property regimes) to instead more closely examine the experiences of working-class college students.[3] I had to do that, because I needed to understand for myself and my family whether my educational success was worth it. I came to the realization that it was, but only if I could spend my academic career trying to do something about class inequities.

Because of who I am, a working-class academic, a person who has crossed class lines by some objective measures but who will always remain loyal to and cognizant of the working class, I know that talking about class is a deeply political act, one that many people would prefer we did not do. Claims of a middle-class society or a classless society serve those with the most class privilege and do no favors to the majority of us – poor, working-class or middle-class. We inhabit a social structure that is deeply unequal, and we still struggle with properly articulating the ways this is so. Until we do, however, we cannot hope to change it. It will not be enough to describe, measure, and understand how race, gender, nationality, and other markers of identity are used to stratify us, if we fail to recognize stratification itself as the problem. This is what talking about class can help us do. Talking about class forces us to confront stratification head on. Class is a system in which we are all entangled. It cannot be understood without paying attention to how resources and opportunities have been unfairly distributed historically, so it necessarily includes discussion of slavery, patriarchy, and racial capitalism. Getting all of our students to talk about class, about their own positions in the system of privileges and resources, opens their eyes to larger systems of oppression. Even as the system may do more harm to some of us than others, it deeply deforms all of us as human beings. Or so is my opinion, having experienced class from multiple positions.

Additional Resources

If you, the reader, find yourself in a similar situation, or want to support students (particularly graduate students) who are struggling to reconcile working-class pasts and middle-class futures, there are thankfully now some organizations and places you can turn to for guidance and support. Join the Working-Class Academics Section of the Association of Working-Class Studies![4] Attend a workshop or use the resources of the organization, Class Action (www.classism.org).

Edited Volumes of Working-Class Biographies

Readings

Adair, V.C., & Dahlberg, S.L. (2003). *Reclaiming class: Women, poverty, and the promise of higher education in America*. Temple University Press.

Dews, C. L. B., & Law, C.L. (1995). *This fine place so far from home: Voices of academics from the working class*. Temple University Press.

Grimes, M.D., & Morris, J. (Eds) (1997). *Caught in the middle: Contradictions in the lives of sociologists from working-class backgrounds*. Praeger Press.

Mahony, P., & Zmroczek, C. (1997). *Class matters: Working-class women's perspectives on social class*. Taylor & Francis

Oldfield, K., & Johnson, R.G., III. (2008). *Resilience: Queer professors from the working class*. SUNY Press.

Ryan, J., & Sackrey, C. (1984). *Strangers in paradise: Academics from the working class*. South End Press.

Samarco, C. V., & Muzzatti, S.M. (2005). *Reflections from the wrong side of the tracks: Class identity and the working class experience in academe*. Rowman & Littlefield.

Tokarczyk, M.M., & Fay, E.A. (1993). *Working-class women in the academy: Laborers in the knowledge factory*. University of Massachusetts Press.

Van Galen, J.A., & Dempsey, V.O. (Eds) (2009). *Trajectories: The social and educational mobility of education scholars from poor and Working-class backgrounds*. Sense Publishers.

Welsch, K.A. (2005). *Those winter sundays: Female academics and their Working-class parents*. University Press of America.

Working-Class Academics and Others Who Have Moved Out of Poverty/the Working Class

Readings

Bowker, A. (1993). *Sisters in the blood: The education of women in native* America. Center for Bilingual/Multicultural Education.

hooks, b. (1994). *Teaching to transgress: Education as the practice of freedom*. Routledge.

Hurst, A. L. (2008). "A Healing Echo: Methodological Reflections of a Working-Class Researcher on Class." *The Qualitative Report, 13*(3): 334–352.

Hurst, A. L., & Nenga, S.K. (Eds) (2016). *Working in class: Recognizing how social class shapes our academic work*. Rowman & Littlefield.

Lubrano, A. (2004). *Limbo*. John Wiley & Sons.

Jensen, B. (2012). *Reading classes: On culture and classism in America*. ILR Press.

Rose, M. (1989). *Lives on the boundary: The struggles and achievements of America's underprepared*. Free Press: Collier Macmillan Publishers.

Thatcher, J., Ingram, N., Burke, C., & Abrahamson, J. (2016). *Bourdieu: The next generation*. Routledge.

Villanueva, V. (1993). *Bootstraps: From an american academic of color*. National Council of Teachers of English.

Zandy, J. (1995). *Liberating memory: Our work and our Working-class consciousness*. Rutgers University Press.

Talking About Class with Students

Readings

Collins, C., & Yeskel, F. (2014). *Class lives: Stories from across our economic divide*. Cornell University Press.[5]

Damaske, S. (2009). Brown suits need not apply: The intersection of race, gender, and class in institutional network building. *Sociological Forum, 24*(2): 402–424.

Bageant, J. (2011). *Rainbow pie: A redneck memoir*. Scribe.[6]

Hurst, A.L. (2010). *The burden of academic success: Loyalists, renegades, and double agents*. Lexington.[7]

Lacy, K. (2007). *Blue-chip Black: Race, class, and status in the new Black middle class*. University of California Press.[8]

Leondar-Wright, B. (2014). *Missing class: Strengthening social movement groups by seeing class cultures*. ILR Press, pp. 9–37.[9]

McCabe, J., & Jackson, B.A. 2016. Pathways to financing college: Race and class in students' narratives of paying for school. In *Social Currents*, pp. 1–19.[10]

Moss, K. (2003). *The color of class: Poor whites and the paradox of privilege*. University of Pennsylvania Press.[11]

Streib, J. (2015). *The power of the past: Understanding cross-class marriages*. Oxford University Press, pp. 188–220.[12]

Audiovisuals

People Like Us (n.d.) [TV Series]. PBS. www.pbs.org/show/people-us/[13]

To prepare for the educational trajectory exercise, there are numerous possible readings, but I recommend pulling a chapter from Jonathan Kozol's *Savage Inequalities: Children in America's Schools* (2012). There is also an excellent PBS documentary hosted by Bill Moyers that includes an interview with Kozol and has graphic representation of the savage inequality Kozol discusses: https://billmoyers.com/content/children-americas-schools/

Finally, if you are feeling brave and want to discuss the Trump phenomenon directly, and the argument that white working class voters are racist, I recommend the short piece by Williams, J. (2016). What So Many People Don't Get About the U.S. Working Class, Harvard Business Review (November 10) plus my (2018) review of Williams' related book *White Working Class*.

Notes

1 Sanders, B. (2019). "The straightest path to racial equality is through the one percent." *Washington Post* July 10, 2019.
2 I use the U.S. here, only as the default. The exercise can be structured to take other national (or regional) contexts in mind. In the text, I have bracketed "American" when referring to this default option, to remind readers that modification here is possible.
3 You can read what I found in my 2010 publication, *The Burden of Academic Success: Loyalists, Renegades, and Double Agents*, published by Lexington Books.
4 https://wcstudiesassociation.wordpress.com/
5 This is a collection of first-person accounts. All are recommended but three in particular have worked well together for the focus group exercise: 1) Introduction: "Caviar, College, Coupons, and Cheese" by Yeskel (pp. 1–12); 2) "Oreo? A Black American Experience" by John Vaughn (pp. 150–155); 3) "Born on Third Base" by Collins (pp. 165–171).
6 Bageant is a harsh critic of American capitalism, and not at all shy in discussing the ways in which those at the bottom are warped and deluded by our meritocratic myths. Some of this book may be too much for undergraduate students, but I recommend the chapter "Lost in the American Undertow" as a good introduction to Bageant's work.
7 This is a study of how a racially diverse group of working-class college students experience college and identity reformations. Several of the chapters can be used singly. I also recommend the stand-alone chapter "Border Country" in my 2012 *College and the Working Class*. Rotterdam: Sense, pp. 65–82.
8 (1) Introduction, pp. 1–17; (2) "Social Organization in Washington's Suburb," pp. 51–71; (3) Conclusion, pp. 219–226. I often use Lacy's excellent ethnography to displace students' expectations that race and class map onto the class system in any easy to define ways. It is also nice to talk about class and class distinctions without foregrounding whiteness.
9 An investigation of how class intrudes into the efficacy and practices of several different activist groups, the pages recommended here are a brilliant introduction to how adding a class lens to gender and race frames deepens our understanding of differences and conflicts within organizations.
10 This is a short and succinct research article based on interviews with a racially diverse set of working-class and middle-class students. I have used this several times since its publication, and students always pay great attention to how other students are paying for college. It is also a good example of how to do sociological research.
11 This is a study of how poor white people understand their position in U.S. society conducted by an educated Black man who was taught as a child to stay away from "poor white trash." The following pages in particular are good examples of Moss' reflectivity and can be used in the focus group exercise: pp. 1–5, 14–17, 94–99.
12 In this book, sociologist Streib interviews heterosexual married partners whose class backgrounds differ. The recommended pages summarize the main findings. I have found that this book provokes a great deal of discussion, particularly allowing students to reflect on parental conflicts they observed (over how to spend money, how much to helicopter parent, etc.)
13 There are several parts to this documentary series. I recommend A Nation of Tribes (9m); Tammy's Story (8m) and Tammy's Story Part II (10m). I have used these selections alongside with parts of the documentary Born Rich (by Johnson & Johnson heir, Jamie Johnson), which includes a cameo appearance of a young Ivanka Trump.

References

Bourdieu, P. (1977). *Outline of a theory of practice*. Cambridge University Press.
Bourdieu, P. (1986). "The forms of capital." In J. G. Richardson (Ed.), *Handbook for theory and research for the sociology of education* (pp. 241–258). Greenwood Press.
Bourdieu, P. (1993). *Sociology in question*. Sage.

11 Teaching About Race in the Historically White Difference, Power, and Discrimination Classroom
Teacher as Text

Bradley Boovy and Nana Osei-Kofi

For faculty who teach on topics of race and racial justice at historically white institutions such as ours, questions often arise about how to more effectively engage students in learning about the social construction of race in ways that foster comprehension of the realities of racialization and racism among white students, while at the same time validating the lived experiences of the often-few students of color in a class. In social justice teaching more broadly, faculty frequently face the challenge of white students refusing to believe that systemic and institutional racism are more than historical artifacts, and that racism has severe material consequences for people of color today. In light of this reality, some of the key questions that arise in relation to our teaching include: How do we as educators make race legible to students who have not experienced being minoritized as a function of racialization? How do faculty – both those whose white bodies are presumed to "belong" in the classroom and those who are seen as "guests" as a function of the color of their skin – teach race effectively? What pedagogical strategies can we rely on? How must these strategies differ for faculty of color and for white faculty, in particular in cases where the latter are not aware of how their own investment in whiteness (Lipsitz, 2006) informs their presence in the classroom? Based on our teaching practices and classroom experiences, we argue in this chapter that, in order to make processes and impacts of racialization legible to students for whom this is unfamiliar, it is critical that we as faculty come to an understanding of the ways our bodies are read by students in the classroom (Lewis, 2011).

We write this chapter from our respective positions as faculty at a historically white institution, who regularly teach Difference, Power, and Discrimination (DPD) program courses that center interlocking systems of oppression such as racism, heterosexism, classism, and ableism. We also co-facilitate the DPD Academy, a year-long faculty development program out of which stems the book in which this chapter appears. Although we teach in the same program (Women, Gender, & Sexuality Studies) and at the same institution, our presence in the classroom is informed by visible embodied differences that we see as a

DOI: 10.4324/9781003091998-14

generative source of comparative pedagogical knowledge about how to engage students in discussions of race and racialization. We seek to draw on the places where our experiences teaching about race and racialization at the undergraduate level have been similar and where these experiences have differed in terms of how our bodies are read by students in the courses we teach. Based on the similarities and divergences in our experiences, we reflect on how the (il)legibility of race and racialization on our respective bodies influences our engagement with students – and their engagement with us – in conversations about race and racism.

We begin by discussing our institutional context as a Historically White Institution, troubling the ways this category can overdetermine the kinds of conversations we have about institutions such as Oregon State University. We then offer a brief review of the literature on *teacher as text*, focusing in on how this concept can be both helpful and limiting when it comes to discussions of visible or otherwise immediately noticeable differences, which not only includes racialized differences, but also differences such as visible disabilities, non-binary gender presentations, and audible accents perceived as "foreign." To further examine the notion of teacher as text, we each share an experience discussing race with white students. Such interactions have provided us with opportunities to reflect on how white students approach us differently based on the embodied markers of racial difference discussed above. We conclude by offering key takeaways based on our often-divergent experience as embodied texts.

Throughout, we draw on Toni Morrison's (1990) *Playing in the Dark* as a critical theoretical framework to understand the legibility – or illegibility – of race and racialization on bodies as texts. Morrison's discussion of the normative whiteness of the U.S. literary canon serves as an evocative metaphor to grapple with the ways classroom spaces in the dominant tradition of U.S. higher education have always been overdetermined by an (un)spoken racial difference, in particular in spaces that are (or are imagined to be) predominantly white. Beyond this, through her careful analysis of core texts that comprise the white U.S. literary canon, Morrison also allows us to interrogate how racialized narratives structure the kinds of embodied interactions that we focus on in this chapter. For both of us, the legibility of different social markers on our bodies as we facilitate student learning about racialization and racism makes it so that otherwise similar topics are received very differently.

About Us

Bradley

As a cisgender white man, white students tend to take my word for it that racial categorization exists in the service of racism. My white masculinity is both a marker of expertise and an indication for white students that my knowledge of race and racism is not informed by an "agenda." By the same token, if I choose to avoid any engagement with racialization and racism and make it something illegible as is common when white educators teach white students, I confirm a post-racial reality as a function of my status as expert. For white faculty like me, discussions of race and racialization need not necessarily happen. As Nolan Cabrera (2017) suggests, we might say that for those of us who are white faculty, we are immune from discussions of race and racialization, and that this immunity is rooted in social realities that exempt us from experiencing racial oppression within and beyond the boundaries of the classroom. It is not uncommon for courses that purport to deal with social justice issues – especially when taught by faculty members who hold dominant identities – to minimize or avoid discussions of race and effectively ignore the intersections of gender identity, sexuality, and other social categories with processes of racialization. In courses led by a white faculty member where white students are in the majority (or where there are only white students), discussions of race often elicit feelings of discomfort that further suggests that white people only talk about race when people of color are present because they feel they are obligated to do so in order to demonstrate their awareness of race and racism. In other words, as a white man, omitting discussions of race and racialization does not appear to detract from my expertise, which is presumed to be grounded not in first-hand experience of racism or racial marginalization but rather in the authority and expertise made legible through visible markers of white male embodiment.

Nana

As a cisgender woman of color, race and racialization are always present in the classrooms in which I teach. For many white students, a person of color at the front of the room is seen as representing a focus on race, regardless of the topic of the class, and more specifically a focus on racism, in ways that are experienced as creating discomfort and bringing forth feelings of guilt. For faculty of color, this creates a context wherein white students' sense of a need or expectation to talk about race is always present, and often this need, borne out of dis-ease, takes the form of arguments for why race is not or should not be a factor in the topic of discussion, separate from whether this is in fact the case or not. Alternatively, I find that racism is engaged as something that is perpetuated by "bad whites" who are repudiated and thought of as separate from those in the class who are also white. Bad whites are typically seen as being part of the larger white community to which students' see themselves as belonging, without holding racist views brought about as a function of a combination of factors such as being of an earlier generation, lacking in education, living in a small town and never having had the opportunity to venture outside this place, or being poor. To these students, "bad whites" are a group that is victim to circumstance, therefore fundamentally innocent, and separate from "real racists," who are a small group of openly proud card-carrying members of contemporary versions of the KKK. Given our geographic location (Oregon), it is not uncommon that I have students of color in class who have grown up in environments where they have not had the opportunity to develop a racial consciousness and who are therefore not yet able to read the world structurally as it relates to race. As a result, they often espouse an ideology of color-evasiveness (Annamma et al., 2017) and individualism, that in practice, aligns closely with the ways many white students engage racialization and racism. For students of color with deep levels of experiential knowledge with racialization and racism, my presence – that is to say, the presence of a faculty member of color at the front of the classroom – can be critical and affirming to many. At the same time, in the absence of healing, I am well aware that presence alone is not enough to advance an anti-racist stance in classroom discussions. I also find that students of color who enter these types of conversations from a place of great awareness and knowledge are often at risk of disengaging out of frustration about the level of conversation in light of the composition of the class. Another pedagogical challenge I sometimes see with students of color is when they expect a faculty member of color to practice a form of racial solidarity above all. Much like the ways white students assume an allegiance and alliance with white faculty, at times students of color can engage with faculty of color in a similar way, assuming that anything and everything is acceptable because of a sense of familial connection, a notion of being on the same side of things, so to speak.

Location, Location, Location

We understand our work as situated within the confines of a historically white institution, rather than the more commonly referenced idea of a predominantly white institution or PWI. Like the notion of teacher as text, whiteness as "predominant" or "historical" also constitutes a matter of legibility or illegibility of embodied racialized differences on an institutional scale. The discursive use of the term PWI, which was originally put in use by higher education scholars based on racial composition data, normalizes the whiteness of a particular geographic or institutional space, reifying these spaces "as 'benign' settings for people to interact across racial and ethnic lines" (Boyd, 2017, p. 161). In contrast, as Carmen Kynard and Robert Eddy (2014) argue, the significance of "draw[ing] on the notion of the *historical*" (p. 268) challenges the idea that the only thing that makes an institution predominantly white is that a majority of students check the "white" box on their applications. Hence, originating with the work of Walter Allen in the early 90s, HWCUs or historically white colleges and universities,

> refer[s] to … institution[s] of higher education whose histories, traditions, symbols, stories, icons, curriculum, and processes were all designed by whites, for whites, to reproduce whiteness via a white experience at the exclusion of others who, since the 1950s and 1960s, have been allowed in such spaces.
>
> (Brunsma et al., 2012, p. 3)

In reference to historical context and language, we also want to note here that we use *students of color* and *faculty of color* throughout to signal our location in the academy and the classroom. We agree with critiques by scholars like Santos F. Ramos (2016) and racial justice activists who contend that "of color" often runs the risk of obscuring Black and Indigenous experiences of racial oppression. We are well aware that as with colleges and universities around the U.S., the origins of our institution points to histories and the ongoing impacts of genocide and dispossession of Indigenous peoples, including most directly the Kalapuya on whose land Oregon State sits. Additionally, histories of enslavement and segregation of Africans and African Americans was foundational to the Oregon state constitution and determined the contours of higher education legislation as discussed in the introduction to this volume. Legacies of exclusion from institutions of higher education rooted in these histories continues to impact enrollment figures and campus climate for Indigenous and Black students and faculty, in particular in a predominantly white state such as Oregon. At the same time, it is important to highlight how racialization and exclusion have and continue to also impact Latinx, Pacific Islander, and Asian American populations in the United States, and particularly on the west coast, a region that, in many ways, diverges from dominant narratives of race and racialization in the United States. In particular, the exploitation of Latinx and Asian migrant labor past and present creates a set of conditions of racialization specific to Oregon. It is for these reasons that we have chosen to use students and faculty of color as terms that build on the concept of women of color as a category of political experience and activism, and thus signal solidarity amongst minoritized groups over and against white dominance (Western States Center, 2011).

Teacher as Text

The idea of teacher as text emerged in the 1990s from a desire of teachers to show up in the classroom in ways that were authentic to their experiences while at the same time allowing them to use their bodies to facilitate students' understanding of complex social issues. Walter Jacobs (1998) developed three pedagogical strategies for revealing and taking advantage of the ways educators are read by students in order to foster learning and critical engagement. He termed these strategies the "three EXs" to refer to exposure, explosion, and explication. As a Black sociologist, Jacobs was most concerned with making himself vulnerable to his students to leverage his embodied experience as a Black educator in order to illustrate how all educators are complicit in systems of power and oppression. Jacobs's framework highlights the importance of being transparent with students about our own positionality, pedagogical approach, and ideological commitments.

Jacobs's conceptualization of teacher as text has been further developed and applied to discussions of the ways students' readings of facilitators' bodies can serve as an important starting point for learning and challenging students to recognize how social systems also structure and influence classroom dynamics. Heather Hartley (1999), for example, applied Jacobs's three EXs in her sociology class to interrogate students' assumptions about her sexual identity based on her gender presentation. In a similar vein, Kate Kedley (2015) argued that K-12 teachers can disrupt accepted "heteronorms" not only by including texts by and about Lesbian, Gay, Bisexual, Transgender, and Queer (LGBTQ) people in their lessons, but also by refusing to confirm student assumptions about the normativity of the teacher's gender or sexual identity. Kedley writes, "Queering the teacher-text suggests teachers explore how resolving unintelligibility and ambiguity works to regulate sex, gender, and sexuality" (2015, p. 373). Although we agree that vulnerability and transparency with our students is critical to effective social justice pedagogies, it is important to distinguish between the legibility of social difference on the bodies of teachers in relation to different histories of oppression and marginalization in the academy. We also assert that it is critical to remain attentive to the ways race, gender, sexuality, (dis)ability, and other embodied markers of social difference are always articulated together and read on the bodies of educators. Where Bradley's whiteness provides the privilege of *not having to* talk about race, in particular with white students, Nana's experience points to the ways race is always legible to students for faculty of color. In distinction to Hartley and Kedley, the legibility of racial difference for faculty of color challenges us to think critically about how we understand the teacher as text.

It is essential, then, to interrogate what we mean by "text" and what such a metaphor does for our understanding of student and faculty interaction in pedagogical spaces that focus on anti-racist social justice learning. Although the notion of teacher as text has a particular resonance in conversations about teachers' embodied presence in the classroom and how vulnerable teachers allow themselves to be with students, the current understanding of teacher-text turns out to be rather limited when we consider teachers' racial identities through a comparative lens. Encounters between texts and readers are dynamic. Readers bring their diverse lived experience to texts, and texts always contain elements that are not under the control of their authors. To continue using "text" as a heuristic for understanding a set of pedagogical practices related to teacher embodiment in the classroom, it is necessary to think critically about the notion of teachers' bodies as texts. Although we are all "authors" of our own embodied texts, we are not always in complete control of how we are read by others or even what visible indicators of racialized difference are legible to different readers in a multiplicity of institutional contexts. Based on the differences in our own experience, on which we elaborate below, it is evident that like texts, there is only a certain part of the teacher-text that we as educators are ever in control of in the classroom. As we hope our narratives below reveal, for white facilitators, whiteness is an unmarked norm that often elides the legibility of race even as notions of "expertise" and "authority" – which adhere to white (cis-male) teacher-texts in particular – rely on racial (and gendered) difference in order to become legible. Drawing on Morrison's analysis, the conditions of this legibility are embedded in histories of racial exclusion in the academy that impact the ways white faculty and faculty of color show up in the classroom and the different approaches they (have to) take in discussing race and racism. More importantly for our argument here, differences in the legibility of race and racialization between faculty of color and white faculty as teacher-texts affects how students read, approach, and interact with teachers both within and outside the classroom.

As previously noted, our assertion is grounded in Toni Morrison's reading of the dominant U.S. literary canon. As Morrison (1990) traces in *Playing in the Dark*, the canon of American literature is only legible because of the constant presence of an unacknowledged, racialized other through which white Americans have come to understand themselves. For Morrison, this racialized other is specifically Black (or "Africanist") and it is through this unacknowledged presence that "American coherence" has come to be organized at all (p. 8). Although Morrison's discussion applies principally to the U.S. literary canon in English, her core insights into the role of race – and specifically Blackness – in determining the definitional possibility of whiteness in the dominant literary imagination extends to all aspects of U.S. social and cultural life, including higher education. We suggest that U.S. higher education relies on similar processes of racialization in the production of "coherent" pedagogical spaces. Moreover, in addition to the institutional and systemic impacts of such racial coherence on faculty and students of color alike, we propose that this coherence emerges from the multiple and often-divergent ways students read educators' bodies. Such everyday acts of reading the signs of racial difference or sameness thus serve, we propose, as an entry point for challenging students (and ourselves) to develop a heightened awareness of the real impacts of processes of racial oppression. As social justice educators, we imagine our roles as those who model such reading strategies as an important starting point for raising students' (and our own) awareness of interlocking systems of oppression at the site of the teacher-text.

The experiences we share in what follows are based on recollections of conversations with students. These conversations were prompted by class discussions on topics of race, racialization, and other concomitant systems of oppression. These conversations are illustrative of the ways students engage faculty on topics of race based on assumptions they make about our embodied identities, assumptions that are ultimately grounded in the racialized interpretive frameworks through which we are socialized to read each other's bodies as texts. The experiences we share stem from conversations we had with students during office hours as we have come to realize that it is often in these moments that students feel most unrestrained and able to share their thoughts and feelings about course topics, in particular race and their own experience of or complicity in systems of racial oppression. Drawing on these experiences behind closed doors, if you will, has offered us valuable lessons and allowed us to make changes in our respective approaches to engaging with students in the classroom, in an effort to be as effective in teaching about race, racialization, and racism as we can be.

Reading and Being Read

Bradley

I regularly teach a DPD course on gender, race, and other systems of oppression in Disney films. Two years ago, a white cisgender male student enrolled in the course and began to visit my office hours regularly after our class meetings. He expressed genuine interest in the topics of the course but admitted to struggling to understand the format of the class and how discussions were structured. As an undergraduate engineering student, he shared his preference for debate-style classes and on several occasions expressed his frustration that I was not encouraging him to "provoke" and "incite" arguments with his classmates. During one of his visits, he told me about a recent experience in a large undergraduate lecture course for which he had been hired to facilitate a discussion section. He related that an Asian American woman student in his discussion section had complained to the professor that he had made a comment that was both racist and sexist. The Asian American student said she no longer felt comfortable being in his group and asked to be moved to another group. The white student in my course faced no consequences beyond a conversation with the professor, yet he was initially very nervous that he might lose his job. He showed little capacity to understand why the student had taken offense and expressed the wish that she had given him the "benefit of the doubt" based on the fact that he did not intend to offend anyone.

What struck me about this exchange was not the content or attitude of the student himself; such defensive reactions from white students are relatively commonplace in DPD courses in discussions of race and white dominance. Rather, it was the way the student approached me as someone he assumed would understand his situation and sympathize. The conversation went on for 30 minutes. In moments when he noticed that I was not going to assuage his anxiety about losing his job or take his side over the student in his discussion group, he dug his heels in further. Indeed, it seemed as if he was trying to draw me out and provoke an argument that I had not let him start in class. I found myself getting impatient with the student and angry at his apparent inability to consider the impact of his words on a student in the discussion section he was facilitating. And, I was upset with myself that I had not somehow made it clear to him through the work we had done in class that I was not the person he should be seeking sympathy from simply because I was also a white man. At what point did his reading of my white masculinity overtake the course learning outcomes, and what could I have done to interrupt such a reading? If I had interrupted his reading of me as somehow sharing his worldview, would I have missed the opportunity to have this conversation with him? Now, a year later, has some part of his experience with the student in his discussion group or of our conversation stayed with him? If so, how does he recall these memories?

I did not express these thoughts to the student. Instead, we talked through the situation and I endeavored to help him understand what he had done wrong. Although I suspect he did not acknowledge his implicit bias or apologize to the student in his discussion section, I hope he came away from our conversation with a bit more self-awareness. For me, the conversation became an opportunity to reflect on pedagogical strategies that reroute white students' expectations that I confirm and validate their racial privilege in pedagogical spaces. Looking back, I wish I had posed more pointed questions to the student, asking, for example, why he felt alright talking with me about these things one-on-one but not with the entire class. I might have asked him to reflect on whether he would have come to my office hours to discuss this had I been a faculty member of color and/or a woman. And I could have challenged him on the assumptions he made that because we were both white men, I was a "safe" person with whom to share his experiences and anxieties.

Going forward, this experience has stuck with me and allowed me to develop a keener sense of the how my body is read by students in ways that overlook whiteness, but that are always just beneath the surface of the text. As a white educator my body is always liable to be read as sharing a particular experience of racial privilege that many white students, whether they're aware of it or not, will try to connect with in discussions of race and racism. To be sure, this experience came among many other missed opportunities to challenge white students in their readings of my whiteness as a marker of seemingly shared perspectives with regard to race and the politics of whiteness in the classroom. (And, I am certain that I'll miss other opportunities in the future.) Yet this experience suggests that white educators can become aware of their own participation in processes of racialization and white dominance and interrogate critically and productively the ways students read and approach us as embodied texts (see Lynch, 2018; Jupp & Lensmire, 2016; Levine-Rasky, 2000).

Nana

As a faculty member of color, I, much like all faculty of color, never have the luxury of being unaware of how academic spaces are marked by my/our presence and the classroom is no exception. As an "outsider within" as Patricia Hill Collins would describe faculty of color, students read the visual and verbal markers of our social locations, in relation to power. We are read in relation to the assumed normative professor, who is expected to be white, male, straight, able-bodied, and middle to upper class. Whether conscious or unconscious, these norms operate in ways that interact with students' own social locations, as they make meaning of ours. If one were to place students' reading practices in relation to faculty of color on a continuum, in a fashion that admittedly lacks sufficient nuance to fully capture reality, yet functions as a useful heuristic tool to understanding how students read us as text, we would have students who mirror the assumed normative professor on one end and minoritized students whose lived experiences have brought with it some level of understanding of Hill Collins' notion of outsiders within. Students who mirror the assumed normative professor are students who challenge the credibility, integrity, and authority of faculty of color (Perry et al., 2009). When taught about matters of race by faculty of color, they report a range of resistant feelings from guilt and shame, to a sense of their identity being under attack, and perform this resistance in a number of ways from disrupting the classroom, to displaying passivity and apathy, to accusations of faculty incompetence (Niemann et al., 2020). On the other end, are the students who like faculty of color, understand that they are outsiders, and for whom too often, this is the first time they "see themselves" or "their people" at the front of the room. These need not be students whose identities match up perfectly to ours, but they are students who read us as sharing a minoritized status in the larger society and place us in the category of role model. In between, we find students with differing racialized identities and varying degrees of acceptance and rejection.

Teaching an introductory course that centers on questions of gender and sexuality a couple of years ago, the make-up of the class was no exception to the aforementioned. It was a 200-level course with 40 students, the majority of whom were white women. Most students regularly showed up to class and engaged in classroom activities and discussions. Having said that, although we took up intersectionality, race would never explicitly come up unless I brought it up in some way, even when it was part of the readings for class. Therefore, like Bradley, one of my most salient experiences with how white students take up race, racialization, and racism took place in a one-on-one conversation with a student during office hours.

A young undergraduate white working-class woman from a small rural community had been struggling for some time to keep up with class assignments. We had met on multiple occasions to talk through ways she could get back on track. During each of our meetings, she would share what amounted to a challenging family situation as a way of explaining why she was having a difficult time completing work on time. It was quite clear that her circumstances were adversely affecting her ability to keep up with her coursework, and so I made every effort to create a situation in which she could successfully complete the course.

Despite my efforts, the student appeared unable to fulfill her commitment. I agreed to meet with her one last time, and it was during this meeting that she voiced what apparently was the ultimate reason why she could not complete her work in the class. Paraphrasing her remarks, what she said amounted to the following: I come from a small rural community and we don't have any people of color there, so I just don't know anything about race, and therefore I am unable to successfully finish the assignments in this class. While race can never be removed from any social analysis where the U.S. is centered, the work the student was unable to complete was asking her to write from her own social identity, without in any way being overdetermined by race. Knowing a little bit about the community from which she came, I was eager to first probe her suggestion that she was from an all-white town before addressing the idea that racial ignorance was limiting her academic capacity. I quickly learned that, sure there were a few Mexicans in her hometown, but if there were inequities within the community, these were class-based, more than anything else.

I grasped onto her comment about class, trying to lift from this, ways one might enter a conversation about identity and social injustice from the perspective of class, while also recognizing how other factors, such as gender, sexuality, religion, and race, are also part of shaping material conditions. She seemed unmoved by this suggestion. I went on to highlight the fact that race was never at the center of the work she had failed to turn in, while at the same time pointing out that to be white is also to be a part of a hierarchical system of racialization that situates whites at the top. Without showing much understanding for the perspectives I was offering, the student agreed she would give the assignments one more try. However, at the end of the day, she never again showed up to class or turned in any work.

What is striking to me about this engagement, and how it overlaps with Bradley's experience, is that it is in the safety of a one-on-one conversation where students are more comfortable to express their "true" perspectives on race, away from the classroom and the possibility of being challenged by the instructor or by other students, in public. It is yet another way shame and guilt around race is manifest, with views fully expressed only in private, unless it concerns affirming one's role as an ally, in contrast to "bad whites" or "real racists."

My conversation with the student illustrates the ways a majority of white students understand themselves simply as being part of the norm, void of a racialized identity, separate from racial thinking, and thus racism. At the same time, the eventual mention of "a few Mexicans" by the student, betrays the ways minoritized groups are often invisible and at the same time hyper-visible. More than anything, what the conversation highlighted for me, was the way the presence of my brown body in the classroom, for this student, meant that the course was "all about race." It was as though my presence represented a hidden curriculum that the student came to read as the official one. That is to say, she believed that when people of color teach, they always make it about race (the hidden curriculum), and that this was now what she was expected to engage as central to the course (the official curriculum).

From a pedagogical standpoint, this speaks in some part to the question of how we teach students to see social structures and understand their own location within these structures, but it is about more than that. It is also about their assumptions about race and power specifically, and how we make this visible to students in order that they may deepen their understanding of the socialization that brings their perspectives into being and from there be able to grapple, both intellectually and emotionally, with the relationship of their world-views to social and economic justice.

How did all this make me feel? This experience left me on the one hand feeling disappointed because the student's academic success mattered to me and I had spent a fair amount of time with her fully expecting that she would be able to complete her work. On the other hand, I felt manipulated and essentialized in hearing that the whole issue came down to one of racial ignorance. At the same time, I continue to hope and maybe even believe that our conversation about class and material realities in some small way opened a door to the student understanding the world and the community in which she grew up slightly differently, even if that realization comes years after our conversation.

Broadening Our Reflections

For me (Bradley), the conversation with my white male student made the interpersonal, affective connections that often exist between white educators and white students visible, where they are often largely rendered illegible to white educators and students alike as part of socialization into white dominance, while for me (Nana), my interaction reinforced an all too familiar way white students frequently respond to being in a class taught by a faculty member of color.

Bradley

Since the interaction described above, now two years ago, I have sought to remain attentive to the subtle modes of interaction through which white students seek reassurance from me as a white-embodied educator in discussions of race, racialization, and racism. Such appeals for reassurance range from modulations in tone of voice, gestures and body language, and, as we discussed above, silence in the face of race as a topic of discussion. Scholars in an increasing number of disciplines have sought to identify some of these strategies (see, for example, Case & Hemmings, 2005; Knowles et al., 2014; Thompson, 2003; Trainor, 2005) and have produced helpful lists of "distancing behaviors" such as the one compiled by Jim Elder and Bruce Irons (see resources). However, it can be difficult to know how to incorporate conversations about these behaviors or discursive cues without singling out or shaming individual students for something they are not likely aware of, especially in the large undergraduate general education courses that we regularly teach. (To be clear, I am not referring here to overtly racist remarks or other kinds of comments that target minoritized students, which do call for the faculty member's direct and immediate intervention.) It is also important to recognize that discussing distancing behaviors can become its own form of distancing from topics of race and racism in cases where whiteness is not the explicit and intended focus of the class or activity.

Beyond the challenges presented by factors such as class size and the dynamics of group discussions, it seems to me to that one of the primary difficulties with addressing these issues head-on has to do with the fact that many white students and faculty alike have not learned to read how their socialization into whiteness shows up on their and other white peoples' bodies in everyday interactions. The question then becomes: how do we teach white students to read race? Returning to Jacobs, I have found it effective to draw on examples from my own experience where I've noticed myself participating in distancing behaviors or other strategies that help me avoid the discomfort of discussing race and racism. There has also been an increase in news coverage, online videos, and popular media representations that explicitly thematize whiteness (see resources). Again, where whiteness is not the express topic of conversation, such resources can further distract white students (and faculty) from engaging with anti-racist dialog and become an exercise in navel-gazing. In an effort to stem these diversions in class discussions, I have found it helpful to offer resources on whiteness through the online learning platform for the course (in both face-to-face and online courses) to which I can direct interested students rather than permitting white distancing behaviors to become the focal point of our conversation. At the same time, incorporating texts that make whiteness legible can be a helpful way of externalizing, through textual representation, processes and impacts of racialization, including white socialization, so that students learn to read, name, and discuss them openly.

Nana

Although the conversation I have described here was incredibly frustrating, it was not a new experience, nor did it surprise me. Rather, what stands out about it is probably the extent to which the student's assumptions were laid bare as a function of being in a one-on-one situation instead of in a shared classroom space. What I took away from it was a reinforcement of the importance of helping students in the classroom realize the assumptions that inform their engagement with course content and with me as a woman of color faculty member. My approach to this is typically shaped by what I see as the power of transparency. When I notice misplaced racialized assumptions operating in a class, I share my observation with the class, and facilitate a conversation around it. These can be difficult conversations and they are only made possible, I would suggest, when preceded by a process of building a sense of trust, respect, and candor among students, along with the necessary scaffolding to make for a meaningful exchange. Work that in part is about aiding students to become comfortable with being uncomfortable as part of the process of learning in situations when it comes to questions of social injustice.

As part of my own process of being comfortable with being uncomfortable, I find that what helps me in managing the emotional labor that this type of teaching entails is refusing to be attached to the outcome of these types of exchanges. I am invested in the process of unearthing racialized assumptions so that students can grapple with them and hopefully engage in some self-reflexivity, but I recognize that what happens in these types of situations is one small part of students' lives. I have no control over the impact it has on them, the timeframe within which they may come to a critical realization, and/or all the other factors that influence their thinking and worldviews. What I can insist on as an educator is that the subject matter, which so often is pushed aside or invisibilized, is engaged. After all, what I ultimately care about is students' understanding the subject matter of the class. I can also facilitate different forms of engagement, as a typical class discussion where anyone who wants to speak can do so anytime they want, can often reproduce ingrained societal inequities. Here I rely on pedagogical strategies that push back against practices that often mirror dominant forms of interaction in society. Examples of activities that I use to create more equitable opportunities for participation and engagement include *a silent conversation, 4-corners,* and *"save the last word for me"* (see resources). I find that when using these activities, not only do more students engage, those who have been most vocal in open discussions, also become more thoughtful in what they share as a function of what the exercises require of them. There is something about these types of practices that helps students who have mis-read my investments in what happens in class, come to realize that I am unattached to outcome (at least in the way they perceive outcome), and it therefore lowers their defensive stances and delegitimizes arguments they may have been eager to make out of willful ignorance and/or simple refusals to see the world as anything other than post-racial. For minoritized students and majority students who recognize how racialization functions, making what can often feel like the elephant in the room, transparent, in my experience, tends to result in a sense of relief from surface level engagements with complex matters and faux conviviality.

Conclusion

The conversations and pedagogical work we have described here seek to provide examples of ways to take into account how we as faculty are read as embodied texts. We offer these anecdotes from our own experience with engaging students in conversations around race and racialization and the actions we have taken as a result, not as models but rather as prompts to reflect further on how race shows up in our work. As we hope our stories have demonstrated, we do not think that faculty as embodied texts are ever *complete*. Every class we teach and every student we encounter presents a new set of challenges and opportunities to understand how we as teachers read and are read by others. These encounters serve as the foundation for ongoing reflection and action as we continue to develop critical, anti-racist pedagogies.

Additional Resources

Activities/Resources Mentioned in the Chapter

A Silent Conversation: www.facinghistory.org/resource-library/teaching-strategies/big-paper-silent-conversation

Distancing Behaviors: www.pcc.edu/illumination/wp-content/uploads/sites/54/2018/05/distancing-behaviors-anti-racism-handout.pdf

Four Corners: www.facinghistory.org/resource-library/teaching-strategies/four-corners

Save the Last Word for Me: www.facinghistory.org/resource-library/teaching-strategies/save-last-word-me

Audiovisuals

Adelman, L. (2003). *Race: The power of an illusion.* California News Reel.

Adelman, L. Companion website launched in 2019: www.racepowerofanillusion.org

Adelman, L. PBS Lesson plans based on the series: www.pbs.org/race/000_About/002_04-teachers.htm

Buzz Feed (2016, February 22). *People of Colour from around the world respond to "white"* [Video]. YouTube. www.youtube.com/watch?v=BZFY0dqC0Ks

Decoded with Franchesca Ramsey [TV Series]. MTV. www.mtv.com/shows/decoded

PBS News Hour (2017, November 30). *What happens when I try to talk race with white people* [Video]. YouTube. www.youtube.com/watch?v=1SynR1NYcpo

*Race – Discussion Starters:*https://dpd.oregonstate.edu/discussion-starters#Race

Web-based Materials

Racial Equity Tools. www.racialequitytools.org/home

Stanford Center for Comparative Studies in Race & Ethnicity RaceWorks Toolkit. http://sparqtools.org/raceworks-scholars/

The 1619 Curriculum Project. https://pulitzercenter.org/lesson-plan-grouping/1619-project-curriculum

Vanderbilt University Center for Teaching – Teaching Race. Pedagogy and Practice: https://cft.vanderbilt.edu/guides-sub-pages/teaching-race/

University of Southern California Resource Guide – Diversity, Equity & Inclusion. Anti-Racist Pedagogy – Further Resources: https://libguides.usc.edu/c.php?g=756583&p=5976573

References

Annamma, S. A., Jackson, D. D., & Morrison, D. (2017). Conceptualizing color-evasiveness: Using dis/ability critical race theory to expand a color-blind racial ideology in education and society. *Race, Ethnicity and Education, 20*(2), 147–162.

Boyd, C. (2017). *Poison in the ivy: Race relations and reproduction of inequality on elite college campuses.* Rutgers University Press.

Brunsma, D., Brown, E., & Placier, P. (2012). Teaching at historically white colleges and universities: Identifying and dismantling the wall of whiteness. *Critical Sociology, 39*(5), 717–738.

Cabrera, N. L. (2017). White immunity: Working through some of the pedagogical pitfalls of privilege. *Journal Committed to Social Change on Race and Ethnicity, 3*(1), 78–90.

Case, K. A., & Hemmings, A. (2005). Distancing Strategies: White women preservice teachers and antiracist curriculum. *Urban Education*, *40*(6), 606–626. https://doi.org/10.1177/0042085905281396

Hartley, H. (1999). What's my orientation? Using the teacher-as-text strategy as feminist pedagogical practice. *Teaching Sociology*, *27*(4), 398–406.

Jacobs, W. R. (1998). The Teacher as text: Using personal experience to stimulate the sociological imagination. *Teaching Sociology*, *26*(3), 222–228. https://doi.org/10.2307/1318836

Jupp, J. C., & Lensmire, T. J. (2016). Second-wave white teacher identity: Toward complexity and reflexivity in the racial conscientization of white teachers. *International Journal of Qualitative Studies in Education*, *29*(8), 985–988.

Kedley, K. E. (2015). Queering the teacher as a text in the English Language Arts classroom: Beyond books, identity work, and teacher preparation. *Sex Education*, *15*(4), 364–377. https://doi.org/10.1080/14681811.2015.1027762

Knowles, E. D., Lowery, B. S., Chow, R. M., & Unzueta, M. M. (2014). Deny, distance, or dismantle? How white Americans manage a privileged identity. *Perspectives on Psychological Science*, *9*(6), 594–609. https://doi.org/10.1177/1745691614554658

Kynard, C., & R. Eddy. (2014). Toward a new critical framework: Color-conscious political morality and pedagogy at historically black and historically white institutions. In R. Eddy, & V. Villanueva (Eds.), *A language and power reader: Representations of race in a "post-racist" era* (pp. 261–294). University of Utah Press.

Levine-Rasky, C. (2010). Framing whiteness: Working through the tensions in introducing whiteness to educators. *Race, Ethnicity and Education*, *3*(3), 271–292.

Lewis, M. (2011). Body of knowledge, black queer feminist pedagogy, praxis and embodied texts. *Journal of Lesbian Studies*, *15*, 49–57.

Lipsitz, G. (2006). *The possessive investment in whiteness*. Temple University Press.

Lynch, M. E. (2018). The hidden nature of whiteness in education: Creating active allies in white teachers. *Journal of Educational Supervision*, *1*(1), 18–31.

Morrison, T. (1990). *Playing in the dark: Whiteness and the American literary imagination*. Harvard University Press.

Niemann, Y. F., Gutiérrez y Muhs, G., & Gonzalez, C. (Eds.). (2020). *Presumed incompetent II: Race, class, power, and resistance of women in academia*. University Press of Colorado.

Perry, G., Moore, H., Edwards, C., Acosta, K., & Frey, C. (2016). Maintaining credibility and authority as an instructor of color in diversity-education classrooms: A qualitative inquiry. *The Journal of Higher Education*, *80*(1), 80–105. https://doi.org/10.1080/00221546.2009.11772131

Ramos, S. F. (2016). Building a culture of solidarity: Racial discourse, Black Lives Matter, and Indigenous social justice. *Enculturation: A Journal of Rhetoric, Writing, and Culture*. http://enculturation.net/building-a-culture-of-solidarity

Smith, S. L. (2014). Oregon's civil war: The troubled legacy of emancipation in the Pacific Northwest. *Oregon Historical Society*, *115*(2), 154–173.

Thompson, A. (2003). Tiffany, friend of people of color: White investments in antiracism. *International Journal of Qualitative Studies in Education*, *16*(1), 7–29. https://doi.org/10.1080/0951839032000033509

Trainor, J. (2005). "My ancestors didn't own slaves": Understanding white talk about race. *Research in The Teaching of English*, *40*(2), 140–167. www.jstor.org/stable/40171701

Western States Center (2011, February 11). *Loretta Ross: The origin of the phrase "Women of Color."* [Video]. YouTube. www.youtube.com/watch?v=82vl34mi4Iw&t=8s

Section 4
Rethinking Approaches to Disciplinary Content

12 Religious Bias, Christian Privilege, and Anti-Muslimism in the Difference, Power, and Discrimination Classroom

Amy Koehlinger and Kryn Freehling-Burton

Religion is one of the most powerful social forces shaping U.S. society. Its effect in the classroom is potent and, at the same time, so diffuse that it is difficult to isolate and dissect in our pedagogies. Mythologies of the Christian founding of the United States are so deeply infused in the national narrative that students are unaware of the ways the historically-false equation of Protestantism with American democracy normalizes an exclusionary white, northern European, English-speaking, male, heteronormative, religiously-narrow nationalism, obscuring the very real pluralism (of belief, gender identity, race, language, social class, and sexuality) that has been embedded in the social and political institutions of the United States from the colonial period onward. Pedagogical strategies for confronting implicit Christian privilege in teaching about American history and society include:

- providing a corrective narrative of the national founding that emphasizes the diversity of persons and perspectives about religion and its usefulness for statecraft that were present during the American revolution;
- equipping students to identify ways Christian privilege operates in contemporary U.S. culture, how it continues to shape social policy, public discourse, and political institutions, and ways of disrupting its hold;
- offering a case study of the origins, depth and omnipresence, tropes and articulations, organizations and leaders, and negative effects of anti-Semitism in U.S. history; and
- demonstrating how these patterns of anti-Semitism in 20th century America prefigure and highlight the form and content of anti-Muslimism in contemporary culture with suggestions for interrupting and challenging it.

Teaching about religion in the social justice classroom often requires transparency about certain facets of identity and the strategic masking of others. For Amy, the disciplinary conventions of Religious Studies and History as academic fields dictate that in the classroom she models neutrality in her approach to religious matters while also offering reflexive awareness of her positionality as a cis-gender, heterosexual, white mother. For Kryn, the disciplinary conventions of Women, Gender, and Sexuality Studies require that she explicitly

DOI: 10.4324/9781003091998-16

position herself as a cis-gender, white, heterosexual, mother who was raised in a conservative, evangelical Christian home but is no longer a Christian.

Drawing on our experiences in the classroom, we created a blended presentation-conversation that emphasizes our experiences in classrooms with content related to religion, Christianity in the U.S., religious privilege, anti-Judaism, anti-Semitism, and anti-Muslimism for both Difference Power, and Discrimination seminars as well as NSF Advance training seminars for senior faculty and administrators in STEM. We organize this chapter in the same way we present in a workshop format. Amy begins with a history of religion in the United States, followed by Kryn's presentation of a series of approaches and activities to working with students and workshop participants on Christian privilege. We then transition to the history of anti-Judaism from Amy and the context for anti-Muslimism from Kryn. Along the way, we share what works in our classes, where students resist or struggle, and how this helps us in facilitating this content with faculty and administrators with resources throughout.

Approach and Perspective

Kryn

I came to feminism by way of feminist Christian and Jewish theology so my engagement in thinking about Christian privilege is intertwined with my journey to intersectional scholarship and activism around difference, power, and discrimination. Teaching at a state university complicates the ways and times I choose to disclose my own religious history, including the name of my undergraduate alma mater, California Baptist University. My particular aversion to fundamentalist and evangelical strains of Christianity makes me not want anyone to make assumptions about my own practices or beliefs and yet I know my white privilege already creates assumptions that I would be Christian. When team-teaching Global Feminist Theologies, I am explicit and provide a complete bio of my spiritual and religious history and how I came to read and know the theologians that we assign. Oregon State University is a place of contradictions – it is situated in a state that has low numbers of church attendance and low numbers of racial diversity (only 17.5% of our student population in fall of 2019 are students of color and .8% are international students), but students also regularly share that our university is the most diverse place many of them have ever lived. When teaching Introduction to Women, Gender, and Sexuality Studies, I am more likely to wait until later in the term to share my own church and Christian history, and often only then in the context of how I learned to talk about abortion and reproductive justice with my evangelical church-going Christian relatives. In Gender and Science, a general education course that meets a science, technology, and society synthesis credit, we explicitly discuss Christianity's impact on health care, scientific research, and technological development. Sometimes it feels appropriate to share my own background and at other times, it feels it would distract from the students' engagement with material. The longer I teach, the more likely I am to share; my age (and the ages of my now grown children) and my race protect me a little from students discounting my own expertise based on racism or ageism, while at the same time my gender and humanities background make me suspect, particularly in the Gender and Science course at a research institution.

It is helpful to work with Amy who reminds us that Religious Studies is an academic discipline and that faith exists beyond the scope of most of these conversations. However, it is my rejection of the Christian church and subsequently Christianity as a faith that led me to the study of religion so my positionality includes this. This rejection began as a simple question about women in leadership at my church, which led to questions about the gender and nature of G*d. I was drawn to anti-war activism after 9/11, standing in weekly vigil with Women in Black. Women in Black was created by Israeli and Palestinian women to mourn loved ones lost to state and militarized violence and call for an end to state violence and war. This personal history influences the ways I approach Christian privilege; I am granted it even though I am not a Christian, and yet mobilize it to interrupt religious bias and anti-Muslimism. I have spent some time in pagan communities but now do not practice spirituality in community.

Resource: "The Danger of a Single Story" Ted Talk

In many of my classes, I find it useful to share Chimamanda Ngozi Adichie's 18-minute Ted Talk, "The Danger of a Single Story" early in the term. It works to challenge students to consider the multiplicity of experiences people who are outside of their own communities have. People in the United States often collapse whole countries and religions into a singular idea of what people from those places or who practice a particular faith are like. Videos literally bring more people and voices into the classroom. Adichie's resistance to simplistic narratives encourages students to see others as three-dimensional. It centers a media literacy approach by asking students to consider where we find information about others and more deeply analyze our own complicity in systems of oppression in our society. In my film classes, we revisit the talk as students work on their own creative film projects to resist a single narrative and incorporate better representation onscreen and behind the camera. In classes where we discuss religion more overtly, like our Disney: Gender, Race, and Empire course, having Adichie as a grounding text allows me to refer back to the danger when we discuss *Aladdin* and *Pocahontas* as films situated in colonial imaginations. In all classes, the value of seeing and hearing a Nigerian woman challenge single narratives pays off throughout the term. As Amy shares the history of religion in the U.S., Adichie's caution can provide some framework for how a single story has distorted reality.

Amy

Teaching in the Religious Studies classroom requires instructors to be creative, flexible, and strategic about providing students information about their personal religious background, experience, and commitments. Often, students are pointedly interested in whether I am a religious believer or a religious skeptic. The model of religious identity as a binary choice between orthodoxy or atheism reveals the limited categories for understanding religious experience that students often bring to their first encounters with Religious Studies as a discipline, but it also reflects a profound misunderstanding of how intellectual positionality is framed in the academic study of religion. My classroom self-presentation attempts to address both of these issues: I model *epoche* (the practice of bracketing, or purposely setting aside metaphysical commitments in order to approach religious phenomena from a neutral position) as the default position of a scholar, but I also strategically disclose specific details of my religious background when doing so helps create a more nuanced portrait of the complicated nexus where religion intersects with innumerable facets of human life.

When students ask point-blank "what do you believe about x?" I typically respond by redirecting them away from my "belief" toward the larger scholarly conversation through presenting a spectrum of two or three distinct, often contradictory interpretations and ask students to defend the position they find most persuasive. When I disclose details of my own experience, I am careful to frame them as multi-faceted points of tension within my biography rather than as elements of a stable religious identity. For example, a student recently asked me to explain the difference between the ethical systems of Protestantism and Catholicism. Instead of solely describing doctrines and practices of these groupings I instead proposed to my class that models of salvation within Christian traditions often influence the ethical systems they implicitly teach. I described how I was raised in a conservative Protestant tradition (Lutheran LCMS) where salvation was understood as a private relationship between an individual and God, but in college I lived for a year in a community of gay Roman Catholic priests living with HIV/AIDS where salvation (itself a fraught concept within Catholicism) was understood through a collective, collaborative lens as the together-striving of the community toward making God more present in the world. So, whereas my Protestant upbringing taught me that helping impoverished people was an act of charity that flows from one's gratitude to God for the gift of salvation, my first sustained encounter with Catholicism focused on caring for others as a way of being Christ to others by advocating for more just social conditions. I offered these examples as an illustration of a larger point about the relationship of redemption to ethics in Christian thought.

My larger goal when teaching about religion in U.S. history is to help students develop a vocabulary and analytical tools for thinking about the intimate terrain where religion intersects with identity, imagination, selfhood, and experience. I introduce religion as a porous, dynamic, and powerful component of culture that influences both how people understand themselves and how they view others. Lectures and readings that focus on Indigenous North American peoples, enslaved Africans, women, ethnic immigrants, queer folx, and religious minorities allow students to see how religion contributed to the socially-constituted stigmatization and oppression of racial, ethnic, gender, sexual and religious groups. But I also balance this focus on religion's contribution to difference and inequality with a simultaneous focus on the role religion has played in allowing stigmatized persons and groups to construct empowering identities and make claims on the nation's political structures. Finally, I encourage students to reflect on how ideas about gender, race, sexuality, and ethnicity have changed from historical moment to historical moment, highlighting the plasticity of the meaning attached to these social and cultural markers of difference. I design my courses to emphasize the intersectionality of systems of oppression in the U.S., highlighting the ways in which social categories like race, gender, class, sexuality, culture, age, and national belonging intersect with and are amplified by religious identities. Students are expected to demonstrate an increasingly complex understanding of religion's contribution to the constructedness of difference.

When introducing religion as a central historical contributor to patterns of discrimination in U.S. history, I often encounter students who have strong preconceived ideas about the value of religion in society. When I taught in the Bible Belt South, the majority of my students identified themselves as people of faith, especially as evangelical Christians. These students assumed that religion was good for society, that faith made people more moral and softened the worst of human tendencies. These students took experiential statements about interactions with God as fundamentally true, and they resisted critical approaches to religion, believing that religion was fundamentally different than other social processes and institutions, that it was *sui generis*, and therefore immune to the interpretive tools we apply in the classroom. Those students imagined religion much like an angel sitting on the shoulder of humanity, whispering words of kindness, encouragement, and tolerance in the ear of the human family. When I moved to Oregon, a state with a much stronger skeptical and secular outlook (where people who claim no religious affiliation or faith are the demographic majority), I instead encountered a significant portion of students who considered religion to be irrelevant at best, and dangerous at worst. These students argued that religion authorized systems of oppression and inequality, that it was responsible for most of the violence humans have visited on each other, and that in the modern world religion is a dangerous impediment to rational and scientific thought. The image these students had of religion was of a Darth Vader-type persona, sitting on humanity's shoulder and egging them on toward bigotry, violence, and irrationality. These students cheered the application of scholarly perspectives to the study of religion, but they balked at taking the perspective of people of faith and their accounts of reality seriously.

In truth, neither of these perspectives is helpful when approaching religion in the classroom. In courses where I do not have time to lay out the full terrain of theories, methods, and approaches to the study of religion (which itself could take a full term), I instead give students three guiding principles to help them navigate their first exposure to the academic study of religion. First, instead of judging religion as either a good or bad actor in human history, strive to appreciate and analyze the sheer power that religion wields in society. Religion shapes legal, social, political, and cultural systems worldwide. And the majority of the world's peoples, both in the past and present, consider religion to be one of the most important human experiences. I ask students to replace images of angel and Darth Vader – which are images of value assessment – with the image of a power lifter, a person with defined muscles, thick arms and thighs, and almost impossible strength. Second, I model for students how to avoid over-generalizations about religious traditions, religious texts, or groups of people of faith. I remind them of the historical specificity of religion to each place and time. I ask them to replace phrases like, "the Bible says...," or "Muslims believe...," with contextualized statements like, "The average Puritan in 17th century New England interpreted Biblical texts to mean...," or "sources suggest that many Muslims from North Africa who were enslaved in 18th century South Carolina believed...." Third, I encourage students to practice *epoche*, to reserve theological questions about God's nature, intentions, actions, and self-expressions for experts in theology, focusing instead on the data of what people in specific places and times have said about divine nature, actions, and revelations. This approach preserves and centers the voices and experiences of religious historical actors, pointing students to traditional historical sources for evidence.

A second early intervention I make when teaching about historical intersections of religion with dynamics of power, difference, and discrimination in the U.S. is to challenge and ultimately dismantle the ahistorical and yet still pervasive false narrative of the United States as a "Christian nation." To undo this mythology – for that is what it is, mythology – I first ask students to tell me what they know about the history of religion in the U.S. Most of the time students mention the Puritans, the Christian faith of the founders, the phrase "One Nation Under God" in the pledge of allegiance and the related motto "In God We Trust" on U.S. currency. They often mention that people were more religious in the past than they are now. Sometimes students mention that Martin Luther King was a minister, and occasionally an especially well-read student will discuss the principle of religious liberty in the Constitution. At this point, I present students with the fact that the story they have just told me is part of a constructed narrative that has only glancing connection to the actual history of religion in the U.S. I ask students to think about how they learned this false story, where they see it repeated in everyday culture, and – most importantly – who benefits from the false narrative.

In place of Christian-mythology, my courses on social justice and structural injustice in U.S. religion provide students with a robust narrative of American religious history that highlights the deep and multi-faceted pluralism that has always characterized U.S. society, arguing that enlightenment skepticism and irreligion rather than Christian orthodoxy characterized religion at the time of the of the nation's founding, and that the subsequent "Christianization" of the nation by white Protestants which occurred in the 19th century was a violent process of racialized conquest that replaced religious pluralism with Protestant cultural hegemony, with disastrous consequences for Indigenous peoples, enslaved Africans, and non-European immigrants, and minoritized peoples of all kinds. The arc of American religious mythology from the Puritans to Martin Luther King implies a teleological progression from a pure but narrow founding orthodoxy toward an expanding and inclusive tolerance; the arc of *actual* American religious history includes the Myth of Ham and the Massacre at Wounded Knee, and tells a less-flattering story of imperialism and intolerance that consistently marks some people as more worthy of religious freedom, liberty, self-determination, legal protection, and basic human rights than others. My goal is for students to realize that false historical narratives like the "Christian nation" story are not neutral in the factual errors they contain. Rather, the construction and replication of historical mythologies is strategic, and the factual errors embedded in them authorize and sustain systems of power in society – in this case, a system of Christian privilege that occludes the longstanding trend of religious, racial, and linguistic pluralism in American society, and marginalizes the stories and contributions of non-white, non-Protestants.

Kryn's work guides us through how this historically-constructed Christian privilege is embedded in present-day institutions, including both undergraduate classrooms and workshops for faculty and administration in higher education. She offers strategies for how to recognize and resist this widespread but little understood form of prejudice.

Christian Privilege

Resources: "Christian Privilege Checklist" and "Guidelines for Christian Allies"

Kryn

The narrative Amy outlines about the primacy and centrality of Christianity in the United States is embedded in overt and covert ways in our society and in our institutions. Examining the ways that Christian privilege functions is a difficult but important exercise not just for students, but for faculty and administrators as well. We can challenge this privilege by calling it out and practicing ways to dismantle or decenter it in our classrooms, laboratories, departments, and even in the academic calendar. Peggy McIntosh's White Privilege article, and particularly the list of ways she experiences white privilege, is a great tool for many audiences and has inspired a myriad of other privilege checklists, including those addressing size, ability, and sexuality.

Lewis Schossler created one for Christian Privilege that includes everything from "I can assume that I will not have to work or go to school on my significant religious holidays" to "I can be sure when I hear someone in the media talking about g-d that they are talking about my (the Christian) g-d" (2003, pp. 48–49). This tool can be used in classrooms or workshops to start conversations about the implicit ways Christianity is privileged in our society. As faculty and workshop leaders, it is important to be aware of the potential over-simplification a single privilege list can elicit and to utilize them carefully to guide a productive conversation that does not end with list discussion. Spending some time with McIntosh's list early in the term or toward the beginning of a workshop provides a context for revisiting privilege as it relates to religion. Asking students to compare the lists, noting where there are overlaps between race and religion, can be particularly instructive around these intersections. Contextualizing them within systems of oppression with attention to intersectionality can help resist their use as boxes to be checked-off rather than inspiration for remaking institutions and ways of being in community with one another.

I emphasize in classes that feminism is not just about the critique but about making society more just; it asks "what do we do to get there?" Ideally, feminism is imagining a world without inequality and inequity and starting to build that world now. Paul Kivel does this with "Guidelines for Christian Allies," by extending Schlosser's analysis into the day-to-day actions we can take to disrupt Christian privilege. Using a list like this can inspire students and workshop participants to identify ways that those of us who "are Christian or were raised Christian [can] counter Christian hegemony" (Kivel, 2018, p. 61).

Centering Indigenous Perspectives and Epistemologies

Resource: "Skywoman Falling" story from Robin Kimmerer's *Braiding Sweetgrass*

Kryn

Assigning this creation story is a good pairing for starting discussions about Christian privilege. It also works well to begin conversations about challenging western epistemologies of science by centering an Indigenous creation story. Skywoman is a common creation story from the Great Lakes region of Turtle Island (North America) that centers relationships between humans, animals, and plants and suggests reciprocity as a way of being in the world. "Like creation stories everywhere, cosmologies are a source of identity and orientation to the world. They tell us who we are. We are inevitably shaped by them no matter how distant they may be from our consciousness" (Kimmerer, 2013, p. 7).

The story of the fall of mankind (I use the masculine intentionally since this is the way that this story is told) as written in the Bible's Book of Genesis, has been used to establish a hierarchy of gender, bodily punishment for women through childbirth, and enmity between man (sic) and the earth through farming. Some Christian denominations use this creation story to literally support the subjugation of women claiming that women were second to be created, but first to sin even though "no weighty accusation of 'original sin' brought about by women is found in the text [of Genesis]. That is a later interpretation" (Niditch, 1992, p. 14). This double punishment, pain in childbirth for women (and desire for her husband) and hard labor (toil or pain) in the fields for men sets up a division between women and their bodies and men and the earth. Ecofeminists note that connecting women and the earth leads to the subjugation of both. If women's bodies are not our own, and the earth passively contains resources to take as needed or desired, it follows that both women and the earth are targets for abuses. Centering a different creation story challenges these intertwined notions by placing a woman as "our ancestral gardener, a cocreator of the good green world that would be the home of her descendants" (Kimmerer, 2013, p. 7). How might this challenge Christian privilege?

For many students in North America, it can disrupt the colonizing aim of Christianity by privileging a narrative that centers a reciprocal relationship between humans and the earth. This is of critical importance for scientists since dominating the earth and its resources has been the West's approach to scientific advancements and technological innovation. The very notion of development is embedded in globalization ideologies that become neocolonial actions enacted by the West on the Global South. Development is based on a white, masculine Christian notion of the primacy of man and the subjugation of nature. It is implicated in the enslavement of Africans (and others) and the methods used in scientific eugenics technologies to further white Christian supremacy through the genocide of Indigenous peoples, particularly in North America where our work is situated. This genocide occurs not only in overt population control that includes forced and coerced sterilization, but also in the destruction of family, language, culture, and community through forced removal of Indigenous nations, theft of native children who were sent to boarding and residential schools, and white state control over water and food to which native communities have access. At the heart of this genocide is a Christian missionizing effort that is often understated or completely ignored in the classroom. In a ten-week course, decolonizing what was implicitly and explicitly a Christian mission in conquest is a complicated task that can be aided with storytelling.

Literally reading the story of Skywoman out loud asks students to be present in a way that disrupts standard university learning. Handing out crayons to have the students draw the main ideas within the story circumvents a colonizing Christian mindset that leads to replicated notions of domination. Crayons give students (and faculty and administrators) permission to have some fun and not be as worried about artistic skill as they might otherwise be. Conversations about the drawings can illuminate ideas worthy of centering in scientific classrooms and programs.

Anti-Judaism and Anti-Semitism

Amy

American anti-Judaism presents an excellent case study for inviting students to explore the complexity of how Christian privilege has operated in the United States' past, and how it continues to operate in the present. I use Richard Hofstadter's 1964 essay "The Paranoid Style in American Politics" to frame a larger classroom exploration of the normalization of white Protestant subjectivity as the idealized marker of citizenship. "The Paranoid Style" traces the perennial power of conspiracy theories in American political discourse. Writing in the midst of resurgent anti-communist paranoia, Hofstadter argues that throughout U.S. history the public imagination has fixated on the specter of a group of people unfit for the demands of democratic citizenship who plot and scheme from the margins of U.S. society to undermine democracy, and overthrow the government to replace it with systems of authoritarian bondage. Hofstadter does not focus on religion but the outlines of his ideas provide a useful model for analyzing how Christian privilege has been weaponized against specific groups in U.S. history.

In the years between 1920 and 1945, prejudice against the Jews reached a peak in the United States. Anti-Semitism has a long history in the U.S., but prejudice against Jews was not especially vicious until the 20th century. There was a simple reason for this: until the 1890s, there weren't enough Jews in America for white Protestants to feel threatened by them. Though the immigration of German Jews in the 1840s and 1850s increased the visibility of Jews in the antebellum United States, the propensity of German Reform Jews to assimilate to U.S. cultural and linguistic norms kept them from being a target of xenophobic harassment. But as the Jewish population grew rapidly from the 1890s to 1920s with the immigration of non-assimilating Jews fleeing the pogroms of Russia and Poland, anti-Jewish sentiment gained a public presence.

The stigmatization of Jews in the U.S. in the early 20th century placed them at the intersection of three distinct tropes that implied that Jews were a danger to the purity and stability of U.S. society. First, Jews were often associated with unskilled industrial labor and with political radicalism, usually socialism or communism. In the early 20th century Americans were increasingly worried about the presence of foreign-born radicals who would stir up political rebellion and economic instability. Jews were often prominent in the organized labor movement and this heightened the fear of many Protestant Americans against them. Second, a more explicitly-religious characterization of Jews portrayed them as the heirs of a curse against those who had crucified Jesus. Since the middle ages, Christians used the Biblical verses Matthew 37: 24–25 to argue that Jews were "Christ-killers" who accepted a blood curse upon themselves during the trial before the crucifixion of Jesus. Protestant and Catholics alike in the early 20th century used this story to explain that hardship or suffering experienced by Jews. Third, anti-Judaism was strengthened by racist ideologies that stigmatized Jews as a specific race of human beings called Semites. Racist anti-Semitism viewed Jews as an inferior racial group with a series of negative attributes.

These intersecting negative ideas about Jews which suffused U.S. popular culture in the early 20th century came into sharp focus with the publication and distribution of *The Protocols of the Elders of Zion*. *The Protocols* is a notorious piece of hate literature, a fabricated anti-Jewish and anti-Semitic text which purports to be the notes of a meeting of Jewish leaders in which they laid secret plans for world domination though destroying Christian civilization and installing a world government run by Jews. *The Protocols of the Elders of Zion* was written in turn-of-the-century Czarist Russia and published and republished, translated and circulated throughout Europe and the Americas in the 1920s and 1930s. The plan for Jewish world domination entails a multi-prong assault on economic stability, political legitimacy, monetary autonomy, legal authority, the family, morality, and education through manipulation of monetary systems and media. To contemporary ears, the story contained in *The Protocols of the Elders of Zion* seems transparently false, but to Americans in the 1920s, immersed in increasingly strident anti-Jewish discourse during a period of intense Jewish immigration (and already inclined toward paranoid delusions about foreign subversion, as Hofstadter notes), *The Protocols* simply confirmed the worst fears of many Christians in the U.S.

The Protocols of the Elders of Zion were given additional legitimacy by automobile business magnate Henry Ford. Ford personally funded the printing and distribution of 500,000 copies of *The Protocols*. Ford further popularized *The Protocols* in his newspaper, *The Dearborn Independent*, through a series of articles presenting *The Protocols* as journalism. Ford required all Ford dealerships and franchises throughout the country to distribute the paper to customers. Ford then re-published the articles as a book, *The International Jew: The World's Foremost Problem*. Through Ford's sponsorship, Americans came into regular and sustained contact with a powerful false narrative about Jewish conspiracies to destabilize Western civilization, conquer Christianity, and replace capitalism with a system of Jewish world domination.

Ford was aided in his mission by religious and political leaders who capitalized on the growing chorus of anti-Jewish and anti-Semitic ideologies. The most famous and influential anti-Semitic religious leader in the 1930s was a Roman Catholic priest, Father Charles Coughlin. Born in Canada, Coughlin lived in Michigan after ordination and won fame as a radio priest, broadcasting inspirational sermons during the Great Depression.

Coughlin was named lead pastor of the Royal Oak parish in Detroit in 1926 and started giving radio sermons that same year. In 1929, the Ku Klux Klan responded to a Catholic priest on the radio by burning a cross on the church's lawn, which only made Coughlin more proudly outspoken about his role as a Catholic with a public audience. Coughlin was a compelling speaker and by 1929 he was broadcasting to Chicago, Cincinnati, Detroit and Cleveland. At the peak of his celebrity, his weekly radio audience was 30 million listeners. He received an estimated 800,000 letters per week and employed a secretarial staff of over 100 people just to answer his mail. (Warren, 1996, p. 164)

Why was Fr. Coughlin so phenomenally popular? He was an effective and compelling preacher with strong populist leanings during a time of political and economic instability. Coughlin offered simple solutions to complex problems. He viewed the world in black and white terms offering a simple choice – Christ or his enemy, Catholic civilization or communism, "Christ or Chaos." In his early years, he was deeply in tune with U.S. Catholics and helped them make sense of the deprivations and upheavals of the Depression in terms of their faith. His message was packaged in emotional, biblical, and nationalistic language that appealed beyond his original Catholic audience to ultimately include a significant number of Protestants.

But Coughlin also offered his listeners a darker source of comfort through the economic upheavals of the 1930s. He offered his substantial radio audience a scapegoat they could blame for their suffering: the Jews. Beginning with the election of Franklin Delano Roosevelt to the Presidency in 1932, and Roosevelt's subsequent appointment of several prominent Jewish businessmen to his cabinet, Coughlin increasingly decried the power of "Jewish moneylenders," who he blamed for the Depression. Coughlin organized his listeners into a political organization, the National Union for Social Justice. In 1938, Coughlin reprinted *The Protocols of the Elders of Zion* in his newspaper, which was called, ironically, "Social Justice." In November 1938, *Kristallnacht*, the night of the broken glass, in which the Germans burned Jewish synagogues, businesses and schools and arrested more than 20,000 Jewish citizens, Coughlin defended Nazism as a defense against the economic suffering imposed on the Fatherland by Jewish communists. He began to speak of "the synagogue of Satan," and to portray Judaism as an explicitly anti-Christian religion. In December 1938, he created a group called the "Christian Front," urging them to "liquidate the Jews in America." (Warren, 1996)

Coughlin's refusal to distance himself from Hitler and the harder edges of European anti-Semitism, ultimately weakened Father Coughlin's hold on public discourse. By 1940, his radio audience had largely evaporated and he had become a pathetic figure and an embarrassment to many Catholics, and in 1942 he was forced to abandon public life and return to his parish, where he served quietly until his death in 1979.

It is tempting to dismiss Coughlin as a lunatic fringe, but the truth is he merely carried to the extreme ideas that enjoyed wide currency among the American people. A 1938 Gallup poll revealed some startling things. About 50% of those polled confessed that they had a low opinion of Jews; 45% thought Jews were more dishonest than Gentiles in business; 35% believed that the Jews in Europe were largely responsible for the oppression that had been heaped on them. And when asked, "Should we allow a larger number of Jewish exiles from Germany come to the United States to live?" 77% said no.

That last question touches on the most devastating consequence of the rise in U.S. anti-Semitism during this period: Americans were, by and large, indifferent to the plight of the Jews in Germany, and this apathy likely contributed to the magnitude of the Holocaust. Specifically, the deep currents of anti-Semitism in U.S. society shaped diplomatic policies that limited the number of Jewish refugees who were permitted to enter the U.S. and Jews who could not officially emigrate were stuck in Europe. Americans like to think of themselves on the right side of history when it comes to the Holocaust. In truth, U.S. anti-Semitism contributed to the ultimate body count of Jews who were murdered in Europe.

When I offer this information to undergraduate students, I return to Hofstadter's "paranoid style," asking students to analyze how this dynamic was at play in American society in the 1930s. And then I ask the most important question: Is the paranoid style still operating in American society? If so, who is the current target? How does it affect American diplomatic policy? Is there a body count in the present moment that results from it? When I first began using this pedagogical strategy in the 2000s, students identified Muslims as the group targeted by Christian privilege and the paranoid style. By early 2012 this had narrowed more specifically (and tragically) to refugees fleeing violence in Syria. After the election of Donald Trump in 2016, students quickly added Mexicans and Central American refugees at the U.S. southern border to the list of people targeted by the paranoid style. And lest we shift the conversation away from anti-Semitism and anti-Judaism completely, violent anti-Semitism in on the rise in the U.S. and in Europe. This was tragically underscored by the mass shooting at the Tree of Life synagogue in Philadelphia in October 2018. I want to equip students not just to be able to see religiously-grounded prejudice in the current political moment of the class, but to have diagnostic concepts – Christian privilege and the paranoid style – that they can continue to deploy throughout their lives to understand the who and why of the always-changing calculus of victimization and marginalization in American policies.

Anti-Muslimism[1]

Resources: Edward Said, "On Orientalism" documentary

Articles by scholars Lila Abu-Lughod, Gayatri Spivak, and Chandra Mohanty

"I'm a Muslim but…" A Response to Buzzfeed video by Fear of a Brown Planet comedy duo

The Arab American Institute's Advocacy Road Map

Kryn

To begin an exploration of Anti-Muslimism, it is necessary to acknowledge that race often becomes a marker for religion and the intersection of the two creates particular manifestations of racism and religious bias. I situate this section in the context of legacies of colonization and orientalism and the implications of Christianity in the ways that Europe and subsequently the

United States mobilized (and continues to mobilize) Christian ideas and expectations for domination.

The colonization of the Global South by Europe from the 16th century onward was undertaken with explicit Christian missionizing goals. "Studies of imperialism show that from ancient to contemporary times three main factors have repeatedly motivated and justified imperialism: God, glory, and gold" (Dube, 2000, p. 47). Adding a fourth G for gender recognizes that, while oppression based on gender exists for both colonizer and colonized, "colonizing women, too, partake of its colonial harvest" (Dube, 2000, p. 76). The primacy of the United States on the global stage today was made possible by the genocide of Native Americans and the enslavement of Africans and continues under the explicit racism of immigration policies and neocolonialism within and beyond our borders.

Edward Said's *Orientalism*, written in 1978, helps contextualize the West's imagined Middle East and the ways this contributes to Anti-Muslimism. In this, and subsequent writing, Said explores the ways the east, or "the Orient," was created in diametric opposition to the West. His writing notes

> the basic distinction between East and West as the starting point for elaborate theories, epics, novels, social descriptions, and political accounts concerning the Orient, its people, customs, "mind," destiny and so on.... Orientalism provided a rationalization for European colonialism based on a self-serving history in which "the West" constructed "the East" as extremely different and inferior, and therefore in need of Western intervention or "rescue."
>
> (Said, 1979, p. 38)

Orientalism creates fear, and at the same time exoticization, of the other. It often conflates religious and racial identities and can excuse the appropriation of religious practices without regard to the spiritual components of the practices or the particular cultural histories in which they were created. Women in particular face exoticization and are often at the center of western justifications for military invasions prompting contemporary postcolonial feminist scholars to critique the ways that white Americans justify saving brown women from brown men. The "saving" is not an accidental word; it is laden with Christian overtones as the missionization aspect of colonization makes clear. Part of the power of Said's analysis is that he used Western art and literature about the Orient in his original writing and continued to add examples from more recent years each time he spoke or was interviewed. This 45-minute interview fits well in a class session leaving time for conversation about the content, which includes visual images of the paintings, art, and recordings of the news reports that Said explores. Students learn media literacy skills when experts like Said show how to analyze images and language in a news item. Placing Said's filmed work alongside articles by Lila Abu-Lughod, Gayatri Spivak, and Chandra Mohanty strengthens students' feminist and decolonial work of investigating Christian privilege and dismantling Anti-Muslimism. Said's conversation was filmed in 1998 and uses the Oklahoma City bombing as a key example. It can help students make their own connections to the ways that the United States responded to terrorism immediately after 9/11 and even the lack of response to the refugee crisis in Syria. Said's presentation provides a powerful prompt for conversation about Disney's *Aladdin* and films like *Wadjda* (directed by Saudi Arabian woman director, Haifaa Al-Mansour) and *A Girl Walks Home Alone at Night* (directed by Iranian-British director Ana Lily Amirpour) that I have shown in my Women in World Cinema classes to reframe Muslim and Middle Eastern women-centered stories.

Exploring this context assists in contextualizing how current anti-Muslimism is not a new form of religious bias and racism. Starting with a definition of anti-Muslimism – the fear, hatred, and mistreatment of Muslims, as a teacher/facilitator, I show a short video created by a comedy duo in 2015 in response to a Buzzfeed video titled "I'm a Muslim but I'm not a Terrorist" (Fear of a Brown Planet). It features Muslims sharing what they want people to know about their faith, cultures, and the impact of common myths about Islam. Videos like this bring voices and perspectives into the room that are likely to be absent and humanizes Muslims for audiences that might not have met or been in community with Muslims.

Depending on the length of the training or the content of the course, it can be appropriate to share some basic information about Islam – when it began, its holy texts, faith practices and how they vary. For instructors who are not experts in Islam, this can be tricky territory. Students tend to focus on particular textual details or cultural practices so I reserve this context for theology courses. Focusing on the Quran or Sharia law can distract from how we ask students and workshop participants to examine anti-Muslimism as a systemic racist ideology grounded in white supremacy that needs to be dismantled. In theology courses, we do tackle questions about G*d, what G*d and sacred texts say about justice and gender, histories, and how Muslim, feminist, and postcolonial theologians are challenging violent or sexist interpretations (Amina Wadud, 1999, and Riffat Hassan, 2008, in particular)

A good follow-up strategy to the video is to share statistics that disrupt stereotypes and myths about Muslims and people from the Middle East. Muslims follow Islam and the five pillars of profession of faith, prayer, charity, fasting, and pilgrimage. According to research published by the Pew Research Center, there are 1.8 billion Muslims in the world, or 24% of the world's population. Islam is the second largest religious tradition and Muslims are the fastest growing religious group in the world (Pew Research, 2017). Contrary to what many people believe, most Muslims are not from the Middle East and North Africa; 62% live in Asia-Pacific countries. Providing a list of the countries with the largest Muslim populations and asking students to make observations about the list is helpful to dispel some of the assumptions that are held about Muslims. The country with the highest Muslim population is Indonesia, followed by Pakistan, India, Bangladesh, Egypt, Nigeria, Iran, Turkey, Algeria, and Morocco; 2/3 of the world's Muslims live in these ten countries. Students are often surprised to realize that while most Arabs are Muslim, most Muslims are not Arab. A large Muslim population within a country does not necessarily mean that the country is Muslim majority, e.g., although India has the third largest Muslim population, Muslims are a minority within the country representing only 13.4% of the population. And as we will discuss below, minoritized populations within a country experience religious bias and anti-Muslimism in ways that often are sanctioned and institutionalized within histories particular to that country. About 20% of Muslims in the United States are black (Pew Research Center, 2017).

Since Arab and Muslim identities are often conflated, a discussion about Arabs and Arab Americans is helpful. The term Arab predates Islam and today is an ethnic term that does not connote religion or politics. People who are Arab come from an Arab nation and usually speak Arabic, though this varies as there are 22 Arab League nations with a range of religions and languages. Latin America has the largest Arab population outside of the Arab World. Though many Arabs are Muslim, millions are Christian and thousands are Jewish.

In the United States, there are 3.7 million Arab Americans; 35% are Muslim. Two-thirds of Arab Americans live in just ten states with 1/3 living in Los Angeles, Detroit, and New York City. Most of these people were born in the United States and 82% are U.S. citizens. Two-thirds are Christian. The Arab American Institute's *Advocacy Road Map: A Local Action Toolkit for How You Can Make a Difference* is a helpful resource for use in classes and trainings. During a Difference, Power, and Discrimination class or seminar, it is not enough to learn facts and context, we also need tools to forge a society that values our differences. Resources like this provide tangible ways for people to act toward a more just society.

Anti-Muslimism is rooted in the structural racism of U.S. history and permeates every aspect of our society. The state creates and maintains racism and anti-Muslimism and individuals act on these ideas and beliefs. Critical theorist and legal scholar Khalid Beydoun details how the structural anti-Muslimism of state policies and the private anti-Muslimism enacted by individuals work in a dialectical way to maintain and support one another. Often it is individual anti-Muslimism that gets highlighted by news media coverage eclipsing the ways that the state endorses and authors negative stereotypes of Muslims. Current anti-Muslimism is part of the legacy of historical white supremacy enacted through colonialism and the slave trade. Scholars believe that as many as 10–15% of the Africans enslaved in the U.S. were Muslims who continued to practice their faith traditions while enslaved and after emancipation. Beydoun (2018) notes how Arabs became legally defined as white by the mid-20th century because whiteness was a requirement for U.S. citizenship and Christian Arabs leveraged their Christianity to argue for their whiteness. Additionally, anti-Black racism is connected to anti-Muslimism in the ways that Muslim = Arab or Middle Eastern is often falsely assumed, thereby rendering Black Muslims who have always been in the United States invisible. Anti-Muslimism and the targeting of Muslims and people from the Middle East through the Muslim and refugee ban is connected to broader racist ideologies that also manifest in recent and increasing targeted attacks on African-American, Jewish, and Latinx people.

Indeed, the most recent data indicate an overall increase in hate crimes: a 6.8% increase from 2014 to 2015, and another 5% increase from 2015–2016. In 2016, nearly 60% of hate crimes reported to the FBI were based on ethnicity, and over 20% were based on religious affiliation.

(Arab American Institute, 2017)

It is critical to dismantle anti-Muslimism like other forms of racism, to recognize that it continues to be connected to broader white supremacy and is tied to law, policies, and state structures. "[W]e need critical Muslim representation, not tokenized representation in media, academia, and in every sphere of American society" (Beydoun, 2018).

Conclusion

Religion is intricately wrapped up in a society's construction of power and invisibly indicates ideas about race, class, gender, and history. Untangling these ideas can be some of the trickiest work in a DPD classroom but well worth the effort as it leads not only the student, but also the teacher/facilitator into new understandings of how religious difference shapes a multitude of discriminations and can lead to new ways of dismantling religious oppression through individual and institutional solutions.

Additional Resources

Audiovisuals

Adichie, C. N. (2009, July). *The danger of a single story* [Video]. TED Conferences. www.ted.com/talks/chimamanda_ngozi_adichie_the_danger_of_a_single_story

Religious Studies and American Religious History

Readings

Holmes, D. (1996). *Faiths of the founding fathers.* Oxford University Press.
Johnson, S. A. (2007). *African American religions, 1500–2000: Colonialism, democracy and freedom.* Cambridge University Press.
Prothero, S. (2007). *Religious literacy: What every american needs. To know – and doesn't.* HarperOne.
Prothero, S. (2020, May 15). *Religious Literacy Quiz.* https://assets.pewresearch.org/wp-content/uploads/sites/11/2007/12/protheroquiz.pdf
Richter, D. (2003). *Facing east from indian country: A native history of early America.* Harvard University Press.

Christian Privilege

Readings

Kivel, P. (2018). Guidelines for Christian allies. In M. Adams et al. (Eds.), *Readings for diversity and social justice* (4th ed., p. 329). Routledge.

Schossler, L. (2003). Christian privilege: Breaking a sacred taboo. *Journal of Multicultural Counseling and Development. 31*(1), 44–51.

Centering Indigenous Perspectives and Epistemologies

Readings

Kimmerer, R. (2013). *Braiding sweetgrass: Indigenous wisdom, scientific knowledge, and the teachings of plants.* Milkweed Press.

Niditch, S. (1992). Genesis. In C. A. Newsom, & S. H. Ringe (Eds.), *The women's bible commentary.* Westminster/John Knox Press.

Anti-Judaism and Anti-Semitism

Readings

Dinnerstein, L. (1994). *Anti-Semitism in America.* Oxford University Press.

Jeansonne, G. (1997). *Gerald L. K. Smith: Minister of hate.* Louisiana State University Press.

Hofstadter, R. (2003). *The paranoid style in American politics.* Vintage Reprint.

Simonelli, F. J. (1999). *American fuehrer: George Lincoln Rockwell and the American Nazi Party.* University of Illinois Press.

Wallae, M. (2003). *The American axis: Henry Ford, Charles Lindbergh and the rise of the Third Reich.* St. Martin's Press.

Warren, D. (1996). *Radio priest: Charles Coughlin, the father of hate radio.* Free Press.

Wenger, B. (Ed.) (2007). *The Jewish Americans: Three centuries of Jewish voices in America.* Doubleday.

Audiovisuals

Father Coughlin Before the 1936 Election (2007, August 11) [Video]. YouTube. www.youtube.com/watch?v=IS9_gqCytV4&feature=youtu.be

Father Couglin In Action (2010, October 30) [Video]. YouTube. www.youtube.com/watch?v=uFDuGNCxyl0&feature=youtu.be

Anti-Muslimism

Readings

Abu-Lughod, L. (2002). Do Muslim women really need saving?: Anthropological reflections on cultural relativism and its others. *American Anthropologist*, 104(3): 783–790.

Arab American Institute's Advocacy Road Map (2017). www.aaiusa.org/advocacy_road_map

Associated Press (2019, October 9). Shooting latest indication of increasing anti-Semitism. https://apnews.com/6a969f460f8e426eba75872289168f87

Beydoun, K. (2018). *American Islamophobia: Understanding the roots and rise of fear*. University of California Press.

Dube, M. (2000). *Postcolonial feminist interpretation of the Bible*. Chalice Press.

Hassan, R. (2008). *Exploring Islam in a new light: An understanding from the Quranic perspective*. Brainbrow Press.

Mohanty, C. (1984). Under western eyes: Feminist scholarship and colonial discourses. *Boundary 2*, *12*(3)–*13*(1), 333–358.

Said, E. (1979). *Orientalism*. Random House.

Spivak, G. (1988). Can the subaltern speak? In C. Nelson and L. Grossberg (Eds.), *Marxism and the Interpretation of Culture*. Grossberg, IL: University of Illinois.

Wadud, A. (1999). *Qur'an and woman: Rereading the sacred text from a woman's perspective*. Oxford University Press.

Audiovisuals

Abdel-Magied, Y. (n.d.). *What does my headscarf mean to you?* [Video]. TED Conferences. www.ted.com/talks/yassmin_abdel_magied_what_does_my_headscarf_mean_to_you

Edward Said On Orientalism (2012, October 28) [Video]. YouTube. www.youtube.com/watch?v=fVC8EYd_Z_g

"I'm a Muslim, but…" – A response to Buzzfeed (2015, October 16) [Video]. YouTube. www.youtube.com/watch?v=lWVV-jBz2_E

Note

1 We use anti-Muslimism instead of Islamophobia for several reasons. It centers the conversation on how people are directly impacted by the bias and oppression rather than on the religion. It also avoids the use of "phobia" that has been critiqued by disability advocates as appropriating a description of a mental illness.

References

Abdel-Magied, Y. (n.d.). *What does my headscarf mean to you?* [Video]. TED Conferences. www.ted.com/talks/yassmin_abdel_magied_what_does_my_headscarf_mean_to_you

Abu-Lughod, L. (2002). Do Muslim women really need saving?: Anthropological reflections on cultural relativism and its others. *American Anthropologist, 104*(3), 783–790.

Adichie, C. N. (2009, July). *The danger of a single story.* www.ted.com/talks/chimamanda_ngozi_adichie_the_danger_of_a_single_story

Arab American Institute's Advocacy Road Map (2017). www.aaiusa.org/advocacy_road_map

Associated Press (2019, October 9). Shooting latest indication of increasing anti-Semitism. https://apnews.com/6a969f460f8e426eba75872289168f87

Beydoun, K. (2018). *American Islamophobia: Understanding the roots and rise of fear.* University of California Press.

Dinnerstein, L. (1994). *Anti-Semitism in America.* Oxford University Press.

Dube, M. (2000). *Postcolonial feminist interpretation of the Bible.* Chalice Press.

Edward Said On Orientalism (2012, October 28) [Video]. YouTube. www.youtube.com/watch?v=fVC8EYd_Z_g

Father Coughlin Before the 1936 Election (2007, August 11) [Video]. YouTube. www.youtube.com/watch?v=IS9_gqCytV4&feature=youtu.be

Father Couglin In Action (2010, October 30) [Video]. YouTube. www.youtube.com/watch?v=uFDuGNCxyl0&feature=youtu.be

Hassan, R. (2008). *Exploring Islam in a new light: An understanding from the Quranic perspective.* Brainbrow Press.

Hofstadter, R. (2003). *The paranoid style in American politics.* Vintage Reprint.

Holmes, D. (1996). *Faiths of the founding fathers.* Oxford University Press.

"I'm a Muslim, but…" – A response to Buzzfeed (2015, October 16) [Video]. YouTube. www.youtube.com/watch?v=lWVV-jBz2_E

Jeansonne, G. (1997). *Gerald L. K. Smith: Minister of hate.* Louisiana State University Press.

Johnson, S. A. (2007). *African American religions, 1500–2000: Colonialism, democracy and freedom.* Cambridge University Press.

Kimmerer, R. (2013). *Braiding sweetgrass: Indigenous wisdom, scientific knowledge, and the teachings of plants.* Milkweed Press.

Kivel, P. (2018). Guidelines for Christian allies. In M. Adams et al. (Eds.), *Readings for diversity and social justice* (4th ed., p. 329). Routledge.

McIntosh, P. (2019). White privilege: Unpacking the invisible knapsack and some notes for facilitators. *National Seed Project.* https://nationalseedproject.org/Key-SEED-Texts/white-privilege-unpacking-the-invisible-knapsack (original work published 1989).

Mohanty, C. (1984). Under western eyes: Feminist scholarship and colonial discourses. *boundary 2, 12*(3)–*13*(1), 333–358.

Niditch, S. (1992). Genesis. In C. A. Newsom, & S. H. Ringe (Eds.), *The women's Bible commentary* (pp. 10–25). Westminster/John Knox Press.

Prothero, S. (2007). *Religious literacy: What every American needs to know – and doesn't.* HarperOne.

Prothero, S. (2020, May 15). *Religious literacy quiz.* https://assets.pewresearch.org/wp-content/uploads/sites/11/2007/12/protheroquiz.pdf

Said, E. (1979). *Orientalism.* Random House.

Schossler, L. (2003). Christian privilege: Breaking a sacred taboo. *Journal of Multicultural Counseling and Development. 31*(1), 44–51.

Simonelli, F. J. (1999). *American fuehrer: George Lincoln Rockwell and the American Nazi Party.* University of Illinois Press.

Spivak, G. (1988). Can the subaltern speak? In C. Nelson, & L. Grossberg (Eds.), *Marxism and the Interpretation of Culture* (pp. 267–310). University of Illinois.

Richter, D. (2003). *Facing east from Indian Country: A Native history of early America*. Harvard University Press.

Wadud, A. (1999). *Qur'an and woman: Rereading the sacred text from a woman's perspective*. Oxford University Press.

Wallace, M. (2003). *The American axis: Henry Ford, Charles Lindbergh and the rise of the Third Reich*. St. Martin's Press.

Warren, D. (1996). *Radio priest: Charles Coughlin, the father of hate radio*. Free Press.

Wenger, B. (Ed.) (2007). *The Jewish Americans: Three centuries of Jewish voices in America*. Doubleday.

13 ¡Sí, se puede! Teaching Farmworker Justice in the Land-Grant University

Ronald L. Mize

Over the past two decades, a resurgent scholarly interest in farmworker justice organizations has resulted in a renewed focus on the perennial plight of migrant farm workers. In the past decade, from history to journalism, the David versus Goliath story of the United Farm Workers (UFW) union has been scrutinized in terms of its long-term effect on the working conditions of farm workers, internal struggles of leadership, problematic heroic status of César Chávez, UFW 'purge', and unabated exploitation of farm labor (Bardacke, 2012; Ganz, 2009; Garcia, 2012; Mize & Swords, 2010; Pawel, 2014, 2010; Shaw, 2008). In university classrooms, a small group of scholars are teaching courses on farmworkers to keep pace with universities' demands for service, experiential, engaged, and transformative learning opportunities. These farmworker courses, taught at University of Connecticut, Cornell University, University of North Carolina, Pennsylvania State University, and Duke University to name a few, build on longstanding relationships between university students and farmworker justice organizations to take classrooms to the fields and bring the fields to the classrooms.

At Oregon State University (OSU), I have led the farmworker justice movements course since 2016, a course that fulfills the DPD Baccalaureate Core requirement, to focus on social justice learning in the context of land-grant universities whose mission is often counter to farmworker interests and more often diametrically opposed to farmworker justice movements. The course was conceptualized, developed, and initially taught with Larry Kleinman, who is a co-founder of Oregon's largest farmworker union. Students learn about the varied organizing strategies of the Pineros y Campesinos Unidos Noroeste (PCUN), United Farm Workers (UFW), Farm Labor Organizing Committee (FLOC), Coalition of Immokalee Workers (CIW), and Migrant Justice/Justicia Migrante. Students work directly with Oregon's largest Latinx organization (PCUN) to advocate for the improvement of the daily lived experiences of Oregon's migrant farmworker community. In this chapter, I discuss the challenges of teaching farmworker justice in the land-grant university context as well as the positive student learning and community partner outcomes that belie such obstacles. I begin with a brief overview of farmworker justice movements and the rise of the UFW in California, continuing through the development of

DOI: 10.4324/9781003091998-17

FLOC headquartered in Toledo, Ohio and PCUN in Oregon, then addressing the more recent rise of the CIW in South Florida and Migrant Justice/Justicia Migrante in Vermont. These organizations become the comparative case studies that comprise the materials of my course, which I distinguish from farmworker courses taught at other (mostly land-grant) universities. I then focus on how the OSU farmworker justice movements course was initially designed in collaboration with a PCUN co-founder, its learning outcomes, my pedagogies and curricular choices, and its relationship to OSU's Difference, Power, and Discrimination learning outcomes. Finally, I discuss the differences between service and experiential learning and how this decentering of the curriculum, the primacy placed on experiential learning opportunities that are derived by our community partners, shifts transformative learning in the direction of the democratization of knowledge.

Farmworker Justice Movements

When most people think about farmworker justice movements, if they are at all aware of these longstanding social movements, it is most likely the story of the United Farm Workers (UFW) and its two most recognized leaders: César Chávez and Dolores Huerta with which they are familiar. In scholarly literatures, this focus on the UFW first peaked in the 1980s with the work of sociologists interested in whether the UFW did or did not constitute a social movement and which theory of social movements best accounted for their successes (see Jenkins, 1985; Jenkins & Perrow, 1977; Majka & Majka, 1982; Mooney & Majka, 1995). In the decade of the 2010s, a group of historians at the confluence of ethnic history and labor history revisited the UFW, often in conversation with public intellectuals, journalists, and other scholars, by turning a more critical eye to account for what some describe as the union's spectacular downfall (Bardacke, 2012; Ganz, 2009; Garcia, 2012; Mize & Swords, 2010; Pawel, 2014, 2010; Shaw, 2008).

There was a significant popular literature while the UFW movement was gaining traction. Early documentation of the successes of the UFW almost always attributed the union's success to its most prominent leader, César Estrada Chávez. Early accounts by Mattheissen (1969) and Levy (1975) certainly portray a glorified version of UFW history with both accounts putting Chávez front and center, and La Causa following obediently behind. This uncritical brand of hero worship was a problem in popular literature and documentaries on the UFW that still carries a certain cachet to this day (see Ferriss & Sandoval, 1997; Garcia, 2008; Griswold del Castillo & Garcia, 1995; Levy, 1975; Mattheissen, 1969; Rosales, 1996; Ross, 1989; Stavans, 2008). As more children's stories are written dedicated to Chávez's accomplishments, acclaimed Chicano author Gary Soto sums up the genre best with the title: *Cesar Chavez: A Hero for Everyone* (Soto & Lohstoeter, 2003). No person could possibly live up to this idol status, though Chávez's ideas on nonviolence put him in direct conversation with influential thinkers such as Dr. Rev.

Martin Luther King, Jr. and Mohandas Karamchand Gandhi (see Orosco, 2008). Not coincidentally, a historical revisionism was required when the marital infidelities of MLK surfaced. Yet, the criticism of Chávez as a dogmatic or authoritarian leader very quickly goes too far down a very well-worn path (see Pawel, 2014, 2010; Krikorian, 2017). Genuine criticisms must be reconciled with the long history of character assassination that UFW leaders received from Republican leaders such as then-California governor Ronald Reagan and then-President Richard Nixon, California growers, and national agribusiness industry groups. In the course I teach, we balance this overcorrective by identifying that the UFW was a movement, not a single-leader model, so we include writings and perspectives from Dolores Huerta, Larry Itliong, Philip de la Cruz, Jerry Cohen, Jessica Govea, Marshall Ganz, LeRoy Chatfield, Eliseo Medina, Randy Shaw, and David Bacon to counterbalance the one-man hero myth that often is deployed to undercut the mass mobilizations that movements constitute, while still recognizing that leadership matters.

Scholarly interest in the UFW found its resurgence first in 1980s sociology of social movements, branding the UFW an unqualified success and in 2010s history at the confluence of ethnic (Chicano) and labor history as success but also as cautionary tale. Always preoccupied with "unruliness" and LeBon's (1895) foundational position that mass crowds breed violence, for social movement theorists such as J. Craig Jenkins, the UFW stood out for its commitment to nonviolence but also as a key example of resource mobilization theory: "The United Farm Workers' Union, for example, has not only constructed a formalized, centrally controlled organization but has used this structure to organize successful mass strikes" (Jenkins, 1983, p. 545). And most importantly, these protests did not devolve into violence even when they were met by state or grower violence. The UFW resisted the temptation to respond in kind. They were most successful in channeling insurgency (boycotts, strikes, pilgrimages, hunger strikes, and marches) into union contracts, essentially mobilizing their limited resources to secure major wins through collective bargaining and lobbying to change California state law (Jenkins 1985, 1983; Jenkins, & Perrow, 1977; Majka, 1981; Majka, 1980; Majka, & Majka 2000, 1982; Mooney & Majka, 1995). Only Majka and Majka (1992) followed through on the UFW post California Agricultural Labor Relations Act in 1975 that brought collective bargaining rights to the state's farmworker population in many ways to thwart union poaching, ending the practice of the Teamsters Union signing sweetheart deals with growers to undercut UFW contracts. Though they do not get into the details of the internal meltdown of the UFW, the authors claim the union fell into disrepair and decline as a result of channeling their energies from organizing to lobbying and policy making (see also Bardacke, 2012, pp. 509–536). Rather than try to cover these first two eras of UFW analyses, I find excerpts from three documentaries that convey these eras well and then I introduce the newest analyses that problematize prior scholarly and popular depictions of hero worship and resource mobilization (see Pearcy's 1975 *Fighting for Our Lives: The United Farm Workers'*

1973 Grape Strike and the Wrath of Grapes, Galan's 1996 "The Struggle in the Fields," Part 2 of *Chicano! History of the Mexican-American Civil Rights Movement*, and Telles' 1996 *The Fight in the Fields: Cesar Chavez and the Farmworkers' Struggle*). The work of historians Matt Garcia and Mario Sifuentez, following the pathway first treaded by Chicano historian David Gutiérrez (1995), attempts to strike a balance between "triumph and tragedy" in the words of Garcia (2012). A much more critical analysis of the UFW questions the decisions made by Chávez, in a manner that questions his almost mythic heroic status.

> Unlike the overwhelming majority of authors who have written about the United Farm Workers, I explain how and why the union achieved most of its goals through 1970, *and* how and why it failed to live up to its tremendous potential after that…. What is missing [in the literature] is a consideration of how Chávez employed strategies and management techniques that compromised the union.
>
> (Garcia, 2012, pp. 4–5)

Garcia and Sifuentez (2012) compare UFW and PCUN to distinguish the two organizations' differing focus on Mexican-American U.S. citizens (UFW) to the focus on Mexican immigrants (PCUN) from the outset. It should be noted, many in the movement disagree with Garcia and Sifuentez's bifurcation, and think the distinction is overblown. The period from 1977 to 1981 was an exceptionally trying era for Chávez as a leader and for the UFW as a farmworker union. The more critical journalists and scholars refer to this time period as "the purge." Marshall Ganz (one of those who was 'purged'), refers to it as "the transformation" (Ganz, 2009, pp. 243–248) when those who expressed opposition to Chávez's tactics, his adoption of Synanon game to distinguish loyalists from those labeled "agents" or "assholes" who took oppositional positions, were fired from the union.[1]

I have weighed in on this debate with my co-author Alicia Swords in *Consuming Mexican Labor* (2010). We argued that in an ad in their trade journal, *El Malcriado*, the UFW clearly did not consider Braceros as "workers" – or at the very least not "our workers"; they are characterized in the ad as simply a weapon in the growers' arsenal. The organized labor divide between Mexican Americans and Mexican immigrants, as Chicano historian David Gutiérrez (1995) first noted, highlights that common ancestry is a tenuous link when labor, border, citizenship, and assimilation pressures are all operating. The UFW's actions represent some of the most positive successes for Mexicans residing in the United States and some of the worst ways in which the Mexican-origin population is internally divided by excluding immigrant workers. As the UFW came to seriously consider the challenges offered by fellow Mexican American organizations, its organizing strategy eventually shifted to an organizing-*sin-fronteras* (without borders) approach.

Today, each of the farmworker organizations (including the UFW) place immigrant rights at the center of their campaigns and given the changing workforce in farm labor, they simply have no other choice. Initially, the two organizations that very much modeled themselves after the UFW were FLOC in Toledo, Ohio and PCUN in Woodburn, Oregon. Long-time FLOC President Baldemar Velásquez followed the AFL-CIO labor union affiliated route of the UFW but quickly distinguished itself by negotiating contracts that most often placed small farmers and farmworkers on the same side of the bargaining table, as third-party contracts were negotiated with the corporations on the top of food chains – in their case first Campbell's Soup and then Vlasic Pickles and Heinz. From 1970 to 1990, FLOC boycotted these corporations and eventually signed contracts by bringing together small farmers and farmworkers in common cause, pressuring the top of the food chain to bargain wage, hour, health, and safety concessions (Barger & Reza, 1994, pp. 52–53). When FLOC followed the pickle chain, their organizing work took them to North Carolina and the Mount Olive Pickle Company. But entering the South, and the right-to-work state of North Carolina, what significantly posed initial challenges were twofold:

1 the North Carolina Growers' Association was often the employer of record in cucumber production, and
2 most workers were temporary visa holders from Mexico who were recruited as part of the H-2A program.

As David Griffith (2009) notes, "The core of FLOC's membership in North Carolina are H-2[A] workers" (p. 59). This occurred because H-2[A] workers comprised the majority of cucumber workers that FLOC targeted in their boycott of Mt. Olive Pickle." Both non-citizens and agricultural workers do not have guaranteed rights to collective bargaining, yet FLOC has been quite successful in their North Carolina organizing efforts.

On the other side of the nation, it's the work of Oregon's PCUN that centers immigrant rights in farmworker organizing. The first book-length treatment of PCUN was penned in 2016 by historian Mario Sifuentez.

> PCUN challenged the idea that the absence of citizenship made undocumented workers vulnerable to deportation and thus unorganizable. Its commitment to organizing all workers regardless of citizenship made PCUN a leader among groups that were rethinking the relationship between farm work and immigrant rights.
>
> (Sifuentez, 2016, p. 4)

University of Oregon anthropologist Lynn Stephen and her students have been key in providing broader exposure to the history of PCUN and more recent organizing campaigns (Stephen, 2012, 2007). One of the unique opportunities afforded by partnering directly with the organization one is studying is unparalleled access to primary documents, even as they are being created as part of its daily operations. Students are able to secure unparalleled access to PCUN co-founder Larry Kleinman's writings (both past and current), sometimes given extra copies of primary documents, and watch sources be created before their eyes.

The Coalition of Immokalee Workers is finally receiving the scholarly interest it has earned given its unique approach to farm labor as an international human rights issue. CIW activists analyze the food chain closely to leverage their unique power in representing workers who supply the vast majority of winter tomatoes produced in the United States. Deploying varied strategies of "truth tours" in supportive churches and universities, boycotts of fast-food conglomerates such as Yum Brands! (Taco Bell, KFC, Long John Silver's, A&W, and Pizza Hut) and eventually every other major fast food and grocery chain, marches to the state capital, and a collection of allies from Eva Longoria and Eric Schlosser (see Rawal's 2014 *Food Chains*; Estabrook, 2012, pp. 53–54) to former UN High Commissioner for Human Rights and president of Ireland Mary Robinson; the CIW truly approaches organizing from a David versus Goliath perspective. The Campaign for Fair Food started as the penny per pound campaign that successfully brought on Yum!, McDonalds, Burger King, Subway, Chipotle, Whole Foods, Trader Joe's, and Walmart as partners meaning their agricultural suppliers must adhere to a code of conduct and third-party monitoring system that includes wage increases, health and safety, anti-slavery, ongoing audits, and complaint resolutions. Long-time activists with CIW were contacted a few years ago by a workers' center in Vermont who were hearing increasing complaints about working conditions from the state's dairy workers.

Out of that training came Migrant Justice/Justicia Migrante and a landmark third party certification system signed by Ben and Jerry's Ice Cream and Vermont state's dairies. Since the agreement is so new (October, 2017) and scholarship is slow to catch up with these fast-moving events, students learn about Migrant Justice from their own social media, media coverage in *New York Times*, and direct testimony from Migrant Justice organizers. Their agreement is as follows:

> The Milk with Dignity program is now fully operational in Ben & Jerry's northeast dairy supply chain, covering 100% of the company's dairy volume.
>
> - 70+ dairy farms in Vermont and New York are covered under the program;
> - 300+ dairy workers are now protected by the Code of Conduct; each worker has received an education session, a rights booklet, and access to a 24/7 worker support line;
> - The newly formed independent 3rd party monitor, the Milk with Dignity Standards Council (MDSC), has responded to dozens of worker calls and is working with farmers and farmworkers to define concrete plans to resolve all reported violations of the MD Code of Conduct;

- The MDSC will audit all eligible farms by the end of 2018 and create detailed Corrective Action Plans (CAPs) to achieve full compliance with the Code.[2]

Very much modeled after the CIW's Fair Food Program, the efforts of Migrant Justice actually coincide with UFW efforts to organize dairy workers employed in Washington state that focus on the Darigold cooperative that controls the supply chain and its largest recipient, Starbucks. The challenge is the vast majority of the literature has and continues to be focused on the UFW, whereas literature on Migrant Justice has yet to be published. Yet, it is nonetheless these five movements for social justice that comprise the comparative case studies for the Farmworker Justice Movements course at Oregon State University. But before I discuss that course, it's important to note the predecessors that made it possible.

Prior Farmworker Courses

Farmworker courses, taught at University of Connecticut, Cornell University, University of North Carolina, Pennsylvania State University, and Duke University to name a few, build on longstanding relationships between university students and farmworker justice organizations to take classrooms to the fields and bring the fields to the classrooms. Craib and Overmyer-Velásquez (2012) discuss their respective farmworkers courses at Cornell University and University of Connecticut by noting the UConn course was based on the Cornell offering. I should note that I participated as a guest speaker in the Cornell farmworkers course when I was on the faculty there but did not contribute extensively to it while the College of Agriculture and Life Sciences (my then-home college) was leading efforts to disband the Cornell Farmworker Program by firing or forcibly retiring its staff who ran afoul of the New York Farm Bureau.

There is a smattering of course offerings across the country on farmworker issues. Legal and public health clinics (such as programs at Villanova and Emory universities) connect students to offer short-term legal advice and health care to neighboring farmworker communities. Good resources also are provided by the Student Action with Farmworkers organization.[3] At Penn State, the agricultural college sponsors a service-learning course called "Service-Learning with Pennsylvania Farmworkers." The course centers around college students teaching basic English literacy to Latina/o immigrant dairy workers in terms that will help make a more efficient and safer workforce. The course is designed to

> help students gain a deeper understanding of the agricultural workforce and make connections between immigrant farmworkers' lives and the global forces of the agri-food system, and to support the local agricultural community by increasing workers' confidence in their language skills, thereby supporting farm viability.[4]

In the Cornell farmworkers course,

> Service requires a significant investment of time. The key issue the course confronts each year is how to ensure that students take seriously both the service and classroom aspects of the course and work persistently to integrate them… Other assignments include having students research and present a brief history of one family member that places that individual's story of migration to the United States within the context of the major themes and issues of the course.
> (Craib & Overmyer-Velázquez, 2012, p. 263)

Finally, referring to course assignments in the UConn course, students

> hand-deliver their letters to legislators during a field trip to the state capital during the last week of class and send the letters to the Washington, DC, offices of federal legislators. This culminating exercise draws on the knowledge students have gained in their classroom and service-learning experiences and connects it with urgent contemporary realities.
> (Craib & Overmyer-Velázquez, 2012, p. 263)

Each of these courses make key decisions about who has input in the course, whose interests are served by course content, how farmers are represented, how one quells the varied interests of institutional actors and academic departments, and what roles students will play in their service-learning efforts. I simply avoided most of these questions by shifting the focus from farmworkers to farmworker justice movements.

Part of the pressure of addressing farmers' interests is certainly related to the history of the land-grant university (LGU). The Morrill Acts of 1862 and 1890 established LGUs and Historically-Black LGCUs when the separate but equal doctrine of Plessy v. Ferguson (1890) required that segregation be permissible as so long as separate institutions were in theory equal. What is often not discussed in the development of the Morrill Act (1862) that established: "An Act donating Public Lands to the several States and Territories which way provide Colleges for the Benefit of Agriculture and the Mechanic Arts" is that many states used prime agricultural lands previously seized from Indigenous communities. Today, when we compel LGUs to land recognition statements, that history becomes visible. Cornell University was founded on Haudenosaunee Confederacy (Iroquois) lands. The University of Connecticut was built on the lands of the Mohegan, Mashantucket Pequot, Eastern Pequot, Schaghticoke, Golden Hill Paugussett, and Nipmuc Peoples. OSU's land recognition reads: Oregon State University in Corvallis, Oregon is located within the traditional homelands of the Mary's River or Ampinefu Band of Kalapuya. Following the Willamette Valley Treaty of 1855 (Kalapuya etc. Treaty), Kalapuya people were forcibly removed to reservations in Western Oregon. Today, living descendants of these people are a part of the

Confederated Tribes of Grand Ronde Community of Oregon (www.grandronde.org) and the Confederated Tribes of the Siletz Indians (https://ctsi.nsn.us). OSU was established in 1868 (nine years after statehood) and like other LGUs added extension and outreach to the established activities of teaching and research. Cantor (as cited in Avila, 2017) identifies that the Morrill Act "launched a revolution in higher education by providing for what would become known as 'democracy's colleges'. [These colleges] were aimed simultaneously at spreading innovation through university-community collaboration and fostering access to education for the next generation of farmers" (p. 6). The question that simply took too long to ask is: does LGU democracy extend to those most marginalized in our agricultural systems, those marginalized by race, Indigeneity, class, gender, sexuality, ability, and citizenship?

Answering in the affirmative, courses on farmworkers also question the traditional disciplinary boundaries that make it so difficult to see farmworker experiences in their totality. Examining the relationship between the local and global are highlights of the Cornell and UConn farmworker courses. As the Craib and Overmyer-Velásquez (2012) note, a key

> course goal asks students to critically examine notions of a bounded nation-state and exclusive and exceptional national histories in a Latin American/Caribbean/United States context.… In so doing, our courses endeavor to teach Latin American and Caribbean, US and Latina/o [transnational] histories as often overlapping and mutually constitutive histories.
>
> (p. 267)

Yet, OSU's DPD curricula center domestic (U.S.-bounded) minoritization processes to "address institutionalized systems of power, privilege, and inequity in the United States."[5] I recognize that focusing on immigration is always a transnational endeavor and the linkages between local and global are so deeply interwoven that it's nearly impossible to discuss the United States as a singularly bounded nation. Though we focus on the experiences of migrant justice movements in the United States, these organizations too are not so easily bounded. For example, one of the most important elements in understanding FLOC's current contracts is the assassination of their organizer Santiago Rafael Cruz on April 9, 2007. Cruz was responsible for administering the North Carolina Grower Association's H-2A labor contract from the sending community of Monterrey, Nuevo Leon, Mexico. He was murdered in his FLOC office by assumedly Mexican labor contractors who wanted to send a message to FLOC that they were an unwanted source of competition (see Mize & Swords, 2010, p. 55).

Teaching Farmworker Justice Movements

I should note that I approached this course from the outset with a clear set of goals for student learning that are inseparable from my own life history. As the first generation in my family not required to work in the fields as a farmworker, and also, as the son of an Anglo father and Chicana mother who both spent time in the fields, I certainly approach this topic from a different set of lived experiences. The idea of needing to find a balance between competing interests or maintain a particular heritage of university-agricultural connections simply does not resonate with me. I did elect to work in the table grape industry as part of my doctoral research in Fresno County (see Mize, 2016). By choosing to connect the experiential learning components of the course as well as course reading content with farmworker justice organizations, I know I was consciously making a choice to focus on

1 farmworker advocacy,
2 internal and competing models of organizing, and
3 direct student involvement with social justice organizations.

Justice movements for farmworkers have a long and storied past in the annals of U.S. history. This course begins with the 1960's Chicano civil rights era struggles for social justice to present day. We focus on the varied strategies of five farmworker justice movements: United Farm Workers, Farm Labor Organizing Committee, *Pineros y Campesinos Unidos Noroeste*, Migrant Justice, and the Coalition of Immokalee Workers. This course was co-designed with a founder of PCUN, Larry Kleinman, who actively co-leads the course as his schedule allows. The course is structured around the question of the movement and its various articulations. Together, we cover some central themes and strategies that comprise the core of farm worker movements, but the course is designed to allow students to explore other articulations they find personally relevant or of interest.

In my first summer at OSU, I participated in the DPD Summer Academy to develop the course to meet the required DPD course learning outcomes. I later served on the DPD faculty advisory board for several years. I also participated in the summer ADVANCE workshop based on the DPD Academy curriculum (for more on the ADVANCE program, see Afterword in this volume) and later co-facilitated a summer ADVANCE workshop with engineering professor and former DPD director, Michelle Bothwell. It was with this cumulative experience that I developed the following course objectives to complement the DPD course learning outcomes.

Course Objectives:
Upon completion of this course, students should be able to:

1 Identify the salient ways in which farmworker movements pursue social justice aims.
2 Demonstrate a broad knowledge of tactics and strategies deployed by farmworker justice movements.
3 Distinguish among the five case studies (UFW, PCUN, FLOC, CIW, and Migrant Justice/Justicia Migrante) in terms of shared or distinct tactics and strategies.

4 Apply insights of course readings and classroom conversations into new articulations of the movement and its related themes/topics.
5 Apply critical thinking skills to readings through presentation, discussion, and writing assignments.
6 Meet Difference, Power and Discrimination (DPD) learning outcomes.

The DPD learning outcomes (see the Introduction to this volume) articulate well with insights from ethnic studies so I can draw upon existing literature in my class to discuss the social construction of difference, the historical and contemporary relevance of racism and other forms of institutional discrimination, and how these social categories shape the lived experiences of farmworkers residing in the United States.

The course tends to draw a majority Latinx and farmworker family student population. I wish it was more formally articulated with our College Assistance Migrant Program (CAMP), Educational Opportunities Program (EOP), or Centro Cultural César Chávez but students to this point end up finding the course through word of mouth or on their own. Some students interested in food justice and a few students in horticulture or sustainable agriculture also find their way to the course. The rest of the students are fulfilling their DPD requirement.

Based on my recollections from past student evaluations, I posit that the course tends to be received in three ways. First, Latinx and farmworker family students find a certain validation by seeing themselves in the curriculum. Latina students particularly connect with a Dolores Huerta interview where she discusses a range of issues from being perceived as a bad mother due to her dedication to La Causa, her Republican Party affiliation that was transformed once she started organizing farmworkers, and her middle-class beliefs that were deeply challenged (see Garcia, 2008, pp. 163–167). Sometimes, this is the first and last time they will see their varied experiences and knowledges represented in the classroom. To me, this is the essence of democratizing the classroom and reason enough to continue teaching the course. The second group, almost always non-Latinx, find relevance and connection (particularly through food and labor) and see how farmworker justice movements share a lot of their own values. They often feel like they are making a substantive contribution to the movements. A former student in my honors offering stated "this has been one of the best honors courses that I have taken." Finally, there is a very small group, always white students, who get disgruntled for not being centered in the course. It's often the first time they are the minority in the classroom, and their usual drawing from life experience simply does not deeply resonate with the course materials. The general malaise of having to take racialized minorities seriously and as *the* experts on issues like food and social justice (a position they are accustomed to claiming), showed most clearly in their lackluster final projects.

In the initial course design, Larry Kleinman and I noted the lack of an established curricula in farmworker justice movements. We decided to build with what was already existing in the literature and charge the students with creating new curricula as new sources became available, or their own interests reshaped existing content.

From the outset, we decided this could not be yet another class where students learn *about* farmworkers and to repeat the surface representations of them as the poorest of the poor. This course had to be in conversation with farmworkers, specifically the organizations that are advocating daily for their well-being. We both were familiar with the language of engaged, service, and experiential learning but we sought for this to be a transformative learning experience with substantive engagements directly with the organizations. We started with PCUN in Oregon, due to the obvious distance constraints, but also with the idea that the local impact could be direct, felt, experienced, and replicated from year to year.

Over time, the course outcomes shifted as students' interests varied, abilities surfaced, and farmworker organization connections were solidified. We began with final projects to add:

1 curricula,
2 more public multimedia projects, and
3 the current course companion website.

In the first iteration of the course, students would often create PowerPoint lectures or class activities centered around a topic not discussed in the course. Students certainly learned the difficulty of crafting curricula. But the results remained primarily in the hands of the course instructors as we debated altering course content for the following year.

The second iteration of the course expanded the definition of curriculum development to public education, including video presentations on topics not discussed in class (such as the role of religion in the UFW) and a zine on reproductive justice in the fields. This served a larger purpose of getting students' knowledge to a more public venue and to connect a bit more to farmworker organizations interested in the outputs.

The third iteration of the course was offered as an OSU Honors College offering, and thanks to a grant from the Honors College, I was able to greatly expand the experiential learning opportunities for the class. I was able to videoconference with farmworker organization leaders from CIW organizers Gerardo Reyes-Chaves and Ximena Pedroza; Vice President of FLOC, Justin Flores; UFW Washington dairy organizer Indira Trejo Cordova; and Marita Canedo of Migrant Justice. These videoconferences complemented experiential learning field trips to the PCUN archives at University of Oregon, curated by David Woken, and to Woodburn to meet with PCUN's executive director Reyna Lopez. As a result of the deeper immersive experience, a small group of honors students were able to compile a website that identifies the current campaigns, organizational structure, networks and synergies, labor contracts, and mission and goals of each organization (see https://liberalarts.oregonstate.edu/slcs/farmworkers). Being able to learn directly from movement leaders, the website solidified a relationship of making meaningful student outputs that are actually helpful to farmworker justice movement organizations.

The website intentionally puts each of the movement organizations into direct dialogue and comparison with one another. Each farmworker justice organization approaches its organizing, advocacy, and internal leadership models differently. Current campaigns feature the issues each of the organizations are working on: the VUSE e-cigarette boycott by FLOC, Darigold Dozen by UFW in Washington state, the Ben and Jerry's third-party contract for Vermont dairy workers known as the Milk with Dignity campaign, drivers' licenses for all in Oregon by PCUN and its sister organizations, and CIW's 4 for Fair Food-Wendy's boycott and for ending slavery and sexual harassment in the fields.

Former UFW Director of Organizing and current Harvard Kennedy School faculty Marshall Ganz (2009) notes, in *When David Sometimes Wins*, the ability for organizations to promote positive social change depends upon the leadership and organization in their ability to develop and deploy strategic capacity within larger environmental contexts. We therefore differentiated between affiliated union and nonaffiliated models of organization. The mission, vision, and goals of each organization shape their relationship to farmworkers and the food chains they are located within. This leads into the networks and synergies that define each organization's relationships to farmers, consumers, supply chains, corporations, religious groups, students, and unions. Finally, agreements that farmworker justice organizations enter into vary widely but they are categorized into three categories:

1   collective bargaining agreements,
2   third-party contracts, and
3   third-party certification and compliance regimes.

Conclusion: Service or experiential learning?

Based on my experience at Cornell, I recall first-hand the initial challenge of teaching farmworker issues in a land-grant university. More often than not, the way in which migrant farm labor is often viewed by colleagues in agricultural economics or other related fields is one of two approaches: migrants as either inputs or problems. Many in the agricultural sciences still view migrant labor as yet another input, a cost of production on par with pesticide, fertilizer, seed, tools, and mechanization. When migrant farmworkers or their accompanying issues are viewed solely as problems, the result is a type of service-learning that is then created to address the core problem. One example of the problems-based approach is addressing the language barrier between English-monolingual farmers and Spanish-speaking migrants that often results in college students teaching farmworkers rudimentary English to improve safety on the farm or more nefariously to be more efficient (i.e., exploitable) workers.

I simply have no idea how to square the needs of farmworker communities with the inputs approach. The constant questioning of migrants' rightful place on farms and whether they even belong in local communities is certainly a concern expressed. I simply am not convinced it is a helpful approach to assessing the daily lived experiences of farm workers, let alone ameliorating squalid conditions in the fields and in labor camps. The starting point for me was farmworker justice organizations that put the problem question in starkly different terms and start first from the inherent humanity of farmworkers and therefore never fall into the input way of thinking trap. For me, it all too often comes down to a Faustian bargain when trying to reconcile quality of life for farmworkers with the exigencies of a land-grant university, extension service, and college of agriculture.

This certainly played out when deciding on how we would approach the question of service versus experiential learning. For too long, the charity model of service-learning dominated, particularly at highly selective institutions. When 'serving' communities living in poverty, the prevailing model is too often made to make predominately white, wealth-privileged students proud of themselves for helping out those less fortunate. The poor are all too often fetishized, shockingly discovered to be "human" when students are confronted with their reality, and it's not clear if traditional service-learning models equip students to check their privilege, to address root causes of inequality, or to avoid the logical fallacy of exoticizing or Othering those living in poverty. Without delving too deeply into the extant literature, many point to Zlotkowski's (1995) "seminal" essay that asks, "Does Service-learning Have a Future?" The essay concludes that only if service-learning is rooted in a *"rigorously academic* way" (p. 5) will the pedagogical practice continue.

> As long as service-learning is described and recommended primarily – let alone exclusively – in terms of moral and/or civic lessons and benefits, the vast majority of academicians will do what many typically do now: agree that moral and civic growth is indeed important, recognize its place in the undergraduate (and graduate) experience – and deny that such concerns have anything to do with their own professional responsibilities.
>
> (p. 6)

We took all of these criticisms of service-learning quite seriously when we designed this course. Not only is the farmworker justice movements course rooted in ethnic studies literatures, it's specifically rooted in how we use experiential learning pedagogies to teach ethnic studies at Oregon State University (see chapters by Barnd and Maldonado, this volume).

What I am advocating for in my farmworker justice movements course is not new and it goes by many names: civic engagement, fair trade learning, transformative experiential learning, the list goes on. Because we often study social movements in ethnic studies, it makes sense to include those movements in our courses from the point of inception. We often draw from scholar-activists in our curricula but the terms of scholarship, activism, and organizing can become muddled. Some seek to distinguish activism from community organizing by dismissing the former "as mobilization and protest aimed at fighting those in positions of power, in this case senior administrators" but they prefer the latter as: "In the community organizing approach I use in higher education, however, conversation, political education, deliberation, relationship building, and relational power are the foundation" (Avila, 2017, p. 26). It would be ideal if higher education was tidy and easily compartmentalized but the reality is community organizing often draws the ire of senior administrators and those faculty with entrenched interests in the *status quo*, which are often the situations community organizing seeks to ameliorate.

Fair trade learning seeks similar aims at the global level when articulating the potentially reciprocal relationship between study abroad sites and institutions of higher education, faculty, and students. "Talk of public purposes, reciprocity, and mutual learning is destined to remain only rhetoric when measures of success are centered on student learning, student development, and/or 'exposure' of students to 'high-quality service-learning' (however defined)" (Hartman, 2015, p. 97). The subsequent list of questions[6] to community partners designed by the aforementioned author is instructive, indeed quite helpful, and should be reckoned with any experiential learning project, local or global. I also co-taught the OSU-in-Cuba study abroad course and that experience more directly relates to the concerns raised by fair trade learning but too often fair-trade learning tends to reproduce the very language it seeks to undermine in the relationship between students, community organizations, and study abroad sites. I would challenge the language of "stakeholders," as this corporate concept really has no place in community-engaged learning. It always creeps back in with all its attendant assumptions about solely material self-interest as the basis for measuring stakes, defining students as customers, inattention to power relations by assuming stakeholders all have the same access to having their voices represented, a purported level playing field, etc.

As a result, visits to PCUN are not of the show-and-tell variety. Students are put in the service of the organization. One year, they canvassed local residents during the school board election campaign that inaugurated the first Latinx majority in the history of Woodburn (a district that is 82% Latinx in the student population and 56.3% Latinx in the community). The following year, they cleaned up the PCUN member database to ensure more timely, effective, and accurate communication between staff and its supporters. Students often return on their own to Woodburn to participate in Lazos Universitarios, a program on PCUN's community-powered radio station that features stories of Spanish-speaking students, staff, and faculty at Oregon State University. As director of the CAPACES Leadership Institute and former secretary-treasurer of PCUN, Jaime Arredondo, notes in evaluating our partnership, "your program models that way service-learning ought to happen. Often times (especially with academia), people want us to fit into their agendas instead of the other way around."[7] And this is precisely the point of transformative experiential education, community partners become truly partners in the educative process where students, faculty, and community partners co-create knowledge and tangible results that advance the needs of the community writ large.

Additional Resources

Websites

Archives West. PCUN Records, 2006–2012 (University of Oregon): http://archiveswest.orbiscascade.org/ark:/80444/xv06887
Chatfield, LeRoy. Farmworker Movement Documentation Project: https://libraries.ucsd.edu/farmworkermovement/
Coalition of Immokalee Workers: http://ciw-online.org
Farm Labor Organizing Committee: www.floc.com/wordpress/
Migrant Justice/Justicia Migrante: https://migrantjustice.net
OSU Farmworker Justice Movements course: https://liberalarts.oregonstate.edu/slcs/farmworkers
Pineros y Campesinos Unidos Noroeste: www.pcun.org
Student Action with Farmworkers, Educate: https://saf-unite.org/content/educate
United Farm Workers: http://ufw.org

Notes

1 Synanon was founded by Chuck Dederich in 1958 in response to restrictions imposed by Alcoholics Anonymous. Nominally proclaiming itself as a drug rehabilitation residential program, it also came to be defined as a cult due predominately to the use of "the Game" whereby group therapy, as a form of social control, aimed at criticizing a single-member's weaknesses or shortcomings. All residents were required to play the game and Chávez built a relationship over time with Dederich and transferred the game to UFW leadership meetings.
2 Migrant Justice. The Milk Dignity Program. https://migrantjustice.net/about-the-milk-with-dignity-program
3 Student Action with Farmworkers. https://saf-unite.org/content/educate
4 Duke, A. (2019). Undergraduate students engage with Latino farmworker community through course. *PSU News*. https://news.psu.edu/story/557977/2019/02/07/academics/undergraduate-students-engage-latino-farmworker-community-through
5 The Difference, Power, and Discrimination Program, Oregon State University, https://dpd.oregonstate.edu
6 Hartman (2015, p. 99) identifies 12 key questions that guide fair trade learning that range from: "Do stakeholders, including several and diverse community members, agree on long-term mutuality of goals and aspirations?" to "Do all stakeholders have access to information regarding financial commitments and disbursements that support the partnership, along with opportunities to openly and critically discuss those commitments with the other stakeholders?"
7 J. Arredondo Email communication (July 18, 2019) on file with author.

References

Avila, M. (2017). *Transformative civic engagement through community organizing*. Stylus Publishing, LLC.
Bardacke, F. (2012). *Trampling out the vintage: Cesar Chavez and the two souls of the United Farm Workers*. Verso Books.

Barger, W.K., & E.M. Reza (1994). *The Farm Labor Movement in the Midwest: Social Change and adaptation among migrant farmworkers*. University of Texas Press.

Cantor, N. (2012, May 23). *The public mission of higher education: Barn raisings a century later*. Invited keynote address delivered at the University of Wisconsin-Madison Teaching & Learning Symposium, Advancing the Year of the Wisconsin Idea.

Craib, R., & M. Overmyer-Velasquez (2012). Migration and labor in the Americas: Praxis, knowledge, and nations. *Hispanic American Historical Review*, *92*(2), 245–267. https://doi.org/10.1215/00182168-1545683

Duke, A. (2019). Undergraduate students engage with Latino farmworker community through course. *PSU News*. https://news.psu.edu/story/557977/2019/02/07/academics/undergraduate-students-engage-latino-farmworker-community-through

Estabrook, B. (2012). *Tomatoland: How modern industrial agriculture destroyed our most alluring fruit*. Andrews McMeel Publishing.

Ferriss, S., & R. Sandoval (1997). *The fight in the fields: Cesar Chavez and the farmworkers*. Harcourt Brace and Co.

Galan, H. (Director) (1996). *Chicano! History of the Mexican American Civil Rights Movement*. [Video Documentary] 55 min. KCET Los Angeles: NLCC Educational Media.

Ganz, M. (2009). *Why David sometimes wins: Leadership, organization, and strategy in the California Farm Worker Movement*. Oxford University Press.

Garcia, M. (2012). *From the jaws of victory: The triumph and tragedy of Cesar Chavez and the Farm Worker Movement*. University of California Press.

Garcia, M., & M. Sifuentez (2012). "The foundations of modern farm worker unionism: From UFW to PCUN." In D. Katz & R.A. Greenwald (Eds.), *Labor rising: The past and future of working people in America* (pp. 253–266). The New Press.

Garcia, M.T. (Ed.) (2008). *A Dolores Huerta reader*. University of New Mexico Press.

Griffith, D. (2009). Unions without borders: Organizing and enlightening immigrant farmworkers. *Anthropology of Work Review*, *30*(2), 54–66. https://doi.org/10.1111/j.1548-1417.2009.01021.x

Griswold del Castillo, R., & R.A. Garcia (1995). *Cesar Chavez: A triumph of spirit*. University of Oklahoma Press.

Gutiérrez, D.G. (1995). *Walls and mirrors: Mexican Americans, Mexican immigrants, and the politics of ethnicity*. University of California Press.

Hartman, E. (2015). A strategy for community-driven service-learning and community engagement: Fair trade learning. *Michigan Journal of Community Service-learning*, The SLCE Future Directions Project, Fall, 97–100. http://slce-fdp.org/essays/fall-2015/thought-pieces/hartman/hartman-full-text/

Jenkins, J.C. (1983). Resource mobilization theory and the study of social movements. *Annual Review of Sociology*, *9*, 527–553. www.annualreviews.org/doi/pdf/10.1146/annurev.so.09.080183.002523

Jenkins, J.C. (1985). *The politics of insurgency: The Farmworker Movement in the 1960s*. Columbia University Press.

Jenkins, J.C. and C. Perrow. (1977). Insurgency of the powerless: Farm worker movements (1946–1972). *American Sociological Review*, *42*(2), 249–268. www.jstor.org/stable/2094604

Krikorian, M. (2017, March 31). Hail Cesar! *National Review*. www.nationalreview.com/2017/03/cesar-chavez-illegal-immigration-foe/

Levy, J. (1975). *Cesar Chavez: Autobiography of La Causa*. W.W. Norton and Company.

Majka, L.C. (1981). Labor Militancy Among Farm Workers and the Strategy of Protest: 1900–1979. *Social Problems*, *28*(5), 533–547.

Majka, L.C., & T.J. Majka (2000). Organizing US farm workers: A continuous struggle. In F. Magoff, J.B. Foster, & F.H. Buttel (Eds.), *Hungry for profit: The agribusiness threat to farmers, food, and the environment* (pp. 7–21). Monthly Review Press.
Majka, T. (1980). Poor People's Movements and farm labor insurgency. *Crime, Law and Social Change, 4*(3), 283–308.
Majka, T., & L. Majka. (1982). *Farm workers, agribusiness, and the state.* Temple University Press.
Majka, T., & L. Majka. (1992). Decline of the farm labor movement in California: Organizational crisis and political change. *Critical Sociology, 19*(3), 3–36. https://doi.org/10.1177%2F089692059201900301
Matheissen, P. (1967). *Sal si puedes (escape if you can): Cesar Chavez and the new American revolution.* Random House.
Mize, R.L. (2016). *The invisible workers of the U.S.-Mexico Bracero Program: Obreros olvidados.* Lexington Books.
Mize, R.L., & A.C.S. Swords (2010). *Consuming Mexican labor: From the Bracero Program to NAFTA.* University of Toronto Press.
Mooney, P.H., & T.J. Majka. (1995). *Farmers' and farm workers' movements: Social protest in American agriculture.* Twayne Publishers.
Orosco, J.A. (2008). *Cesar Chavez and the common sense of nonviolence.* University of New Mexico Press.
Pawel, M. (2010). *The union of their dreams: Power, hope, and struggle in Cesar Chavez's farm worker movement.* Bloomsbury Press.
Pawel, M. (2014). *The crusades of Cesar Chavez: A biography.* Bloomsbury Press.
Pearcy, G. (Director). (1975). *Fighting for Our Lives: The United Farm Workers' 1973 grape strike and the wrath of grapes.* [Video Documentary]. Paper Tiger Television, Inc.
Rawal, S. (Director) (2014). *Food chains.* [Video Documentary]. Screen Media.
Rosales, F.A. (1996). *Chicano! The history of the Mexican American Civil Rights Movement.* Arte Publico Press.
Ross, F. (1989). *Conquering Goliath: César Chávez at the beginning.* El Taller Grafico Press.
Shaw, R. (2008). *Beyond the fields: Cesar Chavez, the UFW, and the struggle for justice in the 21st Century.* University of California Press.
Sifuentez, M. (2016). *Of forests and fields: Mexican labor in the Pacific Northwest.* Rutgers University Press.
Soto, G., & L. Lohstoeter (2003). *Cesar Chavez: A hero for everyone.* Aladdin Paperbacks.
Stavans, I. (Ed.) (2008). *Cesar Chavez: An organizer's tale speeches.* Penguin Books.
Stephen, L. (2012). *The story of PCUN and the Farmworker Movement in Oregon.* University of Oregon Center for Latino/a and Latin American Studies. https://cllas.uoregon.edu/wp-content/uploads/2010/06/PCUN_story_WEB.pdf
Stephen, L. (2007). *Transborder lives: Indigenous Oaxacans in Mexico, California, and Oregon.* Duke University Press.
Telles, R. (Director). (1996). *The fight in the fields: Cesar Chavez and the farmworkers' struggle.* [Video Documentary] 1hr 56min. Paradigm Productions.
Zlotkowski, E. (1995). "Does service-learning have a future?" *New England Resource Center for Higher Education Publications, 16.* http://scholarworks.umb.edu/nerche_pubs/16

14 Listen up, STEM
We Don't Just Teach Facts

Glencora Borradaile

If you suggest incorporating social context into Science, Technology, Engineering and Mathematics (STEM) teaching, you will likely face the maddeningly common ethos of "we teach facts." This problematic worldview makes bringing Difference, Power, and Discrimination (DPD) education into STEM classrooms a charged topic. Sadly, in computer science, this worldview completely ignores the immense social impact that digital technology has had and continues to have on the world. Even when teaching the most theoretical of topics, this worldview avoids the question of whose work we are teaching and whose work we are not (Harding, 2006). Unfortunately, even among the faculty who agree our students should engage with understanding the role that power plays in our society, many feel this has no place in the STEM classroom and should be left to the domain of the liberal arts and social sciences. However, DPD provides a rigorous framework of analysis for any discipline, and, I argue, DPD is best taught this way: as a lens through which to view your field. The DPD program at Oregon State University asks students to critique institutionalized systems of power, privilege, and inequity in the United States. The geographical focus prevents the othering of the problem. Discrimination and oppression isn't something that (just) happens somewhere else. STEM as an educational, research and development field is a microcosm of broader systems that generates discrimination and oppression, both internally and externally. While all our undergraduate STEM students at Oregon State University are required to take a course with a DPD learning objective as part of our Baccalaureate Core, a STEM student's chosen "DPD course" is likely to be far removed from their main studies. This others the problem, sending a message to STEM students that difference, power and discrimination is something that happens outside of their major.

In this chapter, I report on and compare two teaching experiences. In the first, I taught a one-credit seminar class on DPD and Ethics to Electrical and Computer Engineering (ECE) and Computer Science (CS) graduate students. This class did not focus on any particular topic within ECE or CS, but presented DPD largely as a standalone topic. In the second, I designed and co-taught a three-credit course introduction to digital security appropriate for non-majors that explores uses of surveillance to suppress social movements both historically and contemporarily. For both courses, I describe a set of teaching activities designed to engage students with the materials deeply. At the end of the chapter, I reflect on these very different teaching experiences and how they have been received by the School of Electrical Engineering and Computer Science (EECS) and the College of Engineering at Oregon State University.

My path to teaching DPD in the STEM classroom grows largely out of first-hand experience with sexism as a female-identified mathematician and computer scientist. My scholarly interests drifted over the years (from physics to applied mathematics to mathematical programming to theoretical computer science to user-centered privacy and security), but much of that drifting was the result of sexism, and often very explicitly so. I have blogged about some of these experiences (Borradaile, n.d.), but have only privately shared my experience with gender-based violence in the STEM setting. My experiences are not dissimilar to those of whom have bravely shared their experiences in the #metoo era.

Sadly, most efforts I had seen in trying to address sexism in the sciences while I was a trainee had been directed at women. This is typified by Sheryl Sandberg's *Lean In*: for women to succeed, they just need to be more like men (Sandberg & Scovell, 2013). The critiques of Sandberg's advice give some insight in how to better address the dearth of women in tech fields. Author bell hooks argues that *Lean In* ignores "the concrete systemic obstacles most women face inside the workforce" (bell hooks, n.d.). Kathleen Geier critiques Sandberg's idea that more women in leadership would advance women generally, saying

> there is little reason to have faith that Sandberg-style 'trickle-down' feminism will benefit the masses any more than its economic equivalent has [...] her advocacy of a depoliticized strategy that focused on self-improvement rather than collective action troubled many feminists on the left.
>
> (Geier, 2014)

These critiques ask us to dig deeper – to uncover the structures of oppression and address those. To me, education – of everyone, not just the oppressed – is an important ingredient to changing the culture of STEM.

DPD as a Standalone Subject

Starting in 2015, an ad hoc committee at Oregon State University came together to consider adding a DPD learning outcome for all graduate students as a mechanism for reducing an observed rise in discrimination in our graduate program uncovered by surveys of graduate students. The proposed Graduate Learning Outcome (GLO) was to:

> recognize difference, power and discrimination within social systems and their influence on people of diverse backgrounds both inside and outside their discipline.

In the fall of 2015, several academic programs across Oregon State University piloted initiatives to experiment with delivering this GLO. As part of this effort, I taught a one-credit graduate seminar in the School of Electrical Engineering and Computer Science (EECS) devoted to the above learning outcome along with the Responsible Conduct of Research GLO (that was already required by our graduate school). Thirty-one students took this seminar, representing approximately one-third of our incoming graduate students in our Electrical and Computer Engineering and Computer Science graduate programs for that year. Following the pilot, I, and a full professor in EECS, proposed requiring a three-credit version of this course for our ECE and CS graduate students, in the interest of getting ahead of the potential Graduate School requirement and designing a curriculum that would best serve our own students. In the end, neither the Graduate School nor the School of EECS adopted a DPD graduate learning outcome, however, there is a grassroots effort emerging among STEM students which I will comment on in the conclusion of this chapter. In this section, I give a synopsis of this seminar, describe several classroom activities designed to get students engaged with the material in an active way, and reflect on the pilot seminar as a whole.

Seminar Synopsis

Our graduate programs in EECS are highly international: a quarter of our students are Chinese nationals, one fifth are from India, one tenth are from the Middle East, and one tenth from Southeast Asia. Teaching technical classes to such a diverse group of students is challenging enough: there are often big differences in educational preparation, even among those whose degree is Computer Science or Electrical Engineering. Also, language differences can play a major role in sowing confusion while teaching. In preparing to teach about identity, privilege, and discrimination, I sought to create a space for students to discuss these ideas with each other as many students were engaging with this material for the first time. In addition to the varied cultural and language backgrounds of the students, as the seminar met for just one hour per week for the ten-week quarter, I was limited to covering the material at a rather shallow level. In the following, I describe the class activities that focus on the DPD learning objective of the seminar. The full course materials for the pilot seminar are available on the course website (Borradaile, n.d.).

History and Identities

To motivate the DPD learning objective in our first meeting, I started with a short history of computation (Figure 14.1) with a few motivating questions. I started with the bold items and described the discrimination that Alan Turing experienced as a result of his sexual orientation and asked: What advances would Turing have made if not for discrimination and his ultimate suicide? I then pointed out that the history in bold is stunted both by colonialism and

Babylonia	-2000	Babylonian base-60 numerals	
South America	-300	Mayan base-20 numerals	
India	200	Brahmi numerals	
Persia	870	Arabic numerals	
Americas	900	Khipu abacus	
China	1200	Suan-Pan abacus	
France	1700s	Jacquard loom (punch cards)	
UK	1800s	Babbage's Analytical Engine	
		Computer Algorithm (Ada Lovelace)	
UK	1936	Turing Machine	
Europe	1940s	Electronic computers	*computer and*
Europe/US	1940s	Von Neumann architecture	*telecommunication*
USA/Europe/USSR	1950+	Modern computers	*operations by women*
	1952	*Compilers (Grace Hopper)*	
	1984	*40% of computer science graduates are women*	

Figure 14.1 The standard history of **computation** does not reflect on important contributions from non-Western cultures (pre-1700) or more recent contributions by *women*

patriarchy. I added in the earlier points, noting that computational devices (abaci) existed before computers and that positional number systems are requisite for computation. These contributions are non-Western and we can ask the question: What advances would, for example, Mayan mathematics have made had their civilization not been decimated by colonialism? Finally, I added the italicized points acknowledging contributions by women to computer science and asked: What research and development would we be pursuing if women were equally represented among computer scientists?

Vocabulary for Diversity

For our second meeting, I assigned a list of vocabulary (Figure 14.2) for students along with readings (Diangelo & Sensoy, 2014) to help them understand their meanings. In addition to a round-robin exercise to go over the definitions during our meeting, we had an open discussion about some of the more challenging definitions (institutional versus structural discrimination, internalized oppression, and hegemony).

To further reinforce these ideas during out meeting, I had students draw an identity map, placing aspects of their identity on a spectrum from a cause of discrimination to a source of privilege; and deciding which identity attributes should or could be included was itself a fruitful source of discussion. This was a particularly interesting exercise among a largely international group of students who have not been in the U.S. for long. Since identity-based privilege is highly place-dependent, students learned not only about how identity is viewed across the international stage, but also how one's privilege changes as they change locations.

After this meeting, I assigned students to read "Never Meant to Survive" by Evelyn Hammonds, a first-person account of a black women who studied physics and eventually left physics, despite academic success in graduate school. When I read this interview, I was struck by how many aspects of discrimination were described and yet, because it is an older article and an interview as opposed to a scholarly article, it doesn't use a lot of the terminology that we use today (such as implicit bias and intersectionality). I assigned students to annotate instances of the above vocabulary for diversity, further reinforcing these concepts and providing a common framework for the remainder of the seminar.

Explicit and Implicit Discrimination

Over three meetings, we dug into various ways in which discrimination rears its head, from the explicit to the implicit. We discussed overt sexism in sciences, starting with three assigned readings describing contemporary comments by prominent male scientists spanning academia, industry and government.

affirmative action	bias	discrimination	institutional discrimination
gender identity	hegemony	Ideology	imposter syndrome
dominant group	racism	intersectionality	internalized oppression
positionality	privilege	minoritized group	structural discrimination

Figure 14.2 Common vocabulary used when teaching classes with a difference, power and discrimination focus

- In 2015, Nobel laureate Tim Hunt remarked to an international convention of senior female scientists and science journalists "Let me tell you about my trouble with girls ... three things happen when they are in the lab.... You fall in love with them, they fall in love with you and when you criticise them, they cry." Hunt stood by these comments when later pressed (Ratcliffe & agencies, 2015).
- In 2014, Microsoft CEO Satya Nadella gave career advice at an event for women in computing, saying "It's not really about asking for the raise, but knowing and having faith that the system will actually give you the right raises as you go along" adding that not asking for raise was "good karma" that would help a boss trust an employee (Staff & agencies, 2014).
- In 2005, then Harvard President Larry Summers (former treasury secretary under President Clinton and eventual Director of the National Economic Council), at a private conference on the position of women and minorities in science and engineering hosted by the National Bureau of Economic Research, argued that men outperform women in math and sciences because of biological difference and discrimination is no longer a career barrier for female academics (Goldenberg, 2005).

We engaged with these comments through a spokescouncil consensus-building activity I describe in the next section. Although the third example is older, it was in the news when I was a graduate student and was hotly debated in the hallways of my building. These conversations and the media reaction to Summers dug up evidence to counter his arguments that I had never seen before, and this personal connection allows me to more easily start a discussion.

We then turned to everyday incidents of discrimination, from micro- to macro-aggressive moments and workshopped practicing taking action, also described in the next section, with the goal of instilling the idea that it is not enough for one to not engage in racist or sexist behavior, but one must also respond to such acts on the behalf of oppressed groups. In the final seminar, Anne Gillies from our Office of Equity and Inclusion gave an overview of implicit bias, what it is, how it arises and how we can overcome it. Students were expected to try the Implicit Association Tests (*Project Implicit*, n.d.) before class.

Questioning the Production of Knowledge

In retrospect, the session in which I asked students to dive deepest was that in which we considered the basic assumptions of the production of knowledge in their field. We held a silent discussion. The following prompting questions (which came from the Faculty DPD Academy) were written on large pieces of paper around the classroom, and students circulated to first write their own responses (ignoring the comments of others) and then to reflect and respond, in writing, to other students' responses.

- Who funds research in your discipline?
- How is knowledge passed on in your discipline?

- How is knowledge in your discipline disseminated?
- Who created and defined your research discipline?
- Whose perspectives were and are ignored in the development of your discipline?
- How does this affect the knowledge that is created?
- Who has access to this knowledge and who doesn't? Who controls this?
- Whose interests does your discipline serve?
- What are your advantages/disadvantages in your field?
- Who is advantaged in your field? Who is disadvantaged?
- Are some people systematically disadvantaged by the way knowledge in your discipline is produced and/or taught?
- How does your discipline support and help maintain the dominant culture?
- In what ways could your discipline challenge the dominant culture?
- What are the ethical considerations implicit in your discipline?
- How might your discipline play a role in effecting social justice?

Unfortunately, I did not adequately prepare the students for this activity. While students were able to engage in the first four questions, largely about the mechanics of the production of knowledge. Their limited experience within their disciplines, I believe, did not prepare them to engage deeply with the remaining questions.

Classroom Activities: Learning to Respond

One goal for this seminar was to empower students to respond to incidents of discrimination, as this persists as a contributing factor to the under-representation of women and minorities in STEM fields. In this section, I describe two classroom activities designed around that goal.

Spokescouncil Consensus Building

After reading the description of sexist comments by Hunt, Nadella and Summers, representing notable academic, industry and political leaders, I asked students to imagine themselves as the scientific community, to decide if and how to respond, and to try to build consensus in the classroom on a response. To do so, I adapted a spokescouncil forum to the classroom setting. Spokescouncils have been used to extend the consensus-building techniques of the Quaker movement to larger assemblies of people with a higher level of heterogeneity of affinity. The spokescouncil model is usually attributed to the antiglobalization movements of the late 1990s and early 2000 (Haworth & Elmore, 2017). Each affinity group assigns a spokesperson who participates in inter-group discussions (which may or may not be heard by other members of the affinity groups). Discussions alternate between intra-group discussions within each affinity group and inter-group spokescouncil discussions among the spokespeople that attempt to come to consensus on a decision across the groups.

I tasked the students in the class to:

> Decide if and how to respond to sexist statements made by notable academic, industry and political leaders. Try to build consensus in the classroom on the proposed responses. Use the three articles as examples in your discussions; that is, how would you respond to these incidences as part of a group effort.
>
> (from syllabus)

I also asked the students to form their own affinity groups, and alternated between 10 minutes of intra-group discussions and five minutes of spokescouncil discussions with the following instructions:

- Spokespeople must faithfully represent and advocate the opinions and decisions of their small group, even if these conflict with their opinion.
- Small group discussions should generate new ideas and reflect on the opinions of other groups as expressed during the spokescouncil round. New arguments and counterarguments may be generated to respond to other groups in the next spokescouncil. Proposals should arise from small group discussions and only be communicated during the spokescouncil.
- Consensus is not majority rule. Supporting a consensus opinion does not necessarily mean that the proposal being considered is one's first choice. When deciding to consent to a proposed solution, you should consider the question "Is this proposal something I can live with?" rather than "Is this proposal the best proposal in my opinion?"

I adopted this as a way to organize classroom discussions for two reasons. First, it allows a mixture of small- and large-group discussions. The former is more accessible to students who may be shy speaking in front of large groups. The latter allows sharing of ideas more broadly, and, given the nature of the spokescouncil model, would also allow all student views to be represented, not just those who typically speak up in large groups. Second, by allowing the students to form their own affinity groups, I hoped that students would be able to speak more freely. This seemed to work with everyone speaking at some point during small group discussions.

The opinions that were voiced during the spokescouncil were mixed at first; there was an opinion of protecting free speech and one that damage control should be sought to detach the commenting individual from the institution. While a specific consensus action was not decided upon, opinions did converge on acting, noting that the statements by notable, high-profile people descends from protected free speech to the creation of hostile environments. This was heartening: that given time to discuss issues students in the class generally agreed with supporting minority rights.

Practicing Taking Action

Prior to one meeting, I asked students to read "Challenging Homophobia, Racism and Other Oppressive Moments" (LeFavour, 2002). During our seminar meeting, students broke up into small groups of at most five. Each group was given a scenario describing a real incident of sexism or racism that has happened at OSU or at another university, including:

- A female student raises her hand in a tutorial session and asks a question. A TA, instead of answering the student's question says "Little girl, you will have to work a lot harder to keep up with the men in the class."
- A small group of graduate students are talking informally about their job prospects. One student says to a female student "well, you don't have to worry, you'll get a job through affirmative action."
- Graffiti has appeared in multiple bathrooms on campus. The graffiti encourages violence against minorities and uses racial slurs.
- In a small group with several graduate students and one faculty member, the faculty member indicates that the Black student in the group was admitted because he was Black.

Each group was asked to brainstorm ways in which they would respond to these situations in one of several roles: as a fellow student, as a teaching assistant, or simply as a member of the community. After 15–20 minutes of small group discussion, we went from group to group, sharing the incident each group discussed and their ideas on responses. The task required action as the default response.

There was some thoughtful discussion on when is the best time to respond, with some (often valid) concern that responding in the moment, in certain situations, could make matters worse. We also discussed, in the graffiti example, whether one should draw attention to it, so that people know this kind of thing happens, or if one should quietly remove it, to minimize the damage it does. Unlike when teaching many technical topics, here there isn't a yes or no answer.

This type of activity is commonly a part of bystander intervention trainings that have more recently been introduced across U.S. universities to prevent sexual assault. I highly recommend this activity in a classroom setting. I think it is very helpful to:

- hear about bigoted moments;
- imagine what it would be like for these kinds of things to happen on a daily basis; and
- prepare oneself to respond as an ally.

In the incidents of sexism that I have suffered, I felt utterly alone as those around me failed to respond. I am hoping that with a little preparation, our graduate students would have the confidence to speak out against bigotry. On the other side, I have also felt utterly unprepared, in the past, to respond to sexist comments, and practice has made this easier.

Lessons Learned

As a STEM educator, teaching non-technical topics is far outside my comfort zone. If I stumble when teaching technical material, I can draw on years of experience to recover. However, in teaching this seminar, I was relying mostly on the two-week Faculty DPD Academy as preparation, which pales in comparison to my academic preparation. Technical courses rarely have discussion-based lectures, so even basic classroom management was something I needed to learn on the fly. There is also a lot more emotion tied up with ideas of discrimination and privilege, and it is really difficult to see myself as perpetuating systems of oppression. While student resistance was covered in the Faculty DPD Academy, I can't say that it prepared me for the classroom.

Likewise, students in the seminar are STEM students are not all accustomed to non-technical classes. When asked to comment on various aspects of the class, several students in the class referred to the amount of reading being burdensome. However, the same students noted that their reading skills improved. Students found first-person narratives most helpful, commenting in particular on "Never Meant to Survive" which I think stood out because there was a deep-reading assignment to accompany it, helping to focus the reading (Sands, 2008).

DPD as a Teaching Lens

In 2013, CIA employee and subcontractor Edward Snowden disclosed to the public documents detailing hosts of global surveillance programs that have since prompted a global discussion about the balance between privacy and security (Greenwald, 2015). Among colleagues and students, though, I was disheartened to hear variations on the nothing-to-hide argument (Moore, 2010): of course, there is surveillance, but I'm not doing anything wrong so I don't need to worry about it. This attitude was in stark contrast to the range of reactions from members of environmental and social justice movements: from vindication and a complete lack of surprise to anxiety and restraint.[1] Knowing the extent to which surveillance has historically played a role in suppressing social movements (Boykoff, 2007), and also knowing that even non-technological methods of suppression of civil dissent have continued into the modern day (Potter, 2011), I recognized that modern surveillance gives government and corporations unprecedented capabilities to control the public (Zuboff, 2015).

Thus motivated, community organizer Michele Gretes and I created a freshman-level communications security course that includes lessons on the societal impacts of surveillance and the protective roles encryption technologies can play. We use the well-documented state repression of the U.S. Civil Rights

Movement and other contemporary Black liberation movements via the FBI's counterintelligence program (COINTELPRO) (Select Committee to Study Governmental Operations with Respect to Intelligence Activities, Senate, 1976) as our primary historical example for contextualizing potential and known present-day, post-9/11-era abuses of power facilitated by global surveillance. The course was first offered in Spring 2017.

In contrast to the afore-described one-credit graduate seminar, this three-credit class allows us to dive deeper into the DPD learning objective by using it to guide the motivational context of global mass surveillance and historic abuse of surveillance in the suppression of U.S. social movements. Our course has an additional aim of enabling students to provide guidance and rationale to others in the selection and use of digital security tools with the following learning objective: Describe and contextualize uses of surveillance to suppress social movements both historically and currently. This learning objective and the DPD learning objective mesh well as many social movements are based in rebalancing power or fighting for the rights of the discriminated. We limit enrollment in the course to 20–25 lower-division Engineering majors and 20–25 non-Engineering majors, to encourage a mix of perspectives in the classroom. A large majority of the former are taking the class in order to meet their DPD requirement and a large majority of the latter are Liberal Arts majors taking the class to meet their Computer Science requirement.

In the section that follows, I give a synopsis of *CS175: Communications Security and Social Movements* and describe classroom activities that support the above learning outcome. These learning activities were developed with Professor Marisa Chappell, a historian who helped us navigate covering the historical perspective of our class responsibly and rigorously and who guest-lectured for the first two offerings. All teaching materials are available on the course website (Borradaile & Gretes, n.d., a) and the course textbook, which is published as an open educational resource (Borradaile, 2021).

Course Synopsis

CS175 aims to teach students the technical basis and practical use of privacy-enhancing online communication tools and explore their utility in the context of widespread state surveillance. To understand the importance of digital self-defense tools in an age of ubiquitous and reportedly suspicionless surveillance, we spend roughly two weeks of the ten-week course on understanding the historic and contemporary asymmetry in power between governments and large corporations on the one hand and grassroots social and political movements on the other. The remainder of the course is spent on the practical use and understanding of several communications security tools. The course culminates in student projects which demonstrate and explain to their peers a secure communications tool or other privacy-enhancing digital technology and a discussion of a social-movement context in which the tool would be useful.

These activities are in support of the following course learning objectives:

1. Understand concepts of communication security and basic encryption.
2. Effectively use and explain to others secure online communication tools.
3. Describe and contextualize uses of surveillance to suppress social movements both historically and currently.
4. Identify existing and potential uses of secure online communication tools to enhance the effectiveness of social movements.

The third and fourth learning objectives serve as a means to motivate student learning; that is, to give students a reason to value communications security and to overcome the trap of the nothing-to-hide argument. Additionally, the DPD learning objective helps to situate the motivational context of the course: social-movement suppression made possible or facilitated by surveillance.

For students to comprehend the severity of overreach involved in the FBI suppression – deemed illegal and unconstitutional in a U.S. Senate investigation (Select Committee to Study Governmental Operations with Respect to Intelligence Activities, Senate, 1976) – of Black social movements, we examine the grievances that gave rise to the direct actions taken by activists in the Civil Rights Movement and the conditions that produced Black Nationalism and various Black Power approaches. We spend six contact hours in our class discussing a portion of the history of Black America, beginning with the Reconstruction Era. We discuss the nationwide institutionalization of White supremacy in the U.S. political economy (e.g. Jim Crow and voter suppression laws, exclusion from federal social insurance and labor laws, residential segregation and redlining (Coates, 2014)), how these mechanisms arose, and the varied responses of Black communities via negotiation and resistance (Piven & Cloward, 1978). We argue that the liberal reforms enacted could provide only limited economic and social relief for African Americans, thus groups such as the Nation of Islam and the Black Panthers emerged in a context of severe Black discontent (Bloom & Jr, 2013) The FBI's COINTELPRO targeted both the Civil Rights and Black Power movements (e.g. Martin Luther King Jr. and the Black Panther Party) under the label "Black Nationalist – Hate Group" with the goal to "expose, disrupt, misdirect, discredit, or otherwise neutralize the activities of black-nationalist, hate-type organizations and groupings, their leadership, spokesmen, membership and supporters to counter their propensity for violence and civil disorder" (Hoover, 1967).

Jules Boykoff enumerates six ways in which social movements are demobilized (e.g., diminished solidarity, loss of support from bystander publics, reduced capacity to recruit or develop leadership) and articulates 12 modes of suppression that are used achieve this (Boykoff, 2007). We cover a simplified subset of these modes of suppression which we use as a framework for understanding historical and contemporary surveillance systems: surveillance itself, infiltration, snitch-jacketing, agents provocateurs, Black propaganda, harassment arrests, and mass media manipulation.

Classroom Activities: Engaging with Primary Resources

To responsibly represent history in our STEM classroom, we rely heavily on primary resources in covering the context for discussing the negative impacts of surveillance overreach. In addition to using first-person narratives during lectures, we have students work with two corpora of documents that shed light on historical and contemporary surveillance:

- the FBI's *Vault* (*The Vault*, n.d.) of documents made public via Freedom of Information Act (FOIA) requests that cover FBI's COINTELPRO against groups termed "Black Extremist" (which included Martin Luther King Jr. and the Southern Christian Leadership Conference); and
- a database containing documents disclosed by Edward Snowden and the reporting that followed (Canadian Journalists for Free Expression, n.d.).

We take as our starting point the surveillance-enabled suppression of social movements working to overcome discrimination and systematic social, economic, and political power differences based on race. Since the extent and severity of suppression of Black social movements in the Civil Rights Era are not generally known and might seem implausible, we allow students to explore for themselves through a COINTELPRO document dive. For the most part, society can only surmise present-day harms to U.S.-based social movements and civil society organizations facilitated by global surveillance. Rather than speculate, we ask students if a COINTELPRO-like domestic counterintelligence/social movement disruption program were in effect today, what kind of abuses of civil liberties would be enabled or facilitated by modern surveillance tools? We also ask, had a system of global electronic surveillance been in place in the COINTELPRO era, how much more damage would have occurred? Students are asked to keep these questions in mind during the Global surveillance document dive. Thereby we connect the historic abuses of power in the state-sponsored surveillance and disruption of justice-oriented social movements from the Civil Rights Era to modern global surveillance capabilities.

COINTELPRO Document Dive

The COINTELPRO documents include FBI internal memoranda between field offices and the FBI Director as well as materials collected by field offices and materials prepared by field offices (notably: anonymous, pseudonymous and forged letters and pamphlets used in campaigns of disruption). The materials are sometimes hard to read due to poor photocopying or heavy redacting of the originals; despite this, they provide a striking window into "domestic [U.S.] intelligence activities [that] have invaded individual privacy and violated the rights of lawful assembly and political expression" (Select Committee to Study Governmental Operations with Respect to Intelligence Activities, Senate, 1976). Rather than have students browse the documents electronically, which are divided into inconsistently named PDF files of up to 250 pages, and during which students may be easily distracted by diversions available on their laptops, we opted to print all the documents (roughly 4,000 pages), dividing them into folders of approximately 100 pages, allowing our 40 students to each browse a unique section of the archive. We assign students to small groups and task each group to pick one document from their combined folders that highlights suppressive tactics used in COINTELPRO. Each group is then asked to present the document in-class, comment on the impact the illustrated tactic might have had on the Civil Rights Movement, and describe the mode of suppression that the example represents.

For example, documents from the Black Extremist repository of the FBI Vault uncovered in class include:

- Request for permission to fake a letter from a Mexican sympathizer of the BPP passing on rumors of violence between the Black Panther Party (BPP) and the Peace and Freedom Party (PFP), which has been funding the BPP, in order to "cause a breach between the PFP and BPP" (Section 6, p. 51), an example of Black propaganda.
- A memo sharing intelligence from surveillance of BPP members and how "positive results were gained" including BPP member Bobby Seale passing up "$1130 of badly needed cash" and having "caused a possible rift with his [Students for a Democratic Society] partners" (Section 10, pp. 139–142).
- Director approval for an FBI employee to impersonate an under-age woman who is pregnant following an affair with a BPP member who is on probation and to notify local authorities (Section 7, p. 212), setting up infiltration.

Global Surveillance Document Dive

The global surveillance documents are internal documents (for a large part, presentation slides) from global intelligence and law enforcement agencies (primarily the U.S. National Security Agency) as maintained by the Snowden Surveillance Archive (Canadian Journalists for Free Expression, n.d.). Many of the primary documents are difficult to interpret in isolation as they are heavily laden with jargon, acronyms and technical details. However, each document in the archive includes links to relevant news articles, which provide technical interpretation and contextualization by computer security experts and journalists experienced in national security reporting. Again, students form small groups and each group is asked to examine the global surveillance documents for a given program (e.g., PRISM) representing a specific global surveillance capability that would aid or enable more widespread or sophisticated use of the suppressive tactics uncovered in the COINTELPRO document dive. Students select a primary global surveillance document describing the program and provide an explanation and interpretation of it in class, to their peers.

For this second document dive, we reinforce both technical concepts in network security and provide a framework for more rigorous articulation of social movement suppression. We ask students to discuss the specific attack enabled by the technology or program. For example, programs conducting Man-on-the-Side and Man-in-the-Middle attacks (e.g., QUANTUM INSERT, which redirects targets to malicious look-alike sites for malware deployment (Gallagher, 2014) and TURBINE, which automates the deployment and use of malware, e.g., to corrupt file downloads and website access (Gallagher & Greenwald, 2014), would enable both extensive surveillance and sophisticated impersonation (tactics easily identifiable in COINTELPRO documents). Finally, we ask students to specify the threat posed by this network attack capability, if it were available to a COINTELPRO-like social movement disruption campaign and describe the mode of suppression that the example represents.

Lessons Learned

Our focus on the history of Black-liberation social movements supports this class as a DPD course at Oregon State University. However, the COINTELPRO documents provide a rich starting point for alternate historical contextualizations of social-movement disruption supported by surveillance, such as New Left/Anti-War organizing, labor organizing, and Puerto Rican Independence movements. These contexts may interest different student populations and provide an alternative entry to study in computer security. A university with an appropriate archive may more creatively explore other historical contexts of social-movement suppression.

From our research that accompanied the development of this course, it became clear that teaching Communications Security through the DPD lens was highly appropriate. Muslim populations in the U.S. are subject to heightened surveillance, scrutiny, infiltration, provocation and entrapment (Kundnani & Kumar, n.d.). The Department of Homeland Security monitors those involved with #BlackLivesMatter (Joseph, 2015). Historically, the mass collection of data on targeted populations has facilitated genocide (Black, 2002). Mass surveillance doesn't affect all people equally – mass surveillance is disproportionately directed at marginalized groups, such as people of color (Gürses et al., 2016).

Reflecting on Bringing DPD to STEM

Developing and teaching CS175 has been a much more positive experience than the graduate seminar for three reasons. First, as a white woman, I have not experienced race-based discrimination and violence (the main focus of CS175), but I have experienced gender-based discrimination and violence (a prominent focus of the graduate seminar). Second, DPD as a teaching lens rather than a standalone subject allows one to teach DPD by example rather than an abstract concept, and this is generally a more effective introduction to a new topic for learners. Third, the development of CS175 fell within the curricular framework at OSU and did not require creating something new as with the graduate seminar. Let's explore these points further, but also recognize that the graduate seminar met for only ten hours, while CS175 met for 40 hours, which is surely an unfair comparison.

In comparison to my experiences teaching the pilot DPD seminar to graduate students where the focus was often (but not exclusively) on gender discrimination, discussing the causes and effects of oppression in CS175, where the focus is almost exclusively on race, was easier. As a woman in STEM, discussing gender discrimination in STEM in the graduate DPD seminar hit very close to home. At times, student comments were personally offensive, causing a mild panic reaction that made it difficult for me to respond in a constructive way. On the other hand, being both white and Canadian allows me to examine U.S. race issues at arms-length and allows me to address students' fallacies more calmly.[2] As well, because we spend more time delving into the systems of oppression rooted in slavery, we are able to discuss structural discrimination in a way that makes clear the privilege that white skin bestows. And although I was able to bring my lived experience into the graduate DPD seminar, by using audio, video and first-person narratives, we are still able to bring the lived experience of particular Black people into the CS175 classroom.

In CS175, DPD concepts are introduced with concrete examples. The historic oppression of African Americans led to institutional and structural discrimination from which the gains of the Civil Rights Era did little to meaningfully help Black people across the U.S. The activism that challenged the hegemony of the post-Civil Rights era unleashed suppression by those in power. This suppression was aided by surveillance which becomes more sophisticated every year through developments in technology. Every concept that is introduced in the course is illustrated with a historical or contemporary example. No concept is left abstract. This is similar to teaching any material at the introductory level. Conversely, the graduate seminar started with abstract concepts, and, for lack of time, did not give many concrete examples, except through narrative and news readings. While this may be appropriate for the graduate level, graduate STEM students are very likely approaching DPD topics at the introductory level. For that reason, the topics would be more approachable if embedded within a technical class, using DPD as a teaching lens, and drawing on real-world example to illustrate points.

In order to develop CS175, I needed approval only from the undergraduate curriculum committee in the School of EECS and the School Head. This is a small subset of about 10% of the faculty of EECS. Further, the development of CS175 supported the Diversity, Equity and Inclusion principles College of Engineering (COE) Strategic Plan at the time and contributed to the Baccalaureate Core, in which the COE had few courses. By marketing the course as a means to attract under-represented students into computer science, it was an easy sell to develop this course. In fact, its popularity has meant CS175 is now taught every quarter. The graduate seminar, on the other hand, required faculty-wide permission to even run as a pilot. After the pilot, a full professor in the School of EECS and I proposed to the ECE and CS graduate curriculum committees the idea of requiring a three-credit orientation course, that would include DPD as a large component, for all our graduate students. We were emboldened by unanimous support in both curriculum committees and were hopeful as we took this to the faculty at large to enact. However, discussion in the faculty-wide meeting turned sour very quickly, with a few voices dominating the stage: "We teach facts" and "This has no place in our curriculum". It was sent to a vote with the options that the class be:

- a required course for every graduate student to take any time during their studies;
- a required course for every graduate student to take in their first year;
- an optional course;
- not be created at present time.

The vote had 21 of 41 voting for the last two choices. The creation of no other graduate-level class has, in my time in the School of EECS, been up for all-faculty discussion or vote; that a social-justice focused class would be is telling in itself.

The graduate seminar has since been offered every year as a three-credit elective that has now been taught by four different faculty. Prior to the fall 2018 offering, I requested that it be listed as a special topics class and not just as a seminar as the former would allow our graduate students to use the course to satisfy course requirements. I was initially told no because "there were faculty who felt this should not be part of our curriculum" (personal communication). Thankfully, I was able to successfully counter this. As I reflect on this now, I recall the faculty discussions about our proposal for a DPD requirement. While arguments in the faculty meeting on any side were not fully developed, most faculty were promoting the idea that our disciplines are purely objective and value-neutral (something Sandra Harding has critiqued thoroughly (Harding, 2006)). Teaching anything that deviates from fact – equations, procedures, theorems – was argued to be political and that teaching DPD was tantamount to bringing a political agenda into the classroom. One faculty member emailed "When DPD was first started at OSU, some of the materials that they produced where heavily laden with ideology. [...] To the extent possible, we should not be teaching a class that is ideological in nature" (personal communication). Of course, I disagree with these sentiments, starting from the point that our teaching material has no associated ideology, a point that has been argued by others (such as Phillip Rogaway's analysis of cryptography as a field of study (Rogaway, n. d.)) and spawned entire conferences such as the Fairness, Accountability and Transparency Community.

Unfortunately, the graduate DPD learning objective has not yet been adopted university wide. However, there is currently a group of graduate students in STEM who are advocating for this change through a grassroots effort. Since the undergraduate DPD requirement arose through student activism as described in Furman's chapter in this volume, I have new hope that DPD will become part of our graduate education and that my experiences can help inform how best to do so.

Additional Resources

Readings

Borradaile, G. (2021). Defend Dissent. Oregon State University. https://open.oregonstate.education/defenddissent

DiAngelo, R., & Sensoy, Ö. (2014). Leaning in: A student's guide to engaging constructively with social justice content. *Radical Pedagogy, 11*(1), 2–22.

LeFavour, N. (2002, May 10). *Challenging homophobia, racism and other oppressive moments*. Organizing for Power. http://organizingforpower.org/wp-content/uploads/2009/03/challengingmoments.pdf

Sands, A. (2008). Never meant to survive, a black woman's journey: An interview with Evelynn Hammonds. In M. Wyer, & M. Barbercheck (Eds.), *Women, science, and technology: A reader in feminist science studies* (pp. 31–39). Taylor & Francis Group.

Websites

Project Implicit. (n.d.). https://implicit.harvard.edu/implicit/

Borradaile, G. (n.d.). *CS507/ECE507: Difference, Power and Discrimination (DPD) and responsible conduct of research (RCR), Course Webpage.* https://web.engr.oregonstate.edu/~glencora/wiki/index.php?n=Main.CS507ECE507Fall2 015

Borradaile, G., & Gretes, M. (n.d.). *CS175: Communications security and social movements.* https://web.engr.oregonstate.edu/~glencora/cs175/index.php/CourseScheduleSpring2018

The Vault. (n.d.). FBI. https://vault.fbi.gov/vault

Notes

1 Personal communication.
2 Not that Canada is without its race issues.

References

Black, E. (2002). *IBM and the Holocaust: The strategic alliance between Nazi Germany and America's most powerful corporation.* Three Rivers Press.

Bloom, J., & Jr, W. M. (2013). *Black against empire: The history and politics of the Black Panther Party*. University of California Press.

Borradaile, G. (2021). Defend Dissent. Oregon State University. https://open.oregonstate.education/defenddissent

Borradaile, G. (n.d.). CS507/ECE507: Difference, Power and Discrimination (DPD) and responsible conduct of research (RCR), Course Webpage. https://web.engr.oregonstate.edu/~glencora/wiki/index.php?n=Main.CS507ECE507Fall2 015

Borradaile, G. (n.d.). Silent Glen speaks. http://blogs.oregonstate.edu/glencora/?cat=0

Borradaile, G., & Gretes, M. (n.d.) a. CS175: Communications security and social movements. https://web.engr.oregonstate.edu/~glencora/cs175/index.php/CourseScheduleSpring2018

Boykoff, J. (2007). *Beyond bullets: The suppression of dissent in the United States*. AK Press.

Canadian Journalists for Free Expression (n.d.). *Snowden surveillance archive*. https://snowdenarchive.cjfe.org/greenstone/cgi-bin/library.cgi

Coates, T. (2014, June). The case for reparations. *The Atlantic*. www.theatlantic.com/magazine/archive/2014/06/the-case-for-reparations/361631/.

DiAngelo, R., & Sensoy, Ö. (2014). Leaning in: A student's guide to engaging constructively with social justice content. *Radical Pedagogy*, *11*(1), 2–22.

Gallagher, R. (2014, December 13). The inside story of how British spies hacked Belgium's largest telco. *The Intercept*. https://theintercept.com/2014/12/13/belgacom-hack-gchq-inside-story/

Gallagher, R., & Greenwald, G. (2014, March 12). How the NSA plans to infect 'millions' of computers with malware. *The Intercept*. https://theintercept.com/2014/03/12/nsa-plans-infect-millions-computers-malware/

Geier, K. (2014, June 11). Does feminism have a class problem? *The Nation*. www.thenation.com/article/does-feminism-have-class-problem/

Goldenberg, S. (2005, January 18). Why women are poor at science, by Harvard president. *The Guardian*. www.theguardian.com/science/2005/jan/18/educations gendergap.genderissues

Greenwald, G. (2015). *No place to hide: Edward Snowden, the NSA and the surveillance state*. Hamish Hamilton, an imprint of Penguin Books.

Gürses, S., Kundnani, A., & Van Hoboken, J. (2016). Crypto and empire: The contradictions of counter-surveillance advocacy. *Media, Culture & Society*, *38*(4), 576–590.

Harding, S. G. (2006). *Science and social inequality: Feminist and postcolonial issues*. University of Illinois Press.

Haworth, R. H., & Elmore, J. M. (2017). *Out of the ruins: The emergence of radical informal learning spaces*. PM Press.

hooks, b. (2013, October 8). Dig deep: Beyond lean in. *The Feminist Wire*. https://thefeministwire.com/2013/10/17973/

Hoover, J. E. (1967). Memorandum from Director, FBI to Special Agents in Charge. https://genius.com/Federal-bureau-of-investigation-authorization-of-cointelpro-for-black-liberation-movement-annotated

Joseph, G. (2015, July 24). Exclusive: Feds regularly monitored Black Lives Matter since Ferguson. *The Intercept*. https://theintercept.com/2015/07/24/documents-show-department-homeland-security-monitoring-black-lives-matter-since-ferguson/

Kundnani, A., & Kumar, D. (n.d.). Race, surveillance, and empire. *International Socialist Review*, *96*. https://isreview.org/issue/96/race-surveillance-and-empire

LeFavour, N. (2002, May 10). Challenging homophobia, racism and other oppressive moments. *Organizing for Power.* http://organizingforpower.org/wp-content/uploads/2009/03/challengingmoments.pdf

Moore, A. (2010). *Privacy rights: Moral and legal foundations.* The Pennsylvania State University Press.

Piven, F. F., & Cloward, R. (1978). *Poor people's movements: Why they succeed, how they fail.* Vintage.

Potter, W. (2011). *Green is the new red.* City Lights Publishers.

Project Implicit (n.d.). https://implicit.harvard.edu/implicit/

Ratcliffe, R., & agencies (2015, June 10). Nobel scientist Tim Hunt: Female scientists cause trouble for men in labs. *The Guardian.* https://www.theguardian.com/uk-news/2015/jun/10/nobel-scientist-tim-hunt-female-scientists-cause-trouble-for-men-in-labs

Rogaway, P. (n.d.). The moral character of cryptographic work. https://web.cs.ucdavis.edu/~rogaway/papers/moral.html

Sandberg, S., & Scovell, N. (2013). *Lean in: Women, work, and the will to lead.* Knopf.

Select Committee to Study Governmental Operations with Respect to Intelligence Activities, Senate (1976). *Intelligence activities and the rights of Americans.* U.S. Government Printing Office. www.senate.gov/about/powers-procedures/investigations/church-committee.htm

Staff, & agencies (2014, October 10). Microsoft CEO Satya Nadella: Women, don't ask for a raise. *The Guardian.* www.theguardian.com/technology/2014/oct/10/microsoft-ceo-satya-nadella-women-dont-ask-for-a-raise

The Vault (n.d.). FBI. https://vault.fbi.gov/vault

Zuboff, S. (2015). Big other: Surveillance capitalism and the prospects of an information civilization. *Journal of Information Technology, 30*(1), 75–89. https://doi.org/10.1057/jit.2015.5

15 "Show, Don't Tell"

Teaching Social Justice at the Source

Marisa Chappell and Linda M. Richards

The history classroom can be a powerful space for learning about the structural and cultural origins, evolution, and manifestations of inequalities. If students are guided to connect the past to the present, then exploring the operation of painful and destructive processes and systems of oppression in the past can disrupt common assumptions about meritocracy and white victimization that shape popular and political culture in the United States. But learning about historical injustice didactically, whether in the form of a lecture or an authoritative scholarly reading, allows students to distance themselves; history class becomes just another exercise in intaking information. As Natalia Fernández explains in this volume, using primary sources and archival research gives students greater agency in their own learning and provides a crucial tool that can make a history class into a Difference, Power, and Discrimination (DPD) class.

Using primary sources and archival collections with undergraduates has been standard practice in history classes for at least a generation, perhaps because it works. It works to turn students on to history by putting history into their hands. It works to break apart old narratives of the past and to create new ones. Archives, often themselves spaces that reflect privilege, create a reflexive space for students to evaluate their own perspectives, passions, and concerns in the context of, and in conversation with, the past. Primary sources, when engaged from a social justice lens, help students to see the multiple dimensions of systemic and pervasive mechanisms of oppression in operation on multiple scales, in the past and present (Adams, 2007; Hardiman, et al., 2007).

In seeking ways to cultivate our students' curiosity, self-awareness, empathy, and understanding (of the past, of human nature, of the world in which they live), we have both experimented with using primary sources and archival collections in our classrooms. Exploring the past through historical materials allows a process of *encounter* and gives students agency in the learning process. Students can learn to identify and critique the historical narratives that shape understandings of the past and present, uncover the origins of contemporary injustices, trace the evolution of systems of oppression over time, appreciate and weigh multiple perspectives, and find inspiration in courageous and resilient people and communities who have worked – in all historical eras – for justice and peace. This approach is not limited to the history classroom. By

DOI: 10.4324/9781003091998-19

engaging with primary sources, instructors in virtually any discipline, from the humanities and social sciences to natural sciences and engineering, can facilitate students' development as they uncover the complex pasts that shape the present.

In Part I, Linda Marie Richards describes some of the ways she uses DPD research and archival materials in her "Why War?" course to deepen students' understanding of the power of historical narrative. In Part II, Marisa Chappell discusses some of the ways she uses primary source documents in her U.S. History Survey class to further the goals of the DPD program. We emphasize how the strategies we discuss illuminate histories of racial inequality, but in these and other exercises we also highlight a broader nexus of oppression and address the complexities of intersectionality. We present these cases not as idealized models but as experiments that can serve as a basis for conversation and invention.

Part I: Narrations of War (Linda Marie Richards)

Research and teaching are inseparable from identity. DPD training brings forward the necessity for placing ourselves as instructors in front of our classrooms with our motives and privilege disclosed, not hidden behind academic distance. As the sociologist Mandy D. Tröger (2012) points out, academia conditions instructors to ignore their own bias "by making the personal peripheral" (p. 175). Academic culture can disguise "the objectives that stand behind the work we do" to "make us self-ignorant of the personal motives that drive our research" (p. 175). It takes privilege to abide by the academic tradition of objectivity.

Dr. David G. Lewis, an expert on Oregon tribal history at OSU, comments that much more discussion is needed about objectivity. Just how are academics and others shaped by implicit levels of bias? We are operating in a discourse "that is male centered, Western civilization centered, dominance centered, privileged centered, nationalist centered, religious centered, single-perspective centered, human centered. We cannot escape from who we are socialized to be even if it is assumed we are unbiased and objective scholars and scientists," says Lewis (personal communication, January 21, 2020). Academia continues to be deeply embedded in a hierarchy of racism and classism surrounded by a cacophony of isms, from ableism to sexism.

Social justice education demands my honesty. My biases and white privilege, converge with prejudice against me as a bisexual woman, magnified by a Trumpian abrogation of human and bodily rights (Adams, et al., 2007). My students know my feelings against war the first day of class, because I have the privilege to disclose who I really am. I also don't want to lie; I want to learn. I tell them I have been trying to end war since I was nine. My father was deployed in Vietnam in 1972 when I saw the iconic photo of Kim Phuc, running as her body was being burned by napalm. Her image seared me with an obsession to atone for injustice and violence by creating a better world as a peace activist.

But I could never find a satisfying answer to the question: why is there so much violence? Is it built into structures by how we are taught to think? When my neighbor, the young, lively Jacob Simpson, died in Iraq serving in the military in May 2005, part of me gave up. I had failed miserably at ending war. At the age of 45, I stumbled into higher education by chance, still hoping to find a way out of war. One day, standing in the plaza of the OSU Valley Library, I looked down and read the engraved words of Minoru Yasui: "At least I tried. Too many people go through life without ever having made an intense enough effort to be called a failure" (Kessler, 2005, pp.172–173). Yasui had tried to stop the internment of Japanese Americans in World War II. I realized I would continue to fail, in new ways I could not yet imagine.

History was offering important lessons. As a teaching assistant for Mina Carson's DPD U.S. history class, I discovered her "people's history of the United States" model full of inspirational stories of courage and resistance. The DPD structure paired with access to archives creates a beacon for repairing inequality and moving toward peace, in and out of the classroom. Archival collections could be used to repair wrongs, show the subjectivity of historians, shatter preconceived narratives, and widen the view and priorities of education – could it steer us towards survival?

A 2011 visit by Perry H. Charley, faculty of Diné College, sealed for me the power of the OSU archives. He held Linus Pauling's two Nobel Prizes, transforming the past to honor the present: Charley spent his life working on environmental justice, assessment and pollution cleanup of Tribal lands to bring "Beauty, Balance into Hozho, complimenting and integrating Diné traditional knowledge (Native science) with western science" (Charley, personal communication, July 19, 2020). The OSU archives houses one of the best collections of nuclear history anywhere in the United States. These collections show divergent perspectives, ranging from nuclear engineer Eugene Starr promoting nuclear technology to the Ava Helen and Linus Pauling Papers chronicling the human rights-based struggle to ban nuclear weapons. What might be transformed when documents, artifacts, and ephemera are examined through the lens of DPD?

In HST 317: "Why War?" one of my primary teaching strategies is to expose students to multiple and conflicting perspectives from the archives. Students participate in the process of making history (Hassman & Hassman, 2018). The class focuses on the patterns, causes and consequences of violence and war but it was never just an academic exercise. It was created in the 1980s by Dr Paul Kopperman as a counter weight to hate crimes against the Jewish community and the global context of constant war.

Academia is haunted enough by standards of neutrality and objectivity; I disrupt students' notions of objective research and show them that our research is in fact intimate, value-laden, and rich with struggles and questions of self (Hassman & Hassman, 2018). I utilize various strategies in this effort. My lectures include bibliographies; students see my historical interpretations are based on particular research, primary and secondary sources and an academic's vantage point. My stories, like any other historical narrative, are not simply "the truth" but a series of arguments to find it.

It matters where the story starts and stops. We continually discuss the key question: how can we best test for reliability and verify accounts? I expose students to multiple voices and standpoints. They may hear from a U.S. military veteran one day, an anti-war protester the next; or a Los Alamos nuclear scientist one day and a Siletz tribal member the next. Through these embodied sources, I cultivate humility as an intellectual virtue in myself and my students. Likewise, exposing students to conflicting sources allows them to compare and contrast, to unpack bias, and to escape detachment. I encourage students to sustain a place of uncertainty and questioning – this practice of critical thinking is a tool for lifelong learning.

Our exploration of the Modoc War is a powerful way to bring these lessons together. I begin this section of the course by telling the students I study this particular war because it speaks to my heart through my connection with Taliesin Myrddin Namkai-Meche. He had been a favorite of many on the Briscoe Elementary playground years before. I worked in his Ashland, Oregon K-5 school as a Special Education and Educational Assistant, using conflicts as opportunities to practice and teach nonviolent communication.

Taliesin, with his bright heart and mind, was my co-conspirator; he loved, and was stunningly adept at, helping to resolve conflicts creatively. My fondest memory of Taliesin was scrambling with him over the rocks and trails of the Stronghold on our annual Briscoe Elementary field trip to the Lava Beds, the place sacred to Modocs where the small group defended themselves against the U.S. military for almost six months, despite being outnumbered at times sixteen to one (National Parks Service, n.d.). The last time I saw Taliesin, he towered over me at our annual Hiroshima and Nagasaki vigil in Ashland, leaning way over to give me a hug.

Taliesin was murdered by an avowed white supremacist on May 26, 2017. He was killed protecting two teenagers he did not know while riding on a public transit MAX train in Portland, Oregon. The white assailant threatened the lives of the two women shouting "Go back to Saudi Arabia ... get out of my country" and other slurs (Park, May 30, 2017). Then he attacked those intervening on behalf of the teens, stabbing three men, killing two of them. Taliesin's dying words were "Tell everyone on this train I love them" (Bernstein, May 29, 2017). His death reminds me to love everyone on "my train," all of my students.

The week Taliesin was killed I had been lecturing about the ideas of African American civil rights activists on nuclear war. Some of these leaders, ranging from Malcolm X to Ella Baker to Dr. Martin Luther King, Jr. argued nuclear weapons were a technological eco-cidal extension of white supremacy. The weapons, they said, sustain colonialism, divert resources that could be used for equality, and torture the psyche in irrevocable ways. The reality of their lives predisposed these leaders to be perceptive of the harms caused by the expansive threat of nuclear annihilation. Nonwhites in the United States at any time could be randomly lynched for the color of their skin (Williams, 2011; Intondi, 2015). The expansion of this existential threat posed to all of the earth's inhabitants by nuclear weapons is described by the cry today for emotional justice after the terrorizing lack of accountability in the death of Eric Garner: "It is a forever unsafeness for which there can be no real preparation" (Armah, July 19, 2019).

The story of Taliesin's murder explains to my students why I ask the questions I do. My choice of "drishti" (Sanskrit for where to focus one's gaze) is directed by my memory of Taliesin's child self, running amuck on the terrain of the caves at the Lava Beds, and his bearded self, standing for global nuclear weapons abolition, urging me to teach as a radical act of love (Anzaldúa, 2007; hooks, 2003). Can we trace the Modoc Wars to white supremacy, to the war on people of color, to terror, torture and nuclear war?

After explaining my standpoint, I ask, "Who knows about the Modoc Wars?" No hands go up. The war in 1872–1873 was startling, and divisive, with most of the sympathy directed to the Modocs initially. It was one of the first wars covered in the international media with photos. "Okay, who has ever *heard* of this war?" Occasionally, one or two hands out of 50 reluctantly go up. "What did you learn about it?" I ask. Most relate they just know the name. Some laugh and say they are googling it on Wikipedia as we talk. About one in three hundred students say they saw the Oregon Public Broadcasting Modoc War documentary. "Tell me about it," I say, but they are usually too shy.

We then look at the Modoc War from several perspectives. By viewing multiple narratives of the war, students discover the importance of historical narratives, often dangerously subjective, in enforcing oppression, maintaining stereotypes, and re-inscribing prejudice. The most common type of war in the last 500 years has been violence made upon small Indigenous communities, just as in the Modoc War; these add up to irrevocable losses and genocide of Indigenous peoples and cultures all over the world (Hinton, 2002). But that is not the type of war most realists and political scientists have focused on to explain war. In fact, at the war crime trial of Kintpuash (Captain Jack, the leader of the Modoc band involved) the *New York Tribune* editorialized the Modocs were marauders, arguing only nations had status to declare war (Foster, 1999). This contributes to an agnotology, a constructed ignorance, of what causes war (Proctor & Schiebinger, 2008).

As a class we start to piece together a story that can be told many ways, focusing on who is doing the telling and why. First, we look at the Oklahoma Modoc Nation's tribal history website, supplemented by recent published authors and academic historians with their arguments and authorship identified on my slides (Modoc Nation, 2020; McNally, 2017; Cothran, 2014; Compton, 2017; James, 2008). In these narratives the war begins with an onslaught of resettlers abusing safe passage through Modoc lands. The fulcrum for the Modoc telling is a massacre of Modoc families in 1852 by the notorious vigilante "Indian Killer," Ben Wright. Wright used the white flag of peace to lure families out of their homes so that he could slaughter them

(Modoc Nation, 2020). In some versions, this is perhaps out of revenge for an earlier massacre of white resettlers in which the Lost River Modocs had no role.

The Lost River murders are followed by numerous conflicts and violence. Resettlers, miners, and land speculators coveted Modoc land while the U.S. government failed to honor their duties in two different 1964 Treaties concerning the Modocs. The Modocs were forced onto the Klamath Reservation where they were treated badly, living with the Klamath, a traditional foe. There was starvation and strife because the U.S. government promised money, food and resources that did not arrive. Why should anyone stay on the Klamath Reservation when the Americans did not honor the Treaty? Some Modocs did stay but Kintpuash's band fled back to their traditional home at Lost River to feed themselves and live unmolested. Warfare was sparked when the U.S. military, encouraged by propaganda from resettlers despite their peaceful coexistence, forcibly tried to remove the group. Resettlers were killed by some of the Modocs during their escape.

At the time, this war was one of the most expensive and asymmetrical U.S. military actions in U.S. history. Much of the Modoc resistance took place in the Lava Beds, on the eastern side of the Oregon California border, when they fled to their sacred site for protection and refuge. Modocs fired their weapons from behind the lava rock walls, caves and crevices in the Lava Beds, now a National Monument. For six months, 50 to 60 men of Kintpuash's band fought for their liberty and homeland with their families. They resisted up to 1,000 U.S. troops before their surrender. This narrative interprets Modoc actions during the 1873 war as defensive and largely justifiable (Modoc Nation, 2020; McNally, 2017; Cothran, 2014; Compton, 2017; James, 2008).

Students then explore primary and secondary sources that exclude the longer relationship between the Modocs, Europeans, and the U.S. This version portrays the murder and removal as necessary and justified. Students see this framing in older sources, including *Harper's Weekly* illustrations and stories published at the time of the war, an 1890 official military record of the war, and a 1937 rendition of the war by the National Park Service in Crater Lake. They see a current online Oregon Encyclopedia entry about the war. The entry begins not with the 1852 massacre, a land grab by Jesse Applegate, failed treaty agreements, forced removal, military miscalculations, sex slavery of Modoc women, or continual encroachment on Modoc land. Instead, it begins with the death of General Canby during peace negotiations. It matters where the story starts and stops, in time and in definition. Students can see how this framing offers a much different interpretation of culpability.

When is a "peace negotiation" used to deceive? From the Modoc perspective, given the 1852 incident in which Modoc peoples were slaughtered by a self-identified "peace" delegation, the arrival of hundreds of soldiers with weapons hardly portended peaceful negotiations; Kintpuash band's violence was arguably defensive to fall under the rules of engagement of war, not murder. The U.S. government, however, executed four Modoc leaders for this act as murder; a crowd estimated at either 850 to 2,000 people looked on (James 2008, pp. 164–65; Cothran, 2014, pp. 8–9) evoking spectacles of the lynching of African Americans.

Even after death, abuse and torture of the Modocs continued. We learn from several sources, including the October 25, 1873 issue of *Army and Navy Journal* (p. 169) the heads of the four men were severed from their bodies and sent first to the Army Medical Museum in Washington DC for eugenic studies, then to the Smithsonian (Cothran, 2014, p. 11). David G. Lewis, reflecting on this incident, observes this notion of the Army collecting native remains as objects of scientific study demands closer analysis. "Where else does the U.S. government collect the remains of people for such eugenic 'science'?" he asks. The problem is, "Natives are not seen as 'people' deserving of human rights, including the rights to land, the rights to fair compensation even under treaty, the rights to citizenship, the rights to bury their dead" (personal communication, January 21, 2020). There is no bodily nor land sovereignty accorded to the remaining 155 Modoc peoples of Kintpuash's band. They were again forcibly removed, but this time, two were taken to Alcatraz prison and the rest to Oklahoma in cattle cars. By 1879, only 99 people survived the harsh conditions on the reservation (Modoc Nation, 2020).

Analyzing and contrasting multiple primary and secondary sources together in class, students experience how some aspects are magnified while others are lost. The values of a particular historical moment profoundly shape the way we narrate history – and how those stories can reinforce systemic oppression in ways that reverberate across the years. The 1873 *Modoc Indian Prisoners* legal opinion was a precedent to justify torture against those deemed "homo sacer" (excluded from legal protections but still subject to a sovereign's power) as unlawful combatants in the March 14, 2003 "Torture Memo" by John C. Yoo. The 1873 opinion states "All laws and customs of civilized warfare may not be applicable" to tribal people (Byrd, 2011, pp. 226–227).

I share with students the National Archives "Educator Resources: The Homestead Act of 1862." The website's "Additional Background Information" narrative (Potter & Schamel, 1997) makes little mention of Native Americans, discussing them in one paragraph out of seventeen, obscuring the genocide and forced displacement that made distribution of land to white resettlers possible. Robert A. McNally, author of *The Modoc War: A Story of Genocide at the Dawn of America's Gilded Age*, noted that the words of historian Patricia Limerick ring true for the Modoc War: "The history of westward expansion has ended up divided into two, utterly separate stories: the sad and disheartening story of what whites did to Indians, and the colorful and romantic story of what whites did for themselves" (Juillerat, November 14, 2017, para. 9).

Here my students generally start talking; this conversation echoes aspects about nuclear war and technological white supremacy we discussed earlier. Today, the Manhattan Project National Historic Park's tours, sites and materials excise the atrocity caused by nuclear weapons in Hiroshima and Nagasaki. Instead, for example, the B Reactor at Hanford Nuclear Reservation celebrates the construction of those weapons as a testament to American technological ingenuity, like a gift revealed by God in order to grant such supremacy (Chernus, 1986; Richards, 2016).

The lessons are powerful because students understand the gravity while they explore the documents and historical narratives. During their research, they discover conflicting accounts, missing information, and particular ways of framing history. After this exercise and comparison of narratives, most of the students want to imagine ways to rewrite or repair the Oregon Encyclopedia entry or other renditions. My students start to explicitly ask, who gets to tell their story and why? What do we do? Students *feel* history after these examples with a different tenor. They see how much is at stake.

The students also expressed a shared despair, and wondered aloud how much effort it will take to undo racism, when history becomes such a persistent vehicle for stereotyping and harm, as in the case of the Modocs. In one class, a student (a Veteran) wondered if the Modoc War fit the United Nations definition of genocide, prompting me to introduce a "spectrum line" exercise. This exercise asks students to line up according to their opinion about a particular question, then fold in the middle in order to discuss their position with those on the other side. All the students in this first exercise went to the Yes side, in a bunch. We talked a bit about why. Then the student asked "Is there anyway there can be forgiveness or amends made to Native Americans, yes or no?" The students formed a gradated line from yes to no with a middle. I paired up the opposites for the listening exercise. In the activity, one person talks for one minute or so, while the other listens without interrupting, then the listener repeats back exactly what they heard and they can clarify understanding with each other. Then the roles switch.

In the debrief, the middles had a really rich conversation due to their shared viewpoints; others, originally opposed, shared how they were surprised to find common ground. They said it mattered what the definitions are, and when stories start and stop. A Native American student added that he could never forgive. How could that even be a question to ask, how could that be expected? If a Jewish student were in the room, he asked, would you ask them if they forgive Hitler and the Nazis? He illustrated using the analogy of crumpling a piece of paper: imagine this is the Treaty, the relationship, he said. He held up a piece of paper. Then he mashed it in his hands, "Even if you can uncrumple it and straighten it out, the creases are still there, the scar still hurts." We sat there, grief hanging still and heavy in the room, acknowledging the losses in silence together.

Students feel responsibility for the future. They talk about the OSU Native American Longhouse Eena Haws, their campus activities, the yearly OSU Klatowa Eena Powwow and ways to connect. The lesson ends with noting how Oregon tribal members, after many years, successfully won legislation mandating that K-12 Oregon schools include Oregon history education created by the communities from the Nine Federally Recognized Tribes. How Oregon K-12 teachers may or may not be taught to share this history is another challenge for the future of education. In spring term in 2019, the

Oregon legislature began debating a Memorial to apologize to the Modocs (Withycomb, March 28, 2019). By the end of the multifaceted story of the Modoc War, students see they have a role in unwinding the injustices built into history.

Part II: Voices of the Past (Marisa Chappell)

I came of age in the 1970s and 1980s in an emotionally stable and economically secure family with the privileges of whiteness. I imbibed many lessons about race and class in the world of the U.S. Air Force, where a culture of meritocracy promoted both racial integration and class segregation. Academic study cultivated a nascent feminist and antiracist perspective, which has continued to evolve over the past three decades. Whereas Linda moved from activism to academia, I have been moving tentatively in the other direction. The DPD seminar helped me to refine my understanding of systems of oppression and inspired me to seek new ways to engage students in crucial questions about inequality in the past and the present. I struggle to move beyond my comfort zone in the classroom, a tendency rooted in a resistance to confrontation and a deep-rooted valuation of careful and "objective" academic rigor. DPD inspired me to engage students more explicitly in the historical context of contemporary political debates. Rooting these discussions directly in the past, and in primary sources, has proven a fruitful avenue.

The DPD seminar significantly affected my approach to teaching. As a historian, I was not trained to attend to students' affective experiences. Despite earning a graduate Certificate in Women's and Gender Studies, I had consciously distanced my teaching from an imagined caricature of women's studies – all about feelings and students' own lives and perspectives. History was about other people, about rigorous intellectual questioning and analysis. In the DPD seminar, I began to understand that learning requires heart as well as head, and that students may learn more, and care more, if they can see themselves in history and if they are able to connect emotionally with the material. This insight has manifested in various ways. For example, I find myself turning more often to biography and case studies of individuals as a means of illuminating larger historical events and trends. Second, I have become more intentional in the primary sources I assign and in considering how students interact with them. Assigning multiple primary sources around a specific theme, event, or time period, for example, provides students with opportunities both to empathize with past historical subjects and to critically assess various perspectives against each other and against historians' interpretations.

Primary sources are particularly important for teaching HST 203, a survey of U.S. history since World War I, as a DPD class. The class attracts many non-majors; students tend to be mostly male and overwhelmingly white. Many are majoring in science and engineering fields. I suspect that when students with conservative tendencies or politics assess the list of DPD classes they see U.S. history as a fairly "safe" choice, compared to courses in Ethnic Studies and Women, Gender, and Sexuality Studies, for example. I also suspect that HST 203 is likely to be their only exposure to DPD curriculum. I feel a responsibility to provide opportunities for them to question their assumptions about the past and its relationship to the present and, at the same time, to ensure that students from other social locations see themselves in history. By reading various perspectives on a specific moment, students gain an appreciation for the complexity of these moments and the actors inhabiting them.

One example is my strategy for teaching that difference is socially constructed, a required DPD learning outcome. One of the first moments we tackle in class is the 1924 Immigration Act, which dramatically reduced immigration through the imposition of "national origins" quotas. Students read several documents from the early twentieth century that articulate nativist sentiments – elite and popular opinions that immigrants were dangerous and should not be allowed to enter the country. I assign one document to each of several small groups and ask them (1) to identify language that criticizes particular groups of immigrants and (2) to determine the basis of the criticism (does the document contend that certain immigrants are biologically inferior, culturally problematic, ideologically dangerous, etc.). All of the documents conflate arguments about Southern and Eastern European immigrants' cultural inferiority, political ideology, religion, behavior, economic role, and biological make-up while contrasting them to "Anglo-Saxon" or "Nordic" people. Students see for themselves how these particular groups were racialized as "not quite white," deemed biologically inferior and prone to criminality, in ways that justified exclusion. Because these are groups that subsequently became defined as part of a broader "white" United States of America, students are surprised to discover this process of racialization in action. In the last week of the term, I assign Donald Trump's Fall 2016 Arizona speech on immigration, and students immediately recognize similar processes of racialization and criminalization of Mexican immigrants.

As another example, when I teach the Great Depression, students read political speeches from powerful figures (such as Herbert Hoover, Franklin Delano Roosevelt, Huey Long, John Lewis) and letters from ordinary people situated differently in society. I ask students to represent these positions in a town hall meeting. By debating the causes of and proposed solutions to the economic crisis from these various perspectives, students learn a number of things:

1 that the economic crisis had a differential impact depending on one's social location (including race, class, gender, and geography);
2 that different ideas about who/what was to blame had more or less validity when assessed in conjunction with secondary reading/lecture material on the crisis; and
3 that grassroots interpretations of the crisis affected political and policy responses at the top.

Best of all, students discover these things for themselves (with facilitation and guidance, of course), a much more powerful lesson than if I simply offered a lecture stating these points. Students are often appalled at Henry Ford's suggestion that people become more self-reliant because students have learned about the depth of the crisis and the multiple barriers to economic security facing farmers and workers. We often have vigorous debates in class about the contrasting perspectives of Hoover and Roosevelt that resonate powerfully with current discussions about the meanings of freedom, the operation of a "free market," and the responsibilities of corporations, business, and individuals. Because they are exploring the ideas and words of people in the past, students debate these questions with less at stake than if we were debating current policies.

I have recently experimented with the timing of documents as a way to harness students' sense of surprise and discovery toward deeper understanding. I used to assign a collection of primary sources related to the Black Freedom Movement of the 1960s and noticed that students had difficulty breaking from preconceived understandings to tackle the documents in their historical context. Typically, students would laud Martin Luther King, Jr.'s defense of nonviolent direct action and find other perspectives inscrutable. So, I tried moving the Black Panther Party's Ten-Point Program to the session on the postwar economy. I introduced the class by pairing it with another document, a General Electric advertisement for "A People's Capitalism" – part of a broader, public-private effort to "sell" capitalism to the American people and the rest of the world (General Electric, 1956). The GE document celebrates U.S. American industrial might and ingenuity, capitalistic competition, and consumerism as the fruits of "free enterprise" and offers the supposed "American standard of living" as the inevitable result. In the Ten-Point Program, the Black Panther Party systematically attacks U.S. American institutions for exploiting and oppressing African Americans and offers an expansive vision of freedom rooted in reparations, redistribution, social responsibility, and community control. By juxtaposing these very different analyses of postwar U.S. economy and society, I hope to prompt students' curiosity. They initially find the Panthers' perspective "radical" (by which they mean completely unrealistic and unrelated to real circumstances). Then they learn about the multiple ways in which postwar economic expansion was enabled by vast government expenditures (as opposed to the kind of laissez-faire vision of the GE document), offered government-subsidized avenues for social and economic mobility to White Americans, created drastic racial disparities through racialized homeownership policies, and constructed an urban crisis through systematic disinvestment accompanied by various colonial-like practices including racist policing. When we revisit the documents, students are able to understand (and some even to sympathize with) the Panthers' critique.

In response to the state of racial politics in our current moment, I decided in Spring 2019 to introduce an exercise on Confederate monuments during Week 1 of HST 203; my goal was to show students up front that history is about the present moment as much as it is about the past. The exercise introduced students to the contested nature of historical interpretation through an issue that has been widely discussed in popular media in the past two years. Conflicts over historical symbols of white supremacy erupted nationally and locally in the second decade of the twenty-first century. The most dramatic national incident occurred in August 2017 when a white supremacist murdered antiracist protester Heather Heyer and injured nineteen others during a "Unite the Right" rally in Charlottesville, Virginia (Wallace-Wells, 2017). Locally, in response to protests like a "Students of Color Speak-Out" in 2015, OSU President Ed Ray initiated a process that resulted in his decision to change the names of three campus buildings whose nineteenth century namesakes advocated slavery, removal of Indigenous people, and white supremacy (Rimmel, 2015; Ray, 2017). Through the process of discovering for themselves the motivations for and uses of these monuments and the problematic historical narrative they advanced, I hoped that students would appreciate the importance of history in shaping our world.

I began by asking students to come up with arguments offered by those seeking the removal of Confederate monuments and by those seeking to retain them. The groups reported out, and I listed the arguments on the board. I then introduced them to a specific monument, the statue at the entrance to the University of Mississippi. I passed out several documents to small groups of students: three media reports about the statue's dedication from 1906, including the transcript of the keynote speech given at the ceremony, and a history of Ole Miss from its 1948 yearbook. I asked students to read the documents and make note of aspects they found to be important, interesting, or surprising. The small groups discussed the documents and reported out, and then I facilitated a discussion. The documents colorfully illuminate key elements of the "Lost Cause" narrative and Southern (white) nationalism (Neff et. al., 2016). They reveal that the monument was erected to advance a narrative of the past that would reinforce white supremacy, and that this was occurring not immediately after the Civil War but at a moment in which Southern states were forcefully repudiating any pretense of following constitutional guarantees of equal protection and imposing new forms of racial caste. They also illuminate the centrality of white women, racialized gender ideals, and class identity in shaping white Southern nationalism.

Student responses to the exercise were generally encouraging. Students were able to identify key elements of the narrative. I asked students to spend a few minutes writing about the exercise, specifically commenting on if and how it changed their thinking about the issue. A total of 42 students participated. Six (14%) wrote that the exercise influenced them to support removal of Confederate monuments, while seven (17%) wrote that the exercise reinforced an already existing position in favor of removal. Three students (7%) wrote that they supported maintaining the memorials; one wrote that the exercise had influenced that position. Most responses (26 or 62%) did not clearly identify a before/after position on the issue but offered various comments like the one that said the exercise "gave better context into the issue."

The exercise was not designed to convince students to support either maintaining or removing the monuments. The goal was for students to see that historical narratives are built on specific assumptions about the world and are often constructed with particular political purposes in mind, as well as to begin to teach students how to analyze primary sources. I also used the exercise to introduce the state of racial politics in the United States in the early twentieth century, a necessary context/starting point for understanding the rest of the course. In general, I think it succeeded. But, as a work in progress, it also revealed some surprises and problems.

One interesting outcome is that the exercise evoked empathy from some students for early twentieth century Southern white nationalists and the statues' contemporary defenders. Three students (7%) expressed a version of this view. One student gained "more understanding/ compassion" for the monuments' defenders who "were fully convinced that what they were doing was because it was their culture." Another reported that the exercise helped them to "better understand the level of pride and value" that Southern whites express in these monuments. These few students were affected by the narrative of victimization in the sources. "I don't want to take away such an emotional and patriotic event that could deeply effect [sic] those connected to it," one student wrote; another reported that the exercise made them see "strong reasoning" for retaining the memorials because "the South is very intensely passionate about their efforts in the war."

Historical study is a crucial means for cultivating empathy, a key goal for DPD instruction. But these comments expressed empathy only for people in a position of power, and they illuminated two key problems with the exercise. First, I assigned only sources from white Southern nationalists, offering no access to the voices of African Americans from the era, which would have provided students with perspectives to challenge the "Lost Cause" narrative and revealed more strikingly its purpose as a political tool of white supremacy. Second, I asked the group brainstorming arguments for *removing* the monuments to report first. Arguments for *maintaining* the monuments came second and remained unchallenged by critical analysis as the students turned to the sources. I was very conscious of those arguments sitting on the white board without having been discussed. Finally, this was an introductory exercise during Week 1, before students had been introduced to the history of Reconstruction and its aftermath; without knowing the promise of Reconstruction and the violence and terror used to impose a brutal new white supremacist regime, many students lacked context for interpreting the documents.

I ran the exercise in my upper-division Civil Rights Movement class the same week with a couple of changes. I did not have time to locate primary sources from African American contemporaries (though I will include some in future sessions), but I reversed the order of brainstorming reports and facilitated some discussion about the two sets of arguments. I concluded with a ten-minute talk in which historian William Sturkey challenges monument defenders by highlighting the brutality that the "Lost Cause" narrative helped to provoke and justify and by relating his own emotional responses, as a descendant of North Carolina African Americans, to the monument at the University of North Carolina, Chapel Hill (Sturkey, 2017).

It's not a scientific sample; HST 365 students are more likely to be history majors, and they elected to enroll in a course on the Civil Rights Movement and were thus more likely to begin with some kind of racial justice perspective than were students in HST 203. But the results were encouraging. Of 18 students, one wrote that the exercise changed their view from leaving them up to taking them down, noting "after analyzing these primary documents I began to realize that these monuments are not representations of history but instead political ideas embodied in extravagant figures of art." Fifteen students (83%) wrote that they already favored removal but that the exercise reinforced that position or offered tools for justifying it. One wrote, "I have some actual history that gives my argument some support" while another appreciated getting "better perspective" and an understanding that "this is white history from one sole perspective."

The Confederate Monument exercise seems to be an effective mechanism for teaching about the complexities, subjectivity, and power of historical narrative as well as about the ideological and cultural mechanisms that helped reinforce and maintain white supremacy in the twentieth century United States. This and similar exercises would be useful in courses across a wide range of disciplines in the social sciences and humanities.

Conclusion

Our experiences with these and other exercises utilizing primary sources and archival research with students have convinced us that teaching from the sources can promote critical and analytical thinking about the past and present, cultivate empathy, provoke constructive discomfort, and mobilize historical narrative understanding in service of a more just, equitable, and peaceful future. The philosopher Shai Tubali, redeploying ideas from Hannah Arendt, defined active learning as "a highly engaged form of thinking that prepares one to act in the real world." At this moment in our history, we might feel liberated by crisis to teach (Tubali, 2018, p. 16).

As this chapter went to press, the years of intellectual and organizing work by BLM activists enabled mass, multiracial mobilizations in response to the most recently publicized police murders of Black Americans. Confederate flags and statues were being removed, even in Alabama and Mississippi. Taliesin's murderer was unrepentant but convicted. Portland leader Jo Ann Hardesty said the case was more about how our justice system "tackles hate and racism, or doesn't" (KATU Staff, 2020). Noting a prison sentence cannot repair the tragedy caused by enacting neo-Nazi ideas, the justice system "is currently the only system we have to address these acts of violence" (KATU Staff, 2020). Hardesty invokes us to find new ways to intervene daily to prevent hate with the courage of those who stood up in the past for equality and justice. We know the battle to disentangle higher education from white supremacy is just beginning.

We believe students must learn not only the history that led us to now but the skills – empathy, appreciation of complexity, and critical analysis – that can move us all forward. History classes can play a role in promoting this knowledge and these skills if we are intentional about what we do and are willing to experiment. This is risky. It means we will make mistakes, but this also gives a chance to model recovery from failure and learn to heal with students and each other. As educators, we are obliged to get off the train of thought of U.S. white supremacy; from the debate over the Confederate monuments and nuclear weapons to the blood spilled in the Modoc Wars and on the Portland MAX. In this process we uncover the links of shared humanity that bind us together.

Additional Resources

Readings

Campuzano, E. (2017, May 27, updated 2019, January 9). Taliesin Myrddin Namkai-Meche's friends: 'He's just the best person'. *The Oregonian/OregonLive.* www.oregonlive.com/portland/2017/05/taliesin_myrddin_namkai_meche.html

Lewis, D.G. (2019, October 27). Ignoring tribal history in a contemporary exhibit. *NDNHistory Research Critical and Indigenous Anthropology.* https://ndnhistoryresearch.com/2019/10/27/ignoring-tribal-history-in-a-contemporary-exhibit/

Proctor, R.N. and Schiebinger, L. (Eds.). (2008). *Agnotology: The making and unmaking of ignorance.* Stanford University Press.

SPLC (Southern Poverty Law Center) (2019). New hate map helps users explore landscape of hate. www.splcenter.org/fighting-hate/intelligence-report/2019/new-hate-map

Wesson, S. (2015). National treasures: Help your students travel through time with primary sources from the Library of Congress, *Teaching Tolerance, 49.* https://www.tolerance.org/magazine/spring-2015/national-treasures

Whyte, K.P. (2018). On resilient parasitisms, or why I'm skeptical of Indigenous/settler reconciliation, *Journal of Global Ethics, 14*(2): 277–289. doi:10.1080/17449626.2018.1516693

Websites

Digital Public Library of America: https://teachinghistory.org/best-practices/using-primarysources

Don't Shoot Portland. (2020): www.dontshootpdx.org/

Library of Congress. Primary Source Sets: www.loc.gov/teachers/classroommaterials/primarysourcesets/

National Archives and Records Administration. DocsTeach: www.docsteach.org

Texts and Studies

Withycomb, C. (2019, March 30). A long-ago execution and a modern apology from Oregon. *Mail Tribune.* mailtribune.com/news/top-stories/a-long-ago-execution-and-a-modern-apology-from-oregon

References

Adams, M. (2007). Pedagogical frameworks for social justice education. In M. Adams, L.A. Bell, & P. Griffin (Eds.), *Teaching for diversity and social justice* (pp. 15–34). Routledge.

Adams, M., Jones, J., & Tatum, B.D. (2007). Knowing our students. In M. Adams, L.A. Bell, & P. Griffin (Eds.), *Teaching for diversity and social justice* (pp. 395–410). Routledge.

Anzaldúa, G. E. (2007). *Borderlands/La Frontera: The new Mestiza (3rd ed.).* Aunt Lute Books.

Armah, E. (2019, July 19). From I can't breathe to I can't grieve: Black grief matters." *Warscapes.* www.warscapes.com/column/esther-armah/i-can-t-breathe-i-can-t-grieve-black-grief-matters

Bernstein, M. (2017, May 29). Portland MAX hero's last words: 'Tell everyone on this train I love them'. *The Oregonian/OregonLive.* www.oregonlive.com/portland/2017/05/max_heros_last_words_tell_ever.html

Black Panther Party for Self Defense (1966). *Ten point program.* www.marxists.org/

Byrd, J. (2011). *Transit of empire: Indigenous critiques of colonialism.* University of Minnesota Press.

Chernus, I. (1986). *Dr. Strangegod: On the symbolic meaning of nuclear weapons.* University of South Carolina Press.

Compton, J. (2017). *Spirit in the rock: The fierce battle for Modoc homelands.* Washington State University Press.

Cothran, B. (2014). *Remembering the Modoc War: Redemptive violence and the making of American innocence.* University of North Carolina Press.

Foster, D. (Fall 1999) Imperfect justice: The Modoc War Crimes Trial of 1873. *Oregon Historical Quarterly, 100*(3): 246–287.

General Electric (1956). People's capitalism – What makes it work for you? In P.B. Levy (Ed.), *America in the Sixties – right, left, and center: A documentary history* (p. 8). Praeger.

Hassman, K., & Hassman, B. (2018). TOPIC generation and teaching research as inquiry. In J.L. Mattson and M.K. Oberlies (Eds.), *Framing information literacy: Teaching grounded in theory, pedagogy, and practice* (pp. 47–66). Association of College and Research Libraries.

Hardiman, R., Jackson, B., & Griffin, P. (2007). Conceptual foundations for social justice education. In M. Adams, L.A. Bell, & P. Griffin (Eds.), *Teaching for diversity and social justice* (pp. 36–41). Routledge.

Hinton, A. (2002). The dark side of modernity: Toward an anthropology of genocide. In A. Hinton, (Ed.), *Annihilating difference – The anthropology of genocide* (pp. 1–42). University of California Press.

hooks, b. (2003). *Teaching community: A pedagogy of hope.* Routledge.

Intondi, V. (2015). *African Americans against the bomb: Nuclear weapons, colonialism, and the Black Freedom Movement*. Stanford University Press.

James, C. (2008). *The tribe that wouldn't die*. Naturegraph.

James, W. (1911). The moral equivalent of war. In W. James, *Memories and studies* (pp. 267–296). Longmans, Green & Co.

Juillerat, L. (2017, November 14). New Modoc war book mixes facts with compelling story. *Herald and News*. www.heraldandnews.com/news/local_news/new-m odoc-war-book-mixes-facts-with-compelling-story/article_0a275779-275106f-59df -a9f6-c45e42c78e26.html

KATU Staff (2020, February 21). Portland, Multnomah County officials react to Jeremy Christian guilty verdict. *KATU 2*. https://katu.com/news/local/portland-of ficials-react-to-jeremy-christian-guilty-verdict

Kessler, L. (2005). *Stubborn twig: Three generations in the life of a Japanese American Family*. Oregon State University Press.

Maybury-Lewis, D. (2002). Genocide against indigenous people. In A. Hinton (Ed.), *Annihilating difference – The anthropology of genocide* (pp. 43–53). University of California Press.

McNally, R.A. (2017). *The Modoc War: A story of genocide at the dawn of America's Gilded Age*. University of Nebraska Press.

Modoc Nation (2020). History. Modocnation.com. https://modocnation.com/history/

National Parks Service (n.d.). *Lava beds, A Brief History of the Modoc War: War in the Lava Beds*. www.nps.gov/labe/planyourvisit/upload/Modoc-War-FINAL.pdf

Neff, J., Roll, J., & Twitty, A. (2016). A brief contextualization of the Confederate Monument at the University of Mississippi. https://history.olemiss.edu/wp-content/uploads/sites/6/ 2017/08/A-Brief-Historical-Contextualization-of-the-Confederate-Monument-at-the- University-of-Mississippi.pdf

Park, M. (2017, May 30). Teen on Portland train: 'They lost their lives because of me and my friend.' CNN. www.cnn.com/2017/05/29/us/portland-train-teenager-stabbing/

Potter, L.A., & Schamel, W. (1997, October). The Homestead Act of 1862. *Social Education*, *61*(6): 359–364.

Ray, E. (2017, November 27). To the Oregon State University community. https://lea dership.oregonstate.edu

Richards, L.M. (2016, November). Review: The B Reactor National Historic Landmark. The Hanford Site Manhattan Project National Historical Park, Hanford, WA. *The Public Historian*, *38*(4): 305–317.

Rimmel, A. (2015, November 16). OSU students discuss campus racism. *Corvallis Gazette Times*. www.gazettetimes.com/

Sturkey, W. (2017, August 30). Comments at Beyond the headlines: Confederate monuments, historical memory, and free speech [Video]. YouTube. www.youtube.com

Tröger, M.D. (2012). How can I live with(out) C. Wright Mills. Breaking with the disembodied truth. *Cultural studies – Critical methodologies*, *12*(3), 175–181.

Tubali, S. (2018) Hannah Arendt and the human duty to think: Shai Tubali considers the roots and implications of Arnedt's active philosophy. *Philosophy Now*, *125*, 14–17. https://p hilosophynow.org/issues/125/Hannah_Arendt_and_the_Human_Duty_to_Think

Wallace-Wells, B. (2017, November). The fight over Virginia's Confederate monuments. *New Yorker*. www.newyorker.com/

Williams, P. (2011). *Race, ethnicity and nuclear war: Representations of nuclear weapons and post-apocalyptic worlds*. Liverpool University Press.

16 Afterword

Susan M. Shaw

Oregon State University's Difference, Power, and Discrimination Program (DPD) emerged from a shared student and faculty concern for curriculum transformation that centered issues of power, inclusion, equity, and justice. Recognizing that most faculty have not had educational experiences that asked them to think or teach critically about how power and categories of social difference are operative in their disciplines, the DPD Program features a 60-hour summer seminar, known today as the DPD Academy, to help faculty develop transformed syllabi that center disciplinary content around institutional power and systemic oppression.

I directed the DPD program for two three-year terms in the early 2000s and facilitated the seminar drawing on the work of the first DPD summer faculty seminars led by founding director Annie Popkin. Annie's seminar centered feminist and critical race readings that provided a systems of oppression framework through which faculty could rethink the disciplinary content of their courses. In fact, I co-facilitated one summer seminar with Annie.

The most unique contribution of the DPD Program to curriculum transformation has been the radical reorganization of course content around social justice. For example, one professor teaches microbiology by tracing the progression of disease at the microbial level as facilitated by issues of poverty, race, and gender. A kinesiology instructor examines power and privilege in sport; an agriculture professor centers the ecosystem science of Pacific Northwest Indigenous people. To rethink curriculum content, instructors ask such questions as: What epistemological assumptions undergird your curriculum? From whose perspective is your course taught? Whose interests does your curriculum serve? Who created and defined your discipline, and how did their perspectives and interests affect the ways your discipline was constructed? Whose experiences and perspectives are excluded, marginalized, or minimized in your curriculum? What are the ethical considerations implicit in your curriculum? What happens if you move diverse people to the center of your disciplinary content? The DPD seminar challenges faculty to examine the assumptions embedded in their disciplines as historically practiced to expose the underlying biases toward dominant groups and to imagine transformation by centering the experiences, knowledges,

DOI: 10.4324/9781003091998-20

concerns, and critiques of non-dominant groups. In particular, the seminar pushes faculty to scrutinize the power structures embedded in their disciplines and help students begin to see how systems of power and privilege work in what they are studying.

In the early 2000s, despite cuts to funding, the DPD program persisted. At one point, I was required to offer the seminar based on the ten-hour Writing Intensive Curriculum (WIC) seminar model. What resulted was faculty who felt utterly unprepared to address DPD issues in the classroom with such a minimal introduction, and so the 60-hour seminar was reinstated. Shortly thereafter, when the Faculty Senate asked to revisit the criteria, a committee (on which I served as an ex officio member) led by Human Development and Family Sciences professor Alexis Walker spent a full academic year negotiating the new language of the criteria with faculty across the university. At the final faculty senate meeting of the year, senators overwhelmingly approved a strengthened version of the criteria that included a requirement that DPD courses employ active learning. In 1992, senators had been unwilling to have a criterion related to teaching. By the early 2000s, faculty had come to understand that achieving the goals of DPD depended on learners' active engagement with the material and with faculty and peers.

In 2007, then-DPD director Jun Xing, longtime DPD faculty Judith Li and Larry Roper, and I edited a book about the DPD model, *Teaching for Change*. In that volume, the first generation of DPD directors, faculty, and students laid out the rationale for DPD together with pedagogical innovations, institutional strategies, and the summer faculty seminar. This edited collection represents the next phase of DPD at Oregon State University exemplified by a new generation of DPD faculty and current director, Nana Osei-Kofi. Taken together, the two volumes demonstrate how this innovative faculty development program and undergraduate general education requirement have over nearly 30 years both become institutionalized at the university and pushed against the institution to demand greater accountability to social justice. As the editors of this new volume suggest in the introduction, this continuing exploration of the DPD program demonstrates the necessity that "we as educators keep learning and keep growing in our commitments to facilitating and fostering critical consciousness in our classrooms."

The relevance of the DPD model for social justice educators has become even more evident as recent events including the murder of George Floyd by Minneapolis police officers and the resurgence of nationwide Black Lives Matter protests as well as the disproportionate impact of COVID-19 on minoritized communities, have highlighted the persistence of racial injustice in this country. Furthermore, the disproportionate numbers of missing and murdered Indigenous women and murders of trans women of color underline the necessity of action-oriented intersectional analyses that is at the core of the DPD model. This volume provides both the theoretical and practical guidelines needed for faculty to engage deeply with issues of power, privilege, structural oppression, and resistance in their content and pedagogical practices. This moment provides a powerful opportunity for faculty to engage students in meaningful discussion of contemporary events from DPD perspectives. Students want to talk about these issues, but faculty are often fearful of opening up difficult conversations. I've often heard both students and faculty ask, "What does this have to do with [insert discipline here]?" The DPD model helps faculty imagine how courses in geosciences, computer science, fisheries and wildlife, anthropology, public health, engineering, and psychology can engage Black Lives Matter, queer liberation, disability, gender justice, wealth inequality, Islamophobia, environmental racism, and antisemitism.

As faculty members who are expert in their disciplines but sometimes new to feminist and critical race analysis struggle to address this moment in their teaching, opportunities to learn to apply systems of oppression frameworks and feminist social justice education become even more essential for classroom transformation. Institutional commitments to diversity require faculty development to help teachers learn how to make these disciplinary and pedagogical transformations. The DPD summer seminar offers a model for promoting faculty development in social justice education. Through the years, DPD directors and graduates of the seminar have presented the model at academic conferences and have offered similar seminars at other institutions. In fact, for the past ten years, I have facilitated Diversity Academy for two weeks every summer at California State University Chico. Diversity Academy is open to all Chico State faculty and staff and focuses on transformation within the units represented by participants – from recreation sports to maintenance and janitorial services to the library to academic departments. At Oregon State University, we adapted the model to be the centerpiece for our National Science Foundation ADVANCE Institutional Transformation grant. Across four summers, the ADVANCE team offered two-week seminars focused on inclusion, equity, and justice for university administrators and STEM deans, school directors, department heads, and senior faculty. The seminar focused on using systems of oppression theories to make sense of persistent inequality and lead participants to develop action plans to transform institutional structures within their spheres of influence. As a result of the ADVANCE seminar, colleges changed their promotion and tenure processes, reconfigured their hiring committees, and developed new policies to promote inclusion, equity, and justice. In the summer of 2019, we offered a train-the-trainer seminar for colleagues from other institutions interested in adapting our model for their campuses. Ten participants from six institutions participated, and we have developed an ongoing relationship with these participants that is leading to other collaborations.

This volume offers a glimpse into the content and processes of the DPD model that are relevant to a wide range of audiences. The proven success and longevity of the DPD model demonstrates how such a faculty development and curriculum transformation program can be successfully implemented in an institution. Administrators with responsibilities in diversity, faculty development, and curriculum will find in the volume a ready guide for creating their own institutionalized program for diversity and social inequality in the curriculum. While ideally each institution will adapt such a program to the specifics of its institutional history and location, the volume offers a path toward creating an innovative, powerful, and effective program that is responsive to the needs of the local setting. New, as well as seasoned, instructors and graduate teaching assistants can find ideas and inspiration in the volume, as well as encouragement to try new ways of approaching disciplinary content and including new pedagogical practices that are effective in helping students engage in challenging material. The authors of these essays are testament to the ability of faculty to be successful in pushing the boundaries of traditional disciplines and offering courses that center difference, inequality, and social justice. This volume also speaks to curriculum and pedagogical innovations that community and K-12 educators can adapt to their audiences as well. The foundational ideas of DPD – critiquing traditional disciplinary content, transforming content by centering diverse groups, and building innovative and justice teaching practices – apply to every kind of teaching and learning and can be adapted to different contexts and audiences. In particular, the collaborative nature of the volume demonstrates the power of working across disciplines and academic homes to support one another in bringing these important issues of social difference and institutional power to the center in these challenging times.

One of the goals of OSU's DPD program is interdisciplinarity, and this book provides an entry point to faculty members across the disciplines into the possibilities of curriculum transformation and social justice education in every academic field. No matter the discipline of the writers, the examples and methods they offer can be applied across disciplines. One of the unique aspects of the book is the way it brings together diverse disciplinary voices across a range of issues, such as labor, disability studies, religion, and archives. Often social justice education books focus on the central analytical skills of feminist and critical race studies but do not delve into a wide diversity of issues and academic disciplines. By approaching the task of writing about DPD in such breadth, this book offers an innovative and compelling model of feminist social justice education that can be adapted by educators across all academic disciplines.

The organization of the book also offers educators a blueprint for imagining this work on their on campuses and in their classrooms. Section 1: Archives and Power: Engaging History Collaboratively points to the significance of context for this work. Effective curriculum transformation and social justice education should begin by taking into account the institution – the land on which it sits, its history, mission, faculty and students, and campus activism – as well as the surrounding community and its history, particularly the histories of minoritized populations. Section 2: Frameworks for Transformative Pedagogies offers concrete examples and processes for rethinking and reimagining pedagogical practices, including in online courses, a context. Section 3: Destabilizing Dominant Narratives explores the challenges queer, critical race, and class studies offer to traditional pedagogies by centering non-dominant experiences and perspectives. Finally, Section 4: Rethinking Approaches to Disciplinary Content elucidates processes of transforming disciplinary content with gender, race, class, and issues of power, privilege, and discrimination on center. For readers who cannot participate in a two-week DPD seminar, this book offers a workshop-in-a-volume to guide faculty in a curriculum transformation process that can revolutionize teaching and learning.

In summary, this book suggests social justice educators:

1. Understand your institutional histories. Social justice education starts at home. Educators should learn and teach institutional histories in relation to land, buildings, mission, curriculum, faculty and staff, and students. Assumptions about institutional identities should be made transparent and part of analyses of issues of power and privilege. This can happen through archival research and ethnographic research in local communities. Who an institution is matters.
2. Embrace interdisciplinarity. Interdisciplinary work stretches faculty and should be part of faculty development. It also helps teachers construct with students a broader understanding of the world, even as we teach our disciplinary specialties.
3. Plan for diverse learners. Faculty should examine their own assumptions about who learners are. Often, without thinking about it, especially those of us who are members of dominant groups and teach at predominantly white institutions proceed from assumptions about our students that reflect dominant norms: they will be white; they will understand how universities work; they will have a mother and a father; they will learn well from lectures; they will be able to demonstrate what they've learned by taking a test; they will speak English as a first language; they will be able to hear lectures and videos. A just classroom anticipates diverse students rather than accommodating them when they show up. If we teach as if our students all conform to dominant norms, then we will recreate colonizing educational structures that force learners into dominant ways of knowing and being.
4. Educate the whole person. The DPD approach recognizes that learners are not simply minds to fill but whole beings who bring their experiences and emotions to the classroom. The classroom can become a traumatizing place for traditionally marginalized students if it simply reflects dominant norms. Faculty should facilitate a classroom climate that welcomes and affirms difference, makes space for emotion, and uses learning as one tool for promoting healing.
5. Center difference. By moving gender, race, class, sexuality, ability, age, nationality, and religion to the center of academic analysis across the disciplines, faculty can destabilize the colonizing and oppressive master narratives of traditional academic content. Students can learn how white supremacy, patriarchy, ableism, and heteronormativity have shaped assumptions and practices of academic disciplines and can begin to imagine transformative possibilities within the disciplines.

6 Remember that the personal is still political. The old adage of the Second Wave of the Women's Movement remains true. Who teaches and who learns matters. Who we are as faculty members – our gender, race/ethnicity, ability, sexuality, age, nationality, social class, and religion – affects our every interaction in the classroom. We can use ourselves, as Bradley Boovy and Nana Osei-Kofi suggest in Chapter 11, as "embodied texts," or we may inadvertently reproduce dynamics of dominance and subordination if we ignore the personal and institutional powers that intersect in our identities.

7 Unsettle and transform your disciplinary content. Ask intersectional feminist and critical race questions of your content: Who created your discipline? Whose interests does your discipline serve? Who gets to shape your discipline and who doesn't? Whose voices are heard and whose aren't? What happens if you move gender, race/ethnicity, and other forms of difference to the center?

8 Include experiential learning. Social justice isn't learned well through just a lecture. For social justice learning to be most effective, students need to engage in hands-on, participatory learning. Whether in-class activities, archival research, or participation in communities, experiential learning challenges students to use a variety of learning styles and to stretch themselves beyond their usual comfort norms. The lessons of DPD are most successful when students do as well as listen.

While educators can certainly benefit from reading the book alone, I hope that faculty consider organizing groups to read and discuss the book together, perhaps reworking syllabi as they go. One of the outcomes of the DPD summer faculty seminar is a transformed syllabus for each participant, and, for readers of this book, that could be a worthwhile goal for engaging with this volume. I would also encourage administrators to provide support for faculty to work through this book and revise courses together in small groups. We have always limited participation in the DPD seminar to 15 because we want to foster relationship-building and community among participants and to provide abundant opportunity for conversation, risk-taking, and support. Institutions should draw on the expertise they already have among faculty in women, gender, and sexuality studies, ethnic studies, and queer studies and feminist and critical race scholars in other academic disciplines (and, in the spirit of DPD, these faculty should be compensated for any additional work the institution asks them to do to foster curriculum transformation and social justice education across the institution).

This book is a practical guide to starting these conversations and beginning broad-based curriculum transformation for social justice education and life. Each chapter individually (and the book as a whole) addresses longstanding problems in U.S. higher education. While drawing on relevant theories and research, these chapters also rely on the three-decade experience of DPD at Oregon State University and so bring real life examples, with both their pitfalls, possibilities, and histories, to the conversation.

In his conclusion to *Teaching for Change*, Larry Roper noted that DPD's original vision rested on four important beliefs:

1 Teaching has the power to influence individuals and communities;
2 providing students with background on 'various forms of discrimination and their origins' (from the DPD web page) is important;
3 the university had the necessary capacity to create a meaningful response to those issues about which [students] were concerned; and
4 there would be others in the future life of the university who would share their commitments and work to ensure a sustained effort in regards to these issues.

This new volume attests to the validity of those four original beliefs. In particular, this book represents the imagined future of others who would continue and grow the work of DPD at OSU and around the country. I hope readers use this book to transform their own teaching and to encourage institutionalization of curricula that center difference, power, and discrimination across the disciplines and the practice of social justice in the classroom and across the campus.

Bios

Authors of Foreword and Afterword

Alma Clayton-Pedersen is the Chief Executive Officer of Emeritus Consulting Group, a Chicago-based firm that uses organizational development principles to assist nonprofit, public and education entities in enhancing their efficacy for the public good. She is a former AAC&U Senior Scholar who directed the work of a three-year (2010–2013) project Preparing Critical Faculty for the Future, funded by the National Science Foundation. From 2001 until June 2010 she was AAC&U's Vice President for Education and Institutional Renewal. Clayton-Pedersen joined AAC&U after more than 15 years at Vanderbilt University where she served in senior administrative roles within student affairs, academic affairs, athletic affairs and Vanderbilt's public policy center. She has co-authored many publications including *Making a Real Difference with Diversity: A Guide for Institutional Change*, which focuses on changing the diversity paradigm from an add-on to an essential dimension of 21st century learning and on how to monitor progress in achieving institutional goals for diversity. *Enacting Diverse Learning Environments: Improving the Climate for Racial/Ethnic Diversity in Higher Education* provides a framework of the dimensions of campus climate. She holds a B.S. from the University of Wisconsin-Milwaukee, and both the MEd and PhD from Vanderbilt University.

Frank Hernandez serves as Dean of the College of Education at Texas Christian University (TCU). Prior to his work at TCU, Dr. Hernandez served as Associate Dean & The Harold and Annette Simmons Endowed Chair in Educational Policy and Leadership at the Simmons School of Education at Southern Methodist University. Prior to that, Dr. Hernandez served as Dean of the College of Education at the University of Texas of the Permian Basin (Odessa, TX). Dr. Hernandez' research work has focused on four areas of inquiry: Latinos and school leadership, Latino racial identity development, inclusive leadership for LGBTQ students, and leadership for social justice. He has published extensively on Latino leadership, including two books: *Abriendo Puertas, Cerrando Heridas (Opening Doors, Closing Wounds): Latinas/os Finding Work-Life Balance in Academia* (with Elizabeth Murakami and Gloria Rodriguez) and *Brown-Eyed Leaders of the Sun: A Portrait of Latina/o Educational Leaders* (with

Elizabeth Murakami). Dr. Hernandez received his PhD in Educational Leadership and Policy Analysis from the University of Wisconsin-Madison.

Susan M. Shaw is professor of Women, Gender, and Sexuality Studies at Oregon State University. She holds an MA and PhD from Southern Seminary in Louisville, Kentucky and a BA in English from Berry College in Rome, GA. She is the former director of OSU's Difference, Power, and Discrimination (DPD) Program, and she has led numerous seminars at universities across the country on issues of power and privilege in the disciplines. She is co-author of two introductory women and gender studies textbooks, *Gendered Voices, Feminist Visions: Classic and Contemporary Readings* 7th ed. and *Women Worldwide: Transnational Feminist Perspectives on Women* (both with Janet Lee, published by McGraw Hill). She is also author of *God Speaks to Us, Too: Southern Baptist Women on Church, Home, and Society; Reflective Faith: A Theological Toolbox for Women* and co-author (with Mina Carson and Tisa Lewis) of *Girls Rock! Fifty Years of Women Making Music*, and Intersectional Theology: An Introductory Guide (with Grace Ji-Sun Kim).

Volume Editors

Bradley Boovy is Associate Professor of Women, Gender, and Sexuality Studies and World Languages and Cultures at Oregon State University, where he teaches courses on critical men and masculinity studies, gender studies, queer studies, and German-language literature and culture. His research bridges cultural studies, queer theory, and critical language pedagogies. His work has appeared in multiple peer-reviewed journals and edited volumes, including the *Women in German Yearbook*, *L2 Journal*, *Archival Practice*, *Die Unterrichtspraxis*, and most recently, an article with Natchee Barnd on building transdisciplinary alliances, which appeared in *Seminar: A Journal of German Studies*. He is currently completing a book manuscript titled *Queer Masculinity and the Magazine: Race, Gender, and Belonging in 1950s West Germany*, which examines the role of queer periodical publishing in structuring discourses of sexuality in the early Federal Republic of Germany. He also co-directs the Oregon State Queer Archives with Natalia Fernández, a center for research and resources related to LGBTQ+ communities in Oregon and the Pacific Northwest.

Kali Furman is a doctoral candidate in Women, Gender, and Sexuality Studies at Oregon State University. Her dissertation, "Making Sense of Social Justice Education: A Case Study of the Difference, Power, and Discrimination Program," combines her research focus in social justice education, feminist pedagogies, and history. Kali earned her bachelor's degree in History with minors in English and Gender Studies at Boise State University, her Master of Arts in Women, Gender, and Sexuality Studies and a Graduate Certificate in College and University Teaching at Oregon State University. Kali currently works as the Managing Editor for the *ADVANCE Journal*.

Nana Osei-Kofi is Director of the Difference, Power, and Discrimination Program and Associate Professor of Women, Gender, & Sexuality Studies at Oregon State University (OSU). She holds a PhD in Educational Studies and an MA in Applied Women's Studies, both from Claremont Graduate University. Her areas of scholarly focus in relation to education include critical and feminist teaching and learning, faculty development, the politics of American higher education, and arts-based educational research. Additionally, she works in the areas of AfroSwedish Studies and Black European Studies. Journals in which her work has appeared include *Discourse: Studies in the Cultural Politics of Education*, *Feminist Formations*, and *The Review of Education, Pedagogy, and Cultural Studies*. She is currently completing a book manuscript titled *Identity and Kinship: AfroSwedish Places of Belonging*.

Contributors

Natchee Blu Barnd is a comparative and critical ethnic studies scholar interested in the intersections between ethnic studies, cultural geography, and Indigenous studies. His research focuses on issues of race, space, and Indigenous geographies. His book, *Native Space: Indigenous Strategies to Unsettle Settler Colonialism* (OSU Press, and the First Peoples series) illustrates the ways that Native people in North America sustain and create Indigenous geographies in settler colonial nations. His second book, *A People's Guide to Portland and Beyond* (pre-contract with UC Press), highlights lesser-known sites of social justice and oppression across Portland. He also writes on pedagogy, contemporary media, college cultural centers, and popular culture. His articles and chapters appear in *Journal of Geography*, *American Indian Culture and Research Journal*, *Diversity in Disney Films* (MacFarland), *Teaching Race in the 21st Century* (Palgrave/Springer), *Yearbook of the Association of Pacific Coast Geographers*, *Nexus: Complicating Community and Centering the Self* (Cognella), and *Oregon Humanities*.

Glencora Borradaile is Associate Professor of Computer Science at Oregon State University. She sits on the advisory board of the Civil Liberties Defense Center where she helped initiate and continues to build a Digital Security program to support activists and their lawyers. She has initiated a research program whose mission is to support the digital needs of activists, and ensure that everyone can communicate freely and safely, regardless of their identity. She also created and teaches an interdisciplinary course on communications security and social movements that is offered through the Difference, Power and Discrimination program of Oregon State University's Baccalaureate Core. She was on the program committee of the Conference on Fairness, Accountability, and Transparency (FAT*) and USENIX's Workshop on Advances in Security Education. Her work has been funded by an NSF CAREER award and two collaborative NSF Algorithmic Foundations grants. She is an associate editor of the ACM Transactions on Algorithms and the open access journal Discrete Mathematics & Theoretical Computer Science. Her publications include "Minimum cycle and homology bases of surface embedded graphs" (*Journal of Computational Geometry*, 2017), "Min st-cut oracle for planar graphs with near-linear preprocessing time" (*Transactions on Algorithms*, 2015), and "All-pairs minimum cuts in near-linear time in surface embedded graphs" (*Proc. of the Symposium on Computational Geometry*, 2016).

Marisa Chappell is Associate Professor of History at Oregon State University where she teaches modern U.S. history, women's and gender history, and the history of social policy and social movements. She is the author of *The War on Welfare: Family, Poverty, and Politics in Modern America* (University of Pennsylvania Press, 2010), *Welfare in the United States: A History with Documents*, with Jennifer Mittlestadt and Premilla Nadasen (Routledge, 2010), and numerous book chapters and journal articles, including, most recently, "The Strange Career of Urban Homesteading: Low-Income Homeownership and the Transformation of American Housing Policy in the Late Twentieth Century United States" in the *Journal of Urban History* (2019) and "Protecting Soldiers and Mothers Twenty Five Years Later: Theda Skocpol's Legacy and American Welfare Sate Historiography, 1992–2017" in the *Journal of the Gilded Age and Progressive Era* (2018). She has also published in popular venues including the *Washington Post*, *Jacobin*, and Bunk History.

Sharyn Clough is Professor of Philosophy at Oregon State University, where she teaches courses in the study of knowledge, especially scientific knowledge. Her research examines the complex ways in which science and politics are interwoven, and the notions of objectivity that can be salvaged once this complexity is acknowledged. In her most recent work, she has been investigating the importance of basic peace skills ("Peace Literacy") for deliberations about contentious science policies. She also directs Phronesis Lab where she and her students and community partners research the efficacy of Peace Literacy interventions across the curriculum from K-12 as well as adult and higher education contexts. She is the author of *Beyond Epistemology: A Pragmatist Approach to Feminist Science Studies* (Rowman and Littlefield, 2003) and the editor of *Siblings Under the Skin: Feminism, Social Justice and Analytic Philosophy* (Davies, 2003). In addition, she has written a number of essays on science and political values for journals such as *Social Science and Medicine*, *Studies in the History and Philosophy of the Biological and Biomedical Sciences*, *Metascience*, *Perspectives in Science*, and *Social Philosophy*.

Qwo-Li Driskill is a (non-citizen) Cherokee Two-Spirit and Queer writer, activist, and performer also of African, Irish, Lenape, Lumbee, and Osage *ascent*. S/he is the author of *Walking with Ghosts: Poems* (Salt Publishing, 2005) and the co-editor of *Sovereign Erotics: A Collection of Two-Spirit Literature* (University of Arizona, 2011) and *Queer Indigenous Studies: Critical Interventions is Theory, Politics, and Literature* (University of Arizona, 2011). Hir book *Asegi Stories: Cherokee Queer and Two-Spirit Memory* (University of Arizona, 2016) was a finalist for a Lambda Literary Award in 2017. S/he is the Director of Graduate Studies and the Queer Studies Curriculum Organizer in Women, Gender, and Sexuality Studies at Oregon State University.

Natalia Fernández is an Associate Professor and the Curator and Archivist of the Oregon Multicultural Archives (OMA) and the OSU Queer Archives

(OSQA) at the Oregon State University Special Collections and Archives Research Center. Fernández's mission for directing the OMA and the OSQA is to work in collaboration with Oregon's African American, Asian American, Latinx, Native American, and OSU's LGBTIAQ+ communities to support them in preserving their histories and sharing their stories. Her scholarship relates to her work as an archivist, specifically best practices for working with communities of color. Fernández has published in the *Oregon Historical Quarterly*, *Journal of Western Archives*, *The American Archivist*, *Multicultural Perspectives*, and *Archival Practice*. Fernández holds an MA in Information Resources and Library Science from the University of Arizona (U of A). She graduated from the U of A Knowledge River Program, a program that focuses on community-based librarianship and partnerships with traditionally underserved communities.

Kryn Freehling-Burton earned her interdisciplinary Master's degree in Women Studies and theatre from Oregon State University. In the Women, Gender, and Sexuality Studies program at Oregon State, she teaches a variety of courses including Introduction to Women, Gender, and Sexuality Studies, Women and Sexuality, Women in the Movies, and Gender and Science. Her research and creative writing projects focus on mothering, theatre, activism, and online learning. This research informs her classroom work, and she includes popular culture and student-created art projects as important components of learning in all of her classes. Kryn's book is titled *Performing Motherhood*, co-edited with Amber Kinser and Terri Hawkes (Demeter Press, 2014). Forthcoming is a chapter entitled "Reforming the Evil Mother on ABC's *Once Upon a Time*" in the book *Evil Women, Mean Girls* and an upcoming article, "Gender, Nation, and Belonging: Representing Mothers and the Maternal in Asghar Farhadi's *A Separation*" with colleagues Patti Duncan and Mehra Shirazi.

Allison L. Hurst is an Associate Professor of Sociology at Oregon State University, and currently serves as the Associate Director of the Sociology Program, the President of the Working-Class Studies Association, and a member of the American Sociological Association's Taskforce on First-Generation and Working-Class Persons in Sociology. She has published widely on the issue of working-class college students and the experience of social mobility through higher education: *The Burden of Academic Success: Loyalists, Renegades and Double Agents* (2010), *College and the Working Class* (2012), *Working in Class: Recognizing How Social Class Shapes Our Academic Work* (2016, co-editor with Sandi Nenga), and *Amplified Advantage: Going to a "Good" School in an Era of Inequality* (forthcoming). Her current research focuses on the social and economic changes of the postwar period and how a collective experience of that affluent and relatively egalitarian period has misinformed scholarly and personal understandings of how the social world works.

Stephanie Jenkins is Associate Professor of Philosophy in the School of History, Philosophy, and Religion. She received her BA in Philosophy at Emory University in 2003, her MA in Philosophy from Pennsylvania State University in

2007 and her dual PhD in Philosophy and Women's Studies from Pennsylvania State University in 2012. Her book *Disabling Ethics: A Genealogy of Ability*, argues for a genealogy-based ethics that departs from traditional bioethical approaches to disability. Her research and teaching interests include 20th century continental philosophy (especially French), feminist philosophy, disability studies, critical animal studies, and ethics. In her spare time, she enjoys spending time outdoors (hiking, biking, and running), baking, and listening to live music.

Amy Koehlinger is Associate Professor in the School of History, Philosophy, and Religion at Oregon State University where she teaches courses in North American religious history, American Catholicism, religious history of the American West, and methodological issues surrounding the application of ethnographic methods to historical research and writing. Her research focuses on the culture of American Catholicism, historical intersections of religion and social reform in the United States, and the construction of gender within American religious traditions. Her first book *The New Nuns: Racial Justice and Religious Reform in the 1960s* (Harvard, 2007) documents the involvement of Catholic women religious in racial justice programs during the civil rights era. *The New Nuns* won the 2009 Eric Hoffer Prize in the category of Culture. Dr. Koehlinger's next project *Rosaries and Rope Burns: Boxing and Manhood in American Catholicism, 1880–1970* documents the historical significance of the sport of boxing among American Catholics, exploring boxing's relationship with religious ideas about the redemptive value of physical suffering and blood, and the sport's effect on performances of manhood among particular racial and ethnic groups of Catholics.

Marta María Maldonado is Associate Professor of Ethnic Studies at Oregon State University, where she also directs the Ethnic Studies program and teaches courses on critical race theory, processes of race and racialization, and Latinx Studies. She holds a PhD in Sociology from Washington State University. She has published numerous articles and book chapters in *The Journal of Qualitative Inquiry*, *Latino Identity in Contemporary America*, *Human Organization*, and *Antipode*, among others. Most recently, she co-edited a special issue of *Feminist Formations* titled *Critical Feminist Exits, Re-Routings, and Institutional Betrayals in Academia* (2018), which examines institutional failures to support critical feminist scholars, analysis of the consequences of such failures, and discussions of administrative responses that embrace and support critical feminist scholars and their work. She is currently completing a project on demographic change in Oregon's seafood processing industry, funded by an award from Oregon Sea Grant.

Charlene C. Martinez serves as the Associate Director of Student Experiences & Engagement at Oregon State University (OSU). Charlene has 20 years of professional experience working in cross/multi-cultural centers and student affairs programs at Oregon State University, Sacramento State, Mills College, Contra Costa College, UC San Diego, as well as the Rockwood Leadership Program, a non-profit organization. She is the co-founder of OSU's Multiracial

Aikido, a social justice retreat for participants to unpack multiraciality and develop their agency as emerging social change leaders. She received her master's degree in education with an emphasis in multicultural counseling. Charlene infuses cultural organizing, emergent strategies, and storytelling in experiential learning programs and initiatives. Her research appears in *Building Multiracial Aikido: A Student Social Justice Retreat* (Stylus, 2021, with Stephanie N. Shippen) and *New Directions for Student Leadership: No 163. Centering Dialogue in Leadership Development* (Jossey-Bass, 2019).

Ronald L. Mize is Professor in the School of Language, Culture, and Society. He was trained as a journalist at the University of Colorado Boulder and went on to study Sociology at Colorado State University (MA) and the University of Wisconsin-Madison (PhD). In 2016, he was the Fulbright-Garcia Robles Chair in U.S. Studies at el Instituto Tecnológico Autónomo de México. His scholarly research focuses on the historical origins of racial, class, and gender oppression in the lives of Mexicano/as residing in the United States. He seeks to understand the underlying assumptions about nation, race, identity, gender and class in how the public forms our opinions about immigration and part of his effort is to carve out a new paradigm for understanding both the political economy and culture of immigration as well as their interconnections. He is the author of over 50 scholarly publications, including *The Invisible Workers of the U.S.-Mexico Bracero Program: Obreros Olvidados* (Lexington, 2016), *Consuming Mexican Labor: From the Bracero Program to NAFTA* (University of Toronto Press, 2010, with Alicia Swords), and *Latino Immigrants in the United States* (Polity Press, 2012, with Grace Peña Delgado). Mize's most recent book is part of Polity's Short Introduction Series, titled *Latina/o Studies*.

Jenny N. Myers is an instructor in the Sustainability Double Degree Program at Oregon State University. She earned an MA in environmental philosophy from Lancaster University and is currently completing a PhD in sustainability education at Prescott College. Her research investigates affective place-based relationships as a source of agency in colonized space and illustrates transformative acts of place-making as a pathway for resilience in the face of climate change. Her article "Phenomenology of Place: Re-Grounding Environmental Ethics Through Story" appears in the *Journal of Sustainability Education* (2016).

Erich N. Pitcher, PhD, is the Director of Youth Programs at FosterClub. Previously, Erich served as the Program Lead/Instructor for Adult & Higher Education at Oregon State University. Erich's research uplifts the voices of racially, sexually, and gender minoritized populations and imagines more just futures for marginalized groups in higher education. Grounded in organizational and critical perspectives, Erich has examined how lesbian, gay, bisexual, transgender, queer, questioning, and asexual (LGBTQQA) students successfully navigate higher education environments, as well as how trans academics' experiences are shaped by organizations. Their next research project will focus on the ways that diversity and cultural workers across varied institutional contexts experience and resist fatigue. Prior to Oregon State, Erich worked in student success, service learning, and LGBTQ+ support services. While at Oregon State, Erich also served as the Associate Director for Research and Assessment at Diversity & Cultural Engagement and taught in the College Student Services Administration program. Their publications include the monograph *Being and Becoming Professionally Other: Identities, Voices, and Experiences of U.S. Trans* Academics* (Peter Lang, 2018) as well as numerous articles and book chapters in *Feminist Formations*, *International Journal of Qualitative Studies in Education*, and *Educational Studies*.

H. Rakes is Assistant Professor of Women, Gender, and Sexuality Studies and Queer Studies at Oregon State University. They earned their PhD in Chicago at DePaul University, in Philosophy. Their research areas include disability studies, trans studies, queer theory, queer of color critique, and women of color feminisms—especially the convergences of these fields. They have published in *Disability Studies Quarterly*, the collection *Why Race and Gender Still Matter*, and The American Philosophical Association *Newsletter on Feminism and Philosophy*. Their publication, "Crip Feminist Trauma Studies in *Jessica Jones* and Beyond," is in *The Journal of Literary and Cultural Disability Studies*. They have a co-authored essay in the journal *Criminology and Criminal Justice* special issue "Queer Theory and Criminology" about carceral feminism and its imbrications with racism and ableism.

Linda M. Richards has studied nuclear history, human rights, environmental justice and nonviolence for over thirty years, teaching in the streets and the classroom. She has a PhD in History of Science and teaches in Oregon State University's School of History, Philosophy, and Religion. Her current book project, *Human Rights and Nuclear Wrongs* (West Virginia University Press, forthcoming), explains how nuclear weapons and technology shape human rights today. She is co-principle investigator on a three-year National Science Foundation grant "Reconstructing Nuclear Environments and the Downwinder's Case" concerning the history of Hanford Nuclear Reservation contamination from the production of plutonium for nuclear weapons. She is co-editor with Jacob Darwin Hamblin of "Connecting to the Living History of Radiation Exposure" (*Journal of the History of Biology*, 54(1), April 2021) and is published in *The Public Historian*, *Historia Scientiarum*, *Peace and Change*, and *Chemical Heritage Magazine*.

Martha Smith is the Director of Disability Access Services at Oregon State University. She has been working to support increased access for individuals with disabilities since 1984 and has been working in higher education to make the learning environment more accessible since 1990. Since 1995, she has applied the concepts of Universal Design at state universities for undergraduate and graduate students, at a health sciences university as well as in the workplace for a state agency. Her publications appear in the *Journal of Nursing Education*, the *Journal of Postsecondary Education and Disability*, and in numerous proceedings of the *Innovation in Education* conference.

Index

Page numbers in *italics* indicate figures

ableism, academic 67–68
academic bias 267
Adichie, Chimamanda Ngozi 209
Allen, Elaine 100
Allen, Walter 192
anti-Judaism/anti-Semitism, US 216–219
Anzaldúa, Gloria 149, 151
Arbery, Ahmaud xiv
archivist, faculty collaborations: literary event, archive-centered 28–30; oral histories, student projects 33–35; pedagogical objectives 21–22; photographs, contextual analysis 30–33; professors, preparatory factors 35–36; shared goals 24–28, 36–37; social justice activism 23–24
Arellano, Lucy 33–35
Aristotle 109
Arredondo, Jaime 242
Arts and Social Justice Living Learning Community (ASJLLC) 125, 132–133, 134–135
Association of College and Research Libraries 22
attribution errors 115–116, 117–118

Bañuelos, Peter 45–46, *45*
Barnd, Natchee 26, 57
Benson, Buster 113–114
Benton County Historical Society 44, 51
Beydoun, Khalid 222–223
Black Panther Party 257, 259, 276
Black social movements: anti-capitalist critique 276; Black Lives Matter protests 280; surveillance and suppression 257, 258–259, 260, 261
Bonnichsen, M. 13–14

Boovy, Bradley xvi, 22, 44, 149, 150–151
Bourdieu, Pierre 183
Boykoff, Jules 257
Bracero Program, contextual archives 31–33
Brown, Jasmine 51–53, *52*
Brunsma, David 192
Buccola, Steven T. 12
Butler, Shakti 136
Byrne, John xix, 3, 7–8

Cabrera, Nolan 191
Campbell, Fiona Kumari 67
Canales, Alejandro 167
Cantor, Nancy 236
Center for Applied Special Technology (CAST) 99
Chappell, Paul K. 106–107, 109–112
Charley, Perry H. 268
Chávez, César 229–230, 231
Christian privilege: anti-Judaism/anti-Semitism, ongoing impacts 216–219; Indigenous stories, disruptive critique 214–215; pedagogical confrontation 207, 213–214
class, faulty teaching: class as social construct 183; classroom engagement exercises 178–181; collective *we*, distinctions and use 176–177; discussion resistance 175; family trajectories and personal paths 179–180; focus group, skills and application 180–181; founding theorists' views 175–176; privilege walk, arguments against 181–182; racial connections, importance of 174–175; structural mapping of

divisions 178–179; working class academic, reflective action 183–184
Clough, Sharyn 95
Coalition of Immokalee Workers (CIW) 228, 233, 239–240
cognitive biases: attribution errors 115, 117–118; categorization and stereotyping 114–115, 117; contextual categories 113–114; implicit bias tests 116–117; peace literacy, change factors 106–107, 121; self-serving bias 115–116; structural injustice's invisibility 105, 106
COINTELPRO, FBI surveillance 256, 257, 258–259, 260
Cook, Terry 27
Cornell University 234, 235, 236
Coughlin, Charles 218
Covid-19 pandemic xiv, 284
Craib, Raymond 234, 235, 236
Crenshaw, Kimberlé 149–150
Cruz, Santiago Rafael 236

Dean, Allen 51
De Lauretis, Teresa 144–145
Difference Power, and Discrimination (DPD) Program: Affirming Diversity Course Development Committee, founding proposals 9–12, 16; archives, collaborative student engagement 24–35; archives, partnerships 21, 26, 36–37; collective support 170–171; course criteria and development xix–xxi, 283–285; educators, key guidance 287–288; establishment context xviii–xix, 7–8, 283, 289; faculty focus xviii, 236; funding challenges, debates and solutions 13–16; model promotion and adaptability 285–286; place-based learning 24, 48; student activist support xix–xx, 3, 14–17; UDI seminars 75, 79
Disability Services, universities: ableism, perceptual impacts 68; faculty mindset barriers 73–74; institutional change 83; learning environment, facilitating access 71–72, 75, 78, 79
Disability Studies: academic ableism 67–68; UDI advocacy and challenges 69–72, 74–75; UDI implementation guidance 75–80; UDI pedagogical practices 80–83
Dolmage, Jay 67, 68, 75
DPD Program *see* Difference Power, and Discrimination (DPD) Program

Driskill, Qwo-Li 152–153
Duncan, Patti 146

Eddy, Robert 192
educational technologies: access discrimination 87; non-academic resources 92–93; privacy considerations 90–91; video assignments 90
Equity in Educational Land-Grant Status Act, 1994 xviii–xix
ESOL students 71
experiential learning: educational value 288; farmworker justice movements 237–240, 241–242; institutional discrimination, simulation exercise 95–99; Social Justice Tour of Corvallis project 44–47, 45, 48–54, 52; social situatedness and identity 164–166, 165

fair trade learning 242
Farm Labor Organizing Committee (FLOC) 228, 232, 236, 239–240
farmworker justice movements: immigrant rights, changing attitudes 231–232, 241; OSU course, experiential learning 237–240, 241–242; OSU course objectives 236–238, 241; OSU/PCUN partnership benefits 232–233, 239–240, 242; service or experiential learning debate 240–242; targeted campaigns and programs 233–234, 240; United Farm Workers (UFW), critical analysis 229–231; university courses and coverage 228, 234–236
Ferguson, Ed 29
Fernández, Natalia María 150–151
Floyd, George xiv
Foley, Teresa 70
Ford, Henry 217
fundamental attribution error (FAE) 115, 117–118
Furman, Kali xv–xvi, 54

Gandhi, Mahatma 110, 111, 230
Gann, Tami 54, 55
Ganz, Marshall 231, 240
Garcia, Matt 231
Geier, Kathleen 247
gender bias 93, 100, 116
Gendler, Tamar 114–115, 116
Giraldo, Greg 117–118
Gretes, Michele 255–256
Griffith, David 232

300 *Index*

Gross, Joan 9, 11
Gutiérrez, David 231

Halperin, David M. 145
Hammonds, Evelyn 250
Hamraie, Aimi 75
Hardesty, Jo Ann 279–280
Hartley, Heather 194
Hartman, Eric 242
Heyer, Heather 277
Hill Collins, Patricia 197
historically white institution: legacy influences 192–193; teacher embodiment, racially judged 190–192, 194–195; *see also* Predominately White Institution (PWI); race, faculty teaching
Hofstadter, Richard 216
hooks, bell 89, 136, 247
Huerta, Dolores 229, 238
Hughes, Langston 56
Hunt, Tim 251

identity map 250
Imarisha, Walidah 4, 16
immigration: farmworker organization and rights policies 231–232; Jews and US anti-Semitism 216–219; Latinx workers and labor history 166–168; Oregon State exclusions 24; primary sources and student debates 275–276; racialized narratives 160–161; US policies (1920–39), impacts 275–276
Indigenous peoples: land-grant institutions, racial disparities xviii–xix, 193, 235–236; Modoc War narratives, multiple perspectives 270–274; narratives, challenging Christian privilege 215–216; poetic narratives *58*, 58; Queer Studies curriculum 149; race, faculty teaching 193; teacher positionality 42–43, 109–110, 147–148
institutional histories, research 16
intersectional practices: class, evaluation skills 181; educator guidance 288; intersectionality misinterpreted 149–150; OSU Queer Archives (OSQA) 150–151; photographic archive analysis 32–33; Queer Studies assignments 151–154; Religious Studies teaching 210–214

Jacobs, Walter 193, 201
Jaramillo, A. 7–8
Jenkins, J. Craig 230

Jimerson, Randall 23
Johnson, E. Patrick 145
Justice, Daniel Heath 146–147

Kalapuya people xviii, 5, 193, 235–236
Kedley, Kate 194
Kim, Janine Young 166
Kimmerer, Robin 214
King, Martin Luther Jr. 108, 111, 229–230, 257
Kivel, Paul 214
Kleinman, Larry 228, 232–233, 237, 238–239
Kopperman, Paul 268
Kynard, Carmen 192

land-grant institutions, racial disparities xviii–xix, 5, 235–236
Latinx Studies, pedagogical challenges: ethnoracial positionality and interactivity 160–161; identity and positionality 162–164, *163*; peripheral, requirement course 161–162; racialized lives and spaces 159–160, 162; social situatedness, critical learning/unlearning 164–166, *165*, *167*; teacher's pedagogical practice 158–160; unlearning concept 158; work as racial/gendered, biased understanding 166–168; work, expectations and realities 169–170, *169–170*
Lawrence, Sandra 95, 105
Lawson, James 111
Levy, Jacques 229
Lewis, David G. 267, 272
Lloyd, Deanna 30–33, 36–37
Lorde, Audre 143, 149, 152

Mace, Ron 69
MacNell, Lillian 100
Majka, Linda C. 230
Majka, Theo J. 230
Malcolm X 136, 269
Marks, A. 13
Marx, Karl 175–176
Mattheissen, Peter 229
McDade, Tony xiv
McGuire, Joan 69–70
McIntosh, Peggy 105, 213, 214
McNally, Robert A. 272
Merrett, Chris 59–60
Migrant Justice/Justicia Migrante 228, 233–234, 239
Moraga, Cherríe 151

moral outrage 106, 108
Morrill Land Grant Acts (1862 & 1890) xviii–xix, 235–236
Morrison, Toni xiv, 190, 195
Morris, Sean Michael 91
Myers, Jenny N. 91

Nadella, Satya 251
Namkai-Meche, Taliesin Myrddin 269, 270, 279
National Conference on Race and Ethnicity (NCORE) 130
National Union for Social Justice 217–218
NIMBYism 4

online education: access discrimination 87; classroom environment and engagement 89–92, 100, 101; course design and evaluation 99; instructor decentering 91–92; instructor discrimination 100; instructor presence 90; minoritized communities, knowledge integration 92–95; privacy considerations 90–91; strategy challenges 100; student demographics 88–89; transformational learning, structural bias exercise 95–99
Online Equity Rubric 99
open educational resources 93
oral histories 33–35
Oregon Multicultural Archives (OMA): Braceros photographs, analysis activities 30–33; course-specific instruction 24–26, 27; custodian's mission 23–24; resources and access 22–23, 27–28; "Speaking Justice" workshop/event 28–30
Oregon, racial discrimination legacy 4–5, 24, 46
Oregon State University (OSU): Affirming Diversity Course Development Committee 9–12; Baccalaureate Core Committee (BCC) xix, 8–9; campus racism 1990, responses 6–9; Centro Cultural Cesar Chavez 5, 238; Disability Access Services 71, 73–74; Disability Network 74, 79, 155; DPD Program *see* Difference Power, and Discrimination (DPD) Program; Ecampus program 87, 88, 89, 100, 150; Eena Haws Native American Longhouse 5, 151, 273; Graduate Learning Outcome (GLO) 247–248;
institutional bias 93; legacy of racism xviii–xix, 4–5, 192–193, 235–236, 277; Lonnie B. Harris Black Cultural Center 6–7; student activism, ongoing legacy 3, 5–9, 14–17
Orientalism 220
Osei-Kofi, Nana xvi–xvii, 26, 28, 149
OSU African Students' Association 29
OSU Queer Archives (OSQA): course-specific instruction 24–26, 27; custodian's mission 23–24; founding mission 150–151; resources and access 22–23, 27–28
Overmyer-Velásquez, Mark 234, 235, 236

peace literacy: cognitive bias challenges 106–107; main elements 106; non-physical needs, meeting of 109; phronesis, modern version 109; practical evaluations 112, *112*, 113; skills set 110; structural justice, change factors 106–108, *107*; training and capacity development 111–112, 114, 120–121; trauma, psychological effects 109–110
Penn State University 234
people of color: Oregon's racism legacy 4–5, 24; OSU archives and collaborations 24, 25, 28–30; OSU archives, collaboration and resources 28–30; Queer and Trans Studies 143, 144–146, 147, 149–150, 154, 155; Social Justice Tour of Corvallis project 41, 45–46, *45*, 51–53, *52*, 57–59, *58*; student activism, OSU 5–9, 277; student and faculty identities 193; teacher embodiment, racially judged 191–192, 194–195, 197–198
Pérez, Emma 150
Pesznecker, K. 14–15
Pettigrew, Thomas 116
photographic archives, analysis techniques 31–33
phronesis 109, 110
Pineros y Campesinos Unidos Noroeste (PCUN) 228, 231, 232–233, 239–240, 242
place-based learning: archive collaborations 28–37; archivist's practices 24; DPD Program objective xviii; educator guidance 287; oral histories, student projects 33–35; *see also* Social

302 *Index*

Justice Tour of Corvallis, project program
poetry workshops 28–30
Popkin, Annie 12, 283
positionality: critical pedagogy 170–171; decentering and co-learning opportunities 87, 91, 93–95, 100; instructor influence, ethnic studies 41–43; Latinx Studies, interactivity challenges 160–161, 162–164
Predominantly White Institution (PWI): educator guidance 287; faculty of color, teaching challenges 125–126; Latinx Studies, teaching challenges 160–162, 166; legacy influences 4–5, 89, 192–193; OSU's status 40; white student expectations 149; *see also* race, faculty teaching
primary sources, teaching with: archives, repositories for critical thinking 268–269; educational and social value 266–267, 279–280; framing history and by whom 272–274; historical narrative, formation and legacy 276–279; Modoc War narratives, multiple perspectives 270–272; nuclear history 268, 269–270, 272–273; state surveillance documents, engaged analysis 258–260; student engagement, analysis tool 274–276
Protocols of the Elders of Zion 217, 218

Queer and Trans Studies, OSU: disability and crip theories, analysis 155; Ecampus program benefits 150; instructor backgrounds and influences 147–149; Lorde's "tree of anger" 143; queer theories, critical deshaping 154; queer theory, whitening of 144–145; racialization, disruptive approaches 149–150; racially diverse focus 146–147; scaffolding activities 153–154; syllabi structure 151–154; "Theory in the Flesh" project, situating experience 151–154; trans studies, inclusive 146
queer theory, whitening of 144–145

race, faculty teaching: faculty of color, racially based associations 197–200; historical white institution, legacy influences 192–193; racial empathy expectations 196–197; student interaction strategies 200–202; student's contextual engagement 189–190; teacher as text 193–195; teacher embodiment, racially judged 190–192, 194, 199
racism: anti-Muslimism issues 219–223; anti-police protests xiv; Christian privilege, disrupting of 215; cognitive biases 115–116, 118; Oregon's legacy 4–5; OSU archive resources 24; OSU's student activism and responses 5–9; primary sources, teaching histories of inequality 268–279; Social Justice Tour of Corvallis project 45–46, 51–53, *52, 54,* 56–57; STEM students, teaching approaches 254–261; *see also* Latinx Studies, pedagogical challenges; race, faculty teaching
Ramos, Santos F. 193
Ray, Ed 6, 277
religion, pedagogical strategies: anti-Muslimism, historical legacies 219–221; anti-Judaism/anti-Semitism, Christian privilege's impacts 216–219; Christian privilege 207, 213–214; critical centering of Indigenous narratives 214–215; difference as social construction 210–211; evaluative tools 212; Muslims, identity and ethnicity issues 221–223; single narrative rejection 209; teacher beliefs, contextual sharing 208–209, 210; US as "Christian nation", myth-busting 212–213
Rendón, Laura 128, 129–130
Richards, Linda Marie 29–30
Riesman, David 177
Roberts, Lani, Dr. 14
Robinson, William 162
Rockenbach, Barbara 37
Rodriguez, Eddie 53–54
Roper, Larry 289
Rose, Robin 15

Said, Edward 220–221
Sandberg, Sheryl 247
Sanders, Bernie 171
Santa Ana, Otto 160
Santiago, Diana 53
Sauder, Kim 93–94
Sayre, H. 9
Schossler, Lewis 214
Schwartz, Joan M. 27
Scott, Sally 69–70
Seaman, Jeff 100
self-serving bias 115–116

sentipensante pedagogy: arts and transformative learning 134–135; concept 129; practices and personal accounts 128–131, 136–137; story circles 133–134, 135; student transition and integration 132–133
service learning 240–241
Sesame Street 115
Sheehan, E. 50
Sheoships, Gabe 49
Sifuentez, Mario 231, 232
Snowden, Edward 255
Social Dimensions of Sustainability course, OSU: course objectives and design 88, 101; equitable learning 92; instructor presence 90, 91–92; minoritized communities, knowledge integration 93–95; transformational learning, structural bias exercise 95–99
social justice education, pedagogical aims xiv, xvii
Social Justice Tour of Corvallis, project program: affect and speculative non-fiction 55–59, *58*; conceptual principles 48; educational and social value 40, 59–60; guidebook, archival contribution 26; hands on, critical pedagogy 48–49; instructor positionality and influences 41–44; logistical guidelines 47–48; meaningful learning experience 49–54, *52*, *55*, 59–60; multiple level student participation 41; poetic narratives *58*, 58–59; research and practical evaluations 44–45; stories, samples and significance 45–47, *45*; student's primary narratives 51–53, *52*; tour booklets *42*, *43*, 47
Society of American Archivists 22
Soto, Gary 229
Special Collections and Archives Research Center (SCARC): archive-based workshops/events 28–30; course-specific instruction 24–26, 27; custodian's mission 23–24; DPD Program partnerships 21, 26; faculty partners, shared goals 36–37; oral histories, student projects 33–35; photographs, contextual analysis 30–33; resources and access 22–23, 27
speculative non-fiction, historical narratives 55–59, *58*
STEM students, teaching approaches: discrimination, response activities 254–255; identity and discrimination, discussion exercises 248–252, *249–250*; Latinx Studies, student relegation 161–162; overcoming faculty interventions 261–263; racial bias issues 166; sexism in the sciences 247, 250–251; social movements' surveillance and suppression, engaged analysis 255–261; spokescouncil consensus building activities 252–253; teaching challenges 246, 255, 260–261
Stephen, Lynn 232
Stommel, Jesse 91
story circles 133–134, 135
structural injustice: cognitive biases 113–118; in-class art exercise, lessons learned 105–106, 117–120, 121; moral outrage 106, 108; peace literacy, change factors 106–108, *107*; peace literacy, practice overview 109–113, *112*; stereotyping and attribution errors 115–118; teaching practices 113, 114; ubiquitous presence 105
student activism, Oregon State University: Black Student Union, 1969 5; campus racism 1990, reactive responses 6–9; Concerned Student Leaders xix, 8; DPD Program, creation and support xix–xx, 3, 8–10, 14–17; protest influenced initiatives 5–6; Student of Color Speak Out, 2015 6
student privacy: focus group skills 180–181; online education 90–91; social class stigmas 179–180, 182
Summers, Larry 251
Swords, Alicia 231

Taylor, Breonna xiv
Taylor, Keeanga-Yamahtta 174
teacher as text 193–195
Tena-Enarnacion, Jason *58*, 58–59
Thomas, Dale 29
Tobin, Thomas 71, 79
Tokunaga, Miwa 56–57
Too Black 28–30
Trans Studies *see* Queer and Trans Studies, OSU
Tröger, Mandy D. 267
Trouillot, Michel-Rolph 50
Trump, Donald 219, 275
Tubali, Shai 279

United Farm Workers (UFW) 228, 229–231, 239–240

Universal Design for Instruction (UDI): active commitment 76; assignment flexibility 76–77; course engagement options 77–78; cross-unit collaboration, advocate narratives 65–67; faculty mindset barriers 73–74; implementing actions 75–80; inclusivity interventions 70–71; incremental change 79–80; institutional change and networking 78–79; learning environment, challenging perspectives 71–72; online course compatibility 99; originating principles and adaptions 69–70, 75; pedagogical practice innovations 80–83; policy and training interventions 74–75

Universal Design (UD) 69, 75

University of Connecticut (UConn) 234, 235, 236

University of Missouri 5

unlearning, concept 158

Velásquez, Baldemar 232

war, narrations of: Modoc War, multiple perspectives 270–272; nuclear threat, racial perspective 269–270; personal identification 267–269

Watters, Audrey 87

Weber, Max 175–176

Wendell, Susan 66

Whitebear, Luhui 45, 46

white privilege: "bad whites" as racist 191; education and class status 175, 180, 238; local history narratives 43–44; racial empathy expectations 196–197; racial ignorance issues 198–199; service learning issues 241

white supremacy: anti-protests xiv, 277; Confederate monuments, legacy debate 276–279; social movement suppression 257

wholeness and justice: arts and transformative learning 134–135; connectivity, art and storytelling 131–132; damage, forms and risks 127–128, 137–138; faculty partnerships, working towards 137–138; practitioner's personal journey 137; practitioner's personal journey 124–127; self-work and emotional intelligence 136–137; sentipensante pedagogy, practices and personal accounts 128–131; story circle activities 133–134, 135; student transition and integration 132–133; wholeness defined 127

World Health Organization (WHO) 70

Yasui, Minoru 268
Yasui, Ray 56–57

Zlotkowski, Edward 241

Made in the USA
Monee, IL
04 June 2022